CONTENTS

VOL II.

PART IV.

THE RÁMÁYANA.

CHAPTER I.

THE CITY OF AYODHYÁ.

CHAPTER II.

THE HORSE SACRIFICE OF MAHÁRÁJA DASARATHA.

INDIA OF THE
BRAHMANIC AGE
WITH REFERENCE TO THE RAMAYANA

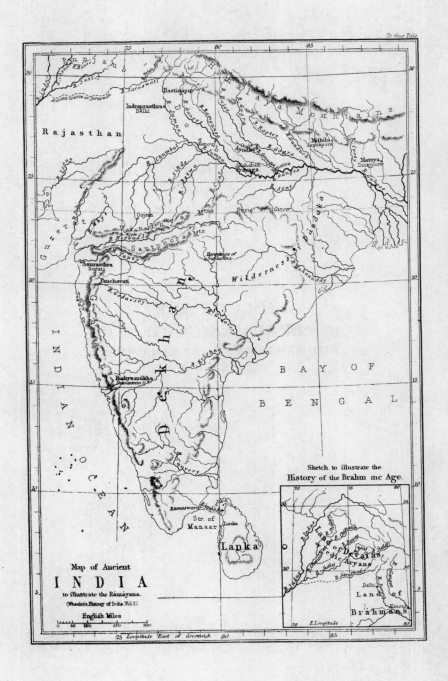

INDIA OF THE BRAHMANIC AGE

WITH REFERENCE TO
THE RAMAYANA
VOL. II OF THE HISTORY OF INDIA

Part-I

BY
J. TALBOYS WHEELER

COSMO PUBLICATIONS
DELHI 6   ●   INDIA
1973

COSMO PUBLICATIONS

10178 LIBRARY ROAD, DELHI-6

SBN 336 00406 0

Printed in India

Published by Mrs. Rani Kapoor, Cosmo Publications, 10178,
Library Road, Delhi-6 and printed by K. L. Sachdeva,
Skylark Printers, 11355 Id-Gah Road, New Delhi-55

viii CONTENTS.

CHAPTER III.

THE CHILDHOOD OF RÁMA.

CONTENTS.

CHAPTER IV.

WARS WITH THE RÁKSHASAS.

CONTENTS.

CHAPTER V.

MARRIAGE OF RÁMÁ.

CHAPTER VI.

RÁMA APPOINTED YUVARAJA.

CHAPTER VIII.

EXILE OF RÁMA.

CHAPTER IX.

JOURNEY TO CHITRA-KUTA.

CONTENTS.

CHAPTER X.

DEATH OF MAHÁRAJA DASARATHA.

CHAPTER XI.

BHARATA REFUSES THE RAJ.

CHAPTER XII.

FUNERAL RITES FOR THE MAHÁRAJA.

CHAPTER XIII.

BHARATA'S VISIT TO RÁMA.

CHAPTER XIV.

RÁMA REFUSES THE RAJ.

Atheistical speech of Jáváli the logician :—

" Whilst your father was alive you obeyed his commands, but now that he is dead they are no longer binding. The relationship of parents to their children is only temporary, like that of the inn to the passing traveller. Take your pleasure in this mortal life of which we know something, and trouble not respecting the life hereafter of which we know nothing. I grieve for those who sacrifice the substantial happiness of this life for a visionary happiness hereafter. Men, it is true, offer cakes to their dead ancestors, but how can those ancestors eat them? If the soul is immortal it must have passed into a new form which cannot eat the cake. If, indeed, the eating of the cake by the cows satisfies the hunger of a dead father, it might also satisfy the hunger of a

CHAPTER XV.

RÁMA'S EXILE.

CONTENTS.

CONTENTS.

CHAPTER XVI.

RÁMA'S WARS RESPECTING SÚRPA-NAKHÁ.

CHAPTER XVII.

RÁVANA'S ABDUCTION OF SÍTÁ.

CHAPTER XVIII.

RÁMA'S SEARCH FOR SÍTÁ.

CHAPTER XIX.

RÁMA'S ALLIANCE WITH THE MONKEYS.

CHAPTER XX.

HANUMAN'S ADVENTURES IN LANKÁ.

CHAPTER XXI.

RÁMA'S INVASION OF LANKÁ.

CHAPTER XXII.

RÁMA'S WAR AGAINST RÁVANA.

CHAPTER XXIII.

TRIUMPHANT RETURN OF RAMA.

PART V.

THE BRAHMANIC PERIOD.

CHAPTER I.

FOUR EPOCHS OF RELIGIOUS HISTORY.

CHAPTER II.

VEDIC AND BRAHMANIC GEOGRAPHY.

CHAPTER III.

RISHIS AND BRÁHMANS.

CHAPTER IV.

VEDIC AND BRAHMANIC CONCEPTIONS OF MANU.

CHAPTER V.

CREATION OF THE UNIVERSE BY MANU AND BRAHMÁ.

CHAPTER VI.

SACRED CHRONOLOGY.

CONTENTS. lvii

CHAPTER VIII.

EIGHT FORMS OF MARRIAGE.

CHAPTER IX.

THE SRÁDDHA, OR FEAST OF THE DEAD.

CHAPTER X.

THE FOUR CASTES.

CHAPTER XI.

THE FOUR STAGES OF LIFE.

CHAPTER XII.

HINDÚ WOMEN.

CHAPTER XIII.

HINDÚ GOVERNMENT.

CONTENTS.

CHAPTER XIV.

HISTORICAL RESUMÉ.

lxviii   CONTENTS.

INTRODUCTION TO VOL. II.

THE previous volume of the History of India comprised an introductory sketch of the Vedic period, and a condensed version of the Mahá Bhárata. The present volume comprises a similar version of the Rámáyana, together with a detailed review of what is termed, somewhat arbitrarily, the Brahmanic age.

The Rámáyana is the second of the two famous Epics, which have been justly regarded by Sanskrit scholars, and by the people of India generally, as the great national treasuries of the traditions and legends of the Hindús. They are indeed the repositories of all that has been preserved of Vedic ideas and institutions, as well as the expression of that later Brahmanical system, which forms the basis of the existing religion and civilization of the masses, ramifying as it does more or less throughout the entire body of Hindú literature. In the authoritative language of the learned Professor T. Goldstücker, "the Mahá Bhárata is the source of all the Puranas, *the* Purana emphatically so called."[1] But

---

[1] *Westminster Review*, April, 1868. The author must acknowledge his sense of the kindness and liberality which so eminent a Sanskrit scholar as Pro-

the Rámáyana differs very considerably in character
and scope from the Mahá Bhárata. The main traditions of both Epics are decidedly Vedic, but they
appear to belong to totally different periods.. The
story of the war of Bhárata refers to the very dawn
of Hindú history, when the Aryan invaders had
only reached the upper courses of the Ganges and
Jumná, and when the plains of Hindústan were a
terra incognita to be converted by the later Brahmanical compilers into a land of myths and fables. The
main tradition of the Rámáyana refers, on the other
hand, to a comparatively recent period of Aryan
conquest, when an Aryan empire had been established
in Oude, and when Vedic rites and institutions had
advanced from the Punjab, or land of five rivers,
into the very heart of Hindústan. Moreover, the
Rámáyana comprises four distinct phases of religion
and civilization. First, there is an old Kshatriya
tradition, replete with Vedic ideas and institutions,
of the exile of Ráma from the Raj of Ayodhyá, or
Oude; and the incidents of this portion of the narrative must be referred to a much later date than
the patriarchal and barbarous age of the war of
Bhárata, although still belonging to the Vedic or
pre-Brahmanic period. Secondly, there is a yet
more modern Brahmanical tradition of a Ráma, who
apparently flourished as the champion of the Brahmanical Linga-worshippers of the Dekhan against
the Rákshasas of the peninsula of India and island

---

fessor Goldstücker has displayed in reviewing the labours of one, who lays no
claim to philological learning, but strictly confines himself to historical investigation and criticism. As regards the Puranas generally, however, it will be seen,
from the opening chapter of the Brahmanic period in the present volume, that
they have by no means been neglected by the author.

of Ceylon; and the incidents of this portion of the narrative must be referred to the Brahmanic or post-Vedic age. Thirdly, there is a Buddhist element, inasmuch as the so-called Rákshasas were evidently Buddhists; and it will be seen, notably in the case of a casuist named Jávali, that Buddhist doctrines are mooted in the presence of the Ráma of the Dekhan, for the purpose of being refuted by that Brahmanical warrior. Fourthly, there is a religious element, belonging to the age of Brahmanical revival; an age when the Brahmans set up the god Vishnu as a higher conception of deity than the old Vedic devatas, and represented the Ráma of the two traditions as an incarnation or avatar of that spiritual divinity.

Here it may be explained that the ancient history of India is divisible into four great religious eras, namely, the Vedic, the Brahmanic, the Buddhist, and the Brahmanic revival. First, the Vedic period was a joyous age of Swayamvaras and Aswamedhas, when Agni, Indra, and other personifications of spiritual existences, were propitiated with feasts and invoked with the enthusiastic hymns of the Rig-Veda. Secondly, the Brahmanic period wás a gloomy sacerdotal age, in which the feasts of the Kshatriyas were converted into sacrifices for the atonement of sins against Brahmanical law; and in which divine worship was reduced to a system of austerities and meditations upon the Supreme Spirit as Brahma; whilst the Bráhmans appeared as a great ecclesiastical hierarchy, and established that hateful priestly dominion which still continues to debase the mind and soul of the Hindú, and renders a foreign rule a necessity to the people at large.

Thirdly, the Buddhist period was characterized by the advent of Sákya Muni as Buddha, and the rapid spread of his peculiar dogmas, that existence was an evil to gods and men: and that there was no deliverance of the soul from the vortex of successive transmigrations, excepting by the annihilation of the passions, and the hushing of the spirit into an eternal rest of dreamy and contemplative repose.[2] Lastly, we have the period of Brahmanical revival; an age when the Bráhmans seem to have abandoned the unpopular worship of their god Brahma, and to have invoked the aid of the old national gods and heroes of the Vedic Aryans against the practical atheism of Buddha, by severally representing Ráma and Krishna as incarnations of the Supreme Being who was named Vishnu.

Válmíki, the author of the Rámáyana, appears to have flourished in the age of Brahmanical revival; and the main object of his poem is to blacken the character of the Buddhists, and to represent Ráma as an incarnation of Vishnu. Before, however, attempting to explain the particular phase of religious belief which existed in the age when the Rámáyana was composed, it may be as well to glance at the general development of religious ideas in India. The earliest stage in the development of

---

[2] The Buddhist period cannot be clearly separated, either from the Brahmanic period which partly preceded it, or from the period of Brahmanical revival which partly succeeded it. Indeed, it will be seen in the so-called history of the Brahmanic age, which forms a portion of the present volume, that Buddhism and Brahmanism flourished side by side. It may, however, be gathered from the traditions connected with the life of Sákya Manu that the worship of Brahma preceded the Buddhist heresy; and consequently it has been found convenient to review the main characteristics of the old Brahmanical period, whilst it was still replete with Vedic ideas and institutions, and before it had passed through a Buddhist crucible.

the religious instinct in the human race appears to
be the worship of the elements, such as fire, water,
and wind, which in their various manifestations con-
tribute so much to the general well-being of man, as
well as to his occasional injury. As, however, individual experience advances, the religious worship
extends to every conceivable thing, visible or invisible, which has been seen or imagined by the
untutored mind; and such objects are personified or
spiritualized, and propitiated with offerings of food
and drink, and other simple gratifications. Gradually, as men separate into families and tribes, they
adopt family and tribal gods, which may ultimately
become the deities of nations and empires. Meantime the exaggerated language of the bards, who
praise their Chief as the Raja of Rajas, and their
Deity as the God of gods, engenders the idea of
monotheism; and this idea rapidly assumes the
form of a substantive conception as it becomes
blended with the idea of a universal ruler. But
having reached this point, the idea of monotheism is
apt to fade away in the progress of human thought
into a mere abstract conception of the Creator of
the universe, the invisible Soul which pervades all
things and animates all things. This is a critical
period in the development of monotheism. So long
as the idea of deity is blended with that of a supreme ruler, who is invested with human sympathies
and national associations, so long his worshippers
will pray to him for all the good things of this life,
as children would address a father. But the mere
abstract idea of a Supreme Deity as the Soul of the
universe, can only be apprehended by the philo-
sophic few; and is so devoid of all human interest,

that it may be approached with childlike awe, but will never be addressed in the language of devotional fervour.   A link is wanting between the human and the divine; a deity incarnate in man, who is invested with sufficient humanity to sympathize with the sorrows and aspirations of human beings, and at the same time so nearly allied to deity that he can mediate between the human race and the Almighty Father.

Such were the conditions of the age in which Válmíki composed the Rámáyana.   During the Vedic period religious ideas had been gravitating towards monotheism, in connection either with the worship of Indra as the sovereign of the gods, or with the worship of the Sun as the Supreme Soul. In the Brahmanic age the notion of a Supreme Soul had reached the form of an abstract idea, which was identified with Brahma, who appears to have been the peculiar god of the Bráhmans.   But this idea of Brahma was divested of all those human sympathies and historical associations which were connected with the adoration of Indra; and utterly failed to kindle those glorious emotions of nature-worship which were poured forth in the daily invocations to the Sun.   The great truth was unknown, or altogether ignored, that it is as impossible to adore the ideal of deity, as it is to adore the ideal of female beauty, excepting through the medium of the concrete.   The worship of an abstract idea like that of Brahma could thus excite neither enthusiasm nor devotion.   The human element was altogether wanting.

At this juncture Buddhism stepped in with its peculiar dogma, that existence was only another name for pain and sorrow. Sákya Muni, the new prophet of Buddhism, appeared as an embodiment of universal benevolence, deeply moved with compassion for suffering humanity, and pointing out the only way by which the soul could be delivered from the vortex of successive transmigrations, and obtain eternal rest. Buddhism thus supplied those human sympathies which were wanting to the worship of Brahma. It denounced the caste system, and admitted Súdras, as well as twice-born men, into the ranks of the priesthood. It thus effected an easy conquest over the worship of Brahma, and for centuries was the dominant faith in Hindústan. The Bráhmans vainly attempted to supply the missing link between man and deity by representing their ancient sages as incarnations of Brahma, the mind-born sons of Brahma; beings who had emanated from the Supreme Soul as Athene had sprung from the intellect of Zeus. But the haughty Kshatriya, the wealthy Vaisya, and the oppressed Súdra, appear to have been alike estranged from the Bráhmans. The worship of ancient sages had no charm for men who were busily engaged in the practical duties of life; and thus the worship of the Supreme Soul rapidly resolved itself into a metaphysical dream.

It was at this epoch that the Bráhmans called in the aid of the gods of the Rig-Veda, and even the gods of the aboriginal races and ancient heroes of the Kshatriyas, as their allies against the power of Buddha. Men had apparently grown weary of the practical atheism of the Buddhists, and yearned after the worship of their time-honoured deities. Moreover Buddhism proved to be a religion for monks and not for soldiers; and the time came when the Kshatriyas, the descendants of the old Vedic Aryans, began to scoff at the Buddhist mendicant, and to engage in schemes of war and conquest. Meantime the struggle between the Bráhman and the Buddhist, aggravated by the religious hate of centuries, burst forth into religious wars and persecutions of the burning and destroying type. But the story of this period still remains for investigation. It will suffice to say here that no records remain of the great conflict, save the charred relics of Buddhist cities and monasteries, and a few vague traditions that in days of old the Buddhists of Hindústan and the Dekhan were driven beyond the seas to Burmah and Ceylon.

When this great conflict was nearly over, and when religious and political ideas in India were in a state of revolutionary chaos, Válmíki appears to have composed his immortal poem of the Rámáyana. The frame-work of his story, as already indicated, was an old Vedic legend of the exile of a Ráma who flourished in Hindústan, combined with a later narrative of the exploits of a Brahmanic champion of the same name, who had helped to drive the Buddhists out of the Dekhan. The people of the south, by whose assistance this Ráma of the Dekhan had achieved his conquest, were popularly regarded as so many Monkeys and Bears, but Válmíki raised them to the rank of divine beings. In like manner the hostile Buddhists were declared to be Rákshasas or demons; and were identified with the Rákshasas or evil spirits of old Vedic tradition. Meantime Ráma was raised to the highest rank of deity as an incarnation of Vishnu.

The conception of Vishnu, as it presents itself to

the mind of the Hindú, is one of the most important of all the religious ideas that have ever been formed by the people of India. An old Vedic personification, known as Vishnu, which was more or less connected with the primitive worship of the Sun, was invested with the attributes of the Supreme Spirit; and the most famous of the national heroes, such as Ráma and Krishna, and even the most popular of the old animal gods of the pre-Aryan races, such as the fish, the tortoise, the boar, and the lion, were associated with the worship of this Supreme Being by being represented as incarnations or avatars of the great god Vishnu. The complicated mythological system connected with the worship of Vishnu through his ten incarnations, will be treated in the third and concluding volume of the present history. It will suffice to state here that the idea which pervades the Rámáyana of Válmíki is that Ráma is an incarnation of Vishnu, who was sent into the world at the earnest entreaty of the Vedic deities, to deliver the Bráhmans from the oppressions of the Buddhists or Rákshasas. The plan of the Epic will be found simple enough; and it will be seen that the presence of supernatural details furnishes the same clue to the discovery of what is and what is not Vedic tradition, as it does in the story of the Mahá Bhárata. The success of the attempt of Válmíki to set up a godman as a representative of the Supreme Being will of course be questioned by the European, who peruses the poem free from all the subjective influences of hereditary teaching and superstitious fear; but it cannot be denied by those who are aware that a hundred millions of human beings are imbued with an unquestioning faith in the divinity of Ráma, and the firm belief that such faith in the heart, accompanied by the frequent invocation of the holy name of Ráma, is sufficient to secure eternal happiness for the soul in the heaven of Vishnu.

But although the historical student may find it necessary to analyze the process by which the national traditions of Ráma have been converted into vehicles for the promulgation of a theological and ecclesiastical system, it by no means follows that the author of the Rámáyana is to be regarded as a mere priestly impostor. On the contrary, the same high religious purpose, which characterizes other great Epics such as those of Homer and Milton, is fully expressed in the Rámáyana of Válmíki. Here it may be remarked that the ordinary conception of the Epic, as an elaborate narrative in elevated poetry, in which free scope may be given to the imagination so long as a moral or religious end be kept in view, has led to a very imperfect estimate of the important part which has been played by the Iliad and Paradise Lost in the history of religious development. The true Epic is the creation of the bard who can elevate his intellect and imagination far above the jarring conflicts of his generation, and afford consolation to the soul in those eras of religious and political revolution, when the progress of human affairs seems entirely opposed to all ideas of a divine government of the universe of being. Such was the age of Milton, and such appears to have been the age alike of Homer and of Válmíki.

The object of these three immortal bards thus appears to have been to exhibit and reconcile the relations between man and deity in accordance with the current religious belief of the ages in which they

respectively flourished. It has already been shown
that the religious yearnings which are common to
every race and creed, namely, the passionate longing to acquaint deity with our sufferings and sorrows, and to induce deity to take a direct and
intelligent interest in our well-being, can never be
satisfied with any monotheism, which takes the form
of an abstract idea. But the Iliad, the Paradise
Lost, and the Rámáyana have each furnished in
turn a solution of the great religious enigma, the
relations between God and man. The conception
of these relations differs widely in each case, inasmuch as each one drew his theological ideas
and personifications from a different mythological
system. But still the same underlying conviction
seems to have been common to all three, that a
necessity existed for reconciling the ways of God to
man. In the days of Homer the Greeks appear
to have invoked and propitiated the Olympic deities
much after the fashion in which the Vedic Aryans
invoked and propitiated the personified gods of the
Rig-Veda. Accordingly in dealing with the tale of
Troy, which had apparently inflicted so much
misery on Greek and Trojan, the popular mind was
consoled by the representation that all the deities of
Hellas had taken an active part in the events which
preceded and accompanied the siege; and that all
the sufferings and sorrows, which were associated
with that contest, were to be ascribed to the warm
interest which was taken by the national deities in
the proceedings of the national heroes. Milton we
know to have been cast upon an evil age, in which
the religious mind found no consolation save what
was to be derived from a living faith in Christianity.

The bard of Paradise Lost must have perceived that
the Commonwealth had failed to save the nation
from civil and religious oppression; and to his pure
mind the restoration of the Stuarts must have been
a restoration of the rule of the sons of Belial. Under
such circumstances the Christian bard naturally
sought to justify the ways of God to man, not by
introducing the action of Deity into history, but by
reproducing, with all the pomp and circumstance of
Epic poetry, the sacred legends which were associated with the expulsion of the evil angels, the
creation and fall of man, and the final redemption
of the human race. The task accomplished by
Válmíki was somewhat different. Like Homer, he
drew the groundwork of his Epic from national
traditions, and his divine personages from a national
Pantheon; but he had to reproduce Vedic traditions
in a Brahmanical dress, and to represent the human
actions of Ráma as the divine actions of the incarnation of Vishnu. It will also be remarked that
there is a considerable change in the deification as
it appears in the story of the exile of Ráma of
Ayodhyá, and in the story of the conquests of Ráma
of the Dekhan. In the narrative of the exile the
Vedic element predominates with its horse-sacrifices
and Swayamvaras; and whilst the language and
incidents have been Brahmanized throughout with
considerable skill, the deification of the hero is artificial and unsatisfactory. Ráma is indeed represented as a Hindú model of a good son and true
husband, but not as a high ideal of youthful deity.
Indeed the interest of this portion of the Rámáyana
turns almost entirely upon the mere human details,
such as the picture of the city of Ayodhyá, the

Aswamedha which resulted in the birth of Ráma
and his brethren, the marriage of Ráma and Sítá,
the claim of Ráma to the succession on the throne,
and the intrigues of his mother-in-law Kaikeyí by
which those claims were set aside, and he himself
condemned to many years' banishment in the jungle.
The subsequent narrative of Ráma's conquest of
Lanka is altogether of a different character. Here
the human element almost disappears, and it is
difficult to arrive at even glimpses of historical truth
beneath the confused overgrowth of fable and exaggeration. Moreover the character of Ráma of the
Dekhan appears to have differed widely from that
of Ráma of Ayodhyá. The Dekhan hero was
apparently a champion of the Bráhmans, but he
was evidently cruel and unscrupulous in the attainment of his ends; and the bard often appears to
labour under the feeling that it is necessary to
explain away the conduct of this Ráma, and he does
not always succeed in the attempt. The deification
of the Ráma of the Dekhan is wild and fantastic,
the product of a superstitious and oppressed age,
when the popular mind could find no hope for relief
excepting in the conception of a friendly warrior,
invested with supernatural power and possessed of
supernatural weapons. The reckless introduction
of fabulous details tends to confirm the theory that
the tradition of the exile and that of the conquest
originated from different sources. Thus it is possible that the wanderings of years could carry a hero
from Ayodhyá to Ceylon, as it has carried Hindú
pilgrims for generations; but the notion of carrying back a warrior and his conquering army from
Ceylon to Ayodhyá was more than the Hindú bard

could explain away. Consequently the conception was introduced of a large chariot, which moved through the air at the will of its driver, and passed like a winged city from the straits of Manaar to the banks of the Gogra. It is also curious to notice that the main plot of this latter tradition, namely, the abduction of Sítá and the siege of Lanka, bears a strong resemblance to the abduction of Helen and the siege of Troy ; saving that whilst the purity of the Hindú heroine was testified by the gods, and she was even then abandoned in the jungle on mere suspicion, the Spartan heroine yielded to every temptation, and was even then received back with favour by her first husband. Again, the war between Ráma and the Rákshasas bears a similar resemblance to that war between the good and evil angels, which finds expression in Paradise Lost ; and which appears to have been borrowed from those ancient legends of the war between Iran and Turan, good and evil, light and darkness, Ormuzd and Ahriman, which still linger in the primitive traditions of the Zoroastrian era.

The abridged version of the Rámáyana now presented to the public is not derived exclusively from the poem of Válmíki, and indeed it is scarcely likely that the story of Ráma's conquests, as related by Válmíki, could ever be rendered acceptable to European readers, nor is such a process necessary for historical purposes. There are three Rámáyanas which are supposed to have been respectively the works of Válmíki, Tulsee Dass, and Vyása. The Rámáyana of Válmíki, as translated by Messrs Carey and Marshman,[3] from the commencement of the

---

[3] The best thanks of the author are due to Mr George Smith of Serampore

poem to the abduction of Sítá by Rávana, has been adopted with some revisions and modifications as the basis of the greater part of the present condensed version. The remainder is given in brief outline from the Bengali version. Moreover a few extracts have been introduced in the text from what is understood to be the north-western version, which furnish particulars not to be found in the poem of Válmíki, respecting the early life, education, and marriage of Ráma, and serve to illustrate the more modern ideas upon these subjects, which are current amongst the Hindús.[4] Again, throughout the present version considerable extracts have been added in the form of foot-notes from the work which is popularly ascribed to Vyása, and which is known as the Adhy-átma Rámáyana. These extracts will be found valuable from the light which they throw upon the modern belief in the deity of Ráma ; but this important point will form a subject of further discussion in the third and concluding volume.[5]

The so-called history of the Brahmanic age, which occupies a large portion of the present volume, requires a few words of explanation. The previous volume opened with a sketch of the Vedic period, which, although somewhat brief, really contained all

---

for having kindly furnished him with a considerable number of sheets of Carey and Marshman's translation which had been printed but never published.

[4] For this portion of the work I am much indebted to the assistance of the same young Sanskrit scholar, Baboo Obenash Chunder Ghose, who had helped me with the Mahá Bhárata. The young Baboo aided me in making a tolerably full translation, which has been subsequently filtered down to suit European tastes.

[5] For the use of this Adhyátma Rámáyana I am indebted to Mr Alonzo Money of the Bengal Civil Service, who has in his possession a beautiful manuscript translation illustrated with native pictures, which appears to have been made about the end of the last century, and which for some months was kindly placed at my disposal.

the results which could be gathered from really Vedic
sources ; in other words, from the hymns of the Rig-
Veda, so far as they had been translated by the late
Professor H. H. Wilson. So far this sketch of the Vedic age served in some measure as a test wherewith to
trace out such Vedic elements as could be discovered
in the Epics, and to separate them from the Brahmanical interpolations with which they were closely
intertwined. In the present history of the Brahmanic
age this process has been carried much farther ; and
consequently it will be found to throw a reflex light
upon the Vedic age ; inasmuch as the main result of
the critical inquiry into the so-called Brahmanic age
is the separation of the ideas and institutions of the
old Vedic period from those which prevailed in the
later Brahmanic period. Hitherto these conflicting
elements have been blended together in the national
literature and belief of the Hindús, in the same way
that they have been blended together in the Mahá
Bhárata and Rámáyana. The publication of the
Hymns of the Rig-Veda first furnished the clue
to this separation, inasmuch as they may be regarded
as the most authoritative expression of the Vedic age,
just as the laws of Manu may be regarded as the
authoritative expression of the Brahmanic age which
immediately succeeded. This comparison of the
Hymns of the Rig-Veda with the Laws of Manu, has
of course been carried out by the light of the data
already gathered from the Epics, and from a tolerably comprehensive investigation of the Puranas ;
and by this process results have been gained which
may possibly be regarded as discoveries, or at any
rate may perhaps be received by Sanskrit scholars
as confirmatory of similar results which have been

worked out by comparative philology. It will be seen that from this simple comparison of the Hymns of the Rig Veda with the Laws of Manu, without any reference to the important results which have been worked out by the great schools of modern philology, it appears to be established that the Rishis belonged to the Vedic age, and the Bráhmans to the Brahmanic age; that polyandry, or the marriage of several brothers to one wife, which is explained away by the Brahmanical compilers of the Mahá Bhárata as purely exceptional and confined to the sons of Pandu, was in fact an old Vedic institution which finds expression in the hymns of the Rig-Veda; and that the Aswamedha, or sacrifice of a horse, and the Swayamvara, or self-choice of a husband by a marriageable maiden, were purely Vedic institutions; originally unknown to Brahmanism, and finding no place in the laws of Manu, but forming prominent features in Epic traditions, and being duly recognized in the Vedic Hymns. From these data it may be easily inferred, that if an investigation of the Brahmanic period can throw so much light upon the period which preceded it, so in like manner further materials for the earlier history of India may yet be gathered from an investigation of the ideas and institutions of the Buddhist period, and of the later age of Brahmanical revival through which the national mind has been slowly passing, since the downfall of Buddha in India, to emerge, it is to be hoped, in the dawn of a brighter and purer day.

J. Talboys Wheeler.

HISTORY OF INDIA.

PART IV.

THE RÁMÁYANA.

CHAPTER I.

THE CITY OF AYODHYÁ.

THE story of the Rámáyana opens at the famous city of Ayodhyá, the modern Oude, which is situated upon the river Sarayú, the modern Gogra, about three hundred and fifty miles to the south-east of the great city of Delhi. In the present day the city of Ayodhyá has disappeared, and little is to be seen of the ancient site beyond a shapeless heap of ruins, a mass of rubbish and jungle, which stretches along the southern bank of the Gogra river. But in olden time this city was one of the largest and most magnificent in Hindústan,[1] and its memory is still preserved in

Opening scene of the Rámá-yana at Ayod-hyá, the modern Oude.

Present appear-ance of the ruins.

Ancient magni-ficence.

---

[1] Abul Fazel, in 1582, thus describes the city. "Oude is one of the largest cities in Hindústan. In ancient times this city is said to have measured 148 coss (296 English miles) in length, and 36 coss (72 miles) in breadth. Upon sift-ing the earth which is round this city, small grains of gold are sometimes found in it. The town is esteemed one of the most sacred places in antiquity."

HISTORY OF
INDIA.
PART IV.

Geographical
position indica-
tive of Aryan
advance from
Delhi to Oude.

every quarter of the Indian peninsula. Its geographical position is highly significant of the progress
of Aryan invasion between two great epochs, namely,
that of the war of Bhárata, and that of the birth of
Ráma.   In the Mahá Bhárata the Aryans had apparently advanced no farther towards the south-east
than the neighbourhood of Delhi ; but in the Rámáyana they seem to have established 'a large and
substantial Raj in the very centre of Hindústan, and
to have founded a metropolis which must ever be
famous in the ancient history of India.

The Raj of
Kosala.

The Raj thus indicated was known as the Raj of
Kosala. Its boundaries cannot be strictly defined, but
it evidently covered a considerable area. In one direction it certainly stretched from the banks of the Gogra
to·those of the Ganges ; for there is distinct mention
of a frontier town which was seated on the Ganges,
and which separated the territory of Kosala from the

Lack of family
traditions.
Rajas descended
from the Sun.

country of the Bhíls. The early history of the Raj of
Kosala is, however, almost a blank. The Rajas claimed
to be descendants of the Sun, in the same way that the
Rajas of Bhárata claimed to be descended from the

The Sun
descended from
Brahma.

Moon ; and the Bráhmans improved the genealogy
by representing the Sun to have sprung from a Rishi
named Kásyapa, who in his turn was the grandson
of Brahma. Thus while the Rajas of Kosala retained
their ancient claim of being descendants of the Sun,
an attempt was made in the national epic to represent
them as children of the peculiar deity of the Bráh-

Earliest tradi-
tion connected
with Dasaratha,
the father of
Ráma.

mans. But scarcely a trace of an authentic family
tradition is to be found in the Rámáyana earlier than
Dasaratha, the father of Ráma ; and in this respect
the story of Ráma differs somewhat widely from that
of the Kauravas and Pándavas. The poem com-

mences with a glowing description of the Raj of
Kosala, the city and people of Ayodhyá, and the
virtues and accomplishments of the reigning Maháraja, the mighty Dasaratha; and this description
may now be presented almost exactly as it stands in
the original Sanskrit, with all those Brahmanical
exaggerations of ancient Hindú glory and caste distinction, which could scarcely have had any existence excepting in the profuse imagination of a
Brahmanical bard:—

HISTORY OF INDIA. PART IV.

Commencement of the Rámáyana.

In ancient times there was a great country named Kosala; and that country was happy and joyous, and abounded in
cattle, and grain, and riches. And in that country on the banks
of the river Sarayú, was a famous city named Ayodhyá; and
there all the houses were large and beautifully arranged, and
the streets were always watered, and there were very many
temples richly decorated, and stately palaces with domes
like the tops of mountains, with pleasant gardens full of
birds and flowers, and shady groves of trees loaded with
delicious fruits, and above all there were the sacred and resplendent chariots of the gods. And the tanks in that city
were magnificent beyond all description, and covered with
the white lotos; and the bees thirsted for the honey, and the
wind drove the white lotoses from the bees, as modesty
drives away the coy bride from her husband. And the ducks
and the geese swam upon the surface of the tanks, or dived
under the clear waters; and the brilliant kingfishers were
wroth as they beheld their own reflection in the bright wave,
and under pretence of catching the fish they beat the water
with their wings. And the plantain trees round the tanks
were bending with the weight of the fruit, like reverential
pupils bowing at the feet of their preceptors. The whole
city was adorned with gems, so that it resembled a mine of
jewels, and it was like unto Amarávati, the city of Indra.
It was perfumed with flowers and incense, and decked out
with gorgeous banners; and it was ever filled with the sweet

Description of the Raj of Kosala and city of Ayodhyá.

Houses, streets, temples, palaces, gardens, groves, and chariots of the gods.

The tanks.

The lotoses.

The wind and the bees.

The ducks and geese.

The kingfishers.

The plantain trees.

Gems.

Flowers, incense, and banners.

Fortifications.
The moat.

The gates.

The guards.

The people of
Ayodhyá.

The Bráhmans
and their three
classes of
disciples, viz. :

Servants,

Students,

Brahmachárís.

The Kshatriyas.

The Vaisyas.

The Súdras.

Virtues of the
people.

sound of music, the sharp twanging of bows, and the holy chaunting of Vedic hymns. The city was encompassed round about with very lofty walls, which were set in with variously-coloured jewels ; and all round the walls was a moat filled with water, deep and impassable ; and the city gates were strongly barred, and the porticoes of the gates and the towers on the walls were filled with archers, and stored with weapons of every description. Every quarter of the city was guarded by mighty heroes, who were as strong as the eight gods who rule the eight points of the universe, and as vigilant as the many-headed serpents who watch at the entrance of the regions below.

The city of Ayodhyá was full of people, and every one was healthy and happy, and every one was well fed upon the best of rice ; and every merchant in that city had store-houses filled with jewels from every quarter of the earth. The Bráhmans constantly kept alive the sacrificial fire, and were deeply read in the Vedas and Vedángas, and were en-dowed with every excellent quality ; they were profusely generous, and were filled with truth, zeal, and compassion, equal to the great sages, and their minds and passions were under perfect control. All these Bráhman sages had three classes of disciples ; first, the youths who served them as servants serve their masters ; then the students who were receiving instruction ; and then the Brahmachárís who maintained themselves and their preceptors by collecting alms. Next to the Bráhmans were the Kshatriyas, who were all warriors, and were constantly exercised in the practice of arms in the presence of the Maháraja. After these were the Vaisyas, or merchants, who sold goods of every description, and who came from every corner of the earth. Last of all were the Súdras, who were ever engaged in devotion to the gods, and in the service of the Bráhmans. Besides these there were jewellers and artificers, singing men and dancing women, charioteers and footmen, potters and smiths, painters and oilmen, sellers of flowers and sellers of betelnut. In all that city of well-fed and happy people, no man was without learning, or practised a calling that did not belong to his family or caste, or dwelt in a mean habitation, or was without kinsmen. There were no misers, nor liars, nor thieves, nor tale-bearers, nor swindlers, nor boasters; none that were arrogant, malevolent, mean, or who lived at another's expense; and no man who had not abundance of children, or who lived less than a thousand years. The men fixed their affections upon their wives only; the women were chaste and obedient to their husbands; and all were patient and faithful in the discharge of their several duties. No one was without a marriage crown, or ear-rings, or a necklace, or jewels for the hands. No one was poor, or wore tarnished ornaments; and no one was without fine raiment and perfumes, or was unclean, or fed on unclean things, or neglected the sacrifice, or gave less than a thousand rupees to the Bráhmans. All the women in Ayodhyá were extremely beautiful, and endowed with wit, sweetness, prudence, industry, and every good quality; and their ornaments were always bright and shining, and their apparel was always clean and without a stain. In all Ayodhyá there was not a man or woman who was unfortunate, or foolish, or wretched, or uneasy, or diseased, or afflicted with fear, or disloyal to the Mahárája. All were devoted to truth, practised hospitality, and paid due honour to their superiors, their ancestors, and the gods. All the four castes—the Bráhmans, the Kshatriyas, the Vaisyas, and the Súdras, were devoted to the Mahárája. No caste intermarried with any other caste; and there were no Chandálas [2] in all the city, either by birth or as a punishment for crime.

In the midst of that great city was the magnificent and *Palace of the Mahárája.* resplendent palace of the Mahárája, encompassed by walls, which were so high that the birds could not fly over them, and so strong that no beast could force its way through them. And there were two gates in the palace walls, one *Temples and treasures.* on each side; and over the gateways the music of the moho-

[2] Chandálas strickly speaking were the offspring of a Súdra father by a Bráhman mother, but the name is generally applied to all low-caste or out-caste tribes. Manu says:—"Even as a Súdra begets on a Bráhmaní woman a son more vile than himself, thus any other low man begets on women of the four castes, a son yet lower."

Throne of the
Mahárája.

Palace guards.

Virtues of
Mahárája
Dasaratha.

Virtues of his
Ministers.

Eight special
Counsellors.

Two priests and
preceptors.

bat was playing at every quarter of the day and night; and within the walls and round about the palace were many temples to the gods, and hundreds of treasuries filled with treasure. In the midst of the palace was the throne of the Mahárája, set upon pillars, and many other pillars were round about the throne; and all the pillars and the throne were covered with precious stones. And the palace was guarded by thousands of warriors who were as fierce as flames of fire, and as watchful as the lions that guard their dens in the mountains.

In this palace reigned the mighty Dasaratha, the Mahárája of the country of Kosala, and of the city of Ayodhyá;- and he was the son of Aja and descendant of Ikshwáku. And Dasaratha was very wise in the Vedas and Vedangás,[3] and had great foresight and ability, and was beloved by all his people. He was a perfect charioteer, a royal sage, famous throughout the three worlds, the conqueror of his enemies, ever loving justice, and having a perfect command over all his passions. In riches and magnificence he was equal to Indra, and he protected his subjects like another Manu. In supplying the wants and necessities of the people, he proved himself to be their true father, rather than the real father who only begot them; and he took tribute from his subjects, not for his own use, but to return it to them again with greater beneficence, as the sun drinks up the salt ocean to return it to the earth as vivifying rain. His Ministers were likewise possessed of every excellence, wise, capable of understanding a nod, and constantly devoted to their beloved Mahárája. And Dasaratha had eight special Counsellors who were ever engaged upon his affairs, and the chief of all was Sumantra; and his two chosen priests and preceptors[4] were Vasishtha and Vámadeva. Possessed of such Ministers

---

[3] The Vedángas are not distinct treatises like the four Vedas, but sciences. Thus the six Vedángas comprise (1) pronunciation; (2) metre; (3) grammar; (4) explanation of words; (5) astronomy; and (6) ceremonial. Müller's *Hist. of Sanskrit Lit.* p. 108 *et seq.*

[4] These two chosen Bráhmans, who are here called priests and preceptors, were perhaps Purohitas or family priests; although there are some indications that Vasishtha was regarded as a Guru.

and priests Dasaratha ruled the world virtuously, and rendered it very happy. Inspecting the world by his spies, as the sun inspects it by his rays, the great Dasaratha found no person of hostile mind, and he shone resplendent and illuminated the whole earth.

The foregoing description of a city, a people, and a Maháraja is perhaps without a parallel in the whole range of Brahmanical literature. Ayodhyá is the Hindú ideal of perfection, in which the Kshatriyas and Bráhmans alike performed their respective duties of protection and worship, and the twanging of bows was heard as constantly as the chaunting of Vedic hymns. It was a city of large houses, well-watered streets, decorated temples, stately palaces, pleasant gardens, shady groves, spacious tanks, and impregnable fortifications. A poetical sympathy with external nature is also displayed both here and in other portions of the Rámáyana, which is singularly illustrative of the dreamy character of the Hindú, and is rendered doubly curious from its occasional subordination to Brahmanical ideas. The Brahmanical conception of marriage involves a display of extreme modesty on the part of a girl wife; and thus the wind that drives away the white lotos from the thirsty bees, is likened to the modesty which drives away a coy bride from her ardent husband. Again, the respect due to Brahmanical instructors is indirectly enforced by the simile that the plantain trees bent with the weight of their fruit, like reverential pupils bowing at the feet of their preceptors. Further on the three classes of disciples or pupils are distinctly indicated, namely, the youths who acted as servants, the students who received instruction, and the Brahmacháris who col-

Review of the foregoing description of a Raj, a people, and a Mahár234.

Hindú ideal of a city.

Poetical sympathy with external nature subordinate to Brahmanical ideas.

Coy brides.

Reverential pupils.

Disciples of the Bráhmans.

HISTORY OF INDIA. PART IV.

The people.

Stress laid upon caste distinctions.

Model of a Hindú Mahá-raja.

Military and religious character.

His Counsellors.

His two Purohitas.

Real nature of the palace enclosure.

lected alms for themselves and their preceptors.[5] The description of the people is equally significant. They possessed every moral and religious virtue; they were learned, well fed upon the best of rice, free from disease, and lived for a thousand years. Every man had abundance of children, jewels, and clean raiment. Above all, every one was so rich and so pious, that no one ever gave less than a thousand rupees to the Bráhmans. A great stress is also laid upon caste distinctions. Every man belonged to a family and caste; no man followed a calling that did not belong to his caste, and no child born of mixed castes was to be found throughout the city. As for the Maháraja, although he subsequently appears in a very different light, he is praised here as possessing every virtue, military and Brahmanical. He was at once famous as a charioteer and as a sage, a mighty warrior and a controller of his passions, endowed with great foresight, and well versed in the Vedas and Vedángas. His court was of course intended as a model for all Hindú Rajas to follow. He had eight chosen Counsellors, of whom his charioteer Sumantra was the chief; and he had two priests, who acted on all occasions as his particular guides and advisers. His palace was magnificent and resplendent, but in describing the walls the Brahmanical bard has indulged in a simile which furnishes a glimpse of the reality. They were so tall that the birds could not fly over them, and so strong that no beast could force its way through them. From this it is evident that the walls could not have

---

[5] The name of Brahmachári is generally applied to all religious students whilst living under a Bráhman master or Guru. All Brahmacháris wait upon their masters, study the Vedas, and collect alms.

been made of brick or stone; for in that case the attempt of a beast to force his way through them would never have entered the mind of the bard. In all probability the palace was surrounded by a hedge, which was sufficiently strong to keep out wild beasts or stray cattle. In other respects however, the picture is sufficiently imposing. The treasuries, which probably contained the land-revenue of rice and other grain, were placed for security within the inclosure;[6] and little temples to the different gods, each perhaps containing a single image before which the worshipper performed his devotions, were set up in the same area. In the middle of the palace was the throne of the Mahâraja raised upon pillars, and surrounded by pillars, and both the pillars and the throne are said to have been adorned with precious stones. The statement that the Mahâraja inspected the world with his spies, as the sun inspects it with his rays, may seem a dubious mode of government to the European; but a strict and universal system of espionage is perfectly in accordance with Hindú ideas, and its organization was considered to be one of the first duties of a Hindú sovereign.

Treasuries and temples within the enclosure.

Throne in the centre of the palace.

Hindú idea of the necessity for spies.

---

[6] In ancient times the land revenue seems to have been generally paid in kind; the Raja being entitled to a certain share of the grain, which was collected at harvest-time.

CHAPTER II.

THE HORSE SACRIFICE OF MAHÁRAJA DASARATHA.

Performance of
an Aswamedha
to obtain a son.

THE first act of Maháraja Dasaratha which is recorded in the Rámáyana, was the performance of an Aswamedha, or horse sacrifice, to obtain a son. Here it is curious to observe that the rite is invested with a meaning totally different to that which appears in the Aswamedha described in the Mahá Bhárata. The horse was loosened for an entire year, but no allusion whatever is made to any conquests over the neighbouring Rajas, nor to any other incident which would connect the ceremony with an assertion of sovereignty. The Aswamedha was performed for the sole and obvious purpose of procuring sons; and this point will be discussed at length after the ceremonial has been described. There is also a curious episode in the narrative which will require special notice. It is the legend of a young Rishi who had passed the earlier years of his life in the hermitage of his father in the jungle, and who had consequently never seen the face of a woman. This youthful Rishi was subsequently enticed by a number of young courtesans to accompany them to the city of Anga, where he married the daughter of the Raja, and was subsequently engaged to perform the Aswamedha of Maháraja Dasaratha. With this brief

Episode of a
Rishi who had
never seen a
woman.

Narrative of the
horse sacrifice of
Dasaratha.

introduction, the narrative of the horse sacrifice may be related as follows :—

Now the Maháraja had three Ránís, and their names were Kausalyá, Kaikeyí, and Sumitrá ; but no son was born to him to perpetuate his race. So he took seven hundred and fifty women into his palace, but still none of them gave birth to a son ; and the thought arose in the mind of the Maháraja that he would perform an Aswamedha sacrifice, and thus propitiate the gods to give him a man-child. And the Maháraja told to his priests and preceptors that he would sacrifice the horse, and the priests bestowed great praises upon Dasaratha, and said to him :—" Let all things necessary be prepared, and the horse be let loose, and let a place for the sacrifice be appointed on the north bank of the river Sarayú : And you, O Maháraja, who have formed this holy resolution to perform an Aswamedha, will assuredly obtain the sons whom you desire." Dasaratha then rejoiced greatly, and he ordered his Counsellors to do as his preceptors had commanded ; and he went to his beloved Ránís and said :—" I will perform a sacrifice to obtain a son ; do you therefore commence the preliminary rites." And the beautiful faces of the Ránís brightened at his words, as the lotos is brightened at the coming of the spring.

Then Sumantra, who was the chief of the Counsellors, said to Dasaratha :—" It was predicted in the ancient chronicles that you should perform an Aswamedha to procure a son, and that the sacrifice should be offered by the Rishi Sringa. Now Sringa was born in the forest, and lived in the hermitage of his father, who was a great sage ; and he never saw any man save his father ; and he never saw any woman, young or old. And it came to pass that the Raja of Anga desired to give his daughter Sántá in marriage to Sringa ; so he sent young courtesans into the forest, and they allured Sringa away to the city of the Raja of Anga ; and Sríuga is still dwelling with the Raja of Anga."

The Maháraja replied :—" Let the story of Sringa be told at length ! " And Sumantra told the story thus :—

Drought caused by the wickedness of the Raja of Anga.

The Raja advised by the Bráhmans to marry his daughter to Rishi Sringa.
Refusal of the Raja's servants to bring Rishi Sringa from the jungle.

Damsels sent to entice Sringa from his father's hermitage.

Gambols of the damsels in the absence of Sringa's father.

Sringa invites them into the hermitage.

" In the Raj of Anga there was a great drought, because of the wickedness of Lomapáda, who was the Raja of Anga. And Raja Lomapáda called to the Bráhmans, and said:— ' You are learned in the Vedas, and acquainted with the customs of men; tell me then, I pray you, how I may expiate my sin that the rain may again fall upon the land.' The Bráhmans answered the Raja:—' Bring the young Rishi Sringa out of his father's hermitage, and give him your daughter Sántá in marriage according to the ordinance.' The Raja agreed, but none of all his servants would go into the jungle and bring away Srínga, lest the father of Sringa should see them and pronounce a curse upon them. So the Bráhmans and Counsellors took counsel together, and they remembered that Sringa was an inhabitant of the forest, and that he had never beheld the face of a woman. Accordingly by their counsel the Raja prepared large boats, and planted fruit trees and sandal trees therein, and filled them with perfumed liquors and delicious fruits; and he collected together a number of beautiful young damsels and sent them in the boats to the hermitage of the Rishi to entice away Sringa from the abode of his father. When the damsels came to the hermitage they trembled with fear lest the father of Sringa should discover them, and they hid themselves in the forest beneath the wide-spreading creepers and climbing plants; but when they learned that the sage had gone out of his hermitage, and left his son alone, they came out of their hiding-place and went before the hut; and they were adorned with necklaces of flowers, and with musical bells upon their ancles, and they began to sing and play in the view of Sringa; and they indulged in many sportive gambols, and danced together, and pushed one another about, and threw garlands of flowers at each other and filled the air with music and perfumes. And Sringa, was amazed at the sight of beings of such slender waists and exquisite adornments; and when the damsels saw his surprise they sung a soft slow air, and approached him, and said:—' Who is your father, and why do you wander in this forest?' Sringa replied:—' My father is a great sage of the family of Kásyapa, and his name is Vibhándaka: Why do you come here thus suddenly? Enter into the hermitage, I pray you, and I will entertain you all.' The damsels then went into the hut, and Sringa offered them seats, and brought water to wash their feet, and gave them fruits and roots; and they smiled upon him, and said in soft accents: —'O sinless son of the sage, if it be agreeable to you, eat now some of the fruits of our own abode!' And they gave *Sringa fascinated with sweetmeats, wine, and caresses.* him delicious sweetmeats resembling fruits, and wine as sweet as honey; and they smiled upon him and caressed him, and putting their fragrant mouths to his ears they whispered soft words to him; and when they departed they pointed to their boats in which they abode, and which were very near the hermitage.

"When it was evening time the sage Vibhándaka re- *Alarm of Sringa's father on discovering what had occurred.* turned to the hermitage, and he saw that his son Sringa was very melancholy and absorbed in thought, and he said: —'Why do you not rejoice at my coming? I perceive, my son, that you are immersed in a sea of anxiety, so tell me why you are changed.' Then Sringa said:—'O divine father, some men with beautiful eyes came here and embraced me very often, and sung soft and ravishing music, and sported before me, and moved their eye-brows in a surprising manner.' The sage replied:—'O my son, the Rákshasas have come to you in this manner to disturb your devotion; and it is not proper for you to trust them in any way.' The sage thus comforted his son, and he stayed in the hermitage all that night, but when it was morning he returned again to the forest.

"Then Sringa, seeing that his father had gone out, went *Sringa carried away to Anga by the damsels.* away to the boats which the damsels had pointed out to him, and they entertained him as before, and led him to a very pleasant boat, and seated him therein, and carried him away to the city of Anga. And when Sringa entered the city, the *Rain falls on the approach of Sringa.* clouds became black with rain, and Raja Lomapáda went out to meet the young Bráhman who had thus brought the rain, and worshipped him with his head bowing to the earth, and presented him with water for his feet, and with the

HISTORY OF
INDIA.
PART IV.
————
Sringa married
to the Raja's
daughter Sántá.

argha ; and the Raja then with serene mind gave his lotos-eyed daughter Sántá in marriage to Sringa. And the father of Sringa, by the force of his devotions, knew all that had taken place, and he dismissed all anxiety from his mind, and abode in the hermitage as before."

Review of the
foregoing
episode of Rishi
Sringa.

Power of pro-
curing rain
assumed by the
Bráhmans.

The foregoing episode is a specimen of those amusing stories which seem to have been occasionally converted by the Bráhmans into vehicles for the promulgation of their own peculiar ideas. The real object of the legend is to enforce the belief that drought is occasioned by the sins of a Raja, and that a young Bráhman Rishi could produce rain. It is perhaps scarcely necessary to dwell upon the vital importance of seasonable rains in every quarter of India. A long-continued drought implies the greatest calamity that can befall a nation. The Ryot loses his crop, the Raja loses his revenue, and parents

and children are literally starving. In ancient times the god of the firmament was Indra; and the hymns of the Rig-Veda are filled with prayers to Indra for rain, or with praises of Indra as the giver

Bráhmans
assert a supe-
riority to Indra.

of rain. But one of the earliest means by which the Bráhmans established their ascendancy over the masses was by arrogating to themselves a power to bring down rain, which was superior to that of

Indra.[1] In the legend of Sringa the Bráhmans have endeavoured to enforce this view; and by their own showing appear to have taken a singular advantage of the superstitious fears of the Raja on account of the drought. They not only declared

---

[1] The legend of Devayani (see vol. i. page 508) contains a curious picture of the arrogant pretensions of a Bráhman to bring down rain by the efficacy of his incantations; and of the ludicrous alarm of the Raja and his Council, lest he should depart out of the Raj, and leave them to procure rain by their own devices.

that the drought was occasioned by his sins, or in other words by his derelictions from Brahmanical laws and observances; but also urged that he could only expiate his sins by giving his daughter in marriage to the young Rishi; and the subsequent appearance of Sringa simultaneously with the rain cloud must have confirmed the general belief in the rain-procuring powers of the Bráhmans. The means by which Sringa was induced to leave the hermitage of his father are more than questionable; but the idea that they involved any immorality does not appear to have crossed the mind of the Brahmanical author.[2]

Having thus disposed of the episode respecting Sringa, the main narrative of the Aswamedha may be resumed as follows:—

Now when Sumantra had related to Dasaratha the story of the Rishi Sringa, he said to the Maháraja:—" O Raja of Rajas, go now to the city of Anga, and bring hither the Rishi Sringa and his wife Sántá, and appoint Sringa to be your own Guru." So Dasaratha took counsel of his priest Vasishtha, and with his approval he went away to the delightful city of Anga, and was entertained for eight days by Raja Lomapáda; and having obtained the consent of Lomapáda he returned to his own city of Ayodhyá, taking

---

[2] A similar legend has been adopted by the Buddhists. It is told not of Sringa, but of his grandfather Kásyapa, and is intended to enforce the sin of animal sacrifices. Kásyapa had acquired great religious merit by strictly keeping all the Buddhist precepts; and the Raja of Benares sent a nobleman to request him to come and offer a sacrifice in his behalf of all kinds of animals from the elephant downwards. Kásyapa refused, upon which the Raja sent his daughter in charge of the nobleman, to tempt the Rishi by offering him half the Raj and the hand of the Princess if he would comply. The scruples of the Rishi were overcome by the sight of the Raja's daughter, and he hastened to the place of sacrifice; but just as he lifted up his hand against the elephant, the affrighted beast set up a loud lamentation, in which all the other animals joined. This brought the Rishi to his senses, and he threw down the knife and fled back to the forest, and resumed his religious devotions. See Hardy's *Manual of Buddhism*, p. 50.

with him the Rishi Sringa and his wife Sántá.[3] Then the Maháraja approached Sringa with obeisance and adoration, and appointed him to be chief priest or Hotri in the Aswamedha.

Preparation for loosening the horse.

When the dewy season had passed away, and the spring had arrived, Sringa requested the Maháraja to collect all the things necessary for the loosening of the horse, and to bring together Vasishtha and Vámadeva, and all the most excellent of the Bráhmans. And when the Bráhmans had all assembled, the Maháraja paid them respectful homage, and spoke to them as follows:—" Although I have been ever most desirous of offspring, none has ever been granted me: I have therefore determined to perform an Aswamedha; and through the favour of the illustrious Rishi Sringa, and of you, O Bráhmans, I intend at this time to sacrifice the horse: In this thing, therefore, I pray you to be gracious to me, your humble dependant." At these words Vasishtha and the other Bráhmans cried out " Excellent! excellent!" And they did obeisance to the Maháraja and shouted forth his praise. Then the Maháraja said to Sumantra and his other Counsellors:—" Let abundance of all things necessary for the sacrifice be speedily provided by you under the direction of these Bráhmans: Let the horse be untied and suffered to go wherever he pleases, accompanied by a Bráhman."[4] And all the preparations were made as the Maháraja had commanded, and on the night of the full moon of the month Choitro, the horse was let loose for an entire year, and the preliminary ceremonies were all performed.

Respectful homage of the Maháraja to the Bráhmans.

The Maháraja's directions to his Counsellor.

Loosening of the horse.

Preparations for the sacrifice of the horse.

Now when the year was fully over, and the spring had again arrived, the horse was brought back to the city of

---

[3] It is stated in the Rámáyana that Sántá was only the adopted daughter of the Raja of Anga, and that her real father was Maháraja Dasaratha. But the passage must be regarded as an interpolation merely intended to associate the father of Ráma with the family of Kásyapa, of whom Sringa was the grandson. The adoption of daughters is foreign to Hindú ideas excepting perhaps in the case of dancing-girls.

[4] The statement that the horse was accompanied by a Bráhman, and not, as in the Aswamedha of Yudhishthira, by a warrior at the head of an army, is a curious instance of the Brahmanisation of the description of the ancient rite.

Ayodhyá, and all the preparations were completed for the sacrifice. Pavilions were set up for the accommodation of the Rajas, and hundreds of booths were constructed for the Bráhmans, and provisions were provided in great abundance. And amongst the Rajas that came to that sacrifice were the Raja of Mithilá, and the Raja of Kási, and the Raja of Anga, and the Raja of Magadhá, and the Raja of Sindhu, and the Raja of Saurashtra, and all the Rajas of the Dekhan. Thousands of Bráhmans were feasted by themselves, and the most delicious viands were served up to them on dishes of gold and silver by the Kshatriyas, who were superbly adorned with gems. And the place for the sacrifice was made ready on the northern bank of the river Sarayú. Twenty-one sacrificial posts were set up ; and each post was twenty-one cubits high, and was overlaid with gold, and adorned with a cloth and fragrant flowers; and the birds and animals for the sacrifice were tied to the posts, and the horse was tied in like manner. And the sacrificial pits were prepared according to the ordinance, and they were eighteen in number and arranged in three rows, in the form of the bird Garura ; and the pits that represented the wings of the bird were lined with bricks of gold. And the sacrificial fire was kindled by the Bráhmans, and the horse was led round the sacrificial fire and immolated with the sacred scimitar, whilst the Udgatri chaunted the Vedic hymns. And the first and second Ránís were placed by the side of the dead horse, and remained there all night. And the different portions of the horse were placed upon the fire according to the ordinance by the Hotri and the Brithi ; and the Brithi repeated the appropriate mantras, whilst giving the flesh to the fire. Thus the Aswamedha was duly performed, and Maháraja Dasaratha gave large presents to all assembled ; and he gave many provinces to the officiating Bráhmans, but they would not accept the land, because they were unable to rule, and were devoted to the study of the Vedas ; and he gave them instead a million of cows, and a hundred million pieces of gold, and four hundred million pieces of silver.

HISTORY OF INDIA. PART IV.

Place of sacrifice. Twenty-one posts.

The eighteen sacrificial pits.

The sacrifice.

The Ránís placed with the dead horse.

Presents of provinces refused by the Bráhmans.

HISTORY OF
INDIA.
PART IV.

Second sacrifice
performed by
Rishi Sringa.
Assembling of
the gods.

After this Rishi Sringa said to the Maháraja :—"I will perform another sacrifice to secure you a son." And the Rishi proceeded to do as he had said. And there were collected all the gods, together with the Gandharvas, or celestial musicians, and the Siddhas, or saints who dwell in the sky, and the seven celestial Rishis; [and there came Brahma, the sovereign of the gods, together with Siva and Vishnu;[5]] and there also came Indra, the glorious one, surrounded by the Maruts. Then the Rishi began the sacrifice according to the ordinance, and supplicated the assembled deities that they would be pleased to grant four renowned sons to the Maháraja. And the gods replied:—" Be it so, O Bráhman, for thou art ever to be regarded by us as men regard a Raja." So saying, the gods received their shares of the oblation, and then disappeared with Indra at their head.

The gods
receive their
shares and
disappear.

The gods pray
to Brahma for
protection
against Rávana.

Rávana,
rendered
invulnerable to
the gods, had
made the gods
his slaves.

Now when Indra and the gods left the place of sacrifice, they proceeded to the heaven of Brahma, the lord of mankind and giver of blessings ; and they went before Brahma with joined hands, and addressed him thus :—" O Brahma, that Rákshasa, named Rávana, to whom in your kindness you granted the blessing that he should be invulnerable to the gods and demons, has in his great pride oppressed all the universe, and deprived the gods of their shares of the sacrifices : O divine one, save us from Rávana, who fills the world with noise and tumult, and who has made the gods his slaves : By his power he has delivered his subjects, the Rákshasas, from the sway of Yama, and made Yama himself the cutter of grass for his steeds : He has compelled the Sun to shine mildly over his city of Lanká, and the Moon to be always at the full throughout his Raj : The six Seasons attend him as his servants, and appear whenever he commands them : Agni burns not in his presence ; and Váyu blows gently in Lanká : He has compelled his brother Kuvera to quit Lanká, and take refuge in the Kailása mountain : No one can perform a sacrifice through fear of him : He is al-

---

[5] This passage is so evidently an interpolation, that it is inserted in brackets. It will be seen presently that when the gods left the sacrifice they proceeded first to the heaven of Brahma and then to the heaven of Vishnu, in order to propitiate those deities.

ways oppressing the gods, the Bráhmans, and the cows: He has taken away several of our wives by force : Secured by your blessing, he treats us with disrespect and has no fear for us : O Brahma, we pray you to devise a scheme for delivering us from the oppression of this Rávana."[6]

Brahma, hearing these words, conducted Indra and all the gods to the ocean of milk, the abode of Vishnu; and the gods propitiated Vishnu, whom they could not see, with loud praises. Then Vishnu the glorious, the lord of the world, arrayed in yellow raiment with ornaments of pure gold, riding upon Garura as the sun upon a cloud, appeared with his shell, chakra, mace, and lotos in his four hands ; and his wife Lakshmí was sitting upon his knees. And all the gods fell prostrate before him, and choked with grief they thus addressed him with joined hands :—" O Vishnu, you who are able to remove the afflictions of those who are distressed, we entreat you to be our sanctuary : You are the lord of this universe, and you already know the reason of our coming ; and we only give utterance to our wants that we may relieve ourselves from the burden which lies heavily upon our minds : Brahma has blessed Rávana the Rákshasa with a life which cannot be taken away by any celestial being; and Rávana in his pride has taken advantage of this blessing to oppress the gods, the Bráhmans, and the cows: Brahma is unable to recall the blessing which he has bestowed upon Rávana, and you are our only resource : Save us and your creation from the oppression of Rávana ! "

At this prayer, Vishnu smiled, and said :—" Be not terrified ; I have already devised a scheme for delivering you from the oppression of Rávana : In his pride Rávana would not request Brahma to secure his life from men and monkeys, for he thought in his heart that they were beneath his notice : I will take advantage of this omission, and cause the destruction of Rávana without casting aside the blessing

Side notes:
Brahma conducts the gods to the abode of Vishnu in the sea of milk.

Vishnu appears upon Garura with Lakshmí upon his knees.

Prayer of the gods to Vishnu against the oppression of Rávana.

Vishnu promises to overthrow Rávana by mortals and monkeys.

---

[6] The ancient gods of the Vedas are here represented as supplicating Brahma, whose worship is of more modern origin, and thus virtually acknowledging his superiority. Yama is death ; Agni is fire ; Váyu is the wind ; and Kuvera is wealth. The Asuras and Dánavas were aboriginal tribes, who were popularly regarded as demons.

which has been bestowed upon him by Brahma : I will go to Ayodhyá and divide myself into four parts, and take my birth as the four sons of Maháraja Dasaratha': Thus by becoming man I shall conquer in battle Rávana, the terror of the universe, who is invulnerable to the gods ; go you meantime upon the earth, and assume the shape of monkeys and bears that you may render me service in my battle with Rávana."

The gods, hearing those words, rejoiced exceedingly ; and they sounded the praises of Vishnu, and went their way and did as he had commanded them.

Meanwhile the Rishi Sringa had performed the sacrifice for obtaining sons for Maháraja Dasaratha ; and when he had finished, celestial music was sounded in the heavens, and a divine being came out of the fire arrayed in incomparable splendour ; and he was as lofty as a mountain, as mighty as a tiger, as bright as the ardent flame, and his shoulders were like those of the lion. This wondrous being was clothed in red, and he wore ornaments on his hands, and on his neck was a chain of twenty-seven pearls, and his teeth resembled the stars in heaven. Thus glowing in brightness, this celestial being held in both hands, like a beloved wife, a large golden vessel filled with the divine páyasa, the rice and milk of the immortal gods.

This celestial being said to the Rishi Sringa, who was the Hotri at the sacrifice :—" O Sage, I am an emanation of Brahma come hither to you : Do you receive this vessel of páyasa from me, and present it to the Maháraja." The wise Rishi replied :—" Be pleased yourself to deliver this surprising vessel to the Maháraja." Then the emanation of Brahma spoke thus to Dasaratha :—" O Maháraja, I present to you this food of ambrosial taste ; it is the fruit of the sacrifice : Receive, O Maháraja, this páyasa prepared by the gods which ensures prosperity : Let it be eaten by your beautiful consorts, and from them you will then obtain the

sons for whom you have performed the sacrifice." And the Maháraja bowed his head, and received the golden vessel full of celestial food which had been given by the gods ; and he rejoiced like a poor man who has obtained wealth; and the emanation of Brahma became invisible to mortal eye.

The apartments of the ladies of the Maháraja were now illumined with joy, as the atmosphere is illumined by the bright autumnal moon; and the Maháraja entered therein with the son-producing páyasa, and he gave the half to Kausalyá and the other half to Kaikeyí; but when Sumitrá came forward, the Maháraja requested his two elder Ránís to give her a portion of their own shares. And Kausalyá and Kaikeyí each divided her portion with Sumitrá, so that whilst they each had one quarter of the páyasa, Sumitrá had two quarters. And when the Ránís had eaten of the sacrificial food, they each one conceived; and the Maháraja, beholding his wives about to become mothers, enjoyed a pleasure of mind equal to that of Vishnu when adored by Indra and the sages. After this the Ránís bore four sons; Kausalyá gave birth to Ráma, and Kaikeyí to Bharata; and Sumitrá having received two quarters of the páyasa food gave birth to two sons; from the quarter which she received from Kausalyá she gave birth to Lakshmana, who became the ever faithful friend of Ráma; and from the quarter which she received from Kaikeyí she gave birth to Satrughna, who became the ever faithful friend of Bharata. And on the birth of these four sons there were great rejoicings in the city of Ayodhyá amongst all ranks of people, and the streets were filled with dancers and musicians, and decked out with flowers and banners.

Eleven days after the birth of the four sons, the priest Vasishtha performed the ceremony of giving them names. To the son of Kausalyá he gave the name of Ráma, which signifies "the delight of the people;" to the son of Kaikeyí he gave the name of Bharata, which signifies "filling the world with his name;" and of the two sons of Sumitrá he named the elder Lakshmana, which signifies "beautiful to behold," and he named the younger Satrughna, which signifies "the destroyer of his enemies." When the names had been thus given, the Maháraja feasted the Bráhmans, and all the citizens of Ayodhyá, and all the people of the Raj of Kosala; and he gave abundance of jewels to the Bráhmans.

Review of the foregoing description of the Aswamedha.

The foregoing description of the Aswamedha comprises two distinct narratives of two different sacrifices, namely :—

Two sacrifices involved.

1st, The horse sacrifice.

2nd, The homa and páyasa.

The offering of homa is not indeed explicitly stated; but still it seems that the second sacrifice of Sringa involved no slaying of animals, but was simply an offering of oblations to the Vedic deities.

Real character of the sacrifice of the horse.

The sacrifice of the horse can be easily realized. The posts to which the birds and animals are tied, and the pits in which the meat is cooked, are perfectly intelligible, and in general conformity with the arrangements made in the Aswamedha of Yud-

Strange rite of the Ránís and the dead horse.

hishthira. The object of the sacrifice, however, was not an assertion of sovereignty, but the birth of sons; and one of the rites for the attainment of this object was that the Ránís should pass the night with the dead body of the horse. Of this disgusting ceremony there is no reference whatever in the Rig-

Probably a later Brahmanical invention.

Veda; [7] and it is difficult to avoid the suspicion that the rite is a pure invention of the Brahmanical author intended to disguise the real meaning of the

Flesh of the horse probably believed to stimulate conception.

Aswamedha. At the second sacrifice, or offering of the homa, the object was attained by giving a portion of sacred food, known as páyasa, and consisting of rice and milk. The idea of food is here involved; of stimulating food which would promote

---

[7] See Wilson's remarks in the introduction to his second volume of translations of the Rig-Veda. Some revolting impurities appear to have been connected with the rite which need not be particularized.

conception.   Now the flesh of the horse was probably
regarded as highly stimulating; and the sacrifice of
a horse for the purpose of procuring such stimulating
food for the Ránís appears to be equally probable.
But such a belief would be very obnoxious to the
later Bráhmans, who were opposed to the slaughter of
animals; and hence the páyasa was substituted, a
divine food which is still prepared and cooked at
Brahmanical sacrifices.

The narrative of the offering of homa is a very
remarkable one.   It exhibits the peculiar genius of
Brahmanism in transmuting a mortal hero into the
Supreme Being, with the ultimate object of convert-
ing his history into a vehicle for the promulgation of
Brahmanical views.   It is an attempt to represent
the four sons of Dasaratha, and especially Ráma, as
incarnations of Vishnu; to connect those incarnations with the offering of homa; and to exhibit the
superior efficacy of the páyasa, or sacred food.   The
belief in the possibility of a direct incarnation of
Deity in the womb of a woman is an important
article of faith in many religions, and indeed is the
foundation of Christianity itself.   But the process by
which that incarnation is effected has always been
treated as a mystery or miracle.   In the Rámáyana
it is surrounded by circumstances which are well calculated to impress a simple and childlike people.   The
object of the incarnation is fully explained, whilst
the incarnation itself is treated with singular delicacy.   A terrible Rákshasa named Rávana devotes
many years to the performance of religious austerities ; and by the power of those austerities he secures
the favour of Brahma, who thereupon, at his request,
renders him invulnerable to gods and demons.   Rá-

Ravana
oppresses the
Vedic deities.

vana now considers himself to be immortal; the gods and demons are unable to harm him; and men and beasts are so much beneath his notice, that he has not stooped to pray for immunity from their attacks. Accordingly, he oppresses the gods; not indeed the great Brahmanical gods, Brahma, Vishnu, and Siva, but the ancient gods of the Rig-Veda, whom he compels to do as he pleases. Death is not allowed to afflict his subjects the Rákshasas; the burning Sun is required to shine mildly over his city; the Moon is obliged to be always at the full throughout his Raj; the Seasons come and go at his command; Fire burns not in his presence; and the Wind is forced

Complaint of
the Vedic gods,
an acknow-
ledgment of
their inferiority
to Brahma, and
of the inferiority
of Brahma to
Vishnu.

to blow gently. Accordingly the gods complain to Brahma, who acknowledges the superiority of Vishnu, by conducting them into the presence of that deity; and since Rávana has not been rendered invulnerable to men and animals, Vishnu resolves to become incarnate as the four sons of Dasaratha, and especially as Ráma; and the gods descend on earth and beget monkeys and bears in order that their progeny may be ultimately formed into an army, and effect the destruction of Rávana under the leadership of Ráma.

Vishnu becomes
incarnate
through the
agency of
páyasa.

Vishnu having thus granted the prayer of the gods, takes advantage of the sacrifice to become incarnate. An emanation of Brahma appears out of the sacrificial fire and presents the páyasa; and the Ránís conceive by merely eating the sacred food; a process which has the merit of preserving decency, although somewhat at variance with physiological laws. Henceforth the great difficulty of the author of the Rámáyana, and his subsequent editors, has been to bring the life and character of Ráma into harmony with his assumed incarnation.[8]

[8] The reconciliation of the divine character of Ráma with that of his mortal career upon earth, appears to have been a task of considerable difficulty. Certainly it has not always been effected by Válmíki, the author of the larger Rámáyana, which forms the text of the present paraphrase. There is, however, a remarkable abridgment of the story, the authorship of which is attributed to the mythical Vyása, in which the whole has been spiritualized, and every conflicting incident either explained away or omitted, whilst the greatest possible stress has been laid upon the character of Ráma as a saviour and deliverer. This work is entitled the Adhyátma Rámáyana, and may be regarded as the testament of the Vaishnavas, or worshippers of Vishnu. It is indeed chiefly valuable from a religious point of view.; but still it may be convenient to exhibit occasionally some of its spiritualizations in connection with the traditional incidents to which they refer. The narrative is put into the mouth of the god Siva, who is supposed to be relating the Rámáyana to his wife Párvatí.

The following extracts exhibit the religious ideas which are popularly associated in the present day with the birth of Ráma :—

"Hear now, O Párvatí! an account of the sacrifice celebrated by Raja Dasaratha. The gods attended in their proper persons, and sitting in a row, took with their own hands their respective shares. The Tirthas, or places of pilgrimage, attended in person. There was such a crowd the earth trembled; the shock was so great that no one could withstand it. So much homa was thrown into the fire that at first it appeared inauspicious. When the sacrifice was completed, the god of Fire (Agni) appeared bearing in each hand a cup of rice and milk. Agni said to Dasaratha :—'Take this rice and milk, O Raja! from me: go into thy female apartments and give it to thy wives; the fruit of it is great, of its effect there cannot be a doubt.' The god of Fire then vanished. Vasishtha and Sringa then went into the female apartments, and gave a portion to the three wives Kausalyá, Kaikeyí, and Sumitrá. All three became pregnant, and when Vishnu entered into the body of Kausalyá, Brahma and the gods mounting their cars, stood on the heavens above the city of Ayodhyá, and repeated numberless praises to Ráma; and then returned to their own abodes in a transport of joy. At a most auspicious hour Ráma was born of Kausalyá. His body was like a cloud; on his head was a crown set with jewels; his four arms were extended; in one hand he held the holy shell, in another the circle, in the third the war mace, and in the last the lotos. In his ears were rings in the form of a crocodile; he had a string of rubies and Vaijayanti seeds on his neck; his forehead was ornamented with a stripe of saffron and sandal wood. A yellow cloth was girded round his loins, a veil of brocade covered his shoulders; his two locks of hair hanging down on his cheeks were like the waving spikenard. He was covered from head to foot with ornaments of gold, jewels, and pearls. The beauty of his person appeared with resplendent grace; his eyes were like the lotos. The figure of Lakshmana sat on his left hand, the form of the sage Bhrigu on his right. His lips were as red as the rubies of Badakshan. At his feet was the form of the lotos, because the whole world finds an asylum at his feet. A million suns and moons would hide their diminished heads before the light of his countenance. In this form he appeared before his mother Kausalyá, who knew him to be the godhead. With joined hands she bowed down and began to praise and adore him. (Here follows a prayer of Kausalyá to the infant deity, concluding with the following words) :—

" 'Thou, O Lord! hast now four arms, be pleased to assume the shape of an infant that I may nourish thee with maternal affection, my happiness will then be perfect.'

" Ráma, highly pleased, explained to his mother the cause of his assuming a human form, and then concealed his four-armed shape, and assumed the form of a new-born infant, and began to cry aloud. Raja Dasaratha heard the sound, and his joy was indescribable. He distributed innumerable treasures in alms. Vasishtha also caused him to perform such ceremonies as were necessary on this occasion. The rejoicings in the city of Ayodhyá were such as it is impossible to describe. On every gate kettledrums in thousands sounded the joyful tidings. The inhabitants placed the boughs of the mango-tree at their doors; they fixed flags and ensigns of brocade and embroidery on the tops of their houses. The sprightly dancers danced in every street; the shop-keepers went about uttering praises and thanksgivings; the eunuchs performed various dances and received great rewards.

" Brahma and the gods received intelligence of the birth of Ráma with joy unbounded. They stood on the heavens above Ayodhyá, and showering down Parijata flowers, they exclaimed with a loud voice,—' May thy prosperity endure for ever.' After giving praise to him they. made obeisance and retired to their own abodes."

CHAPTER III.

THE CHILDHOOD OF RÁMA.

THE narrative of the Aswamedha of Dasaratha and subsequent birth of his four sons, is followed by an interesting account of the early years of Ráma, from the days when he lay a helpless infant upon his mother's knee, until the time when his education was completed, and his marriage was contemplated. This account is valuable on two grounds. First it exhibits that love of children and sympathy with childhood, which are almost peculiar to Hindú bards ; and which find expression, not so much in conceptions of a boy-saint or infant deity, as in genuine pictures of infants and children drawn from a close observation of real life. Secondly it exhibits the domestic life of the Hindús in a succession of scenes representing every stage in the progress of the child from infancy to manhood ; and Ráma appears in every character with a downright realism which may seem somewhat puerile to men of sterner mould, but which has endeared him to the hearts of Hindú mothers for countless generations. Every scene is perfect. Ráma trying to put his toe into his mouth ; Ráma laughing and trotting away when called by his parents ; Ráma snatching a morsel out of his father's hand and eating it with a laugh ; Ráma pointing out

Hindú love of children.

Realism in the descriptions of domestic life.

Progressive incidents in the infancy, childhood, and boyhood of Ráma.

his eyes, nose, mouth, and ears, when called upon by his mother; Ráma crying for the moon; Ráma beginning to say "pa" and "ma;" Ráma sitting on his father's knee in the Council-hall; Ráma and the other little boys making clay images and worshipping them after the manner of the family Bráhman; Ráma going to school with his brothers and learning his letters; Ráma and his brethren dressed in different coloured frocks, and carrying their satchels and ink bottles; Ráma's progress in grammar, science, and accomplishments; Ráma examined in his proficiency by the Mahárája in the Council-hall; Ráma playing in mock battles and at being Mahárája; Ráma invested with the sacred thread; and Ráma perfectly educated, and arrived at a marriageable age;—all these are described with a natural simplicity, of which perhaps no parallel can be found in European literature.[1]

Narrative in the Rámáyana.

The story of Ráma's childhood may now be related as follows :—

Description of the four babies during the first year of infancy.

Now the four infant sons of the Mahárája were exceedingly beautiful, and the three Ránís took very great delight in nursing their respective children. And Ráma, more than all the others, was a very lovely babe, and as he slept in a white cot he appeared like a blue lotos floating upon the pure water of the Ganges; and sometimes he would lift up his foot and put his toe into his mouth, as if to taste what it was in his toe which drew so much reverence from all who

[1] The incidents of Ráma's early life are probably a later interpolation. They are not to be found in the Bengal edition of the Rámáyana, but only in what is called the North-West recension. Accordingly, they are not reproduced either in Carey's English version, or in the French translation of M. Fauche, or in the Italian translation of Gorresco. Moreover, Professor Williams seems to make no allusion to this portion of the narrative in his useful analysis of the Rámáyana. In the Adhyátma Rámáyana there is some allusion to the youthful sports of Ráma, but they have evidently been borrowed from the life of Krishna.

beheld him. When Mahárája Dasaratha, accompanied by the priest Vasishtha, went to see his infant sons, the priest pointed to Ráma, and said :—" O Mahárája, I perceive from the marks on Ráma that he is no ordinary child ; and I am nearly assured that he is an incarnation of Vishnu : Behold his beautiful colour, like green grass, his fine hair glossy and curled, his large head and high forehead, his brow radiant with the signs of royalty, his face smiling like the full moon, his large dark eyes, his lips red as the Bimba fruit, his nose like that of the green parrot, his neck like that of a shell, his long hands and red palms bearing the marks of the chakra, lotos, and circle on the tips of his fingers, his wide breast, his legs resembling plantain trees, his feet red as the rising sun, bearing the marks of the shell, the chakra, the mace, and the lotos : Behold all these, and you will see that he is full of marks belonging to Vishnu."

When the four little boys were sufficiently grown to be able to run about, they were the delight of their mothers and of the Mahárája. Sometimes the Mahárája would call Ráma, and Ráma would turn his back and laugh and run away ; and if his mother Kausalyá or his father the Mahárája ran after him, he would run all the faster, and afterwards would come back to them of his own accord. Sometimes Ráma would snatch a morsel of his father's food, and going to a distance from him, he would eat it up and laugh at the Mahárája all the while. Sometimes his mother would ask him to point out his eyes, nose, mouth, ears, or other parts of his body, and he would do so by touching those parts with his forefinger. Sometimes the women of other households would come to the palace, and ask Ráma who his mother was ; and then he would smile and run to his mother and sit upon her lap. And it so happened that one evening, whilst the Rání Kausalyá was nursing Ráma in the inner court of the palace, the full moon arose in the east in all its splendour, and Ráma felt a very strong desire to have the beautiful moon to play with as a toy. And he put out both his little hands towards the moon, in order to obtain it ; but his mother could not understand what it was that he wanted, and thereupon he tried to

HISTORY OF INDIA.
PART IV.

Ráma identified by the priest Vasishtha as an incarnation of Vishnu.
Distinguishing marks.

Ráma and his brethren begin to run about.
Anecdotes of Ráma.

Story of Ráma crying for the moon and refusing to be comforted.

Kausalyá fails
to comfort him.

beat her. And Kausalyá asked him many times what he
wished to have, and he continued to point to the moon, so
that at last she came to understand what it was that he
wanted, and she then spoke to him in mild terms as follows :—"Do not desire, O my child, to possess the moon,
because it is thousands of miles off, and it is not a plaything
for children, and no child ever got it : If you wish I will
bring you some jewels that are brighter than the moon, and
you can play with them." So saying she brought some
beautiful jewels, and placed them before the little boy; but
Ráma threw them away in anger, and began to cry until his

The women of
the palace fail.

eyes were red and swollen with weeping. Now by this time
a number of women were gathered around him, but no one
could console him. One said :—" Perchance he is hungry ;"
and Kausalyá tried to give him suck, but this he utterly
refused to take. Another woman said :—" Perchance he is
sleepy ;" and she took him in her lap and sung the lullaby,
but she could not quiet him, and he still continued to cry.
Then one of the women said :—"The goddess Sustí has
become unpropitious, and must be propitiated with offerings
of curds, plantains, and fried paddy." Another said :—"A
ghost is troubling him; so send for a man who can repeat a
mantra and drive the ghost out." But though all these
means were tried they were all of no effect, and Ráma was

The Maháraja
tries and fails.

still as unpacified as before. So the Rání Kausalyá sent for
the Maháraja, and when the Maháraja heard that Ráma was
ill he went to him immediately, and tried his utmost to console the child ; but he could do no more than those who had
tried before him, and Ráma continued to cry and would not

Sumantra, the
chief Coun-
sellor, pacifies
Ráma with a
mirror.

be comforted. Then the Maháraja sent for his chief Counsellor and told him all that had taken place ; and when
Sumantra heard that Ráma was crying for the moon, he
desired those about him to bring a mirror. So a mirror
was brought and placed in the hands of Ráma ; and when
Ráma saw the image of the moon in the mirror, he was fully
satisfied, and left off weeping, and was soon as merry as
before, and the whole family were at ease.

When Ráma and his brethren had reached their second

year, they could not say the words " peeta" or " father," or " mata" or " mother," and therefore they called their parents " pa " and " ma." And if any one asked Ráma what his name was, he would answer " Ama," for he could not pronounce the letter " R." Sometimes the three mothers would sit together and make their four sons dance in a circle, whilst they clapped their hands. Sometimes the Maháraja would tell Ráma to bring him his sandals, and Ráma would take up the Maháraja's sandals with both his hands, and carry them to his father, to the great delight of all who saw him. At other times the Maháraja would take Ráma into the Council-hall, and keep the little boy on his knee during the Council; and Ráma listened to all that was going on, and as he sat upon his father's knee, he appeared as beautiful as a new rain-cloud when seated on the golden mountain of Sumaru. Meantime his mother the Rání would be impatient at his absence, and would send her maid servant every minute to the Council to bring away Ráma; for a moment's absence from her son appeared like an age in her eyes.

HISTORY OF INDIA. PART IV.

Second year of infancy : Ráma and his brethren begin to talk.

Anecdotes of Ráma.

When the sons of Dasaratha were in their third year, the Maháraja performed the ceremony of piercing their ears; and the rite was celebrated with great magnificence. After this the brethren began to play with other little boys of their own age. They made images of clay, and offered clay offerings to the images, after the manner that they had seen the priest of their father offer up sacrifices to the gods in behalf of the household. They would first entreat the images to eat the offerings which they offered, and then when the images did not move they would put the offerings into their mouths; and when the images would not eat the offerings, they were very angry and broke up the images into pieces. Sometimes Ráma would see his own reflection in a crystal pillar, and he would say to his mother Kausalyá :— " A second Ráma is come, so keep him here that I may play with him." But seeing in like manner the reflection of his own mother, he would say :—" Why have you left me and gone to the other Ráma : Do not take him in your lap ! "

HISTORY OF
INDIA.
PART IV.

And with these words he would take hold of her cloth and pull her away.

At five years of age Ráma and his brethren are educated by Vasishtha.

Rites of initiation.

When Ráma and his brethren were five years of age they commenced their education according to the rule. Vasishtha was appointed to be their preceptor, and he initiated them in their studies in the accustomed form. He first worshiped the divine Saraswatí, the goddess of all learning, and afterwards directed the four brethren to make offerings of flowers and leaves of bale fruit to the goddess. He then took a chalk stone, and drew the vowels upon the floor, and directed the boys to run over each letter three times ; and when this lesson was over, the Mahárája gave many rich presents to Vasishtha, and from that time they went every day to the house of Vasishtha, to receive his instructions. And the four lads were dressed by their mothers in clothes of different colours ; and Ráma was dressed in yellow, Lakshmana in purple, and Bhárata and Satrughna in green and red. And they had hundreds of servants at their command, but still each one carried his ink bottle in his right hand, and over his left shoulder was his satchel containing books, reeds, and white palm leaves. In this manner they went out of the palace every morning, and proceeded with other school-boys to the house of their preceptor ; and sometimes when a boy strayed away from school without the leave of his preceptor, they were commanded by Vasishtha to go out into the street and bring the truant in. And when they knew all the vowels, they were taught all the other letters of the alphabet ; and when they knew these also, they began to teach the smaller boys under the direction of Vasishtha. And Ráma never disobeyed his preceptor, nor did aught that would excite his displeasure. And when he had learnt all his letters, he began to read the grammar ; and in a short time he learnt eighteen languages, as well as the arts of singing, playing on musical instruments, dancing, and painting, and every one of the sciences. And at certain times the Mahárája would send for his sons, and examine them in the Council-hall before his Council ; and the boys always acquitted themselves to the admiration of all present, and the Ministers and

Dress of the four boys.

Daily attendance at school.

Progress in their studies. Alphabet.

Grammar.

Arts and sciences.
Examinations in the Council-hall.

Chieftains expressed their great surprise at the proficiency of the sons of the Maháraja.

When the four brethren had passed out of their childhood, they were exercised in the use of arms and in military and royal games. At times, having obtained the permission of Vasishtha, they would go out and play at hide-and-seek; or they would form themselves into two parties, and engage in a mock combat; and it was agreed amongst them that the party who was defeated should carry the victor upon his shoulders for a hundred cubits; and when Ráma was defeated he was not excused on account of his being the son of a Maháraja, but he was obliged to carry his victor like any other boy. Sometimes, however, Ráma would play at being the Maháraja; and some of his play-fellows would be his Ministers, and others his subjects, and some would hold the umbrella of royalty over his head, whilst others fanned him with the chámara. Then some would bring offenders before him, and submit their complaints for his decision; and Ráma would listen to the whole of the case, and at the end he would deliver his judgment, and would award appropriate punishment to the guilty party.

Exercises in arms and games.

Hide-and-seek and mock battles.

Ráma's play at being Maháraja, with play fellows for Ministers.

Thus passed away the lives of Ráma and his brethren, until the time drew nigh when each one was to be invested with the sacred thread. Accordingly their heads were shaved by the barber, and they were clothed in red silk; and they went to the house of their preceptor Vasishtha, and were invested with the sacred string which was made of the skin of the antelope. Vasishtha then taught them the holy Gayatri; and throughout that day they became Brahmachárís according to the ordinance, and each one carried his bag amongst his kinsmen to receive alms. First, Ráma went to his mother Kausalyá, and she gave him the dole of rice, and with it many precious jewels; and in this manner all the brethren went round and received alms and rich gifts from all present, from the subjects of the Maháraja, as well as from the Ministers, Chieftains, and ladies; and all the riches they received they gave to their preceptor Vasishtha.

Investiture with the sacred thread, and the attendant rites.

Ráma and his brethren Brahmachárís for the day.

After the four sons of Dasaratha had been thus invested

Study the Vedas.

HISTORY OF
INDIA.
PART IV.

Virtues and
accomplish-
ments of the
four Princes.

with the sacred thread, they began to learn the Vedas; and
in due time they grew up like four heroes, and were possessed of every virtue and every accomplishment. They
were bright as the moon, skilful in archery, expert in mounting the elephant, the horse, and the chariot; and they were
devoted to all the wishes of their parents, and became deeply
versed in the Vedas. But Ráma excelled all his brethren,
and was as conspicuous amongst them as a flag upon a
tower; and whilst all grew up in loving attachment to
each other, Lakshmana was the special companion of Ráma,
and rejoiced to perform whatever was pleasing to him.

Superiority of
Ráma.

Legend of the
great bow of
Siva preserved
by Janaka,
Raja of Mithilá.

Now it happened one day that Ráma was shooting with
a bow that belonged to a companion of his, and he bent the
bow with so much strength that it broke in two pieces. And
his companion said to him :—" You have strength enough
to break my bow, but if you would manifest your full might,
you should go to the city of Mithilá, and break the great bow
of the god Siva, which is preserved in the household of Raja
Janaka." And Ráma answered :—" Tell me the story of the
bow." Then his companion said :—" Janaka, Raja of
Mithilá, has a beautiful daughter named Sítá, or the ' white
one,' and he has vowed to give her in marriage to that man
who can break the great bow, which belonged in former
times to the god Siva, and which the Raja worships every
day with flowers and incense." And Ráma pondered over
these words in his heart, but he said nothing, for the time
had not yet come.

Review of the
foregoing narra-
tive of Ráma's
early life.
The blue-
coloured babe.

The foregoing narrative of the childhood of
Ráma is so plain and simple as to require but little
comment. The picture of the dark-coloured babe,
lying in his white cot like a blue lotos floating upon
the pure water of the Ganges, is perhaps somewhat
foreign to European ideas accustomed to the pink
complexion of western babies. Moreover the picture is somewhat marred by the description of the
marks from which Vasishtha the priest is supposed to

have identified the infant as an incarnation of Vishnu.
The story of Ráma crying for the moon is peculiarly
Hindú. The inability of the mother to console the
little boy, and the suggestions of the other women,
are precisely the every-day occurrences in the houses
of Hindús. When a child of tender years is fractious, and refuses to eat or to sleep, the women immediately begin to propitiate the goddess Sustí; a
primitive household deity who finds no place in the
Vedas, but who is largely worshipped by the females
of Hindústan. If the child still refuses to be comforted, a Bráhman is sent for to exorcise him with
mantras. Lastly, if these resources fail the husband
is sent for to bring about a pacification. In the
present instance the story turns upon the wisdom of
the Chief Counsellor in sending for a mirror, and
satisfying the child with a reflection of the moon.
This idea again is essentially Hindú. No one but a
Hindú, with his passionate fondness for children,
and his traditions of patriarchal life, would conceive
the idea of a sovereign sending for his Prime Minister to pacify a fractious child. In like manner the
scene in which the little boys make clay images and
propitiate them with clay offerings, in the same way
that they had seen the family Bráhman propitiate the
household gods, could only take place in an Indian
household. But yet the realism of Hindú childhood
in trying to make the idols eat the offerings, is
paralleled by European children, who will give oats
to a wooden horse, or bread and butter to a stuffed
bird; and it is thus exquisitely true to human nature, whilst furnishing a significant travestie of the
original ceremonial.

The education of Ráma, which commenced

The marks of
Vishnu.
Incidents con-
nected with
Ráma's crying
for the moon
common to
modern Hindú
life.
Worship of
Susti.

Exorcising.

Hindú idea of
the Chief Coun-
sellor being
called in to
quiet Ráma.

Realism of
Hindú child-
hood as dis-
played towards
the clay images.

Life of Ráma a
type of the
modern Hindú.

HISTORY OF
INDIA.
PART IV.

Custom of
becoming
Brahmacháris
at the investi-
ture with the
thread.

according to rule in the fifth year of his age, is the
exact routine pursued by Hindú preceptors ; and the
scenes enacted in Vasishtha's school-room are precisely such as still take place in purely Hindú
schools.[2] So, too, the investiture with the sacred
thread is celebrated in the present day, in the case
of all Bráhmans and Kshatriyas, precisely as it is
described in the Rámáyana ; the boys becoming
Bramacháris or religious mendicants for the day,[3]
and carrying about bags in which they receive presents from their relatives and friends. The remaining details call for no remark, the incidents described in the narrative being sufficiently clear to explain
themselves.

[2] The worship of Saraswatí by Hindú students is dying away in English
schools, and books are no longer regarded as sacred things ; probably because the
printed English volumes are treated as altogether different from the ancient
manuscripts. Once a year there is a festival to the goddess Saraswatí, on which
day most school-boys enjoy a holiday, for every book in the house should
be laid before the image of the goddess and remain there for the day. English
books, however, are not always offered, especially if the parents are anxious for
their children's progress in education ; but idle school-boys will on such occasion
rise early in the morning and place all their books, English included, before the
goddess ; after which they are perfectly safe, as no one would be profane enough to
remove the volumes which have been once offered.

[3] The Brahmachárí is a religious pupil who studies the Vedas, who also col-
lects alms for his own subsistence, and for that of his master or Guru. In the
present instance the Guru was Vasishtha.

ROUTE OF RÁMA FROM AYODHYA TO MITHILÁ (Chap. IV.)

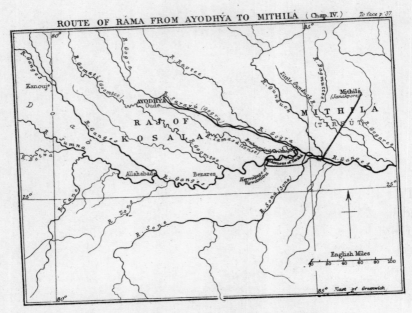

ROUTE OF RÁMA FROM AYODHYA TO CHITRA-KÚTA (Chap. IX.)

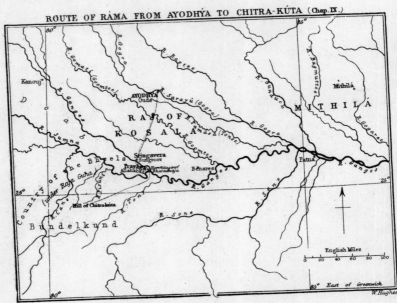

CHAPTER IV.

WARS WITH THE RÁKSHASAS.

THE story of Ráma's boyhood is naturally followed by the story of his marriage; but an interval occurs during which he appears to have acted as the protector of the Bráhmans against the Rákshasas, or aborigines of the country, who seem to have persecuted the Bráhmans by polluting their sacrifices.

Interval
between Ráma's
boyhood and
marriage
employed
against the
Rákshasas.

It has already been seen that a considerable confusion exists respecting the aboriginal inhabitants of India. They are alluded to under different names, such as Rákshasas, Asuras, Daityas, and Dánavas. Sometimes they are popularly regarded as ghosts or demons. At other times they are represented as forming different families, who have descended from Bráhman sages, and have acquired supernatural weapons or supernatural powers by the worship of Brahma. Thus the terrible Rávana is said to have been the grandson of the sage Pulastya, who was the son of Brahma; and to have obtained invulnerability as regards gods and demons as a reward for his severe worship of Brahma. It seems probable that originally the names Rákshasa, Asura, Daitya, and Dánava were applied with some strictness to different tribes of aborigines, but that at a subsequent period the names were indiscriminately applied to the

Confusion
respecting the
aboriginal
inhabitants of
India.
Different
appellations.

Regarded as
ghosts or
demons.

Represented as
descendants
from Bráhman
sages, and as
worshippers of
Brahma.

aborigines in general. As, however, the popular belief attributed supernatural powers to the aboriginal inhabitants, the Bráhmans took care that those powers should be derived from the faithful worship of Brahma; although it is exceedingly improbable that the aborigines had any knowledge of Brahma, excepting that which they may have subsequently derived from the teachings of the Bráhmans.

Origin of the
opposition of
the Rákshasas
to the Bráh-
mans, and to the
Brahmanical
sacrifices.
The origin of the opposition of the Rákshasas to the Bráhmans is no doubt to be referred to the natural opposition of the people of the country to the advancing tide of Aryan invasion. The opposition to the Brahmanical sacrifices seems to be more obscure, but may perhaps be ascribed to the superstitious fears of a race of savages at finding their country overrun by powerful invaders, whose irresistible might may have been derived from the rites in question.

The establishment of Brahmanical hermitages in the midst of an aboriginal population, also opens up a curious field of inquiry, but must be reserved for future discussion.

Narrative in the
Rámáyana of
Ráma's expedi-
tion against the
Rákshasas.
The narrative of Ráma's expedition against the Rákshasas and of the circumstances which led to it, may now be related as follows:—

Anxiety of the
Maháraja
respecting the
marriage of his
four sons.
Visit of
Viswámitra.
When Ráma and his brethren were approaching their sixteenth year, the Maháraja became very anxious respecting their marriage. It so happened that one day when he was discussing the subject with his Counsellors in the Council-hall, the great sage Viswámitra arrived at the gate of the palace, and desired the door-keeper to go within and tell the Maháraja that Viswámitra the son of Gádhi, was

there. When the Maháraja received the message, he rose up with his two priests, and went out to meet the sage, rejoicing as Indra at the coming of Brahma; and he received Vaswámitra with every honour, and presented him with the argha, and said respectfully:—"Your coming, O great sage, is as grateful to me as amrita, as the fall of rain in the proper season, as the birth of a son to a childless father, as the recovery of lost treasure, as the dawning of a mighty joy! Tell me, I pray you, what important request you have to make, and I shall grant it with great delight." Now Viswámitra was a very illustrious sage, for in former times he had been a Kshatriya and a great warrior; but after practising many religious austerities in the Himálaya mountain he had become a Bráhman. His hermitage was situated on the southern bank of the Ganges river; and many other Bráhman sages dwelt there likewise, and passed their days in devotion and sacrifice. And Viswámitra said to the Mahárája:—"O Raja of Rajas, our sacrifices are spoiled by the Rákshasas, who pour blood and flesh upon the homa; and they are commanded by two chieftains, named Márícha and Suvahu, who have been commissioned by Raja Rávana to destroy all the sacrifices of the Bráhmans: I therefore pray you to suffer your son Ráma to return with me to my hermitage, for he is young, great, and valiant, and the Rákshasas will never be able to stand against him." At these words the Mahárája was exceedingly sorrowful, and he said:—"My son Ráma has not yet reached his sixteenth year: I will therefore send a great army with you, but I cannot give up Ráma." Then Viswámitra was in great wrath, and as fierce as a sacrificial fire when fed with abundance of ghee; and the whole earth was moved, and even the gods were in great fear. And he said:—"O Mahárája, you have given me your promise, and you cannot depart from your word: Make haste then, and send Ráma, and I will so protect him that he shall never be overcome by the Rákshasas." So the Mahárája sent for Ráma and Lakshmana, and delivered them up to the sage; and the two Princes took leave of their parents, and made ready to go with Viswámitra to the place of his abode.[1]

HISTORY OF
INDIA.
PART IV.

The Mahárája volunteers to grant his request.

Viswámitra originally a Kshatriya.

Requests the Mahárája to send Ráma to protect his Brahmanical settlement against the Rákshasas.

Sorrow of the Mahárája.

Viswámitra claims the fulfilment of the Mahárája's promise.

Ráma and Lakshmana permitted to accompany Viswámitra

---

[1] The following extract from the Adhyátma Rámáyana explains the circumstances which induced the Mahárája to part with Ráma in a somewhat different

Departure of
the three for
the hermitage of
Viswámitra.
Poetical descrip-
tion of autumn.

Now it so happened that as the three went out of the
city it was the beautiful season of autumn; and the pure sky
was free from clouds, as the pure mind of the devotee is free
from all passions; and the rains were over, and the high
winds had ceased, and the breezes were blowing gently at
the approach of the cold season, as the riotous and tumultuous assume a gentler aspect when they enter the company
of wise men. The water in every river, lake, and pond was
pure and transparent; and the beauty of the clear wave was
increased by the presence of the full-blown lotos, as the
beauty of a pure mind becomes increased by faith in God.
Thus Ráma and Lakshmana, and the sage Viswámitra,
journeyed along the south bank of the river Sarayú, towards
the spot where that river joins its waters with those of the
Ganges; and on their way they beheld the vast fields of rice
bending down with the weight of the grain, like a modest
man bending his head at the recital of his own praises. And

Viswámitra acts
as Guru.

Viswámitra instructed Ráma on the way, and performed all
the duties of a Guru. And when evening was come they
slept on grass beds by the side of the river Sarayú.

Journey to the
Brahmanical
settlement at
the junction of
the Sarayú and
Ganges.

Now when the light of morning began to dawn, the sage
Viswámitra awakened the two young heroes as they lay
upon their beds of grass, and directed them to arise and
perform their morning ablutions, and repeat the holy Gayatri according to the ordinance. After this the three pro-

---

manner. "The Maháraja with troubled mind consulted his preceptor Vasishtha :—
'If,' he said, 'Viswámitra should take Ráma away, I cannot survive the loss; If
I should not permit him to go, this sage, who is a strenuous adorer of the deity,
doubtless will utter a curse against me : This idea of danger afflicts my soul; besides Ráma is delicate in his frame, how then can he destroy that giant who resembles the mountain elephant?' Vasishtha answered :—'I will disclose this
secret mystery; this son of thine, who is named Ráma, is the Omnipotent Being
in whom the universe is comprehended.' The sage then told the Maháraja the
whole story of Brahma's application to Vishnu, and spoke as follows :—'Know, O
Maháraja, that Ráma is the Almighty, the Incomprehensible, the Supreme Soul;
that Lakshmana is an incarnation of Sesha-nága; Bharata an incarnation of the
shell, and Satrughna an incarnation of the circle : His primeval affection has
assumed a female form, and is born in the house of Raja Janaka : Now if Ráma
goes with Viswámitra he will obtain the hand of Raja Janaka's daughter Sítá
in marriage : Be not therefore under any apprehensions or grieved in thy mind, no
danger can accrue to Ráma : I have given thee that advice which I deemed most
proper; keep it concealed in thy own heart.' "

ceeded on their journey as before, until they came to the HISTORY OF INDIA. PART IV. place where the waters of the river Sarayú are joined with those of the Ganges; and there they saw a sacred hermitage where many holy Bráhmans practised religious austerities. And Viswámitra told the two Princes that here was the holy spot where the great god Siva was wounded by the love-inspiring Káma with the arrows of desire, and in return burnt up the god of love with the fire of his anger. And Viswámitra and the two Princes were hospitably entertained by the Bráhmans in that hermitage, and there they slept that night, and prepared to cross the river in the morning.

Legend of Siva smitten by the love-inspiring arrows of Káma.

Hospitable reception.

Now when the morning had come, the sage and the two Princes left the hermitage at the union of the two rivers, and entered a boat for the purpose of crossing the river Ganges, in order that they might proceed to the hermitage of Viswámitra, which was situated on the southern bank of the holy stream.[2] And as they crossed the river they heard the roaring of the waters, which is made by the conflict of the river Sarayú with the river Ganges; and having made obeisance to the two sacred rivers, they reached the other side, and entered a dreadful jungle which was called the wilderness of Táraká. And that jungle was as black as a cloud, and very dense, and filled with the voices of birds, and the notes of insects, and the noise of the wild deer, and the roaring of lions and tigers, and bears, and wild boars, and elephants, and rhinoceroses. Now in that jungle dwelt a terrible female Rákshasi, named Táraká, and she was the mother of Márícha; and Viswámitra said to Ráma :—" This cursed Táraká ravages all this country : Do you, O Ráma,

Passage over the Ganges to the southern bank.

Roaring of the waters.

Dreadful jungle of Táraká.

Viswámitra requests Ráma to slay Táraká, the Rákshasi.

---

[2] The route followed by Viswámitra and the two Princes on this occasion is easily traced. According to the Adhyátma Rámáyana the hermitage of Viswámitra was situated on the site of the modern town of Buxar, which is situated in the district of Shahabad. The distance from the site of the city of Ayodhyá, near Fyzabad, to the junction of the Sarayú (Gogra) and the Ganges, is about a hundred and seventy miles, a journey which must have occupied several days, although only two days appear to be indicated in the Rámáyana. From the junction of the two rivers to the modern town of Buxar, the distance is rather more than forty miles in a retrograde direction from east to west along the southern bank of the Ganges. This latter portion of the journey is said to have occupied two days, which approximates to the actual distance.

HISTORY OF INDIA. PART IV.

for the sake of the Bráhmans, destroy her : Such an act is not to be abhorred by you, as though it were the murder of a woman; but must be performed as a duty which all Rajas are bound to fulfil for the public good, whether it appear merciful or cruel, innocent or blamable." Ráma replied :— "I am bound to obey your command." And Ráma said to Lakshmana :—"Behold this misshapen Rákshasi : My heart relents at killing her because of her female nature, but I will deprive her of her strength and power." And the hero grasped his bow and twanged the string ; and Táraká heard the sound, and was filled with wrath; and presently she came to that place, roaring out with a loud voice; and she rushed upon Ráma with her arms lifted high in the air, and she rained a shower of stones upon the two sons of Dasaratha. Then Ráma took a missile weapon and cut off her two arms, so that they fell upon the earth. Then Lakshmana cut off the ears and nose of Táraká, and she disappeared, and again by the power of sorcery caused a fearful shower of stones to fall upon the two heroes. Then Viswámitra cried out to Ráma :—" Your unwillingness to kill this impious sacrifice-destroying Rákshasi is very wrong : Instantly slay her, for the evening is coming on, and in the darkness it is difficult to overcome the Rákshasas." Then Ráma thus encouraged drew forth a powerful arrow, with a head shaped like a crescent, and he discharged it at the misshapen and vengeful Táraká as she advanced upon him ; and she was dreadfully wounded by this tremendous arrow, and vomiting out blood, she fell down and expired. And Viswámitra rejoiced at the death of Táraká, and he kissed the head of Ráma, and said to him :—" To night, O Ráma, we will remain here, and on the morrow we will proceed to my own hermitage." And the sons of Dasaratha remained that night with the sage in the wilderness of Táraká.[3]

Combat between Ráma and Táraká.

Ráma's unwillingness to slay a woman.

Slays Táraká at the instigation of Viswámitra.

Divine weapons given to Ráma by Viswámitra.

Next morning the sage Viswámitra gave Ráma many

---

[3] In the Adhyátma Rámáyana everyone who is slain by Ráma, or who dies in his presence, or with the name of "Ráma" on his lips, ascends at once to the heaven of Vishnu. Accordingly a beautiful form, arrayed from head to foot with jewels, is said to have risen from the dead body of Táraká, and worshipped Ráma and then to have ascended to the abodes of bliss.

famous weapons endowed with divine energies, and irresistible even against the gods; and he turned to the east and taught him two powerful mantras. By the utterance of the first mantra all the weapons appeared before their master, and awaited his orders; and by the utterance of the second mantra, all sense of hunger, or thirst, or desire of sleep, passed away from the body. So Ráma uttered the first mantra, and all the mighty weapons which had been given to him by Viswámitra presented themselves before him, and stood with joined hands, and said :—"Command us, O Ráma, of mighty arm!" And Ráma examined them all, and said :—"Whenever I call you to remembrance, then do you wait upon me." Then all those mighty weapons bowed their heads and went their way.

The two heroes and the sage then proceeded on their way until they saw a mountain which appeared like a cloud, and near it a most exquisitely delightful grove, filled with deer, and enlivened by a variety of tuneful birds. And Viswámitra said to Ráma :—"This is my hermitage, and it is thine even as it is mine." And Viswámitra related the following holy legend to the two young Princes :—

"In ancient days, before the glorious Vishnu became incarnate as the Dwarf, this was his holy hermitage, and here he practised sacred austerities as an example to all others. And it came to pass that Bali, the mighty Raja of the Asuras, conquered Indra and the gods; and the gods came to this hermitage and prayed to Vishnu for succour : And Vishnu was born on earth in the form of a Dwarf, and he assumed the dress of a mendicant, and went to the abode of Bali, and prayed Bali to give him as much earth as he could step over in three steps : And Bali granted his request : Then Vishnu took upon himself a mighty form, and took three steps; and the first step covered the earth, and the second covered the heavens, and the third was on the head of Bali : And Vishnu bound Bali, and sent him and all his legions to the realms below the earth, and once more restored the universe to the rule of Indra." [4]

HISTORY OF INDIA. PART IV.

Two powerful mantras.

Arrival at the hermitage of Viswámitra.

Legend of Vishnu in the Dwarf incarnation taking three steps for the destruction of Bali.

---

[4] The meaning of this myth is not very obvious. It is said to have originated

HISTORY OF
INDIA.
PART IV.

Reception of
Ráma by the
sages at the
hermitage of
Viswámitra at
Buxar.

The sacrifice
assailed by the
Rákshasas.

Victory of
Ráma over
Máricha and
Suvahu.

Ráma and
Lakshmana
proceed with
Viswámitra to
the sacrifice of
Janaka in
Mithilá.

When Viswámitra had finished speaking, all the sages who were dwelling at his hermitage came up and welcomed Ráma, and they presented him with the argha, and with water to wash his feet, and entertained both him and his brother Lakshmana with every hospitality. And the two Princes dwelt at the hermitage of Viswámitra for six days, whilst the Bráhmans made preparation for the sacrifice. The altar was covered with kusa grass, and made ready, together with the sacrificial ladles, the wood and the flowers, and on the seventh day the sacrifice was begun. Then when the fire was blazing upon the altar, Máricha and Suvahu and their evil crew of Rákshasas rushed to the altar, and tried to defile the sacrifice with bones and blood, but were prevented by Ráma. And Máricha beheld the heroic Ráma, who was of the colour of azure, speaking to his brother Lakshmana, who was as resplendent as burning gold; and Máricha was filled with contempt, and began to seize the Bráhmans, when Ráma hurled a mighty weapon at the breast of Máricha, and drove him far out into the ocean.[5] Ráma then discharged a fire-producing weapon at the breast of Suvahu, and brought him to the ground; and he fell upon the sacrifice-destroying Rákshasas, and slew them all. Viswámitra then bestowed great praises upon Ráma; and Ráma and Lakshmana were honoured by all the sages, and passed the night in great satisfaction and joy.

Now when the morning had dawned, and the sons of Dasaratha had performed their devotions, the sages, with Viswámitra at their head, spoke to the two Princes as follows:—" Janaka, the Raja of Mithilá, is about to perform a great sacrifice, which we shall attend, and you may ac-

---

in an obscure Vedic idea that Vishnu as the Sun took three steps; viz., first on the earth at his rising; secondly in the heavens at noonday; and thirdly on the under-world at his sitting. (See Wilson's Rig-Veda, Vol. I, p. 53, *note.*) The legend however is exceedingly popular, probably on account of the successful trick played against the giant; and a festival is still celebrated in memory of the so-called event.

[5] Máricha is an important character. He is not slain, but only driven some hundreds of miles out at sea. In the sequel he reappears in the character of Minister to Raja Rávana.

HISTORY OF INDIA. PART IV.

company us: And Raja Janaka will show you the great bow of Siva, which neither man nor god can bend." So Ráma and Lakshmana, and Viswámitra, and all the sages, journeyed from that place towards Mithilá, which is now the country of Tirhut. And the first night they slept on the bank of the river Sone, where Viswámitra told them a wonderful legend respecting the foundation of the city of Kanouj.[6] And the second night they approached the river Ganges,[7] and the sage told the sons of Dasaratha how the river Ganges had descended from the Himalaya mountain upon the head of the great god Siva. And Viswámitra said:— " The cloudless sky was illuminated by the porpoises, the serpents, and the fishes, as they darted through the air like bright sparks of lightning. The white foam of the flowing waters, and the flocks of water-birds, filled the air like autumnal clouds. The water falling from the head of Siva, and thence to the earth, ran in some places with a rapid stream, and at others in a tortuous current; sometimes it was widely spreading, and sometimes it descended into caverns and again spouted upward. The sages, the Gandharvas, and the inhabitants of the earth touched the holy water, knowing its purifying power. Those who had fallen from heaven to earth performed ablution in this stream, and became free from sin, and returned again to heaven. And all the people of the earth rejoiced in this illustrious river,

Country of Mithilá, the modern Tirhut.

Legend of Kanouj.

Legend of the descent of the Ganges on the head of Siva and thence on the earth.

---

[6] This legend is told at a wearisome length in the Rámáyana, but is utterly worthless. A sage has fifty beautiful daughters. Váyu, the god of wind, makes some amorous proposals which they very properly reject, declaring that they will only accept such husband as their father may give them, and will never receive any other. Váyu, in his wrath, renders them hunch-backed. Subsequently they are all married to a young sage who cures them by a touch; and the city in which they dwelt was henceforth called Kanya-kubja, which signifies the "hunchbacked" girl, and still goes by the name of Kanouj. The legend has been modified by the Buddhists, who say that in this city there was formerly the hermit' of the great tree, who cursed ninety-nine damsels, so they all became hunch-backed; hence the name. See Fa Hian's Travels, chap. xviii. *Klaproth's note.*

[7] The route from Viswámitra's hermitage at Buxar can be distinctly traced. The party proceeded *viá* Arrah to the Sone river, which they crossed. Next they proceeded, still in an easterly direction, along on the bank of the Ganges, until they came to the neighbourhood of Patna, where they probably crossed the river to the northern side, and thus entered the country of Tirhut or Mithilá.

for by performing ablution therein, men became freed from all impurity and sin.[8]

When Viswámitra had finished his relation, it was early morning, and Ráma said to the sage :—" O Bráhman, most astonishing in this admirable story of the sacred descent of Ganga : Revolving your words in my mind, the night has appeared but an instant." Then Ráma and the rest performed their morning ablutions, aud crossed the pure river in a boat provided by the sages, and departed to the pleasant city of Visálá ; and Viswámitra related to Ráma the wondrous story

The party cross
the Ganges and
halt at Visálá.

---

[8] The story of the descent of the Ganges is of no real value, excepting that it is universally believed by the Hindús. According to a primitive myth, the Himavat mountain had two daughters, Ganga and Uma ; and Ganga is the river, whilst Uma, under the numerous names of Párvatí, Dúrga, &c., is the wife of Siva. The story of the descent is also connected with another legend, which fills up a great space in the Rámáyana. Sagara, an ancient Raja of Ayodhyá, determined on performing an Aswamedha. The horse was accordingly loosened, but was subsequently carried away by the great Serpent Anantra. The sixty thousand sons of Sagara sought throughout the universe for the horse, and at length beheld it feeding by the side of Kapila, the sage. Accordingly they charged Kapila with having stolen the horse, upon which he consumed them with the fire of his wráth, and reduced them to ashes. Subsequently Sagara discovered that his sons could only obtain salvation by being purified by the Ganges water. But Sagara died, and two or three generations passed away, and still his sixty thousand sons continued to be mere heaps of ashes. At length a Raja Bhagiratha entrusted the Raj to the care of his Counsellors, and spent a thousand years in severe austerities upon a mountain. In the hot season he surrounded himself with great fires, and had the sun over his head ; in the cold seasou he laid himself in the water ; and in the rainy season he exposed himself to the descending clouds ; and he fed on fallen leaves, with his mind restrained, and his senses kept under the most perfect control. After a thousand years Brahma was propitiated, and referred him to Siva ; and now Bhagiratha had to propitiate this deity, which he did by standing with uplifted arm day and night without support on the tip of his great toe, as immovable as a dry tree, and feeding only on air. Siva accordingly called upon the Ganges to descend upon his head, which she did, and was detained in the recesses of his jata, or knot of hair on the back of his head, and wandered there for ages. At length the river descended upon the earth, and all the gods and divine beings came to behold the wondrous sight. After descending to the earth the Ganges followed the car of Bhagiratha ; and all the gods, demons, serpents, apsaras, fishes, and water-birds followed the car of Bhagiratha in like manner. Unfortunately the Ganges in its progress watered the sacrificial ground of the sage Jahnu, and Jahnu in his wrath drank up the whole river. However, the gods worshipped Jahnu, and he relented, and discharged the river from his ears. After this Bhagiratha moved his chariot towards the sea, and the Ganges followed and watered the sixty thousand sons of Sagara, who were at once purified by the sacred water from all their sins. Accordingly their souls ascended to heaven, and Bhagiratha performed their funeral ceremonies.

of the churning of the ocean by the gods and demons, and HISTORY OF INDIA. PART IV. the production of amrita in the following manner :—

"In days of old there was war between the gods and the demons; and Indra, the sovereign of the gods, was overcome in battle by the demons.[9] And Indra and the gods fled for refuge to Brahma, and Brahma conducted them to the abode of Vishnu in the sea of milk, and prayed to Vishnu. And Vishnu manifested himself to Brahma and the gods, bearing in his four hands the shell, the chakra, the mace, and the lotos. And Vishnu commanded the gods to ally themselves with the demons, and to throw every kind of medicinal herb into the sea of milk; and to take Mandara mountain for a churning stick, and the serpent Vásuki for the churning rope, and to churn the sea for the production of amrita, which should render them mighty and immortal. And Vishnu said :—'The demons shall share the labour of churning, but I will prevent their tasting of the amrita, which shall be drank only by Indra and the gods.' So the gods allied with the demons, and did as Vishnu had commanded; and as they churned there appeared many wondrous things rising out of the sea. The goddess Váruní, the deity of wine, arose in sweet intoxication, and was joyfully received by the demons. Next rose the beautiful Apsaras, who became the nymphs of Indra's heaven. Then rose the great goddess Lakshmí, radiant with youth and beauty; and a crown was upon her head, and bracelets upon her arms, and her form was covered with ornaments of pearls; and her jetty hair flowed in long ringlets, whilst her complexion resembled molten gold; and thus attired and decorated she took up her abode on the bosom of Vishnu. Lastly appeared the physician of the gods, bearing in his hand the golden cup which contained the divine amrita. Then the demons

Legend of the churning of the ocean by the gods and demons for amrita.

Indra and the gods fly for refuge to Brahma, who refers them to Vishnu.

Churning of the sea.

Ascent of Váruní the deity of wine.

The Apsaras.

Lakshmí, beautiful and youthful, rises out of the sea, and becomes the wife of Vishnu.

The amrita.

---

[9] In the present myth the wars of gods and demons are plainly alluded to, just in the same way as gods and demons are implied in a previous myth, in which Vishnu promises the gods that he will become incarnate. But very often the gods are called Devatás, and seem to represent a superior tribe of mortal men; whilst the demons are termed Daityas, Dánavas, Asuras, or Rákshasas, and appear to represent the aborigines of India.

Indra and the
gods quaff the
amrita and
overcome the
demons.
Hospitable
entertainment
of the party at
Visálá.

fought lustily; but Vishnu assumed the form of a captivating damsel, and stole away the amrita. Vishnu then gave the amrita to Indra and the gods; and Indra and the gods quaffed the amrita, and fought and overcame the demons, and Indra once again recovered his rule."

Now when Viswámitra had finished speaking, he told the two Princes that they would rest that night in the city of Visálá. And when they arrived at the city, the Raja of Visálá came out to welcome the sage, and presented him with water and the argha; and the Raja wondered as he beheld the two heroes, and at his request Viswámitra related to him who they were, and wherefore they had come to the city of Visálá; and they were hospitably entertained by the Raja, and passed the night there.

When morning had come, Ráma and Lakshmana, accompanied by the sage Viswámitra, proceeded towards the beautiful city of Mithilá; and on the way Ráma saw a hermitage in the midst of a grove, and he inquired of Viswámitra respecting that hermitage, on which the sage related to him the sacred story, as follows :—

Legend of the
adultery of
Indra with the
wife of
Gautama, the
sage.

"This holy hermitage, adorned with trees, fruits, and flowers, belonged in ancient times to the sage Gautama; and here the sage remained for many thousand years with his wife Ahalyá in the performance of religious austerities. One day when the sage was absent from his dwelling, the mighty Indra passed by, and burned with an impure passion for the wife of Gautama; and he entered the hut in the disguise of the sage, and began to entreat Ahalyá; and Ahalyá, knowing him to be the Raja of the celestials, in the wantonness of her heart yielded to his desires. Then the sovereign of the gods left the hermitage, but at that moment Gautama entered, and he was invincible even to the gods through the power of his austerities. Perceiving him, Indra was overwhelmed with sadness; and the sage, beholding the profligate lord of gods in his disguise, thus ad-

dressed him in words of dreadful anger :—' O depraved wretch, assuming my form you have perpetrated this great crime ! Therefore from this moment do you become a eunuch!' The great sage then pronounced this curse upon his wife Ahalyá:—'O sinful wretch, for thousands of years shall you remain in this forest, abandoned by all and invisible to all, until Ráma, the son of Dasaratha, shall enter here, and you from beholding him shall be cleansed from all sin, and again approach me without fear.' With these words the illustrious Gautama abandoned this hermitage, and performed religious austerities on the summit of the Himálaya mountain.''[10]

HISTORY OF INDIA.
PART IV.

The wife of Gautama rendered invisible until the arrival of Ráma.

Having heard this holy legend, Ráma entered the hermitage, preceded by Viswámitra; and at that moment, Ahalyá was released from her curse, and became visible to all; and a shower of flowers fell from heaven, and divine music was heard in the sky. Then the illustrious Gautama, beholding with divine eye that his consort was cleansed from all sin, repaired again to his hermitage; and having paid due honours to Ráma, he engaged in sacred austerities with his purified spouse. And Ráma proceeded to Mithilá with his brother and Viswámitra.

The foregoing narrative of Ráma's expedition against the Rákshasas, and subsequent journey to the city of Mithilá, offers but few points worthy of consideration. The character of Viswámitra is an anomaly. He is said to have been originally a Kshatriya, and to have subsequently practised so many religious austerities, that he ultimately became a Bráhman; but his case must be regarded as altogether exceptional, as no other similar change of caste appears to have been recorded.[11] The geo-

Review of the foregoing tradition of Ráma's expedition against the Rákshasas.

Anomalous character of Viswámitra.

---

[10] This curious myth of the seduction of the wife of a sage by Indra, the god of the firmament, probably originated in the opposition of the Bráhmans to the worship of Indra, to which reference has already been made, and which will form the subject of discussion hereafter. The prophetical curse pronounced by the sage, that his wife should remain in the forest until the advent of Ráma, stamps the whole as a mythical interpolation.

[11] The difficulty in connection with Viswámitra's change of caste, is to apprehend the reason why a Kshatriya should desire to become a Bráhman. In ancient times the Bráhmans were certainly regarded by the Kshatriyas with a certain

HISTORY OF
INDIA.
PART IV.

General truth-
fulness of the
geographical
references.

Large interpo-
lation of un-
historical
myths.

graphical references are generally exact, and present no difficulty; a circumstance which seems to indicate that the Rámáyana was composed in the neighbourhood of the scenes to which it refers. The main feature of the story is the abundance of wearisome and unmeaning legends, which Viswámitra persists in relating to Ráma at every opportunity, and in which Ráma professes to be deeply interested. These episodes, however, appear to be entirely devoid of historical value, and accordingly only a few have been retained in a condensed form as specimens of the remainder. Thus the legend of the descent of the river Ganges upon the head of Siva, and that of the churning of the sea by the gods and demons for the production of amrita, have been preserved in the foregoing relation, not because they possess any hidden meaning, or throw any light upon the religion or civilization of the people, but simply because they are wonderful products of Hindú imagination, which from some cause or other have been frequently brought before the notice of European readers, whilst traditions of infinitely greater importance and significance have been wholly ignored.

---

amount of contempt, and it is evident that Viswámitra is to be referred to a tolerably remote period, for he was the reputed father of Sakuntalá. It seems not unlikely that he was one of the Kshatriyas who had adopted Buddhism, but who from some cause or other deserted to the side of the Bráhmans, and henceforward became a favourite hero in Brahmanical tradition.

CHAPTER V.

MARRIAGE OF RÁMA.

THE story of the marriages of Ráma and his three brethren, naturally forms one of the most attractive and favourite portions of the Rámáyana. In all civilized countries the story of a marriage is universally interesting to young and old; and amongst western nations it is generally adopted as the climax of every romance and every drama. In India this interest is intensified from causes which are by no means difficult of apprehension. The sympathies which in Europe are permitted to spread through large communities, are concentrated in the family or household; and the consequence is that family events, such as births, deaths, and marriages, assume an importance in the family which is unknown elsewhere; whilst they are accompanied by a multitude of rites and observances which still further add to the gravity and significance of the occasion. Marriages especially are the all-absorbing topic in every Hindú household; from the little girl who is looking forward to the day when she will be arrayed in jewels and fine clothes, and be seated by the side of her future husband, to the aged matron who can remember every recurrence of the ceremony in the family for many generations. Indeed the marriage

HISTORY OF INDIA. PART IV.

Interesting story of Ráma's marriage.

General interest attached to marriages intensified in India.

The all-absorbing topic in Hindú households.

Paramount duty of Hindú parents to arrange the marriages of their children.

of sons and daughters is a paramount duty which
every Hindú father must fulfil, who would escape the
censure of his fellow-men and the anger of the gods;
whilst it is the one great event in the life of every
Hindú boy and girl, without exception, throughout
the land.

But the marriage of Ráma and Sítá possesses
attractions far above those of any ordinary tradition. It is not a mere union of a boy and girl,
which can only be consummated in after years; but
it is the union of a young hero to a marriageable
maiden, and of a hero who has won his prize by a
feat of arms. Moreover the holy legend calls up

associations and sympathies which no other story
can awaken. It describes not only the union of the
heroic and beautiful, but the marriage of the greatest
of gods with the kindliest of goddesses; of the personification of all that is handsome and glorious in
the god-man, with all that is lovely and light and
graceful in a goddess-maiden; of the divine incarnation of the immortal Vishnu with the divine incarnation of the equally immortal Lakshmí. Accordingly,
that indescribable charm which is thrown round
every marriage in which the lovers are young and
fair, is invested with a higher interest from the deep
religious feeling which is stirred within the breast of

all who listen to the sacred song. The mother remembers when she too was a bride; the daughter
sighs for the day when she too will be given to a
husband; whilst the poor widow's heart is bursting
at a glimpse of happiness which is denied to her for
ever. But still with all these natural emotions,
there is mingled a deep religious joy and exultation

in all the more important turns in the narrative; and especially when Ráma triumphantly bends the fabled bow, or takes the hand of his beautiful bride in the presence of the sacred fire.

It must, however, be confessed that the religious sentiment above indicated is not expressed in the Rámáyana in the degree to which it is felt by a sympathetic audience of Hindús. Thus the narrative to a European reader is a mere ordinary story of a Hindú marriage, in which the allusions to the divinity of the married pair are strained and artificial. But in this respect the associations in the mind of the Hindús supply all that is wanting. From their earliest infancy they have been taught to repeat the sacred name of Ráma, and to believe in his divinity; and not a single doubt as to the truth of that divinity is ever felt or uttered. When, therefore, the Hindú poet fails, as he must fail, to indicate that incarnation of deity in which he fully believes, and which indeed he is desirous of enforcing, the belief of the reader or hearer is in no way affected by the deficiency. To him the divine Ráma is an incarnation of the eternal, the immortal, and the invisible; whilst Sítá is a personification of a corresponding female nature, who is mystically regarded as the primeval affection or divine love of Ráma.

The story of the marriage of Ráma is comprised in three distinct narratives, as follows:—

1st, The circumstances which led to the marriage, and the ceremony of the marriage, all of which took place in the city of Mithilá.

2nd, The return journey of Mahárája Dasaratha

from the city of Mithilá to the city of Ayodhyá, accompanied by his four sons and their respective brides.

3rd, The honeymoon of Ráma, which did not commence until after the arrival of the party at the city of Ayodhyá.

1st. Tradition of the winning of Sitá by Ráma, and the subsequent marriage.

The first portion of the narrative, comprising the story of how Ráma won his bride, and how the marriage ceremony was performed, appears to be a rélic of the original tradition, and may now be related as follows :—

Confusion of the women of Mithilá on hearing of Ráma's approach.

When the women of Mithilá heard that the handsome and heroic Ráma was entering the city, they hastened out of their houses to behold him ; and so anxious were they to gaze upon his countenance, that in the confusion some put their anklets on their arms and their bracelets on their ancles ; and some put the ornaments for their heads on their bosoms, and others fixed the ornaments for their bosoms on their backs.[1]

Raja Janaka respectfully receives Viswámitra and inquires respecting Ráma and Lakshmana.

And when Raja Janaka heard that the sage Viswámitra had come to his city, he hastened to receive him with every token of great respect, and he said :—" O chief of sages, I am truly blessed, seeing that my place of sacrifice is thus honoured by your presence and that of the sages." And when the Raja saw Ráma and Lakshmana, he said to Viswámitra :—" Who are those two illustrious youths who are as majestic as elephants, as heroic as tigers, and as beautiful as the two Aswins ?" Viswámitra replied :—" They are the sons of Maháraja Dasaratha, and the conquerors of the Rákshasas, and they are come hither to inquire about the great bow."

Exhibits the great bow of Siva.

And Janaka showed to the sons of Dasaratha the great bow with which Siva had destroyed the gods at the sacrifice of Daksha, and which had ever since that day been preserved in the royal

---

[1] This passage respecting the women is evidently a later interpolation, for it is scarcely possible that they should have been acquainted with the merits of Ráma, whilst their Raja Janaka was compelled to ask Viswámitra respecting his identity.

house of Mithilá, and worshipped with every honour.[2]   And
the bow was laid in a huge chest, which moved on eight
wheels; and it was drawn into the presence of Raja Janaka
and the two Princes by eight hundred men, who were tall
and strong, so heavy and stupendous was that great bow.
And Raja Janaka said to the two heroes :—" I have pro-   Sitá promised
mised to give my beautiful daughter Sítá in marriage to   to that Raja who could bend the bow.
that Raja who shall succeed in bending the bow; and all
the Rajas of the earth have come hither, and not one has
ever been strong enough to lift that bow from the ground."
Now when Ráma saw the bow, he lifted it with one hand   Ráma bends the bow.
from the ground in a sportive manner; and a great multi-
tude in deep amazement looked on.   Then Ráma made the
bow ready with a smile, and putting forth all his strength
he bent the bow until it broke in the midst, and the noise
thereof was like the crash of a falling mountain, or the
roar of the thunder-bolt hurled by Indra.   And all the
people were stunned and fell down, excepting only Viswámitra and Raja Janaka, and the two sons of Dasaratha.

Then Raja Janaka said to the sage :—" This deed of Ráma   Raja Janaka sends messengers to inform Dasaratha.
is without a parallel, and he shall receive my daughter Sítá
in marriage : With thy permission, O sage, let messengers
on swift horses go hence to the city of Ayodhyá, and
acquaint Maháraja Dasaratha with all that has occurred, and
bring him to this city."   And Viswámitra agreed, and the
messengers were mounted on swift beasts, and in three
nights they arrived at the city of Ayodhyá; and they
entered the royal palace, and delivered their message to the
Maháraja.   Then the Maháraja consulted Vasishtha and the
other priests, and they were highly pleased, and said :—
" On the morrow we will go to Mithilá."   And the messengers from Raja Janaka were entertained in the palace with
great respect, and remained there all that night.

Early the next morning the happy Maháraja set out   The Maháraja goes to Mithilá, and is received by Raja Janaka.
with his priests, and his treasures, and all his army, and in

---

[2] The story of the sacrifice of Daksha is connected with the worship of Siva.
Daksha performed a sacrifice, and invited all the gods excepting Siva and his wife
Sáti; and Siva, at the instigation of Sáti, became so highly offended at this
omission, that he destroyed the sacrifice.

four days he arrived at the pleasant city of Mithilá; and Raja Janaka came out to meet him, and received him with every honour. And Raja Janaka said to Dasaratha :— "Happy am I this day, and delivered from every kind of distress, for by this alliance my family will be honoured and purified."

On the morrow Raja Janaka commanded his Chief Counsellor to bring Maháraja Dasaratha together with his son Ráma and priest Vasishtha. Then the Maháraja, attended by his two priests, and all his friends, went to the place where Janaka was; and the great sage Vasishtha recited to Raja Janaka the names of all the ancestors of Dasaratha, and Janaka recited to the Maháraja the names of

all his own ancestors. Then Janaka proposed to give his daughter Sítá in marriage to Ráma, and her sister Urmilá in marriage to Lakshmana; and he also proposed that the two daughters of his brother Kusadhwaja should be married to Bharata and Satrughna. And Viswámitra and Vasishtha approved of the marriages of the four damsels to the four sons of Dasaratha. Then Maháraja Dasaratha, having requested leave of the Raja of Mithilá, departed to his own lodgings, preceded by Vasishtha and all the sages; and

there the Maháraja performed a great Sráddha to the ghosts of his deceased ancestors, and gave four lakhs of cows with their calves to the Bráhmans, being a lakh for each son, and each cow was adorned with horns of pure gold.[3]

When the night had passed away, and Maháraja Dasaratha had fulfilled his morning duties, he went out attended by his sons richly adorned with jewels, and preceded by Vasishtha and the other sages; and he proceeded to the place of sacrifice, and approached the Raja of Mithilá in due form, and thus addressed him :—" O Raja, peace be to you! We are come into your assembly to perform the nuptials, and now therefore introduce us and our friends into your own house." Then the eloquent Raja of Mithilá thus

---

[3] It is customary to perform a Sráddha, or feast to the souls of departed ancestors, on the eve of a marriage. For a description of the ceremonies of the Sráddha, see chapter xii.

replied to the generous words of Dasaratha :—"What
porter have I placed at the gate, and who considers about
entering his own house? My daughter is standing at the
foot of the altar, and I am prepared and waiting for you."

Meanwhile Vasishtha had erected the altar in the chamber of the gods, and adorned it on every side with fragrant
flowers. And there were cooling jars of water, and pots
filled with branches of trees, and pots of incense, and vessels of shells, and spoons and ladles for pouring the homa
upon the fire, and vessels of fruit, and milk, and honey, and
rice, and parched barley. And the kusa grass was spread
upon the floor, and the fire was lighted upon the altar with
all the due formulas, and the homa consecrated with mantras
was placed upon the flame. Then whilst Ráma stood on the
eastern side of the altar, Raja Janaka brought his daughter
Sítá, adorned with every ornament, into the presence of the
sacred fire, and placed her opposite to the heroic son of Dasaratha; and he spoke to the lotos-eyed Ráma as follows :—
"This is my daughter Sítá, endowed with every virtue:
Take her hand in yours, O son of Dasaratha, and she will
ever attend you like a shadow : Maintain her for life, and be
not offended if she ever commits a fault." Raja Janaka in
like manner desired Lakshmana to take the hand of his
other daughter Urmilá, and Bharata and Satrughna to take
the hands of the two daughters of his brother Kuradhwaja.
Raja Janaka then sprinkled the bridegrooms and their
brides with water consecrated by the utterance of holy
mantras; and the trumpets sounded, and each of the four
sons of Dasaratha led his bride three times round the fire
upon the altar, and round the Raja, and performed the nuptial ceremonies according to the ordinance. A shower of
flowers then fell from heaven upon them all, and celestial
music was heard in the sky, and the Apsaras danced for joy,
and the Gandharvas played sweet and solemn music.[4]

Preparations made by Vasishtha the priest for the nuptial ceremony

Janaka places Sítá before the altar.

The bridegrooms take the hands of the brides, and are sprinkled with holy water.

Walk three times round the fire.

Joy of the gods.

---

[4] The marriage of Ráma and Sítá is somewhat differently related in the
Adhyátma Rámáyana, as will be seen from the following extract :—

"Satánanda, the son of Gautama, the priest of Janaka, being satisfied as to
the propriety of the day fixed for the marriage, said to Janaka :—'Let a proper
canopy be erected in thy house; cause four pillars to be raised and adorned with

Ceremonies in
the inner apart-
ments.

Now when the ceremonies of the marriage had been all performed, the bridegrooms led their brides into the inner apartments, and each one seated his bride on his left side, and the women tied their garments together; and the women removed the veils from the brides, and desired both the brides and bridegrooms to look each other in the face for the first time; and each of the sons of Dasaratha gazed upon the face of his own bride, and she in like manner gazed upon the face of her husband; and they exchanged garlands

jewels, with fringes of pearls, embroidery, and brocade.' The marriage procession was then made ready; they first rubbed Ráma's body with meal and oil; after which he bathed and was dressed in clothes of gold brocade. He had a crown of pearls on his head; earrings of exquisite richness hung from both his ears; his eyes were rubbed with antimony, and his hands and feet with henna. He wore a string of pearls and flowers round his neck, and an ornament of pearls on his forehead; a stripe of saffron was marked in the centre of his forehead; and his two locks of hair hung in curls on his cheeks. Being thus adorned he mounted his horse, the kettle-drums and shells sounding on every side; lights innumerable accompanied him, and immense quantities of fireworks were displayed. The dancers performed various dances; the gods appearing in the heavens sounded their shells, and showered down flowers upon Ráma. Thousands of elephants resembling mountains, and of horses also swift as the wind, were led before him; horsemen and footmen without number attended him. In this manner was the marriage procession of Ráma conducted.

"The wife of Janaka, having adorned Sítá with jewels and rich clothes, placed her under the canopy. Millions of suns and moons would bow down in subjection before the faces of Ráma and Sítá. When the procession came to the palace, Janaka went forth to meet Ráma; he brought him and his attendants into the house, and having seated Ráma with Sítá under the canopy, the Bráhmans commenced reading the Vedas. At the sound of the Vedas the fire was kindled, and the sacrifice placed therein. The whole assembly walked round them seven times. The Rája then tied the clothes of the bride and the bridegroom in a knot, as having bestowed them on each other, and Janaka delivered Sítá to Ráma. At that time the world was filled with the sound of ' May thy prosperity endure for ever.' The gods sounded their kettle-drums and showered down flowers. Alms were distributed in such quantities that no one could complain of want in future, all were happy.

"On the second day Janaka assembled Vasishtha, Viswámitra, and the other holy men, and gave them an account of the birth of Sítá, saying :—' Sítá was not produced, holy men! from the body of any one. One day I cleared a spot of ground for a sacrifice, and turning up the earth with a plough-share, a silver vessel sealed on the top was rooted up. When I opened the seal, a virgin beautiful as a hundred moons rose from out of that vessel. I brought her to my house with the affection of a father, and my wife and I adopted her, and we considered her as our daughter.' Janaka then stated that Nárada had related to him the whole story of the incarnation of Vishnu in Ráma and his brothers, and the primeval affection in the form of Sítá, who was to be married to Ráma. He added that he had commenced the Swayamvara in order to discover Ráma."

together, and every other rite was performed according to the ordinance.

The foregoing narrative of the marriages of Ráma and his brethren, comprises some exaggerations as regards the great bow of Siva, and perhaps has been slightly Brahmanized by some later editor, but otherwise it bears the impress of being based upon an authentic tradition. That Ráma should have performed some wonderful feat of arms at the court of Mithilá, and by these means should have obtained the hand of the beautiful daughter of Raja Janaka, is perfectly in accordance with the traditions which have been preserved of the Swayamvara. Again, it will be noticed that the Bráhmans play little or no part in the ceremony. Vasishtha, indeed, is introduced as reciting the ancestry of Ráma, and even as preparing the altar and performing the homa; but it is Janaka, the father of the bride, who performs the actual ceremonies of the marriage; and this circumstance is alone sufficient to indicate that the original tradition refers to a period when the authority and dignity of the Bráhmans were by no means so firmly established as they were in later years.

Review of the foregoing tradition of the marriages of Ráma and his brethren.

Authentic character of the narrative.

Marriage ceremony not performed by the Bráhmans but by Rája Janaka.

As regards the ceremony itself, it seems to have included four important rites, viz. :—

1st, The procession of the bridegroom and his relatives and friends to the house of the father of the bride.

2nd, The placing of the bride and bridegroom before the sacred fire which has been kindled on the altar.

3rd, The bridegroom taking the hand of the bride in the presence of the fire.

4th, The sprinkling of the bride and bridegroom with water which has been consecrated by the utterance of verses from Vedic hymns.

Resemblance
between the
ancient Aryan
ceremony and
the modern
Christian rite.

Here it is impossible to avoid noticing the striking resemblance between the ancient ceremony as it was performed by our Aryan forefathers in their private dwellings, and the more modern rite as it is performed in Christian churches. In Protestant countries the fire on the altar has been rejected as Jewish, and the use of holy water has in like manner been abandoned as Romish. But still in all essential particulars the ceremony is the same. The bridegroom and the bride are still placed before the altar; and the father of the bride still gives away his daughter; whilst the bridegroom takes her hand in his, and pledges his troth in the presence of the altar, although the fire is wanting.

The second section of the story of Ráma's marriage comprises the return journey of Maháraja Dasaratha from the city of Mithilá to that of Ayodhyá, in which he was accompanied by his four sons and their respective brides. This journey is of minor importance; but it contains a curious account of a meeting between the two Rámas; that is, between Ráma the Kshatriya and Ráma the Bráhman; or in other words, between the present Ráma, who was the son of Dasaratha, and another Ráma, who was the son of a sage named Jamadagni, and was known by the distinguishing appellation of Parasu Ráma, or Ráma "with the axe." This Parasu Ráma is said to have been a great warrior as well as a Bráhman. He was a worshipper of Siva, from whom he obtained his celebrated axe; and is especially renowned for his prowess against the Kshatriyas. These latter circumstances seem to have placed him in opposition to Ráma. As a worshipper of Siva he was opposed to Ráma as an incarnation of Vishnu; and as a Brahmanical slaughterer of the Kshatriyas he was opposed to Ráma as the son of Mahárája Dasaratha. A further inquiry into his real character will be attempted hereafter. For the present it will be sufficient to reproduce the simple narrative, which is as follows:—

Now on the morning after the marriages of Ráma and his brethren, the sage Viswámitra took leave of the two Rajas and went his way to the northern mountain. And Mahárája Dasaratha also took leave of Raja Janaka, and Raja Janaka gave to each of the four brides many rich presents of clothes, deer-skins, jewels, soft silks, garments of various colours, beautiful ornaments, together with a hundred thousand cows.[5]

Then Mahárája Dasaratha departed out of Mithilá in great splendour, preceded by his preceptor Vasishtha and the other sages, and accompanied by his sons and daughters-in-law. And as the Mahárája was returning to his own city of Ayodhyá, he saw the birds gathering together on his

---

[5] The author of the Adhyátma Rámáyana exhibits a much more brilliant imagination. He states that Sítá's portion consisted of the following articles:—

"One hundred crores of gold mohurs.

Ten thousand magnificent carriages.

Ten lakhs of horses, swift as the wind, with saddles ornamented with jewels.

Sixty thousand elephants, resembling mountains, covered with embroidery and brocade, and with gold chains on their four legs.

One hundred thousand male slaves, beautiful and obedient.

Fifty thousand female slaves, resembling the rising sun, adorned with jewels, and well versed in service.

Two crores of cows giving milk, and lovely as Kama-d'hena.

One crore bales of cloth, such as embroidery, brocade, silk and plain.

One hundred thousand gajmookta, or that species of pearl which is sometimes found in the heads of elephants.

An immense quantity of other kinds of jewels, such as diamonds, emeralds, rubies, topazes, sapphires, and cat's eyes.

Innumerable vessels of gold and silver.

Crores of maunds of sweetmeats and preserves.

Grain not to be reckoned."

HISTORY OF
INDIA.
PART IV.

Evil and good
omens.

Terrible appear-
ance of Parasu
Ráma, son of
Jamadagni.

His wrath
against Ráma
for having
broken the bow
of Siva.

Vasishtha and
the Bráhmans
present the
argha.

Parasu Ráma
challenges
Ráma to bend
the bow of
Vishnu.

right hand, and the peaceful deer of the forest encompass-
ing him round about ; and he was greatly alarmed and said
to his preceptor Vasishtha :—" What mean these omens ? "
And Vasishtha replied :—" The birds, O Maháraja, inform
you of the approach of something terrible, but the deer who
surround you bid you not to be afraid."

Whilst Vasishtha and Dasaratha were thus speaking, a
fierce tempest arose which raised the sand in clouds, and
caused the earth to quake ; and the air was filled with
darkness, and the sun lost its heat, and the country was
filled with dust and ashes, and all were sore afraid, except
Vasishtha, and the sages, and the sons of Dasaratha.
Presently they saw a mighty being, with a jata on his head,
drawing near unto them, tremendous as Indra, dreadful as
Yama coming to destroy the world, arrayed in splendour
greater than human eye could behold, and bright as the
glowing fire. With a mace upon his shoulder, and a bow
resembling the rainbow, and a fiery shaft in his hand, he
advanced like Siva going to destroy Tripura ; and he was
enraged with Ráma, the son of Dasaratha, for having broken
the bow of Siva, and his wrath resembled a fire throwing
out its flames through a cloud of smoke. And Vasishtha
and the sages knew him to be the Bráhman Ráma, the famous Ráma who was the son of Jamadagni, and who in days
of old had slain all the Kshatriyas in a single day. And they
said one to another :—" Will the great Ráma again destroy
the Kshatriyas ? " Thus foreboding, Vasishtha and the
other Bráhmans presented him with propitiatory offerings,
and said :—" O my lord, accept this argha ! O sage, be not
again angry ! " And Ráma, the son of Jamadagni, accepted
the argha without speaking to the sages ; and he turned to
Ráma, the son of Dasaratha, and spoke as follows :—" O son
of Dasaratha, I have heard of your great prowess, and how
you have broken the divine bow of Siva, which was made by
Viswakarma : But another bow was made by Viswakarma
and given to Vishnu, and with this bow I have conquered
the whole earth : Take it now, and if you are able to draw
it I will give you battle." Then the heroic son of Dasara-

tha smiled and took the bow, and fixed the arrow, and discharged it at the sky, saying :—" As you are a Bráhman I will not discharge this fatal arrow at you." Then the son of Jamadagni lost his strength, and knew that Ráma was Vishnu; and he respectfully saluted the divine hero, and went his way to the Mahendra mountain. And Dasaratha was in great joy, and all the sages bestowed many praises upon the heroic son of the Mahárája.

HISTORY OF INDIA. PART IV.

Ráma bends the bow and discharges an arrow.
Parasu Ráma acknowledges him to be Vishnu.

After some days, Dasaratha approached his own city of Ayodhyá, and the city was adorned with banners, and the pleasant streets were watered and strewed with flowers, and the air was filled with the clangour of trumpets, and thousands of citizens went out to welcome back their Mahárája; and the Mahárája was filled with joy, as he saw his people anxious to behold him and to do him honour; and Kausalyá and Kaikeyí, and Sumitrá, together with the other wives of the Mahárája, were ready to embrace their daughters-in-law, the fortunate Sítá, Urmilá, and the two nieces of Raja Janaka. Then the sons of Dasaratha, with their newly-married wives, bowed down to the feet of their mothers; and the Ránís took their sons, and their sons' wives, to the different temples, that they might all bow down their heads to the gods and goddesses therein. Then the brethren and their wives bowed down to the feet of their elders and preceptors, and were conducted to the palace. And all the women of the neighbourhood came and saw the faces of the brides and made them presents according to their rank; and the musicians, and the genealogists, and the eulogists, and all the dancers and singers, were dismissed with rich presents; and the Bráhmans and kinsmen, being well feasted, went their way, and the marriage was over.

Grand entry of the Mahárája into the city of Ayodhyá.
Rejoicings of the people.

The newly-married pairs bow down to their mothers and worship the gods.

Presents and feasting.

The only point in the foregoing narrative which seems to require consideration here is the character of Parasu Ráma. According to an extravagant myth, this Bráhman hero cleared the earth twenty-one times of every Kshatriya, and filled either five or seven lakes

Inference that
his alleged
extirpation of
the Kshatriyas
is historical.

Refutation of
the inference.

Parasu Ráma
the mere hero
of some petty
local tradition,
originating in
the theft of a
cow.

with their blood.[6] From this wild statement it has
been inferred that the extirpation of the Kshatriyas
was an accomplished fact, to be compared with the
downfall of the Greek tyrannies, and that the triumph
of the Bráhmans was a counterpart of the rise of the
Greek republics.[7] Such a view, however, appears to
be contrary to probabilities, and is certainly dis-
countenanced by actual facts. The conflict between
the soldier and the priest, the Kshatriya and the
Bráhman, belongs to the age of Buddhism. In the
earlier age to which Parasu Ráma seems to belong, a
conflict between the haughty Kshatriya and the mendicant Bráhman, could only have had but one result.
Occasionally, however, there may have been trivial
local feuds, in which some warlike son of a Bráhman
may have triumphed over a Kshatriya, and such a
feat would be duly preserved and exaggerated in
Brahmanical tradition. Parasu Ráma was apparently
the hero of some such village feud, which broke out
respecting the theft of a cow, or as some authorities
have it, the theft of a calf. The cow or calf of the
Bráhman Jamadagni was stolen by a Kshatriya. In
revenge Parasu Ráma, the son of Jamadagni, slew
the Kshatriya. Then, by way of reprisals, the sons
of the slaughtered Kshatriya attacked the hermitage
of Jamadagni and murdered him. Finally Parasu
Ráma slew the murderers of his father, and vowed
that he would destroy the whole race of Kshatriyas.
Henceforth it is said that he killed every Kshatriya
whom he met; and, indeed, he appears to have be-

---

[6] The legend of Parasu Ráma, as it is related in the Mahá Bhárata, has been
translated by Professor H. H. Wilson, and is inserted in his translation of the
Vishnu Puráwa, p. 401, 4.to edition.

[7] See Professor Max Müller's Hist. of Sanskrit Literature, p. 17. Whilst
doing full justice to the learning and critical ability of the eminent editor of the
Rig-Veda, it may be remarked that some of his historical inferences appear to be
open to question.

whom he met: and, indeed, he appears to have become so terrible with his axe, as to have been called Parasu Ráma, or Ráma with the axe. That this cattle-lifting story should be exaggerated into a legend that Parasu Ráma extirpated the whole race of Kshatriyas, is only a specimen of Brahmanical extravagance. The Kshatriyas were never extirpated. Those professing Buddhism were defeated, and perhaps driven out of India; but the Kshatriyas, or Rajas, are to this day dwelling as a people in their own country of Rajputána. The legend of Parasu Ráma's interview with Ráma is evidently a myth, introduced to exhibit the superiority of Vishnu over Siva; the comparison being probably invited by the similarity of name. This myth, however, is in singular opposition to another myth by which Parasu Ráma is represented as an incarnation of Vishnu. That the Bráhmans should have elevated their own caste hero to the rank of deity is by no means surprising; but it is impossible to reconcile this idea with the statement that Parasu Ráma was a worshipper of Siva; and as such came in conflict with Ráma, who, like himself, was an incarnation of Vishnu.

The third section of the story of Ráma's marriage comprises the narrative of Ráma's honeymoon, and is especially curious as representing the Hindú ideal of perfect happiness in wedded life. It must, however, be treated as a modern interpolation, and indeed is only valuable as an illustration of modern customs and ideas.[8] The change in the whole tone of the Rámáyana will be at once perceptible; and in this respect the style is similar to

HISTORY OF INDIA. PART IV.

Cattle-lifting story exaggerated into a Brahmanical fable that Parasu Ráma extirpated the Kshatriyas.

3rd. Story of Ráma's honeymoon.

Its modern character.

Contrast between the simplicity of the marriage ceremony, and the ornate story of the honeymoon.

[8] This section is only to be found in what is called the North-West recension of the Rámáyana.

Hindú charac-
ter of the nar-
rative.

Story of the
honeymoon in
the Rámáyana.

Consummation
of the marriages
at Ayodhyá.

Advice given to
Sítá by her
maids.

Timidity of
Sítá.

Remonstrances
of Ráma.

that of the story of the childhood of Ráma. In the description of the marriage ceremony which was performed at Mithilá, there is a certain patriarchal simplicity, which evidently refers to a remote and primitive age. In the following narrative there is all the artificial prettiness and extravagant fancy which belongs to modern Hinduism. No one but a Hindú bard could have pictured forth such details; and perhaps no audience, which was not composed of orientals, could possibly appreciate the description of early married life which is here presented to the eye. The story of Ráma's honeymoon is as follows:—

Now it was not until the day of the return of the brides and bridegrooms to the city of Ayodhyá that the marriages were fully accomplished. And when it was evening some of the maids said to Sítá:—"When your husband comes to see you, do not speak to him too soon, but let him entreat and flatter you for a long while before you open your mouth; and when you do speak you must say but little, for a husband soon becomes weary of a prattling wife." But the other maids said:—"This counsel is not good, and we advise you to talk to your husband, and do your best to please him; for the lotos is never weary of giving honey to the bee, and yet the love between them is never diminished; and if by your wit you can defeat your husband, it will give us all a power over him, and make mirth for the morrow." Sítá blushed at these words, and the maids then brought her to Ráma; but she was fearful of approaching her husband, like one who sees a radiant gem in the head of a serpent, but is fearful lest he should have a poisonous fang. The maids then said to her:—"Wherefore this reluctance? No one will force you into the presence of your husband, just as no one would force another to bathe in the water of the Ganges, but he must do so of his own accord." At that moment a lion roared out in the jungle, and Sítá trembled as she heard the roaring; and the cunning maids said to her:—"The roaring is that of a Rákshasa, and you must now take refuge with him who conquered Táraká and the other Rákshasas, for no one save Ráma can protect you from this great peril." So Sítá approached her husband, and sat blushing near him, and Ráma said to her :—" Why do you sit thus, O my beloved ? Why do you not show your beautiful face to me, and turn upon me the light of your lustrous eyes ? But if you will not look me in the face, at least gratify my passionate heart with the nectar of your words : Yet why be fearful of me ? The lotos is never fearful of the bee." And he took her by the hand, and Sítá trembled like one who shrinks from plunging in a tank on a winter morning.

Meanwhile the bridal chamber was beautifully adorned with flowers and garlands. On the walls were wreaths of flowers shaped like trees, and deer, and birds of bright plumage, and cats, and snakes, and bees, and flags, and mimic gardens ; and there also was the semblance of a pond, the water of which was formed of black crystals, and it was as it were filled with flowers, and on each of the four sides of it were steps for going into the pond. In the middle of the chamber was the bridal couch decorated with garlands, and the legs of it were of purest ivory, and the bed was very soft, and it was whiter than the moon, or the sacred shell, or the whitest of white flowers. Lamps of gold were lighted, and golden pots were filled with water as clear as crystal, and with camphorated and perfumed water ; and betel was prepared, and pots of sandal, with garlands round the necks of the pots. And the entrance to the room was adorned with plantain trees, and with branches of the mango tree arranged in pots, which were adorned with flowers.

Decorations of the bridal chamber.

The bridal couch.

When the night had passed away and the sun was rising in the heavens; the maids went in and awoke the sleeping pair, and they made much mirth at Sítá ; and after this the honeymoon passed away in love and joy, and Ráma was ever happy in the company of his wife. One day Ráma and Sítá sat down to play at dice, and Sítá said to Ráma :—" I do not like to play for nothing." So it was agreed between them that the one who lost the game should give a good gift

Description of the honeymoon.

Ráma and Sítá playing at dice.

Rama's joke.

to the Dwija, or twice born.[9]　And they sat down to play, and the board and the dice were made of ivory, and the balls were of gold.　And Sítá won the game, and Ráma arose and gave her a kiss; and Sítá then said to her husband:— "What does this mean? I defeated you, and then you come and kiss me." Ráma replied:—"I duly paid the wager: I had to give a good gift to the Dwija, but Dwija signifies 'teeth' as well as 'twice born,' and in bringing my lips to your teeth I gave a good gift to the Dwija." Sítá replied:—"I shall not play such a game with you again, for you will ever be the winner; if you lose you will kiss me, and if I lose I shall have to kiss you."

Ráma compares Sítá with different things in nature.

One evening after this, the moon was at the full, and Ráma and Sítá went to the banks of a beautiful pond which was filled with lotos flowers, and Ráma began to compare her with the scenes before them.　He said:—"The lotos resembles your graceful form, the moss is like your hair, the bees are like your eyes, the reflection of the moon upon the water is like your face, the stalks of the lotos are like your arms, and the buds of the lotos are like your bosom." Then

Sports of the married pair in the pond.

they went down into the pond, and threw water at one another; and as their garments hung down from the water, Ráma threw lotos flowers upon his wife's bosom.　Presently Sítá got out of her depth, and caught hold of Ráma's neck, and he was so happy to have his wife's arms round his neck that he was in no hurry to bring her out of the deep water. Then they played at hide-and-seek amongst the lotos flowers, and Ráma went first to hide, and he kept only his face above the surface of the water; and when Sítá went to search for him, she was doubtful whether she saw the face of her husband, or only a blue lotos; and she went to smell the flower, when their lips met, and Ráma kissed her.　Then Sítá went and hid herself in like manner, and when Ráma

Ráma and Sítá drink honey together.

saw her, he kissed her many times, but she remained perfectly still.　At last they came out of the water, and each of

---

[9] The Bráhmans were known as the twice-born. Ráma and Sítá are here represented as playing to see who should give a handsome present to the Bráhmans.

them drank a cup of honey; and the heart of Sítá was exhilarated like one who has drank wine.[10] Thus the heroic Ráma and the beautiful Sítá lived in the highest felicity, even as Vishnu lives with the beautiful Lakshmí.

To review such a narrative as the foregoing from a European point of view is simply impossible. Even an attempt to describe a honeymoon is perhaps scarcely in accordance with modern taste; for whatever may have been the custom of a past generation, modern manners seem to demand that a bride and bridegroom should retire from the view of their relatives and friends after the performance of the ceremony, and live in some degree of privacy until they have settled down to the calm routine of matrimonial life. Then, again, a European newly-married pair are supposed to have arrived at years of discretion, and to follow pursuits corresponding to a mature age. But the story of Ráma's honeymoon is little more than a description of the sportive play of a boy-husband and girl-wife, under conditions altogether foreign to European experience. The scene lies in the inner retreat of a Hindú palace. The complexion, age, dress, and manners of the young couple are all opposed to European ideas. The bridegroom is a handsome boy of sixteen with a blue complexion. He is arrayed in a coat of cloth of gold, and his trowsers are made of dyed cotton or silk embroidered with flowers. He has a golden tiara on his head, earrings in his ears, and necklaces of pearls or gems hanging down upon his bosom. The bride is a delicate young girl of fourteen with a complexion the colour of gold, but

Review of the foregoing story of the honeymoon of Ráma.

Wide difference between a European and a Hindú honeymoon.

Ráma and Sítá little better than children.

Description of Ráma as a Hindú bridegroom of sixteen.

Description of Sítá as a Hindú bride of fourteen.

---

[10] In the original, Sítá is described as being really intoxicated, and as uttering an amount of gibberish which cannot be reproduced in English.

still very fair. She is arrayed in a light shawl-like garment of a rose-red colour, embroidered with gold. Her raven-black hair is wrought into platted locks on each temple, and drawn in graceful curves on either side from her forehead to her ears; whilst the jetty tresses are glistening with jewelled butterflies, and other gossamery ornaments. Her ears and nose are alike resplendent with jewels; her wrists and arms are adorned with bracelets; her slender ancles are circled round with golden rings; whilst little golden bells twinkle upon her toes as she walks with naked feet over the carpeted floor. Such is the model of a Hindú bride, who has only just been carried from the bosom of her family to the house of her husband, or her husband's father. In educational matters she is perhaps more ignorant than a parish girl in England, but in rank and blood and manners she is a perfect Princess, a royal lady, as graceful and charming as a nymph in Indra's heaven, but pure as the driven snow. Such then were the pretty bridal pair, whose presence was the delight of the whole household; a pair of youthful Hindú lovers, who played at dice for kisses, or sported in the pond at moonlight, or drank honey together, with all the innocence of married children, surrounded by all the luxury of a Hindú zenana, and without a single care in all the world.[11]

---

[11] The picture of the married life of Ráma and Sítá is presented in the Adhyátma Rámáyana in a more Brahmanical form, as will be seen from the following extract :—

"When Ráma had married Sítá, and had conducted her to Ayodhyá, he built apartments for her adorned with gold and gems. So great was the quantity of jewels, the reflection from them was far beyond that which could be produced by innumerable tapers; the darkness of night was not known in her mansion. In those apartments a throne studded with gems was erected, on which Ráma sat every day elegantly adorned. Sítá stood at his left side holding in her hands a fan ornamented with precious stones, with which she fanned him. The body of Ráma resembled the lotos; he wore on his shoulders a veil of yellow brocade; earrings in the form of fish were pendent from his ears; a crown of pearls was on his head, and a string of rubies on his neck. His clothes sparkled with every species of jewels, his countenance was luminous as a million suns and moons.

"He was one day sitting in this apartment eating the betel-leaf which he had received from the hand of Sítá; he looked on Sítá's face and smiled; Sítá also looking towards Ráma, smiled in the most affectionate manner. At this time the Bráhman sage Nárada came into the apartment. The body of Nárada resembled the purest crystal; the clothes he wore were as red as the rose. He played on the Vina, and he was chaunting a hymn in which the name of Ráma was frequently repeated, for his whole thoughts were bent on Ráma. Nárada is acquainted with the present, the past, and the future. When Ráma beheld him he descended from his throne, and conducted him into his apartment. Ráma and Sítá placing him on their throne, stood before him with joined hands; they worshipped him with pious affection, and walked round him three times. They washed his feet, they then threw the water on their own heads, saying :—'Thy condescension, Nárada! in exhibiting thyself before us, is unbounded; it is not in our power to account for our good fortune.' These words of respect paid him by Ráma filled the heart of Nárada with delight, and he praised Ráma as the Sovereign Lord and Deity, and identified Ráma and Sítá with each of the deities by name. 'What power,' he said, 'have I to relate thy former history : All the women of the world are stamped with the image of Sítá; all mankind with thine; thus the three worlds, which I have seen, are not in appearance different from Ráma and Sítá.' . . . .

"In this manner did Nárada rehearse the praises of Ráma, while tears of joy fell from both his eyes. Then with joined hands he again addressed him :—

"'Brahma, O Lord! has sent me to present sundry requests to thee; if it be thy pleasure I will mention them.' Ráma said :—'Speak.' Nárada answered :— 'My request is this : Thou, Ráma! hast assumed an incarnation of the flesh for the purpose of destroying Rávana : Thou thyself declarest that thou wouldst perform this deed, and that thou wouldst descend into the world to remove the burden from the face of the earth : Now I understand that Mahárája Dasaratha proposes to resign his throne to thee : Whilst thou art engaged in the government of the kingdom, thou wilt forget to destroy Rávana, and this important event will not be accomplished : Thou, Lord! hast voluntarily entered into this compact, that thou wouldst appear on the earth, and that thou wouldst render light the burden of the world : Confirm the engagement into which thou hast entered : Thy promises ever have from the utmost period of time been sacred; whatever thou hast declared, whatever thou hast designed, that has been carried into effect : We are reduced to great distress; condescend to remove our sorrows : We have taken refuge at thy feet; comply, O Lord, with our petition, and afford us thy assistance without delay.'

"Ráma, on this address from Nárada, considered a little within himself, and thus spoke : —'Be not troubled in thy mind, Nárada! it is my firm and unalterable intention to carry into execution those engagements into which I have entered : Never will I retract my word : I recollect my promise; I will fulfil it in due season : Rávana shall obtain the full reward of such religious observances, charity, and good works, as he may have performed during former births; and when the benefits of his religious acts shall cease I will destroy him.'"

CHAPTER VI.

RÁMA APPOINTED YUVARAJA.

Temporal
prosperity of
Ráma.
Ancient
appointment of
the heir-appar-
ent to be co-
Rája during
his father's
lifetime.

THE marriage of Ráma having been brought to a happy conclusion, there seemed to be only one thing wanting to complete his earthly prosperity, and that was his elevation to the throne. It appears to have been an ancient custom in Asiatic monarchies, for the heir-apparent to be solemnly recognized as such in the lifetime of his father, by being formally installed in the regal dignity, and admitted to a share in the administration.

The object of this custom appears to have been threefold. In the first place, it settled the succession, and prevented any civil war between rival claimants for the throne, which might arise at the death of the sovereign.

Secondly, it furnished an aged or infirm ruler with a youthful coadjutor, who might relieve him of all the more active duties of Government, military as

well as civil. Finally, it familiarized the young Prince with the administration of justice and other branches of government, and enabled him on the death of his father to fulfil with efficiency all the duties of Asiatic sovereignty.

Installed as
Rája under the
title of Yuva-
raja.

Under such circumstances an heir-apparent on attaining his majority would be solemnly installed as Raja; and henceforth he would receive the title of Yuvaraja, or " little

Raja," and would be presumed to act in subordination to his father, who would still retain the title of
Maháraja, or "great Raja."

The installation of a Yuvaraja would naturally
be regarded throughout the Raj as an important
political event; as the accession of a young and
promising Prince would be expected to result in
such an infusion of new blood into the administration as would materially affect the interests of both
Chieftains and people. But in its social aspect
such an event would not fail to excite a far deeper
interest in the court and palace. In cases where
the Maháraja was blessed with a single consort, the
nomination of a Yuvaraja would be commonly
attended with no difficulty, as the eldest son would
naturally occupy the position; although exceptional
cases might occasionally arise, as in the royal house
of Bhárata, in which the claim of a nephew seemed
to override that of a son, and the rivalry ultimately
led to a disastrous war. But in families where the
Maháraja was married to more than one wife, the
nomination of a Yuvaraja would frequently be a
source of intrigues which would keep the inner
apartments in a constant turmoil. The enmities
and heart-burnings of the rival women would be
kept alive by the ambition of the mothers for the
elevation of their respective sons. The apparently
just claim of the first wife to see her son appointed
Yuvaraja might in the case of an aged and uxorious
Maháraja be set aside by a younger and more
favoured rival. Meanwhile, any extra attention
which the Maháraja might pay to a favourite consort
would be construed into an intention to elevate her
son to the throne, and would thus arouse both the

Partisanship of
the slave girls
of the palace.

jealousy of the wife and the wrath of the mother. The slave girls of every Rání would also espouse the cause of their respective mistresses, and by their sympathies and tale-bearings would inflame their wrath to the utmost; until at last the pent-up feelings of the affronted wives would burst into flames, and the peace of the Maháraja would be lost for ever.

Intrigues
embittered by
the conditions
of zenana life.

The passions
stimulated by
want of society
and occupation.

Nor are these circumstances surprising when the conditions of zenana life are taken into consideration. Passions, such as pride, ambition, jealousy, and malice—which in Europe are subdued by the moral influence of general society—become intensified in the confined atmosphere of the zenana, in which that influence is generally wanting. Here a number of ignorant and passionate women are herded in separate apartments, without any accomplishment or duty that would serve to occupy their mind, without any society beyond that of their slaves and parasites who are more illiterate and cunning than themselves, and with all their energies concentrated into one pursuit of so influencing the mind of the Maháraja as to secure the welfare of their own sons

Tenderness of
the woman
changed to the
ferocity of the
tigress.

at the expense of the sons of his other wives. Under such circumstances the feminine mind is left to brood at will over real or imagined wrongs, and the prospect of revenge, until sentiment, kindliness, and even humanity, are utterly crushed in the female bosom, and the woman grows into a cruel and relentless tigress. Moreover, the question of the succession, which under any circumstances would excite the antagonism of rival claimants, becomes of paramount importance on other grounds. The question is not merely whose son shall succeed to

Vital import-
ance of the
question of
succession in
polygamous
households.

Involves the
question of
which wife
shall rule the
family.

the throne, but which wife shall rule the royal household; for the mother of the Yuvaraja would naturally secure that position, whatever might be the claims of the eldest Rání; and· it can easily be imagined that the mortification of an elder wife in finding herself subordinate to a younger and more successful rival would prove a fertile source of protracted misery, and perhaps would entail the most poignant anguish which a woman could be called upon to bear. The mortification of the son would add to the affliction of the mother. She would see him become the obsequious servant of the son of a hated rival, whilst she herself would be compelled to submit during the remainder of her life to the airs and caprices of a detested woman, through whom her son had lost his birthright, and she herself had been deprived of the affection of her lord.

The tradition of the appointment of Ráma to be Yuvaraja furnishes a graphic illustration of the inner life in the zenana of a Hindú Raja, under circumstances similar to those which have been indicated. It must, however, be borne in mind that the object of the author of the Rámáyana was not so much to exhibit the traditionary life of Ráma in all the truthfulness of authentic detail, as to represent Ráma himself as a Hindú model of goodness, who was equally beloved by all, by the people as well as by the Ministers and Chieftains, and even by all the wives and all the sons of the Maháraja. Glimpses however of the ancient and authentic tradition are sufficiently manifest throughout the whole narrative; and it is by no means difficult to perceive that the real state of affairs in the court of the Maháraja was somewhat of the following character. The two claimants for

Opposition of
Ráma to
Bharata.

Relative posi-
tion of their
mothers.

Partisanship of
Lakshmana and
Satrughna.

the dignity of Yuvaraja in Ayodhyá appear to have been Ráma the son of Kausalyá, and Bharata the son of Kaikeyí. The mother of Ráma was the first wife of the Mahárája, and consequently would have the first claim. The mother of Bharata, however, was the youngest wife of the Mahárája, and by means of her youth and beauty she appears to have exercised a considerable influence over the uxorious Mahárája. The two remaining sons, Lakshmana and Satrughna, appear to have had no prospect whatever of succeeding; and although born of one mother, they appear to have taken different sides; Lakshmana being the particular friend of Ráma, whilst Satrughna was the particular friend and follower of Bharata. This point, however, is not clearly stated in the Rámáyana, as, according to the Brahmanical author, both the young Princes, and even Bharata himself, fully recognized on all occasions the superior claims of Ráma.

Progress of the
intrigues.

Opposition of
Kaikeyi, the
younger wife,
to Kausalyá, the
first wife.

Views of the
Mahárája.

The progress of the intrigues in the palace at Ayodhyá may be inferred in like manner, although the particulars are rather obscurely related in the Rámáyana. The young and beautiful Kaikeyí, proud of her influence over the Mahárája, had probably determined from a very early period that her son Bharata should succeed to the Raj. On the other hand, the first wife, Kausalyá, had been nervously jealous lest her more favoured rival should tempt the Mahárája to commit an injustice by setting aside Ráma and appointing Bharata. As for the Mahárája he seems to have been disinclined to admit either of his sons to a share in the administration; and at length only yielded when he found that his Chieftains and people were determined to press the measure. Having seen, however, the necessity for appointing a Yuvaraja, he seems to have preferred Ráma; probably considering him to be the rightful heir as the son of the first wife. With this view he appears to have sent away Bharata and Satrughna to the distant city of Girivraja, which belonged to the father of Kaikeyí, in order that their presence might occasion no interruption to the installation of Ráma.

With these explanations the narrative of the appointment of Ráma to be Yuvaraja may now be related as follows:—

Now Ráma was the son of Kausalyá, and his brother Bharata was the son of Kaikeyí. And it came to pass that Yudhájit, the brother of Kaikeyí, came to Ayodhyá to visit his sister; and the Maháraja received him kindly and entertained him well. And when Yudhájit prepared to return to his father's city, the Maháraja determined that his son Bharata should accompany him; and he sent for Bharata and desired him to take leave of his mother Kaikeyí, and to prepare to go with his brother Satrughna to the city of Raja Aswapati, the father of his mother Kaikeyí. And Kaikeyí rejoiced exceedingly when she heard that her son Bharata was going with her brother to the house of her father. And the Maháraja said to Bharata:—"Go, my gentle one, to the house of your grandfather, accompanied by your brother Satrughna, and revere your grandfather as a deity: Serve the Bráhmans with the utmost assiduity, and ask counsel of them, for they are the gods of the earth: Constantly travel on horse-back, in a chariot, or on an elephant, and make yourself master of singing, and playing, and painting, and dancing, and never sit for a moment in idleness: Never speak a harsh word to any body, for one harsh word will spoil all your good qualities; and ever send messengers to me, as my heart will rejoice greatly to hear of your welfare."

HISTORY OF INDIA. PART IV.

Preference for Ráma.

Bharata sent to the city of his maternal grandfather.

Tradition as related in the Rámáyana.

Visit of Yudhájit, brother of Kaikeyí and uncle of Bharata.

The Maháraja determines to send away Bharata with Yudhájit.

Joy of Kaikeyí.

Commands given by the Maháraja to Bharata.

Departure of
Bharata and
Satrughna.

So Bharata took leave of his father and brethren, and then bowed to his mother Kaikeyí, and the other wives of his father, and departed with his uncle and his brother Satrughna ; and after travelling many days, and passing many delightful forests, rivers and mountains, he approached the pleasant city of Girivraja, and the palace of his grandfather

Arrival at the
city of Raja
Aswapati.

Aswapati. Bharata then sent on a trusty messenger to announce his arrival to his royal grandfather; and the Raja, hearing the words of the messenger, was greatly pleased, and caused the highly honoured Bharata to be introduced

Public rejoic-
ings.

into the city. Then the people of the city watered their streets, and decorated them with garlands of wild flowers, and flags placed on high, and perfumed them with sweet-smelling drugs ; and all the people went out with a number of beautiful dancing girls dressed in gay attire, and welcomed Bharata to the city amidst the sound of trumpets ; and all the heralds and eulogists walked before Bharata and proclaimed the greatness of his name and lineage : In this manner Bharata slowly arrived at the palace of his grandfather, and there beheld the aged Raja, and did him obeisance, and inquired after his welfare. He then entered the inner apartments, and bowed to the ladies of the royal

Bharata and
Satrughna
dwelt in the
palace of Raja
Aswapati.

household. After this Bharata dwelt in the greatest felicity in the palace of his grandfather, who appointed instructors for him ; and Bharata attended upon his instructors with all diligence ; and he studied the Vedas, and the Vedángas, and the Sastras, and perfected himself in all the sciences and

Studies of
Bharata.

the mechanical arts. And he acquired a perfect knowledge of the whole science of archery, and was deeply versed in the duties of royalty, and very skilful in the management of elephants and chariots, and eminent in writing and composition, and accomplished in leaping and vaulting, and perfect in the knowledge of the stars. Then Bharata sent a messenger to his father Dasaratha to acquaint him with all he had done; and the Maháraja and the Ránís rejoiced greatly at the pleasing tidings brought by the messenger, and sent him back with proper presents to his sons Bharata and Satrughna.

And it came to pass that the Chieftains and people of Ayodhyá began to consider which of the Princes should be appointed Yuvaraja, to assist the aged Mahárája in the administration of the Raj, and on his death to succeed him on the throne.

Now Mahárája Dasaratha loved all his four sons, but he had the greatest regard for Ráma; for Ráma was a mine of excellence, eminent in wisdom and religion, learned, generous, of quick perception, pleasing in speech, heroic, but not elated with his own great valour, of incomparable address, reverencing the aged, devotedly attached to those who were devoted to him, the delight of all the people of the Raj, honouring the Bráhmans, compassionate to all who were in distress, and with all his passions under perfect control. And the thought came into the mind of the Mahárája that he would appoint his son Ráma to be Yuvaraja, and his associate in the government of the Raj. And all the Ministers and Counsellors, and all the people of the Raj, consulted together how they should entreat the Mahárája to appoint Ráma to be Yuvaraja. And the Ministers and Counsellors went to the palace, and said:—" O Mahárája, listen to the voice of your people! You are the Raja of Rajas; you are the greatest amongst men: At the sacrifice of your happiness you have governed us for nine thousand years,[1] and under your rule every one has been happy, and no one has ever dreamed even of any misery or misfortune: Now it is the wish of all, that Ráma should be placed upon the throne and entrusted with the government of the Raj, that you may retire from the duties of sovereignty, and spend the remainder of your years in sacrifice and religious ceremony, and so secure heaven in your next life." And the Mahárája was glad at heart to hear these words, but he feigned anger, and replied in severe terms, as follows :—" What faults have you discovered in me? Why do you wish my son to be Raja whilst I am alive? Have I ever deprived any one of his rights, that you now desire me

HISTORY OF INDIA. PART IV.

Question as to which of the Princes should be appointed Yuvaraja.

Partiality of the Mahárája for Ráma.

Virtues of Ráma.

Resolution of the Mahárája to appoint Ráma to be Yuvaraja.

Ministers, Counsellors, and people request the Mahárája to retire in favour of Ráma.

Feigned anger of the Mahárája.

---

[1] This is one of those palpable exaggerations as regards numbers which so frequently deface Brahmanical literature.

A great Council
summoned.

to retire?" Then the Ministers and Chieftains said that they
meant no evil to him, but that they all loved Ráma. So the
Maháraja called together a great Council of all his Ministers
and Counsellors, and all the Chieftains of the Raj, to discuss
the installation of Ráma; and all the officers of the army,
and all the people of the city of Ayodhyá and the country of
Kosala were in like manner gathered together.[2]

Speech of the
Maháraja
expressing a
desire to retire
in favour of
Ráma, and to
appoint Ráma
Yuvaraja.

Now when the Ministers, and Counsellors, and all the
Chieftains were assembled in the Council hall, the Maháraja
addressed them in a grave and majestic voice, as follows :—
" This day I consider myself to be the happiest of all men,
and I am assured that I cannot reward you sufficiently for
the great joy you have given to me by your proposal : I
myself have been for a long while desirous of placing Ráma
upon the throne ; but I would not discover my wish until I
knew what were your thoughts upon the measure : Now
that you have expressed your wishes, let there be no further
delay in the matter : It is well known to all of you that this
excellent Raj was nourished by my royal ancestors as a
father nourishes his sons ; and I have persevered in the
path trodden by my ancestors, and have constantly and
vigilantly preserved my subjects to the utmost of my power:
But this frame of mine has become old under the shadow of
the royal umbrella, and I am worn out with the weight of
the duties of sovereignty, and I desire rest : My excellent
son Ráma I wish to appoint Yuvaraja ; to him I commit the
government of the Raj ; do you accept him for your Raja,
or make known some other measure which will prove better
for the common weal."

Joy of the
assembly.

Then all the Chieftains there assembled rejoiced as the
peacocks rejoice at the coming of rain, and a pleasing sound
like the rushing of chariots ran through the whole assembly. Having heard the desire of the Maháraja, the Chief-

Reply of the
Chieftains that
Ráma should be
coadjutor with
the Maháraja.

tains replied to him as follows :—" O Maháraja, you are
many thousand years old, we pray you to appoint Ráma to

---

[2] The proceedings in connection with the installation of Ráma seem to indicate an attention to constitutional forms. But this point will be noticed hereafter
in reviewing the narrative.

be your associate in the Raj ; we desire that the mighty
Ráma, riding on an elephant, may be overshadowed with
the royal umbrella." The Maháraja, hearing these words,
was gratified in mind ; but still being anxious to know more,
he inquired of the Council as follows :—" O Chieftains, you
desire that Ráma should become Yuvaraja ; but tell me, I
pray you, why do you desire to see my son associated with
me while I govern the Raj in righteousness ?" The Chieftains replied to the Maháraja in these words:—" O Maháraja,
in every divine quality your son Ráma is equal to Indra : The Chieftains recite the many
He transcends in excellence the whole race of Ikshwáku : merits of Ráma.
In wisdom he is equal to the holy Vrihaspatí, the preceptor His wisdom and bravery.
of the gods : His glory and renown are continually increas-
ing, for he reveres the aged, the learned, and the Bráhmans :
In war he is irresistible, whether against gods, or demons,
or men ; for he is skilful in the use of all weapons, whether
human or divine : When he goes out against foreign enemies, accompanied by his brother Lakshmana, he always
conquers their cities ; and when he returns from the battle,
whether he be seated on an elephant or in a chariot, he ever His kind words.
inquires after the welfare of the citizens, like a father
inquiring after the welfare of his children, saying :—' Is it
well with your sons, and your fathers, and your wives, and
your servants ? ' Thus, O Raja of Rajas, does Ráma ever
address us : He is afflicted at our distresses, and he rejoices
in our joys : He is ever truthful, ever attentive to the aged, His truth, con-
a famous archer, never speaking without a benign smile, and justice,
never inclining to the love of women. He is never angry
without a just cause, and never bestows a favour on one
who is unworthy : He upholds the law by protecting the
innocent and destroying the criminal : All the people of the Universal
city and country pray for the health and strength and long popularity.
life of the magnanimous Ráma, whether they be servants or
bearers of burdens, citizens or ryots, young or old : We
therefore supplicate you, O Maháraja, that you will install
your excellent son Ráma as your coadjutor in the administration of the Raj."

The aged Maháraja then said to all his people :—" I am The Maháraja makes known his delight.

Directs his two
priests to
prepare for
Ráma's in-
stallation.

General
acclamations.

Vasishtha, at
the request of
the Maháraja,
recites what
will be necessary
for the cere-
mony.

The installation
fixed for the
morrow.

The Maháraja
sends for Ráma.

transported with delight : It is your desire that my eldest and beloved son Ráma should be my associate in the Raj." Then turning to his illustrious preceptors, Vasishtha and Vámadeva, he said to them in the presence of all the people : —" This delightful month Chitra, in which the forests are adorned with flowers, is sacred and auspicious ; prepare then all things for the installation of Ráma as Yuvaraja." At the words of the Maháraja a mighty shout arose among the people, and when the sound had somewhat ceased, the Maháraja said to Vasishtha :—" O chief of sages, it is proper for you to say what should be the ceremonies performed at the installation of Ráma." Vasishtha then said to the serv- ants of the Maháraja :—" Prepare the gold and the jewels, the purifying bath of the gods, the incense, the garlands of white flowers, the parched grain, the honey, the clarified butter, the insignia of royalty, and all things necessary for the installation of the Yuvaraja, and place them in the house set apart for the sacred fire of the Maháraja : Provide also abundance of food, dressed and seasoned, together with curds and milk sufficient for the wants of a hundred thousand Bráhmans, and fill golden pots with water from the sacred rivers : To-morrow at sunrise the Bráhmans must strew the rice upon the earth, and invoke the blessing of the gods upon the installation of Ráma. Therefore let the Bráhmans be invited to attend, and the throne be prepared, and the banners be elevated on high, and the chief roads be well watered; and let musicians, and beautiful damsels gaily adorned, fill the inner court of the royal palace ; and let rice and other food, with fees for the Bráhmans, and garlands of flowers, be placed on all the temples, and beneath all the sacred trees ; and let heroic warriors, armed with long swords and clothed in clean raiment, enter the first court of the Maháraja.'

Then the Maháraja said to his chosen Counsellor Suman- tra :—" Bring hither the accomplished Ráma ! " And Su- mantra brought Ráma in a chariot to the royal palace ; and the Maháraja, adorned with jewels, and with gratified heart, was sitting in his palace as conspicuous amongst his Chieftains as Indra among the Maruts, when he beheld his god-like son approaching.   Presently Ráma descended from his chariot, and with joined hands followed Sumantra, and entered the palace, which was as resplendent as the summit of the Kailása mountain, and went into the presence of his father, and bowed at his feet.   The Maháraja then took his son Ráma by his two hands, and drew him towards him, and clasped him in his arms, and commanded a throne to be set before him, lofty, brilliant, and adorned with gold and gems. Then the Maháraja, seeing his son standing before him adorned with jewels, like his own image reflected in a mirror, was the happiest of fathers; and he said to Ráma— "All men owe three great debts; the first to the gods, the second to the Rishis, and the third to their ancestors; the first I have paid by sacrifices and ceremonies, the second by learning the Vedas and the Sastras, and your birth has freed me from the third: I have now one wish remaining; listen to my words and promise that you will gratify me: You were born of my first wife, and you are the eldest of my four sons ; and all my subjects and Chieftains and Counsellors are desirous of seeing you upon the throne: I wish you therefore to comply with their request: Do not hesitate to do so on account of my being alive, for it has always been the rule of my race that when a Maháraja grows old, he should give the Raj to his eldest son and retire to the forest: So I wish you to reign in my stead, and relieve me from all my cares, that I may retire to a holy place and worship Vishnu: Three planets are placed in malignant aspect to my star, namely, Súrya, Mungul, and Rahu; and the astrologers say that such aspects generally portend the death of a Raja, and will certainly subject him to dreadful misfortunes: But to-morrow is auspicious, for the moon passes into the favourable mansion of Pushyá; therefore to-morrow I will install you as Yuvaraja : Pass the night with your wife Sítá, sleeping on a couch of kusa grass with a stone for your pillar; and let your friends surround you on all sides, and remain sober, and watch with you: The absence of Bharata is the proper time for your installation; Bharata is obedient to his elder

Ráma arrives at the palace.

Received graciously by the Maháraja.

Speech of the Maháraja to Ráma.

Requests Ráma to become Yuvaraja.

His own planet threatened by three malignant aspects.

Passing of the moon on the morrow into Pushyá.

Ráma directed to keep watch until the morning.

HISTORY OF
INDIA.
PART IV.

Ráma proceeds
to his mother's
apartments.

brother, but still the mind of man is inconstant ; therefore keep watch until the morrow."

Ráma having received the instructions of the Máharaja, bowed his head, and went his way to the apartments of his mother Kausalyá; and there he beheld his devout mother, attired in silk, and supplicating the gods in silence, for the prosperity of her son; and Sumitrá, the youngest of the Ránís, and Sítá, and Lakshmana were attending on Kausalyá, as she sat with her eyes fixed in mental supplication to the gods, and contemplated the great Vishnu. Ráma approached her, and bowed with joy at her feet, and said :—

Acquaints her
of his coming
elevation.

Joy of Kau-
salyá.

"O mother, I am chosen by the Maháraja to govern the subjects of the Raj : To-morrow my installation will take place by the command of my father." Now Kausalyá had been long desirous that her son should obtain the Raj, and she replied to Ráma with tears of happiness, saying :—"O my beloved son Ráma, may your life be long, and all your oppressors be destroyed : Favoured by Lakshmí, who is the goddess of all prosperity, all the kinsfolk of myself and Sumitrá will be filled with joy : O my dear son, surely you were born under an auspicious star, seeing that your father Dasaratha has been moved by your excellent qualities : My devotion to Vishnu has been effectual, since the good genius of the Raj of Ikshwáku[3] will condescend to reside with you."

Ráma's kind
address to his
brother
Lakshmana.

Having been thus addressed by his mother, Ráma turned to his brother Lakshmana with a smile and said :—"O Lakshmana, share the Raj with me : Let my good fortune attend you as my second self : Enjoy, O son of Sumitrá, the pleasures that spring from royalty, for I desire life and a Raj for your sake." Ráma then bowed to the feet of both his mothers, and gave directions to Sítá, and went his way to his own house.

Goes home.

Vasishtha, by
direction of the
Maháraja, visits
Ráma.

Meanwhile the Maháraja called his priest Vasishtha, and said to him :—"Go now and cause Ráma to fast this day according to the ordinance." The divine Vasishtha, profound

---

[3] Ikshwáku was a celebrated ancestor of the Rajas of Kosala, and in all probability was the founder of the royal line; all his predecessors being of a mythical character, consisting of Rishis, who were either the ancestors or the descendants of the Sun.

in the knowledge of the Vedas, replied :—" Even so." And
Vasishtha mounted his chariot, and quickly arrived at the
house of Ráma, which was as resplendent as a bright cloud ;
and he entered the third court, and Ráma hastened to him,
and assisted him to dismount from his chariot.   Then the
venerable Bráhman blessed Ráma, and said :—" O Ráma,
your father is gracious to you : This day you must fast with
Sítá, and on the morrow the Maháraja will install you as his
associate in the Raj."   Then Ráma respectfully bowed his
head, and said :—" It is an auspicious and sacred day." And
Ráma worshipped the sage, and presented him with ten
thousand cows ; and Vasishtha, having laid his injunctions
upon him, took his leave.[4]   Then Ráma bathed himself, and
with devout mind he approached Vishnu with his beloved
wife, and placing on his head the vessel containing the purifying liquids,[5] he offered clarified butter to the gods, and
gave it to the fire according to the ordinance.   He then
meditated on the god Vishnu, and with his passions under

---

[4] The narrative of Vasishtha's visit to Ráma is somewhat differently related
in the Adhyátma Rámáyana for the purpose of laying more stress upon the divine
character of Ráma.   The passage is as follows : —

" Vasishtha then proceeded to wait on Ráma.   The latter went to meet him,
made his obeisance, and conducted him into his apartment, where he placed the
spiritual guide on a seat, brought water to wash his feet, which he poured on his
own head, and then spoke :—' This is a happy day to me, inasmuch as I have
been able to sprinkle the water from thy feet upon my head ; that thou hast
visited me in my own apartment ; I am by this means freed from the bondage of
sin.'   Vasishtha at these words considered a little time within himself, and thus
answered :—' Wherefore hast thou, O Lord ! thus forgot thyself ?   I know thee
well : The Ganges which purifies all things, flowed originally from thy feet, and
the great god Siva, knowing the excellence of it, received it on his head : My
father Brahma ever sprinkles on his head the water with which thou hast bathed
thy feet, being confident he shall be exalted from it : Thou art the Lord of all,
and in accordance with the prayer of Brahma and the gods, hast assumed the
human form to punish the evil-doers, Rávana and his iniquitous followers : I have
taken upon myself an inferior position in this world, and taken upon myself the
priesthood, having learned from Bráhma that thou wouldst appear among the
descendants of the Sun.'   .   .   .   .   .   .
Sítá, the object of thy affection, has thrown the veil of delusion over the senses of
the whole world ; she has done it by means of thy divine power : Desire this
delight of thy soul not to cast the veil over me, that my soul may always be
inclined towards thee : This is the request I had to make."

[5] The purifying liquids are the five products of the sacred cow, viz. milk,
curds, butter, urine, and ordure.

strict control, and his speech restrained, he lay in the temple of Vishnu, on a bed of well-spread kusa grass by the side of the fortunate Sítá, keeping watch the whole night.

Rejoicings in
the house of
Ráma.

All this time the house of Ráma was enlivened with joyful faces, as a lake abounding in water-lilies is enlivened by the inebriated bees; and as Vasishtha left the house and made his way to the royal palace, the high road of the city

Rejoicings
throughout the
city of Ayodhyá.

of Ayodhyá was crowded with a joyful multitude, which moved to and fro like the waves of the sea, whilst their noise was like that of the roaring of a tempest. Throughout the night

Illuminations
and purifica-
tions.

the whole city was illuminated by clusters of lamps, and every road and pathway was cleansed from impurity, and every house was filled with men, women, and children, all longing for the installation of Ráma, and anxiously watching

Adorning of the
city at sunrise.

for the rising of the sun. At the first dawning of the morning all the citizens of Ayodhyá began to adorn the city. They watered the streets with fragrant waters, and strewed the roads with flowers; and they set up glittering banners upon the bright temples of the gods, and at the corners of the streets, and on the sacred trees, and on the tops of stately houses, and at the bazaars and shops, and at the

Young and old
exult in the
installation of
Ráma,

courts of justice and hall of assembly. And the multitudes, young and old, were exhilarated by companies of beautiful dancing-girls, and by singers and musicians; and everywhere the people conversed together respecting the installation of Ráma; and even the children, as they played together in the court-yards or under the porticoes, were ever saying the one to the other:—"This day Ráma is to be

Country people
flock into the
city to behold
the installation.

anointed Raja." Meanwhile the glad tidings of Ráma's installation had been carried far away from the city into the country of Kosala; and the ryots and the husbandmen and the herdsmen were all eager to witness the ceremony, and they flocked into Ayodhyá from all quarters, so that the sound of the multitude was like that of the rushing of the flood-tide rolling in from the sea at the waxing and waning of the moon.

Review of the
narrative in the
Rámáyana.

In the foregoing narrative of the proceedings con-

nected with the appointment of Ráma to be Yuvaraja, a few of the details have been slightly Brahmanized. Thus Vasishtha, the priest, is introduced
for the unnecessary purpose of giving to Ráma almost the same commands as those which had been
previously given to him by the Maháraja; and for
the significant object of representing him as receiving from the young Prince the reverence and worship
which the author of the Rámáyana considered to be
due to so celebrated à Bráhman. Again, considerable stress is laid upon the worship of Vishnu both
by Ráma and his mother; although Ráma is himself
said to be an incarnation of Vishnu. Moreover, the
feigned anger of the Maháraja on hearing the pro-
position that he should retire from the Raj, and that
Ráma should be appointed in his room, was, in all probability a sincere expression of displeasure. But in
other respects the essential details may be regarded
as a relic of the original tradition. The object of
the Maháraja, in sending Bharata to the city of his
maternal grandfather, is sufficiently manifest; and
it will be noticed that the Maháraja expressly desired
Ráma to keep watch during the night which inter-
vened between the great Council and the day of installation; apparently lest Bharata should return
during the interval, and create a disturbance for the
purpose of enforcing his claim to the succession.

But perhaps the most interesting circumstances
in the narrative are those connected with the popular movement in favour of Ráma's installation. Here
a democratic element in the ancient Hindú despot-
isms is distinctly discernible. First of all a deputation of Ministers, Chieftains; and people wait upon
the Maháraja to express the popular will, that he

Brahmanical
introduction of
Vasishtha, a
later interpola-
tion.

Dubious stress
laid upon the
worship of
Vishnu.

Remaining
details a relic
of the ancient
tradition.
Fears as regards
Bharata.

Democratic
element evi-
denced in the
popular move-
ment in favour
of Ráma.

The deputation
which waited
upon the Mahá-
raja.

General
assembly, or
great Council,
convened in
consequence.

Popular interest
in public affairs
converted into a
personal affec-
tion for Ráma.

should retire from the active administration of the Raj, and that Ráma should be entrusted with the reins of power. Upon this intimation the Maháraja summons a great Council or Parliament at which he expresses his intention of appointing Ráma to be Yuvaraja. This popular demonstration in favour of Ráma seems to indicate a direct interest on the part of the people in public affairs; although the Brahmanical author for his own purposes has converted it into a demonstration of personal affection for the youthful hero. That the popular regard for Ráma was not so strong as Válmíki would seem to intimate will be proved in the sequel, in which it will be seen that the same assembly displayed considerable apathy as regards the rival claims of Ráma and Bharata, and were only bent upon a prompt settlement of the question as regards the succession. It should also be remarked, that there is at least one passage in the sequel which would intimate that there was a far greater difference in the ages of the four sons of Dasaratha than is indicated in the mythical account of their birth and origin.[6]

---

[6] See especially a passage in chapter viii., in which Kausalyá requests Ráma to take care of Lakshmana, because the latter is a mere boy.

CHAPTER VII.

INTRIGUES OF KAIKEYÍ.

THE story of Ráma's appointment to be Yuvaraja, and the description of the imposing preparations for the ceremony of installation, would seem to indicate that the young Prince had arrived at the acme of human felicity. His infancy and boyhood had passed away without a cloud. He was happily married to the most beautiful and loving of wives. Another day, another sunrise, would see him installed Yuvaraja of Kosala. It was on the very eve of this brilliant success, that the ancient and mysterious conception of an avenging Nemesis, of the envy of the gods at the prosperity of a mortal, would seem to have found an expression in the Hindú tradition.[1] The city was one blaze of joy and exultation. Throughout the night every street was illuminated with endless clusters of lamps, whilst the vast multitude of citizens were unable to close their eyes for thinking of the approaching installation, and were

Acme of human felicity attained by Ráma.

Conception of the avenging Nemesis.

Brilliant preparations for the installation on the eve of the ceremony, throughout the night, and on the following sunrise.

---

[1] The conception of the avenging Nemesis does not literally find expression in the Rámáyana in its present form. Indeed the religious idea involved is rather that the gods were angry at an event which was calculated to interfere with the fulfilment of the mythical purpose for which Vishnu became incarnate as Ráma, namely, the destruction of the demon Rávana. (See extract from the Adhyátma Rámáyana in the next chapter.) But it is impossible to avoid the suspicion that in the original tradition the sudden adversity which succeeded to so much prosperity was invested with a moral meaning similar to that indicated.

eagerly watching for the rising of the sun. At last the white-robed dawn appeared in the sky, and immediately the people began to decorate the city. They watered the streets, they strewed the roads with flowers, and they set up gay banners in all directions. Meanwhile, fresh crowds of country people were pouring into Ayodhyá; and all the ministers of public rejoicing,—the singers, the musicians, and the dancing-girls,—were delighting the hearts of young and old with music, and song, and exhilarating dances. Even the little children were not forgotten by the Hindú bard, who pictures them sporting together in the court-yards, and under the porticoes, and saying to one another in the midst of their play:—" This day Ráma is to be anointed Raja."

Painful scene
enacted during
the same
interim in the
palace of the
Maháraja.

Meantime, however, from the evening of the preceding day until the rising of the sun on the morning of the installation, a terrible scene had been enacted in the palace of the Maháraja; a scene which is never described to a Hindú audience without calling forth abundance of tears, and many sympathetic

expressions of sorrow and condemnation. But here further remark may cease, and the Hindú bard may be permitted to tell his own story, as follows :—

Scenes within
the palace of the
Maháraja on the
eve of the installation.

Manthará, the
old nurse of
Kaikeyi.

Now on the night which preceded the day of installation, and whilst the city was filled with joy and exultation, the evil aspect of the stars was working woe and desolation in the palace of Maháraja Dasaratha. There was an old nurse named Manthará, who had been the servant of the Rání Kaikeyí, whilst Kaikeyí was still living in the house of her father Aswapati; and when Raja Aswapati gave his daughter in marriage to Maháraja Dasaratha, he presented her with this slave woman as part of her dowry, and Manthará accompanied her mistress to the city of Ayodhyá. This Manthará was very ugly and deformed; her arms were long and thin, her fingers were very large, her chest was narrow, her neck was short, and her breasts were as small as figs, her legs were slender like those of a crane, her stomach was large and projecting, and her back bowed out like her stomach, for she was hump-backed.[2] Now this Manthará ascended to the roof of the palace, and saw all the preparations which were being made for the installation of Ráma, and the rejoicings of all the people of the city, and she inquired the reason thereof; and when it was told to her that Ráma was to be appointed Raja, she was much troubled, and her eyes were red with anger; for in by-gone years she had offended Ráma, and Ráma had smitten her with his foot, and she had leadly enmity against him.[3] So she hastened down from the roof of the palace in a great rage, and ran to the apartment of Ḳaikeyí, and found her reposing upon a couch, and she said to her:—"Rise up, you stupid one! Why do you sleep whilst a tremendous calamity is awaiting you? You are born of a royal race, but your husband has deceived you: The Maháraja is fair in speech but deceitful in deed: He has filled you with vain words, and Kausalyá with riches: He has sent your son Bharata to your father's city, which is far off, that to-morrow he may quietly install the son of Kausalyá in the Raj: You must now so act as to prevent your husband from installing Ráma."

At these words Ḳaikeyí was filled with surprise, and

HISTORY OF INDIA. PART IV.

Her extreme ugliness.

Beholds the preparations for the installation with great wrath.

Attempts to rouse the jealousy of Ḳaikeyí in behalf of Bharata.

Ḳaikeyí professes delight at the news of Ráma's installation.

---

[2] This description of Manthará is interesting as exhibiting the Hindú idea of female ugliness.

[3] That Ráma should have kicked the slave-girl in his boyhood is by no means unlikely, and the incident probably found a place in the original tradition. But such a proceeding was scarcely compatible with his divine character, and accordingly the author of the Adhyátma Rámáyaṇa ignores the occurrence, and supplies the following pious myth as the reason for Manthará's interference :—

"When the gods heard the tidings from Ayodhyá of Ráma's approaching installation, they were overcome with terror. Indra and the rest held a consultation, and then went to Saraswatí and prayed her to obstruct the accession of Ráma. They said :—'Thy lord Brahma has informed us that there is a female slave named Manthará, who waits on Ḳaikeyí, the second wife of Dasaratha. Do thou visit the earth and enter her tongue.' Saraswatí, in obedience to the instructions of her husband, went instantly and took up her abode in the tongue of Manthará."

gave some ornaments to her nurse, and said :—" O Manthará, the information you have given is pleasing to me :
There is no distinction between Ráma and Bharata, and
therefore it pleases me that the Maháraja should install his
eldest son as his coadjutor in the Raj : Let us go to the
house of my eldest sister Kausalyá, and congratulate her on
the installation of her son Ráma."

Then Manthará, full of envy, and mad with disappointment, threw aside the ornaments given to her by Kaikeyí,
and cried out :—" O woman, there is no one so foolish as
you are in all the world : It would have been better for you
to have been slain by the bite of a serpent, or the fall of a
thunderbolt : Kausalyá is very fortunate, for her son is to
get the Raj, and you will be her slave, and your son will be
the slave of her son, and the wife of your son Bharata will
be the slave of her son Ráma : What can be more unfortunate for you than this ? And yet you consider it to be a
cause for rejoicing."

Kaikeyí dilates
on the virtues of
Ráma and his
superior claim
to the Raj.

Kaikeyí replied :—" Why do you cherish so much
hatred against Ráma, who is my beloved son, ever virtuous
and truthful, and who has the best claim to the Raj : He is
the son of the eldest Rání, he is the eldest of the sons of
the Maháraja, and he is in every way fitted to have the Raj :
He treats me with the same respect as he treats his own
mother Kausalyá, and when he gets the Raj he will treat
Bharata as his own son : Ráma is the eldest and Bharata the
youngest of the four brethren ; and there is no harm in
Bharata becoming the dependent and servant of Ráma :
Bharata could only get the Raj with the consent of Ráma :
Why then do you pain my heart by speaking against such a
happy event ? "

Manthará
insinuates that
Bharata and
Satrughna have
been sent away
that Ráma
might be in-
stalled.

At these words of Kaikeyí, the nurse Manthará became
thunderstruck, as if the heavens had fallen upon her head ;
and she began to verify the old proverb, that as a lame man
and a blind man have each a hundred faults, so there is no
limit to the faults of a humpback. She breathed hard, and
in a tone half of anger and half of supplication, she spoke
thus to her mistress Kaikeyí :—" O Rání, have you fallen

into such a misery that you can rejoice at that for which you ought to mourn? Ráma fears Bharata, because the Raj is the common property of all the four brethren; and Bharata, and his loving brother Satrughna, are sent to the city of your father, whilst Ráma remains here to be installed in the Raj; for Lakshmana is attached to Ráma, even as Satrughna is attached to Bharata: Kausalyá is indeed the beloved wife, and to-morrow her son will be installed when the moon enters Pushyá: What good then can attend you when your son Bharata loses the Raj? Like a slave you must henceforth stand with clasped hands before Kausalyá, and you will be her servant, whilst your son Bharata will become the servant of Ráma: All the women in the house of Ráma will be filled with joy, and all the women in the house of Bharata will be filled with sorrow: Ráma and his posterity will become Mahárajas, whilst Bharata will be driven from his father's house; but had Bharata remained in the city of Ayodhyá up to this day, no one but he could have been installed Yuvaraja: How will your son, deprived of wealth, live in subjection to his brother Ráma? It becomes you to save Bharata, who is about to be supplanted by Ráma, as the leader of a herd of wild elephants is driven off by a fierce and roaring lion: When Ráma becomes Raja he will certainly send Bharata into exile and secure the Raj for his own sons: Do you, therefore, procure the Raj for your own son Bharata, and persuade the Maháraja to send Ráma into the jungle: You are a woman of an extraordinary character; for any other woman would rather die than behold the prosperity of a co-wife."

Then Kaikeyí arose from her couch in great alarm, and said:—"How can I persuade the Maháraja to install my own son Bharata in the Raj, and send Ráma into exile?" Manthará, intent on evil, replied as follows:—"O Kaikeyí, hear from me how you may obtain the Raj for Bharata: Do you not remember that when Dasaratha went to the south to join the gods in the war against the demons, he was grievously wounded in the battle, and was carried

Again insinuates that Kausalyá is the favourite wife, and points out the coming elevation of Ráma and degradation of Bharata.

Counsels Kaikeyí to persuade the Maháraja to install Bharata and exile Ráma.

Kaikeyí aroused.

Manthará reminds her of the two boons promised her by the Maháraja.

HISTORY OF
INDIA.
PART IV.

Desires her to
request the
installation of
Bhárata and
exile of Ráma.

off, and preserved by you? Then he promised you two boons, and do you now ask two favours of him, the Raj for your son Bharata, and fourteen years' exile for the son of Kausalyá : [4] Thus whilst Ráma is wandering in the woods, your son will acquire the affection of the people, and enjoy the Raj without molestation : O Ráni, feigning anger, do you go into the chamber of displeasure, and the Raja will come to you and inquire the reason of your grief : You have ever been the beloved of your husband, and he will not dare to see you angry : Should the Mahárája offer you pearls, or gems, or jewels of any kind, pay no attention to him, but only ask for the two boons, the Raj for Bharata, and exile for Ráma; otherwise Ráma will obtain the Raj, and you and your son will become wanderers in the jungle."

Thus excited by her wicked nurse, the beautiful Ráni, intoxicated with wrath and jealousy, ran away to the chamber of displeasure, and threw off her pearl necklace and excellent jewels, and strewed them upon the ground; and she untied her hair so that it fell down dishevelled, and she covered her face with the darkness of anger. [5]

---

[4] This myth is differently related in the Adhyátma Rámáyana, where Manthará is represented as speaking to Kaikeyí as follows :—

"Heretofore, a very long time ago, when there was a bloody warfare between the gods and demons, Indra solicited the aid of Mahárája Dasaratha. At that time the Mahárája really loved thee; he never was separated a moment from thee. He seated thee on his own chariot; he took thee with him to a place where he entered into a dreadful conflict with the demons, during which an iron pin being broken in the wheel of the carriage on the field of battle, thou didst by putting thy hand into its place, prevent the carriage being overturned. He was then so much pleased with thy conduct that he declared he would grant whatever thou mightest request of him. Thou at that time didst require two things from the Mahá-rája, and having taken hold of each other's hands as a bond of agreement, thou didst say, when I require these two things, I will remind thee of thy promise. The time has now arrived; demand from the Mahárája the performance of his contract."

[5] Mr Ward states that an apartment is still maintained in Hindú houses to which the wife resorts when angry with her husband. This assertion must be taken with some qualification. The women will sometimes shut themselves up in a spare apartment, such perhaps as a lumber room; and this room may be called the chamber of displeasure with reference to the story in the Rámáyana. But such a chamber is not maintained as an institution. The dishevelling of the hair, which was carried out by Kaikeyí, is a more significant proceeding. She undid her platted locks, so as to resemble a widow, who is not allowed to wear platted hair.

Meantime, the Mahárája, having commanded the installation of Ráma, proceeded to the inner apartments to
impart the news to his beautiful and beloved Kaikeyí. The
palace was gay with parrots and peacocks, and vocal with
tuneful birds. It was filled with beautiful maidens and
slave girls, and adorned with clusters of climbing plants and
flowers. The painted verandas were supported by pillars of
gold, silver, and ivory. In the garden were trees over-laden
with fruits and flowers, and tanks of transparent water,
with beautiful seats upon the banks thereof. The Mahárája,
full of love for his charming Ráni, entered the magnificent
inner apartment, which resembled the sky when covered
with silver clouds during an eclipse of the moon ; but lo and
behold, he only saw the decorated couch, and the beautiful
Kaikeyí was not lying thereon. And the heart of the Maháraja sank within him, for he was thirsting for the presence
of his beloved; and ever before when he entered that
apartment, his beautiful Ráni had welcomed his coming
with a smile. Then he thought in his mind that perchance
she had gone to the apartment of Kausalyá, to wish her
joy on the installation of Ráma ; and he inquired where his
beloved had gone. Then the door-keeper was terrified, and
with hands respectfully joined, he said :—" O Raja of Rajas,
the Ráni is in a great rage, and she has fled in her haste to
the chamber of displeasure." Hearing these words the
Maháraja was exceedingly troubled, and he went to the
chamber of displeasure, and saw his young wife, dearer to
him than life, lying on the earth in sordid garments and
imagining mischief; and he beheld her, as an elephant
beholds his female mate who has been pierced by the
poisoned arrow of the hunter. And he caressed her, and
tried to arouse her, like one who endeavours to awaken a
sleeping serpent who will cause his death ; and he said to
her :—" Why, my beloved, are you in the chamber of displeasure ? Why are you without ornaments, and why do
you wear sordid attire ? I weep as I behold your misery,
and surely I have never offended you by night or day :
Say if you are sick that I may send for the most eminent

physicians, or that you have been affronted by any one that I may punish him according to your pleasure : I will do whatever you may command : I will slay the innocent or release the guilty, for I am a Raja of Rajas, and you are my most beloved: I will give you whatever you may request, even if it be my own life; there is nothing that you may want that I cannot satisfy." So saying, the Maháraja took her to his bosom, like one who takes up a snake by mistake for a garland, and he wiped her face, and asked her many times what it was that she desired.

Then the wicked Kaikeyí, seeing that her lord was pierced with the love-inspiring arrows of Káma-deva, and infatuated by his love for her, said these dreadful words :— " O Maháraja, I have neither been maltreated nor defamed, but I have formed a wish which I entreat you to gratify ; and if you will solemnly promise to do as I desire, I will

make known my request." Then the Maháraja, sick with love, smiled upon her, and taking her charming locks in his hand, he said to her as she lay upon the ground :—" Know, O haughty one, that no one is more beloved than you, excepting my son Ráma ; and by Ráma, who is dearer to me than life, I swear, O desire of my soul, that I will perform your request : O my beloved, divulge the wish of your heart, and you will relieve mine : May I lose all the merit of every good deed I have done upon earth, if I do not perform your request."

Kaikeyí calls
upon the gods
to witness his
promise.

The merciless Rání then made known her evil intent, in words as terrible as those of Yama. She said :—" Grant me the boon even as you have sworn : Let all the gods, with Indra at their head, the sun, the moon, the gods of the household, and all the regents of the universe, bear witness to this promise of the illustrious, the upright, and the faith-

Reminds the
Maháraja of
his previous
promise to
grant two
favours, and
requests the
installation of
Bharata and
exile of Ráma.

ful Maháraja." Then laying hold of her lord, and entreating him while he was intoxicated with love, she said to him :— " Remember, O Maháraja, what happened in the war between the gods and demons, when you were surrounded by the enemy, and in peril of your life; then when you were preserved by me, you promised me two favours, and these

two favours I now claim: The first favour is that my son
Bharata be installed this day in the stead of Ráma; and the
second favour is that Ráma may embrace the life of a
devotee, and clothe himself in the skins of deer and bark of
trees, and go this day into the forest of Dandaka for fourteen years."

The Maháraja, hearing these dreadful words, was filled
with anguish, and he fell down prostrate upon the ground,
like a plantain tree that has been thrown down by a strong
wind.   Then Kaikeyí was anxious, and said within herself:
—" I shall not be sorry for the death of the Maháraja, after he
has installed Bharata in the Raj; but now I must try and
restore him to his senses."   With these thoughts in her
mind, she attempted to awaken him, as a hunter awakens a
sleeping antelope before he kills it.[6]   Presently Dasaratha
aroused himself, and said:—" Am I tormented by demons,
or has my reason departed from me?"   Then when he fully
remembered all that Kaikeyí had said, he was as distracted
as an antelope at the sight of a tigress, but felt as powerless
as a serpent encircled by the spells of the snake-charmer.
After a long while the Maháraja, full of affliction and anger,
and consuming Kaikeyí with his eyes, thus spoke:—" O
cruel wretch, depraved in heart, and destroyer of this family,
what has Ráma done to you?   He has always paid the same
reverence to you as to his own mother Kausalyá; why then
are you bent upon his ruin?   You, the daughter of a Raja,
have crept into my house like a venomous serpent, in order
to destroy me: For what fault should I abandon my beloved
son Ráma?   I could part with Kausalyá, or with Sumitrá, or
with life itself, but I cannot part with Ráma: Among the
thousands of female slaves and dependents, no charge has
ever been brought against Ráma: He conquers mankind by
his truthfulness, the Bráhmans by his generosity, his preceptors by his attention, and his enemies by his sword and
bow: O Kaikeyí, have pity upon an old man, who is approaching the end of his days, and who humbly supplicates

The Maháraja
falls into a
swoon.

Kaikeyí's
anxiety.

Distraction of
the Maháraja.

He reproaches
Kaikeyí for her
cruelty.

Implores
Kaikeyí to
withdraw her
request.

---

[6] It is a Hindú rule that no man shall kill a sleeping deer.   Accordingly the
hunter must awaken the animal before he may slay it.

you : It would be easier for a fish to live out of water than for me to live without Ráma : Relinquish then this intention, and never let me hear of it again : Moreover, your son Bharata is virtuous, and would never accept the Raj if his elder brother is to go into exile, so that your labour would be lost : The husband is the Guru of his wife according to the Sastras, so you must never violate my orders : Save my life by relinquishing your evil purpose : Take jewels instead, or a thousand cities, or anything else that will satisfy you."

Remorseless obstinacy of Kaikeyi.

Saying these words, the Mahárája fell prostrate at the feet of the Rání, but Kaikeyí was unmoved at his anguish ; and such is the nature of a woman, for when she is bent upon increasing her own prosperity, she will sacrifice shame, honour, respect, or anything else to gain her end. At length Kaikeyí replied :—" I am prompted by no evil intention : I am in full possession of my senses : Every one calls you truthful, and it is said that you always adhere to your promise : You have promised me two favours, and the time has arrived for you to grant them : Why do you humble yourself in order to induce me to absolve you from your promise ? Your saying that the husband is the Guru of his wife is perfectly true ; but virtue is above all things, and never will I obey the words of my husband, if by so doing I lead him into vice : Grant me the two favours, and you are free."

She insists upon the fulfilment of the Mahárája's promise.

At these words of Kaikeyí, Dasaratha became exceedingly wroth, and would hear no more, but cried out :—" Hard-hearted and wretched woman, what has my son Ráma done to you that you wish to send him into exile ? For the sake of riches you are bent upon killing your own husband : Shame be upon that man who dotes upon his wife ; there is no happiness for him in this world or the next : But how can Bharata obtain the Raj during the life of his father ; for as the Sastras have said that a younger son should not marry before an elder brother, so a younger son cannot succeed to the Raj before his elder brother ? Your purpose is equally opposed to law as to religion, and I therefore look to you either to relinquish it altogether or to take my life."

Wrath of the Mahárája.

Reproaches himself for his uxoriousness, and insists upon Kaikeyí recalling her request.

When Kaikeyí heard these words of the Maháraja, she was furious with rage, and said :—" O Maháraja, if after making me two promises you now refuse to perform them, how will you be esteemed among men ?   You must say :— ' I have broken my word even to her who saved my life ; ' and you will become infamous among the Rajas : If Ráma be anointed I will take poison this day : You know that, according to the Puránas, the earth can bear any weight except that of a liar."

HISTORY OF INDIA. PART IV.

Kaikeyí insists upon the Maháraja keeping his word.

Then the Maháraja remained for a time like one convulsed, and his eyes were fixed upon the Rání, and he said nothing ; but after a while he remembered the dreadful oath he had uttered to Kaikeyí, and he fell to the earth like a tree that has been cut down by a woodman.   At length he spoke these words :—" O Kaikeyí, in what evil hour have I entered your apartment ?   I have been entrapped by my love for you, as a mouse is entrapped by the bait : As the ocean contains worthless shells as well as rich gems, so compared with my illustrious ancestors I am but as a worthless shell amongst the gems : The race who have descended from the Sun have been hitherto without stain, but I am the first to pollute it : Never before was it heard that a father sent his eldest son into exile in order to gratify a capricious wife : A wife is bound to serve her husband, and where is the husband who promises her favours in return for her service ?   I would rather go to hell for violating my promise, than consent to the exile of Ráma : Be the consequence what it may, I shall place Ráma upon the throne as soon as it is morning : But I fear lest Ráma should hear of my promise : for then he would of his own accord go into exile, rather than send me who am his father to the pains of hell : O Kaikeyí, relinquish this cruel wish !   How shall I behold the countenance of Ráma changed like the moon during an eclipse ?   How can I see my well-matured measure, which has been confirmed by all my people and Counsellors, thrown into confusion like an army which has been smitten by an enemy ?   What will the Rajas say, when I tell them that, tormented by Kaikeyí, I have given the

Lamentations and remonstrances of the Maháraja.

Raj to Bharata, and sent Ráma into exile? What will Kausalyá say to me, when Ráma is banished to the jungle? Can I survive the sight of Ráma departing to the dreary forest, and the agony of his weeping wife Sítá? You, a widow, will then govern the Raj with your son Bharata, and shall I discard Ráma for you? I am like a man who has drank good wines mingled with poison, or has seated himself on a beautiful carpet which has been spread over a deep well; and you have soothed me with deceitful caresses, like the murderous hunter soothing the antelope with the charms of music: The good will exclaim against me, as they would against a Bráhman who drank strong drinks: The whole world will abhor me, who for the sake of a woman has sent his beloved son into a jungle: If Ráma would refuse to go I should be happy, but at my command that dutiful son will proceed to the jungle without a word of complaint, and then death will soon convey me, execrated by all men, to the abode of Yama, and my beloved Kausalyá will follow me on the funeral pile: Then having sent us to hell you will govern the Raj, but if Bharata be gratified with the exile of his brother, he shall perform no funeral rites for me: But how can the dear Ráma, accustomed to ride in chariots and upon elephants, wander about on foot in a vast wilderness? How can my son, for whom cooks adorned with ear-rings prepared the most excellent food, subsist on the harsh and bitter fruits of the forest? How shall he who has been clothed in costly apparel sit on the bare ground clothed with thick kashaya grass? O Kaikeyí, seek not my destruction: I fall at your feet, be gracious to me: I would that the gods would cause my death this night, and strike with dhmbness all who know of these things, so that Ráma may never hear of my promise, and may become the Raja as determined upon by me."

Thus did the illustrious Maháraja speak whilst prostrate at the feet of the contemptuous Rání; but the wicked Kaikeyí said :—" I have three times repeated my requests and your promises must be fulfilled, or I will take poison in your presence." Then the Maháraja said to her :—" Tha hand of yours, which was consecrated with mantras, and which I accepted in the presence of the fire, I now reject for ever, and with you I reject your son Bharata, albeit he was descended from me." Thus passed away the dreadful night in the palace of Maháraja Dasaratha.

The picture of zenana life presented by the foregoing narrative furnishes a powerful illustration of the intrigues which were not unfrequently carried on in the Courts of Hindú Rajas. The dialogue has been somewhat marred by the palpable exaggerations of the author as regards the goodness and popularity of Ráma. It is impossible to believe that Kaikeyí could have felt all that gratification at the installation of Ráma, which she is said to have expressed to her old nurse on first hearing that he was to be appointed Yuvaraja; and it seems more probable that she was brooding over her imagined wrongs, when Manthará suggested to her the means by which she might work upon the affections of the uxorious Maháraja, and procure the elevation of her own son in the room of Ráma. In like manner it is difficult to believe that the Maháraja could have felt all that overweening affection for Ráma which he is said to have expressed to Kaikeyí; although no doubt he was greatly mortified at being betrayed into making a promise to Kaikeyí, which would upset the matured measure which had been proclaimed in the Council, and to which he was almost irretrievably committed. The story of the two boons is also apparently mythical, and was probably introduced for the simple purpose of strengthening the promise which the Maháraja was induced to make to Kaikeyí in the chamber of displeasure. But in other respects the narrative is marvellously

Review of the foregoing narrative of the intrigues of Kaikeyi.

Exaggerations in the dialogue respecting Ráma.

Real feelings of Kaikeyi.

Real feelings of the Maháraja.

Mythical character of the story of the two boons.

true to human nature. The malice exhibited by the old hag of a nurse, after witnessing the preparations which were being made for the installation of Ráma, is very well indicated, as well as the motives which she brought to play upon the mind of Kaikeyí. The proceedings of Kaikeyí are still more significant, and are precisely what might have been expected from the cunning and obduracy of a petted woman. Her first object was to wheedle the Mahárája into making a promise; her second was to insist upon the fulfilment of that promise. To effect the first purpose she determined to appeal to the affections of the Mahárája. She knew that Ráma was to be installed, and probably expected that the Mahárája would pay her a visit to cajole her into acquiescence with presents and caresses. She accordingly retired to another chamber, and literally sulked; throwing about her ornaments and jewels to show that no presents could console her, and dishevelling her hair to indicate her extreme anger and displeasure. When the Mahárája found her in this state of affliction, and protested his love and affection, and his great grief at her prostration, she said nothing whatever; but when she saw that his caresses had filled him with desire, she seized the critical moment for seducing him into making the promise. The Mahárája having thus committed himself, a woman's obstinacy compelled him to keep his word. He might implore and threaten and try to reason with her, but she was inexorable. He had made the promise and she insisted upon its fulfilment. To all he could urge she had but one answer "Unless Ráma is exiled and Bharata is installed, you will be stigmatized as a liar, and I will take poison."

The great stress which is here laid upon the per- formance of promises is somewhat remarkable, from the fact that it scarcely tallies with the charges which have been so frequently brought forward against the truthfulness of Hindús. But notwithstanding all that has been said upon this subject, it may be confidently asserted that the people of no nation in the world are better acquainted with the value of words, or display a higher regard for those who are scrupulous in keeping their promises.

There is one point in connection with the *Curious Brahmanical interpolation that Ráma was required to become a religious devotee.* Brahmanizing of the original tradition, which is deserving of notice, as being connected with the later worship of Ráma as Vishnu. Kaikeyí not only demanded the exile of Ráma, but required that he should be clothed in the skins of deer and bark of trees, and lead the life of a devotee or Vánaprastha. Now the idea that a man should become a devotee as a punishment involves two conflicting elements, which appear to have escaped the attention of the Brahmanical author. That Ráma should be represented as a religious secluse was no doubt highly desirable, both as giving prominence to his divine character, and as reflecting a glory upon those Bráhmans who betook themselves to the same mode of life. But that Kaikeyí should have insisted upon Ráma's becoming a devotee is altogether incomprehensible; and moreover would destroy any religious merit which Ráma might be supposed to acquire by a religious life to which he was forced by the vindictiveness of his step-mother. However, the notion is so perfectly in accordance *Modern belief in the idea.* with the Brahmanical ideal of Hindú life, that it would be blasphemy to doubt it; and to this day every fanatical worshipper of Ráma exults in picturing the divine hero arrayed in garments of bark, and with his hair braided into a knot on the crown of his head, as a holy devotee and incarnation of Vishnu.[7]

---

[7] The Bráhmans taught that every Hindú of the three superior castes,—the Bráhmans, Kshatriyas, and Vaisyas,—should pass through four orders or conditions of life: namely, that of the Brahmachárí, or religious student; the Grihastha, or household and married man; the Vánaprastha, or hermit; and the Bikshuka, or Sanyási, who is a religious mendicant.

The life of a Vánaprastha is well described in the Vishnu Puraná, as follows :—" When the householder, after performing the acts incumbent on his condition, arrives at the decline of life, let him consign his wife to the care of his sons, and go himself to the forests. Let him there subsist upon leaves, roots, and fruit; and suffer his hair and beard to grow, and braid the former upon his brows; and sleep upon the ground: his dress must be made of skin or of kasa or kusa grasses; and he must bathe thrice a day; and he must offer oblations to the gods and to fire, and treat all that come to him with hospitality: he must beg alms, and present food to all creatures: he must anoint himself with such unguents as the woods afford; and in his devotional exercises he must be endurant of heat and cold. The sage who diligently follows these rules, and leads the life' of the hermit (or Vánaprastha), consumes, like fire, all imperfections, and conquers for himself the mansion of eternity."

CHAPTER VIII.

EXILE OF RÁMA.

THE sensational scene within the palace between the Maháraja and·Kaikeyí, on the night before the expected installation, is followed by a series of touching events, which terminate in the exile of Ráma. This portion of the Rámáyana requires no preliminary explanation; and it will be sufficient to divide it into six sections, as follows:—

HISTORY OF INDIA. PART IV.

Series of six touching events connected with the exile of Ráma.

1st, Ráma's visit to the palace on the morning of the installation.

2nd, Ráma's interview with the Maháraja and Kaikeyí.

3rd, Ráma's interview with his mother Kausalyá.

4th, Ráma's interview with his wife Sítá.

5th, Parting scene, in which Ráma, Sítá, and Lakshmana take their farewell of the Maháraja and his wives.

6th, Lamentations on the departure of Ráma.

The narrative of Ráma's visit to the palace on the morning of the installation may be related as follows:—

Now when the morning had dawned, the sage Vasishtha, surrounded by his disciples, speedily carried the sacrificial articles into the excellent city, which was adorned with flowers and banners, and crowded with people. And all was ready for the installation of Ráma. The golden throne had been set up, with the white umbrella which was the special sign of royalty; and there were the jewelled chámaras of white hair for brushing away the flies from the new Raja, and the sacred tiger's skin, and the bow and scimetar, and the sacrificial fire, and the elephants, and the chariots harnessed with four horses; and there also were the golden pots filled with Ganges water, and with water from other holy places, together with the parched grain, the limes, the ghee, the honey, the milk, the curds, the kusa grass, and the flowers. There too were the Bráhmans, and the Rajas that paid tribute, and the eight chosen damsels,[1] and the large white-humped bull begirt with a golden rope, and the shaggy lion, and the cows with golden ornaments on their horns, and very many musicians with all kinds of musical instruments, and beautiful dancing-girls exquisitely adorned, together with multitudes of people of all the four castes. And at the rising of the sun all were in the street leading to the palace, waiting for the coming of the Maháraja and the excellent hero Ráma.

Sumantra sent by Vasishtha to hasten the Maháraja.

Then Vasishtha said to Sumantra, who was the Chief Counsellor of Dasaratha:—"Go you and hasten the Maháraja, that Ráma may receive the Raj as the moon enters the mansion of Pushyá."[2] Sumantra, filled with pleasure, then entered the palace, and he saw that the gate of the inner apartments was surrounded with aged men armed with staves, and clad in mail and wearing turbans; but they gave way as he approached, for the inner rooms were always open to him. And Sumantra, not knowing what had occurred to the Maháraja, approached the curtain at the door of the chamber where Dasaratha had passed the night,

Sumantra enters the inner apartments and approaches the door of the Maháraja's chamber.

---

[1] At the installation of a Raja, at marriages, and at other seasons of festival, a number of young women are employed to rub turmeric on the body of the person or persons, on whose account the ceremony takes places. Eight are required at the installation of a Raja; on other occasions the number is optional. Widows are prohibited from assisting at this ceremony. Carey and Marshman's *note on the passage.*

[2] This command as given by the priest to the Chief Counsellor is probably a Brahmanical flourish introduced to show the authority of the priest in ancient times.

and praised the Mahárája thus :—" As the ocean when il-lumined by the rising sun gives pleasure to the beholders, so a great Raja by his benign presence diffuses happiness around him : As the charioteer of Indra addressed the mighty god before he went forth and conquered all the Daityas, so do I arouse you : As the Vedas and the Vedán-gas stirred up Brahma, so do I stir up you : As the moon awakens the earth, permit me this day to awaken you : The god of day rises propitious from his couch, may he and all the gods command that success attend you : O Mahárája, all is ready for the installation of Ráma : As feeble cattle with-out a keeper, as an army without a commander, as the night without the moon, as a herd of cows without the lordly bull, so is a country in which the Mahárája does not appear." At these words the venerable Dasaratha was speechless with anguish, but the heartless Kaikeyí said :—"Go you, Suman-tra, and bring Ráma hither, for the Mahárája has something particular to communicate to him." Sumantra replied :— " How can I go unless I have the permission of the Mahá-raja ? " Then Dasaratha said in his grief :—" O Sumantra, go and bring Ráma hither, as Kaikeyí has requested you."

Then Sumantra went out of the palace, and he said to all the tributary Rajas who were there assembled :—" I am going at the command of the Mahárája, to bring Ráma with all haste for the installation." And Sumantra went to the palace of Ráma, which was as resplendent as the palace of Indra ; and the palace was adorned with garlands, and sur-rounded with deer and peacocks. And Sumantra put aside the servants who surrounded the doors, and entered the outer apartment which was guarded by young men who were sober and vigilant, adorned with bright earrings, and armed with swords and bows ; and he then went towards the inner apartments which were guarded by ancient men dressed in red with canes in their hands. And Sumantra said to the old men :—" Quickly inform Ráma that Suman-tra stands at the door." Then Ráma, hearing that the chosen Counsellor of his father was come, ordered that he should be conducted into his presence ; and Sumantra be-

Praises the
Mahárája.

Kaikeyí desires
him to bring
Ráma.

The Mahárája
commands him
likewise.

Sumantra pro-
ceeds to the
house of Ráma.

Beautiful house.

Outer apart-
ment guarded
by young men.

Inner apart-
ments guarded
by old men.

Sumantra
enters the
presence of
Ráma and
declares his
mission.

HISTORY OF
INDIA.
PART IV.

Ráma prepares
to go to the
Maháraja.

held Ráma sitting on a golden couch elegantly adorned, perfumed with sandal and many excellent odours, with Sítá standing by his side fanning him with peacock's feathers. Then Sumantra said to Ráma:—"O Ráma, your father Dasaratha and the Rání Kaikeyí desire your presence: Go thither without delay." And Ráma said to his wife Sítá: —"O divine one, the Maháraja and the Rání Kaikeyí have consulted together respecting my installation: This day the Maháraja will assuredly install me as his coadjutor in the Raj: I will go speedily to the Maháraja, and do you remain here and amuse yourself with your maids." The black-eyed Sítá I followed her lord to the door, saying :—

Prayer of Sítá.

"May the Maháraja bestow the Raj upon you, and esteem you worthy to celebrate a Rajasúya: May the gods of all the four quarters of the universe protect you: May Indra, who wields the thunder-bolt, guard you on the east ; may Yama, judge of the dead, guard you on the south ; may Varúna, god of the waters, guard you on the west; and may Kuvera,

Ráma ascends
his chariot.

lord of wealth, guard you upon the north." Ráma then went out with Sumantra, and ascended his bright and spacious chariot, which was lined with tigers' skins, and adorned with gold and gems, and drawn by horses like young elephants ; and Lakshmana, his younger brother, attended him, standing behind him in the chariot with a chámara in

Acclamations of
the multitude.

his hand resembling the moon. When Ráma came forth, the multitude filled the air with a prodigious burst of acclamations, like the shouts of two armies rushing to battle ; and a mighty crowd surrounded his chariot, and thousands of horses and elephants followed him, whilst a company of heroes armed with bows and scimetars marched before him.

Ráma's progress
to the palace of
the Maháraja.

Thus amidst the glad sounds of music, and the praises of the eulogists, the heroic Ráma proceeded to the palace of the Maháraja ; and the verandas and the house-tops were filled with slender-waisted women, beautifully adorned, who saluted him with eager praises, and threw wreaths of flowers upon him as he passed. Presently the royal palace appeared in view like a vast cloud ; and the pleasure-houses around it were as resplendent as the milk-white cars of the gods.

And Ráma descended from his chariot and mounted his horse, and entered the gateway of the palace, and his form was as bright as the kindling flame. And Ráma rode through the three first courts, which were guarded by archers, and then he dismounted and went on foot through the two next courts, and having passed through all five, he ordered his people to halt, and entered into the presence of his father.

The foregoing narrative of Ráma's visit contains a few particulars which are well worthy of notice. The arrangements for the installation are somewhat obscure, inasmuch as the ceremony was not actually performed, but still they are very suggestive. The golden throne, the white umbrella, the jewelled chámara, and the tiger's skin are perfectly intelligible ; the latter probably being laid on the ground before the throne, and being perhaps deemed a sign of royalty. The bow and scimitar were in like manner emblems of sovereignty and objects of worship. The elephants and chariots were probably required for a procession of the new Raja and the attendant Chieftains. The Brahmanical articles, such as pots of sacred water, grain, fruit, ghee, honey, milk, curds, kusa grass, and flowers, were all doubtless employed in symbolical rites similar to those which were practised at the installation of Yudhishthira, and at the actual installation of Ráma, which appears in a subsequent part of the Rámáyana. The part taken by the white humped-back bull, the shaggy lion, and the cows with golden horns, is somewhat obscure ; unless, like the eight chosen virgins who were appointed to rub Ráma with turmeric, they were merely introduced to impart a sensational character to the ceremony.

Review of the foregoing narrative of Ráma's visit to the palace.

Obscure references to the installation ceremonies.

HISTORY OF
INDIA.
PART IV.

Palace ar-
rangements.
Young men
employed to
guard the outer
apartments and
old men to
guard the
zenana.
Hyperbolical
address of
Sumantra to
the Maháraja.

The references to the palace arrangements are very curious. The outer entrance seems to have been the resort of the house servants. The outer apartments in Ráma's palace were guarded by young men with bows and scimitars; whilst the inner apartments, or zenana, were guarded, not by eunuchs, but by old men with staves. Again, Sumantra does not venture to enter the apartment of the Maháraja, but stands without the door and addresses him in that high-flown language of flattery and religious hyperbole which is so generally affected by Bráhmans when approaching a sovereign.

Picture of
Ráma fanned
by Sítá.

The references to Ráma are very striking, and perfectly in accordance with Hindú ideas. The representation of the divine hero sitting upon a couch, whilst his wife Sítá is fanning him with peacock's feathers, is a favourite picture with Hindú bards, who frequently preach the duty of wives to fan their husbands.

Hindú charac-
ter of the pro-
cession.

The procession formed in full expectation that Ráma was to be installed Yuvaraja is of a very Hindú character. The hero and his brother drive along in a chariot lined with a tiger's skin. They are preceded by a body of soldiers, and followed by a number of horses and elephants. As Ráma drives along the eulogists chaunt his praises, the musicians fill the air with triumphant strains, and the women appear in the verandas in their gayest attire and throw down flowers upon his head. The progress to the palace is one of joy and exultation, and as such forms a bright contrast to the dark events which were about to be disclosed to the public view.

2nd. Ráma's
interview with
the Maháraja
and Kaikeyí.

The narrative of Ráma's interview with the

Maháraja and Kaikeyí may now be related as follows :—

While the whole multitude, filled with joy, were waiting
without the palace, Ráma beheld his wretched father sitting
with Kaikeyí on an elegant couch, his countenance withered
up with sorrow. Then Ráma humbly bowed at the feet of
his father, and at the feet of Kaikeyí ; and the eyes of the
Maháraja were overflowing with tears, and he could only
exclaim :—" O Ráma ! " Ráma, seeing his father's countenance filled with tears, was seized with fear as though his
feet had touched a serpent ; for Dasaratha was convulsed
with grief, like the waves of the sea during a storm, or like
the sun during an eclipse, or like a sage who has told a
falsehood. And Ráma bowed to Kaikeyí, and said :—" O
mother, tell me how I have offended the Maháraja ! " Then
Kaikeyí, void of shame, and relentless as a tigress, replied :—" The Maháraja is not angry. O Ráma, nor is he
in distress ; but he has something on his mind which he
forbears to mention through fear of you, but it is necessary
that you should know it : The Maháraja has made me two
solemn promises, and confirmed them by oath, but he now
repents, like one of low caste : In former times, when I
preserved his life in the war between the gods and demons,
he offered me two boons, and swore to perform them ; and I
have now requested that my son Bharata may be installed
as coadjutor with the Maháraja, and that you may be sent
into exile in the wilderness of Dandaka for fourteen years :
If, therefore, you desire that your father should act according to his oath, you will go out of the city this day,. and
return not for fourteen years, and you will permit Bharata
to govern the Raj."

At this merciless speech, the Maháraja was pierced with
grief, but the words of Kaikeyí had no effect upon Ráma ;
they fell upon his mind like sparks of fire upon the ocean
waves, and he felt no kind of sorrow, but replied :—" Be it
so ! I will depart into the forest that the Maháraja may
fulfil the promise which he has made : But wherefore is he

*Scenes within
the palace.*

*Humiliation
and sorrow of
thé Maháraja on
seeing Ráma.*

*Kaikeyí informs
Ráma of the
promise made
by the Mahá-
raja, and of her
own two re-
quests in
return.*

*Ráma's promise
and cheerfully,
acquiescence.*

distressed? Whatever my father, or my preceptor, or the
Maháraja may command, that I will cheerfully perform:
Let messengers on swift horses be despatched to bring
Bharata from the city of Girivraja, and I will hasten to the
forest of Dandaka, and abide there fourteen years." And

Kaikeyí said :—" So let it be : Let not your father's shame
affect you, but depart immediately, for until you are gone
out of the city your father will neither bathe nor eat."
Thus urged on by Kaikeyí, as a horse is urged on by a whip,
Ráma replied to her thus :—" I obey the will of the Mahá-

raja, for there is no act of virtue greater than that of obeying the command of a father and fulfilling his engagements :
Bear with me whilst I take leave of my mother Kausalyá,
and console my wife Sítá, and then I will this day depart to

the wilderness of Dandaka." With these words Ráma
bowed at the feet of his father, who was lying senseless from
grief, and he prostrated himself at the feet of Kaikeyí, and
went out from the inner apartments, followed by Lakshmana and all his friends. All excepting Ráma were bathed
in tears, but not even the loss of the Raj, or the prospect
of weary exile, could affect the dignity of Ráma, any more
than the taking out of a pot of water can lessen the ocean,
or pouring in a pot can increase it. Withdrawing his eyes
from all the preparations for his installation and the insignia
of royalty, he manifested neither the slightest change of
countenance nor sign of sorrow.

The only point worthy of special notice in the
foregoing narrative is the stress laid upon the stoicism

of Ráma, or rather upon the perfect control which
he maintained over his passions, at the very moment
when the cup of happiness was dashed from his lips,

and he was condemned to hopeless exile. The extent to which this virtue is carried by the Hindús is
perfectly marvellous. The news of sudden and dire
calamity will be received with a composure and
dignity, which no one but an Asiatic could display;

and which arises partly from a belief in the inevit- able and irresistible decrees of fate, and partly from a careful training in the habit of self-command.

The next scene, namely, Ráma's interview with his mother, is even more touching, and may be related as follows :—

When Ráma left the presence of the Maháraja and Kai- keyí, he proceeded towards the apartments of his mother Kausalyá. And as he passed the first apartment, the ancient men standing at the door cried out :—" May he conquer gloriously." And as he passed the second apartment, he saw the Bráhmans, deeply versed in the Vedas, and he bowed to them. Then as he went to the third apartment he saw the maid-servants, and children, and matrons, and those expert at keeping the door ; and the women, full of joy, rushed off to carry to Kausalyá the news of her son's approach. Now all that night the Rání Kausalyá had been en- gaged in religious mortification, and in the morning she was paying divine honours to Vishnu. Desirous of propitiating the bright god in favour of her son Ráma, she had clothed herself in silk, and performed all the ceremonies of thanksgiving and joy, and offered up the burnt-offerings, after they had been duly consecrated by mantras from the sacred Vedas. When Ráma entered the elegant apartment of his mother, he beheld her fanning the fire of the sacrifice, and he saw all that she had prepared for the service of the gods ; the curds, the rice, the ghee, the sweetmeats, the parched grain, the white garlands, the boiled thick milk, the sacrificial wood, and the jars of holy water. The pious Kausalyá had rolled up her silk garment like a rope, and thrown it over her left shoulder, and drawn it loosely under her right arm ; and she was weary with religious observances and internal abstraction of mind, but still eager to propitiate the gods. Seeing her son Ráma, she arose full of pleasure, and as he bowed to her feet she embraced him, and kissed him, and said :— " May you attain the age, the renown, and the virtue of the royal sages of old, and the merit worthy of your race : O

Ráma informs
his mother of
his coming
exile.

Ráma, your father the Maháraja, faithful to his word, will this day install you into the office of coadjutor in the Raj."

Then Ráma, with joined hands, bowed to his mother, and said:—" O mother, are you unacquainted with this heavy calamity now impending, which threatens sorrow to Sítá and Lakshmana ? It is Bharata whom the Maháraja will install as his coadjutor, and as for me, I am to go into exile for fourteen years, and dwell in the wilderness of Dandaka, and perform all the duties of a Vánaprastha, and live on fruits and roots."

Terrible grief of
Kausalyá.

When the Rání heard these terrible words she fell down to the earth, like the bough of a saul tree lopped by the axe of the forester, or like a god who had fallen from heaven ; and Ráma raised her up, and gently stroked her with his hand. At length, in an agony of grief, she spoke as follows :

Her bitter
lamentations.

—" O my son ! O Ráma ! If you had never been born I should have been saved this bitter sorrow : A barren woman has only the grief of being childless, and knows not what it is to lose a son : O Ráma, I am the chief Rání, yet whilst you are here I have been supplanted, and now what shall I have to suffer when you are gone ? My death must be the consequence : Disliked and neglected by my husband, I am already contemned by the servants of Kaikeyí; and now those who serve me will see the son of Kaikeyí installed in the Raj, and will not vouchsafe me a word : O my son, how shall I, thus deeply afflicted, be able to behold the face of the wrathful Kaikeyí ? Seventeen years, O Ráma, have I passed since your birth, hoping that my sorrows would one day end : O Ráma, I am worn with age, and I cannot sustain the loss of you, nor the persecution of my rivals : You, too, doomed to hunger and fatigue, are now sunk in misery with wretched me : Surely my heart is as hard as a rock, since it has not burst ere now like the banks of a river in the rainy season : There must be no room in the mansions of Yama, or death would have seized upon me this day, like a lion springing upon a trembling doe : What is life to me ? The sacrifice performed for obtaining a son has been to me like seed sown upon a barren land : If you go into the wilderness

I will follow you, like a feeble cow following her calf : But, O Ráma, it is not pleasing to me that you should forego the Raj and go into the jungle : The Mahárája is subject to the words of a woman, and has become the slave of Kaikeyí : You, O Ráma, have committed no fault that you should be driven into exile ; and what son who remembers the duties of a ruler, would regard a sovereign who has sunk into his second childhood ? O Ráma, before this matter is noised abroad, do you assume the management of affairs ! Who will oppose you ? If, urged by Kaikeyí, your father should appear hostile, do you slay him without remorse ; enslaved by Kaikeyí he has sunk into childhood, and rendered his old age contemptible in the eyes of men."

Lakshmana then said :—" O mother, your words are perfectly just : You have spoken what is in my mind : I long to see Ráma upon the throne, and should any one come to oppose him, I swear by you and my weapons that he should soon behold the mansions of Yama : So long as I, who am the servant of Ráma, am here, who will dare to give the Raj to any one else ? "

When Kausalyá heard these words, she rejoiced greatly, and thus addressed Ráma :—" O son, you have heard the words of your brother : If you approve, do that which lies before you : It does not become you to depart hence at the unjust words of my rival, and to leave me a prey to grief : If you desire to act rightly hearken unto me ! If the Mahárája is entitled to your respect and obedience, I am, according to the Sastras, entitled to even more ; and I command you not to retire to the forest : If you leave me I will refuse all food, and you will sink into hell."

Ráma then spoke thus to his mother :—" I cannot transgress my father's commands ; and therefore I entreat your permission to depart to the forest : No one is degraded by obedience to the command of a father." Ráma then said to Lakshmana :—" O my brother, the distress of my mother is immeasurable, but truth is founded on virtue, and virtue consists in obedience to a father : Having engaged to obey my father, I cannot render my promise void."

Refuses to per-
mit Kausalyá to
accompany him.

Refuses to
blame his
enemies.

The wretched Kausalyá still implored her son to remain,
or else permit her to accompany him; but Ráma would not,
and said to her:—"The authority of the Maháraja is
superior to all other considerations: He is your husband,
and he is to you as a deity; and how can you condemn yourself to become a widow whilst your husband is still alive?"
He then took his leave, saying:—"Bharata incurs no blame
by accepting the Raj, nor Kaikeyí by accepting the favour
from the Maháraja, nor Dasaratha by giving the Raj to
Bharata rather than break his word." But the words of
Ráma could not remove the heavy grief of Kausalyá; for
she loved her son very much, and she feared that when he
was gone her wicked rival Kaikeyí would heap insults upon
her; and her heart was much oppressed, and she could only
pray for the welfare of Ráma, and engage in religious rites
in the hope of propitiating the gods.

Review of the
foregoing nar-
rative.

Perfect picture
of a Hindú
mother propiti-
ating the gods
in behalf of her
son.

Desperate cha-
racter of Kau-
salyá's proposi-
tions to Ráma.

The foregoing narrative furnishes a perfect picture of a Hindú mother whose whole soul is bound
up in the well-being of her son. Her prayers and
sacrifices to the gods in behalf of Ráma, are precisely
such as Hindú matrons in the present day would
offer up on similar occasions But with her the bitter
disappointment was overwhelming, and she was
wholly unable to exercise that self-control which had
been so nobly displayed by Ráma. In the agony
of her sorrow she suggested disobedience, rebellion,
and parricide; to which, however, Ráma turned a
deaf ear; although the bare fact of her making such
propositions would seem to indicate that such revolu-
tions were by no means uncommon in the courts of
Hindú Rajas. Next Kausalyá prayed that she
might be permitted to accompany Ráma into the
jungle, and thus escape from the contempt of the
palace slave girls, and the exultant face of her detested rival. But Ráma still refused, failing not to

remind her in Brahmanical language of the duty which she owed to her husband, who was to her as a deity. Lastly, in a noble spirit of filial obedience, he absolved his brother, his step-mother, and his father from all blame in the cruel measure which deprived him of a throne and condemned him to a lengthened period of exile.

The next scene, comprising Ráma's interview with his young wife, forms another of those beautiful pictures of a wife's love and devotion, which are so frequent in Hindú poetry. The story is as follows :—

When Ráma had taken leave of his mother, he departed out of the palace, aud proceeded to his own house. Meanwhile, the beautiful Sítá, not knowing what had occurred, and rejoicing in her husband's coming installation, was standing in her own apartment with eyes fixed upon the door, anxious for the return of her lord. When Ráma, with saddened countenance and drooping head, beheld his beautiful wife, dearer than life, modest and adorned with humility, he could no longer restrain his sorrow. Seeing that Ráma was sorrowful, Sítá was anxious, and asked him the reason of his melancholy in these words :—" Why is it, O Ráma, that you are not as yet installed, or is it that the moon has not yet entered the mansion of Pushyá ? Why have you not the royal umbrella over your head, and why are you not fanned by the chámara ? Why do not the bards repeat your praises, and why are you not attended by your servants, and priests, and counsellors ? Why do I not see any signs of your installation ? Let me know all and be relieved from my suspense ! "

At these words of Sítá, Ráma told her of the two promises which Dasaratha had made to Kaikeyí, and how Bharata was to be installed in his room, and he himself was doomed to fourteen years' exile in the jungle. And Ráma said :—" The Maháraja has appointed Bharata to be his perpetual coadjutor in the Raj ; and he is therefore to be honoured by

Desires her to
remain and
devote her life
to religion and
the service of
her mothers.

you : By the command of my venerable father I go this day
into the forest ; it will become you therefore to devote yourself to vows, and fastings, and acts of devotion : My aged
mother, wasted with grief, demands your respectful attention ; my other mothers must also be duly honoured by you
according to their rank ; and my two brothers, Bharata and
Satrughna, should be constantly regarded by you as your
own brothers or sons : O beloved one, I must depart to the
great forest, and do you remain here obedient to the commands of Raja Bharata, and never praise me in the presence
of Bharata, for a Raja cannot endure to hear the praises of
any one beside himself."

Sitá replies that
she must ac-
company him,
and longs to
roam with him
in the forest.

Sítá, angry but yet humble, replied as follows :—" O
Ráma, what words are these ? A wife must share the for-
tunes of her husband ; and if you this day depart to the
forest, I must precede you and smooth the thorns : Wherever
the husband may be, the wife must dwell in the shadow of
his foot : I shall live in the jungle with as much ease as in
my father's house, and shall enjoy happiness with you in the
honey-scented wood : I have no fear, and I long to roam in
the forest with you, and view the lakes and rivers, and the
flowers and water-birds : I will be no burden to you, but if
you leave me I will die."

Ráma recounts
the perils and
sufferings of
jungle life.

Hot sun.

No servants.

Stones and
briars.

Serpents, croco-
diles, and
sharks.

Wild beasts.

Then Ráma, wishing to turn the mind of his wife from
going with him into the forest, spoke to her as follows :—
" O Sítá, the forest is not always pleasant, but I know that
it is always dangerous : You are very delicate, and the beloved daughter of a Raja : You have never been in the sun
out of your own room ; how then can you brave the dangers
of the wilderness ? You are surrounded and attended every
day by your maids ; how then can you go out into the jungle
without a servant near you ? Your feet are as delicate as
the petals of the lily, and the pebbles and the briars will
afflict you grievously : You are like butter which will be
melted away by the sun at noonday : You will have to cross
many rivers, in which there are serpents, and crocodiles,
and sharks : The roaring of the lions and the thundering of
the cataracts are terrible to hear : The roads are infested

with wild elephants and filled with thorns; and the jungle is HISTORY OF INDIA. PART IV.
covered with rank weeds in which venomous snakes lie con-
cealed, so deadly that their breath alone will kill a man: Bad food.
Sometimes you will have to subsist upon grass seed; sometimes upon bitter roots and fruits; and sometimes you will
not find even these things, and will have to fast many days:
At times you will be athirst, and there will be no water:
For garments, you will have to wear the bark of trees, or Coarse garments.
the skin of the antelope; and at night you will have to sleep
upon grass, or upon the bare earth: Reptiles, mosquitoes, Mosquitoes and scorpions.
flies, scorpions, and fierce birds, will bite and sting you, and
afflict you in your sleep: Fearful Rákshasas infest the wil- Rákshasas.
derness, and will eat up a whole man at a single meal: Your
beautiful locks of hair will become a tangled mass, and will
lose their colour from want of oil: Besides all this suffering Solitude.
you will be without friends; and how can this be endured by
a woman? It is my knowledge of all that you will have to
suffer that prevents my taking you with me: Exposure to Exposure.
the heat, cold, and wind renders the frame lean and emaciated: What enjoyment then can you experience in the
forest, whilst I shall be filled with distress at the sight of
your afflictions? You are dearer to me than my own life,
and I cannot consent to your suffering pain on my account;
so take my advice and remain at my house: Though I may Ráma desires Sitá to remain, and urges that separation will increase their affection.
be travelling in distant parts, yet still you shall always be
present in my thoughts; and though separated in our eyes
we shall never be separated in our hearts: Moreover, separation often increases affection, and he alone can perfectly enjoy the felicity of connubial love, who knows what it is to
have been separated from his wife: So bear all these things
in your mind, and relinquish your plan of accompanying me,
and do you determine to remain here."

Hearing the words of Ráma, Sitá was greatly distressed, Sitá replies that in his society all evil will become good.
and her eyes were filled with tears, and she replied in a low
tone thus :—" O Ráma, I am fully aware of all the evil
things that have been described by you, but in your presence all that is evil will be turned into good: The fierce
animals of the jungle, the elephants, the lions, the tigers,

_____

and all the beasts of prey will fly away when they behold you: The grass and the seeds, the roots and the fruits, will in your presence be more delightful than amrita; and if I should fail to procure these things for food, I can never be deprived of the amrita of your words: As for garments of bark and antelope's skin, I am not sorry to wear them, for the goddess Párvatí wore them for the sake of her husband Siva: Sleeping with you upon a bed of grass will give me more delight than sleeping by myself upon a bed of the

Implores Ráma to permit her to accompany him.

softest down: Without you my life is not worth preserving, but with you not even Indra could terrify me: O my lord, by following my husband through affection, I shall be faultless, for the husband is the chief deity of the wife: It is written in the Vedas that the woman who always attends upon her husband, and follows him like a shadow in this life, will in like manner follow him in the world of spirits: It becomes you, therefore, O Ráma, to take me with you that I may share in your pleasures and in your pains, for the desert with all its evils are far better in my sight than all the pleasures of this palace without you."

Ráma still unwilling.

But notwithstanding all the entreaties of Sítá, Ráma was unwilling that she should go into the wilderness; and, beholding her weeping, he bowed down his head, and fell into

Wrath of Sítá.

a deep meditation. And Sítá saw that he was sad, and that he was not inclined that she should go with him; and her face reddened with anger, and the tears fell from her eyes

Taunts Ráma.

like honey from the red lotos, and she said:—" Shame on my father who gave me to a husband who has no spirit within him! Those who say that Ráma is brave, courageous, and strong, speak falsely: He has no power to protect his wife; and surely the Maháraja has acted wisely in not giving him the Raj: Having once married me he now wishes to give me away; and to whom am I to go, and where am I to remain

Checks herself and weeps bitterly.

for fourteen years?" Then she suddenly checked herself, and repented the harshness of her words, and said:—" I have never given you any cause for offence, but if I have done anything wrong I pray you to forgive me: I can bear anything but separation from you: I entreat you to take me

with you : Do not disappoint me, O Rama ! " So saying,
she fell at the feet of her husband, and wept very bitterly.

At these words, Ráma could no longer shut his ears to *Ráma yields to his wife's entreaties.*
the prayer of Sítá. He took her by the hand, and wiped
away her tears, and spoke to her in a mild voice thus :—
" Why, my beloved, do you blame me without understanding me ? My heart's desire is always to remain with you,
and I would not care to attain the exalted position of Brahma
should I be without you : But when I thought over the
perils of the wilderness, and the delicacy of your frame, I
desired for your own sake to prevent you from accompanying
me : Now I am satisfied that you are determined at heart to
go with me, and therefore it is not proper for me to leave
you behind : Go you, therefore, and take leave of all your superiors, and of your mothers-in-law, and throw off all your
ornaments, and present them to the Bráhmans, and to those
who may be in need."

Then Sítá was filled with joy, and did as she was com- *Sítá's joy.*
manded by Ráma. And Lakshmana approached his brother *Lakshmana permitted to accompany Ráma.*
and entreated that he might be permitted to accompany
them into the wilderness, and Ráma gave him leave. Then
Ráma and Sítá gave all their jewels and goods to the Bráh- *Ráma and Sítá give all their jewels and goods to the Bráhmans and the needy.*
mans of their household, and to other Bráhmans, and to
their own servants, and to all the needy who came from afar
to receive presents from Ráma ; and then they took off their
shoes, after the manner of devotees, and went with bare feet
to the palace of the Mahárája to take their leave of Dasaratha.

The foregoing dialogue is almost too beautiful for *Remarks on Sítá's love for Ráma.*
criticism. The delicate girl-wife not only compels
her reluctant husband to take her with him into the
jungle, but even pictures the delights of jungle-life ;
although, to one bred in the luxuries and seclusion of
a zenana, such a life must have presented a thousand
terrors.

Next follows the last scene, the farewell visit of *5th, Farewell visit of Ráma, Sítá, and Lakshmana to the Mahárája.*
Ráma, Sítá, and Lakshmana to take leave of the

Maháraja. According to European ideas, such a visit could scarcely have been expected under the circumstances; and yet it is strictly in accordance with Hindú ideas of the respect due to a parent and a superior, even in such a time of trial. The story proceeds as follows :—

Profound sorrow of the people of Ayodhyá at the exile of Ráma.

Meantime the rumour spread throughout the city of Ayodhyá, that Ráma, and his wife Sítá, and his brother Lakshmana were to be sent out as exiles into the wilderness of Dandaka ; and all the people were thunderstruck at the tidings, for they had been expecting to see the installation of Ráma ; and all of them were grieved to the heart, and became so senseless, that though they had eyes they could not see, and though they had ears they could not hear. And all the inhabitants of the city crowded around the gate-way of the palace ; and even the women came out from their inner apartments, and sacrificed their shame and modesty, and stood round the palace gate-way. Presently the two Princes, and the wife of Ráma, were seen walking with bare feet towards the palace of the Maháraja ; Ráma walking first, and Sítá close behind him, while Lakshmana brought up the rear. At this sight the whole multitude were filled with grief, and bitterly reproached the Maháraja. Some said that he was án old hollow tree, which had generated the fire which was destroying a blooming garden. Others cried out that he was possessed by demons, saying : —" Unless the Maháraja were possessed by demons he could not have sent his son into exile ; since no father is capable of sending away his son, even if that son were full of faults, whilst Ráma is full of every kind of virtue." Some of the people thought of accompanying Ráma into the jungle, taking with them their wives and families, and leaving Dasaratha, and his wife Kaikeyí, and his son Bharata to rule the desert city of Ayodhyá. Others said :—" Why do you blame the Maháraja, when it is Kaikeyí who is the root of all this evil ? She persuaded the Maháraja by sweet and coaxing words to send Ráma away, and to give the Raj

Ráma, Sítá and Lakshmana walk barefooted to the palace.

The people reproach the Maháraja.

Contemplate accompanying Ráma into the jungle.

Reproach Kaikeyí.

to Bharata : Perchance Bharata is in the plot, and therefore HISTORY OF INDIA. PART IV. remains in the city of his mother's father out of shame : If he felt so strong a desire to rule the Raj, he should have asked Ráma for it; and then he would have obtained the Raj without any misfortune befalling Ráma."

Whilst the people were thus lamenting, Ráma approached the apartments of the Maháraja, and heard the lamentations of his father, and the imprecations which he continued to pour upon the wicked Kaikeyí. At length the chosen Counsellor Sumantra made known to Dasaratha that his son Ráma stood at the door; and the Maháraja ordered that all his women should be summoned to that apartment, and that Ráma should then enter the room, for he cared not to be alone when he took leave of his son. Then all the women advanced with a slow pace into that room, and their eyes were red with weeping, and Kausalyá was in the midst of them. Then Ráma, and Sítá, and Lakshmana were conducted into the presence of the Maháraja; and the Maháraja, surrounded by his wives, arose from his seat, and then fell upon the ground in a swoon; and Ráma and Lakshmana ran towards him and embraced him with their arms, and placed him on the royal couch; whilst the cries of that multitude of women filled the palace, and mingled with the clanging of their ornaments. Then Ráma, with joined hands, said to his father : —"I entreat you, O Maháraja, to look with a propitious eye upon me who am ready to depart to the wilderness of Dandaka : Permit also Lakshmana and Sítá to accompany me to the forest : O fountain of honour, command us even as Brahma commands his children."

The Maháraja then gazed steadfastly upon Ráma, and said :—" O Ráma, I have been infatuated with Kaikeyí through the promises I have given to her : O Ráma, set aside my commandment, and become this day the Raja of Ayodhyá ! " Ráma replied, with joined hands :—" My lord the Maháraja has yet a thousand years to live upon the earth, and I will abide in the forest without desiring the Raj : When fourteen years have passed away I shall have

Scene in the palace. The Maháraja summons all his women to be present at his parting with Ráma.

Swooning of the Maháraja on beholding Ráma, Sítá. and Lakshmana.

The Maháraja desires Ráma to seize the Raj.

Ráma refuses.

HISTORY OF
INDIA.
PART IV.

The Mahárája
implores Ráma
to stay one day
longer.

Ráma urges
that he must
not delay.

Seeks to console
the Mahárája.

Intense grief of
all present ex-
cepting Kaikeyí.

Sumantra heaps
terrible re-
proaches upon
Kaikeyí.

completed my vow and will again embrace your feet : Who in this earth will hereafter obey the commands of his father if I now violate them ? " Then the distressed Mahárája said to his affectionate son :—" O beloved one, go without haste in a safe and good road, but go not away to-day : The evening is approaching, and refreshed by the sight of you, let me enjoy one good day more : Spend this night with your mother and me, and to-morrow do as it pleases you : O Ráma, I have been deceived by a woman, who has covered her evil designs, like a fire that is covered by ashes."

Ráma replied :—" To depart hence is my only desire : Let the Raj, with its people and wealth, and waving fields of corn, be given to Bharata ; for my resolution to embrace a forest-life cannot be shaken : O Mahárája, let the promise given by you to Kaikeyí be fulfilled to the very uttermost ! Observing your commandment exactly as it was delivered, I will reside in the forest for fourteen years ; and I swear, O Mahárája, that my only desire is that your word should be fulfilled, and your character be cleared from every stain of falsity : O my lord and father, I cannot stay longer, and I pray you to restrain your grief ; it is no affliction for me to depart : Kaikeyí said to me :—" Ráma, go to the forest ! " I replied :—" I will go ! " I will therefore keep my word : O venerable father, be not distressed ! We shall enjoy ourselves in the quiet forest, filled with gentle deer, and vocal with the song of birds ; and when the fourteen years are expired you shall behold us again, and your promise will have been fulfilled."

At these words all the wives of the Mahárája wept bitterly, excepting only the remorseless Kaikeyí ; and the Chief Counsellor Sumantra wept in like manner. And the Mahárája was overcome with anger, and he moved about his head, and sighed heavily ; and he began to wring his hands, and to grind his teeth, and his colour changed, and his eyes reddened with rage, and he fell anew into the depths of anguish. Then Sumantra, seeing the deep sorrow of the Mahárája, tried to pierce the soul of Kaikeyí with sharp words as terrible as thunderbolts, saying :—"You, who have abandoned Dasaratha, are the murderess of your husband and family; by your vile deeds you have afflicted him who is invincible as Indra, as immovable as a mountain, and as impassable as the sea : The will of the husband ought to prevail over the wife, far above the gratification of her children : Men succeed to a Raj according to their seniority, and is it your wish to annul this law ? But let your son Bharata become the Raja, and let him govern the Raj : Where Ráma goes we will go : No Bráhman will remain in your dominions : We, the inhabitants of the city of Ayodhyá, and all the people of the country of Kosala, will certainly go into the jungle with Ráma : What pleasure then will you have in obtaining a Raj which has been abandoned by all your friends, by all the Bráhmans, and by every good and loyal subject ? Your deeds are so heinous that I wonder the earth does not open at the sight of your abominable conduct : Who but you would fell a mango tree with an axe, and plant a tree of harsh and worthless berries in its room ? O Rání, obey the will of your husband, and be not obstinate in transgression, for a husband is like the sovereign of the gods : Let the lotos-eyed Ráma, the virtuous, the first-born, the generous, the energetic, the mighty, be installed in the Raj; for bear in mind, O Rání, that if Ráma leaves his father and goes into the forest, your infamy will fill the whole world."

Threatens to accompany Ráma with all the people of Kosala, and leave the Raj uninhabited.

Implores Kaikeyí to retract her determination.

At these words of Sumantra the Rání Kaikeyí was neither moved nor distressed, nor was her countenance changed. So the Maháraja said to Sumantra :—" Speedily order the army, composed of four bands, and laden with wealth, to accompany Ráma; let beautiful dancing-girls, and musicians, and rich merchants adorn the train of my son; let the warlike engines follow Ráma, and the citizens also, and all kinds of carriages, with huntsmen and all who are skilled in the chase : Whilst hunting the antelopes, and the elephants, and drinking the wild honey, and beholding the flowing rivers, he will speedily forget the Raj : Let all my storehouses of grain and treasure accompany Ráma, so that he

Kaikeyí unmoved.

The Maháraja orders the army and treasures to accompany Ráma.

may dwell happily in the wilderness; and Bharata shall govern Ayodhyá until the prosperous Ráma shall have accomplished all he desires."

Kaikeyí declares
that Bharata
will not accept
an empty Raj.

At these words of the Maháraja, the Rání Kaikeyí was greatly troubled and sore afraid; and she said to Dasaratha: —" My son Bharata will not accept of a Raj which has been stripped of its wealth, and become like wine which has lost its strength." Dasaratha replied: — " O you vile one, having loaded me with a grievous burden, will you afflict me whilst I am bearing it? What has become of your former pretended love for Ráma?" Kaikeyí said :—" It is meet that he should go into the forest, even as one of your own ancestors sent out his eldest son Asamanja." [3] Dasaratha replied :—" Asamanja was a wicked prince; he caught the children of the people in the streets, and threw them into the river Sarayú; but what has Ráma done that he should be sent into exile? O Rání, to abandon a virtuous son would destroy the splendour of Indra; and I, with all the rest, will turn my back upon the Raj, and pleasure, and wealth, and will follow Ráma this day; and leave you with your son Bharata to enjoy the pleasures of the Raj."

Urges that
Ráma should
go into exile as
Asamanja had
done.

Tradition of
Asamanja.

Ráma refuses to
accept the army.

Then the humble Ráma supplicated Maháraja Dasaratha in these words :—" O Raja of Rajas, what occasion have I for soldiers or for followers, who have abandoned all society and enjoyment to live on the wild productions of the forest? Who, having given away an excellent elephant, is desirous of possessing the grass rope which binds it round? O lord of the world, what occasion have I for troops? Bring hither, I pray you, the raiment of bark, the spade wherewith I may dig for the roots, and the basket covered with leather in which I may carry them; these are for me who am to reside fourteen years in the jungle." Then Kaikeyí, devoid of shame, brought herself the dresses of bark, and said before all the people :—" Put them on ! " And the mighty Ráma received the bark dress from Kaikeyí, and threw off his garment of fine linen, and all his ornaments, even the mar-

Calls for gar-
ments of bark,
and a spade and
basket.

Kaikeyí brings
the bark cloth-
ing.

Ráma puts it
on.

---

[3] This reference to the cruelty of Asamanja is remarkable from its being one of the very few traditions which appear to refer to the ancient Rajas of Ayodhyá.

riage ring given to him by the father of his wife Sítá, and
he put on the habit of a sage. Lakshmana also in like
manner put off his elegant and ornamented dress, and put
on the habit of a devotee in the presence of his father.
Sítá, accustomed only to a silken dress, started at the sight
of the bark raiment, like a deer at the sight of a snare; and
filled with shame, and deeply distressed, she received the
habit from the cruel Kaikeyí. Then with tearful countenance she said to Lakshmana:—"What am I to do with
these garments of bark? I have never worn such clothes,
and I do not know how to use them." At these pitiful
words of Sítá all the women began to cry, and Maháraja
Dasaratha reproached Kaikeyí, saying:—"O shameless
Kaikeyí, you are determined to ruin me; but answer me
one thing: You asked me only for the exile of Ráma; why
then do you give the bark raiment to Lakshmana and Sítá?
Ráma is bound for my sake to wear the garments of a
devotee according to your request; but Sítá and Lakshmana
accompany Ráma of their own accord, and are not bound to
obey your commands." [4]

The sage Vasishtha then said to Kaikeyí:—"O worthless woman, you are the disgrace of your own family, and
you have imposed upon the Maháraja without the shadow
of an excuse: It is improper for Sítá to go into the forest,
and she ought to abide here in the house of Ráma: If Sítá
goes into the wilderness we will attend her, and all the city
will attend her likewise: Even Bharata and Satrughna will
go when Ráma goes, and attend upon their elder brother:
Govern alone then the country when it shall be empty and
destitute of men: You wicked woman, there will be no city
here unless Ráma resides in it, and the wilderness which he
may inhabit will instantly become a great country: You,
rapacious for your own son, have plunged him into misery,
for there is no one in all the Raj who will not follow Ráma:
O Kaikeyí, to-day you will see the beasts, and the serpents,
and the deer, and the birds accompanying Ráma; and even
the trees will turn their faces towards him: Present, then,

HISTORY OF
INDIA.
PART IV.

Lakshmana
adopts the bark
clothing.
Sítá weeps over
it.

The Maháraja
declares that
Ráma alone is
bound to wear
the bark gar-
ments.

Vasishtha re-
proaches
Kaikeyí.

---

[4] The garments here said to have been made of the bark of trees, in all probability, were made of a thick coarse cotton expressly for jungle wear.

O Rání, excellent ornaments to your daughter-in-law, and take away the dress of bark, for she shall not wear it : The exile of Ráma was alone requested by you." [5]

At these words of Vasishtha, the Mahárája ordered his storekeepers and treasurers to present Sítá with clothes and ornaments sufficient to last her for fourteen years; and the men did as they were commanded, and Sítá threw aside the garments of bark, and arrayed herself in excellent attire as before. The Mahárája then said :—" Bring the chariot and take Ráma in it; that he may appear to be going on a pleasure excursion rather than into exile."

Ráma, Sítá, and
Lakshmana
take leave of
Kausalyá.
Her speech to
Ráma.

Then Ráma and Sítá and Lakshmana turned to Kausalyá to take their leave of her; and Kausalyá said to Ráma :— " Sítá is unprotected, and Lakshmana is a mere boy : Do you take care of them in the wilderness, and above all take care of yourself, and never forget me, who am your unfortunate mother." Here she was choked with grief, and could speak no more; and Ráma said to her :— " Lakshmana is my right hand, and Sítá is my shadow; so you need have no fears on their account; For myself fear nothing, but engage yourself wholly in consoling my father Dasaratha : By your favour I hope to be successful at last, and to absolve my father from his promise, and return again to the Raj." Kausalyá then said to Lakshmana :— " I rejoice to see your attachment to Ráma; you should mutually protect each other, and Sítá should be the object of your common care : Consider Ráma as your father, and Sítá as your mother, and serve them as you have served us." Kausalyá then embraced Sítá, and kissed her, and said :— " The nature of women who have been constantly honoured by their beloved husbands, is to neglect their lords in time of trouble; but in the heart of a virtuous woman her husband is esteemed sacred, and regarded as the pure foun-

---

[5] The whole of this episode in which Vasishtha reproaches Kaikeyí is evidently an interpolation in the original tradition. The ideas expressed are almost precisely the same as those which had been previously expressed by Sumantra. In the original story the gift of the dresses to Sítá probably followed immediately after the declaration of the Mahárája that Sítá was not required to wear the garments of bark.

tain of happiness: Thus, though my son Ráma is exiled to the jungle, he is not contemptible in your sight, but is regarded as your deity, in poverty the same as in wealth."

Then Sítá, with joined hands, replied thus to the mother of her husband:—"O excellent one, I will do all you have commanded; for I am acquainted with the duty of a woman towards her lord, and could no more depart from virtue than light could depart from the moon: The lute yields no music if it be divested of its strings; the chariot moves not without wheels; and a woman bereft of her husband has no pleasure though she have a hundred children: Scanty is the joy derived from a father, a brother, or a son; but who does not honour a husband, as the source of happiness without bounds: To the wife a husband is even as a god." After this, Ráma took leave of the other wives of his father, and he said to them:—"Whatever I have done amiss through ignorance while living with you, I entreat you now to forgive." When the ladies heard these pious and humble words, their hearts were penetrated with grief, and they filled the palace with their lamentation and wailing.

The parting was now over, and the unfortunate trio were to be conveyed to the frontier in the chariot of the Maháraja. But the story may be related at once as it is told in the Rámáyana:—

After this Sumantra said to Ráma:—"O Prince, ascend the chariot, and I will drive you whithersoever you desire to go." Then the weapons were placed in the chariot, and all the clothes and jewels which the Maháraja had given to Sítá, together with a strong basket covered with leather, and a spade; and Sítá ascended the chariot, and Ráma and Lakshmana did likewise, and Sumantra mounted the driving seat, and drove the willing steeds with the swiftness of the wind. Then the whole city of Ayodhyá was filled with tumult, and resounded with the noise of intoxicated elephants, the neighing of horses, and the clanging of ornaments; and all the people were in deep affliction, and ran after the chariot like persons running to plunge into water;

HISTORY OF
INDIA.
PART IV.

The charioteer
called upon to
stop.
Grief of the
people.

and they cried out to Sumantra :—" Pull in the horses that
we may behold the face of Ráma ! " The distressed Maháraja in like manner rushed out of the palace crying :—" I
will see my beloved son." And there was a great noise of
weeping women like that of a female elephant-when her mate
is bound by the hunter. But Ráma commanded Sumantra
to drive on, and the dust raised by. the chariot-wheels was
laid by the falling tears of the citizens. The whole city
was steeped with water, for the people were frantic with
grief; and the tears fell from the eyes of the women, as
water falls from the lotos when struck by the leap of a fish.

Affliction of the
Mahàraja.

The Maháraja, seeing that the city was overwhelmed with
sorrow, fell down beneath the affliction like a tree which
has been severed from its roots; and a tumultuous noise
arose behind Ráma from the men who supported the Maháraja in his swoon. And Ráma looked behind him and saw

The Maháraja
and Kausalyá
command Su-
mantra to halt.

his father Dasaratha, and his mother Kausalyá, running
after the chariot, and heard. them calling upon Sumantra to
rein in the horses; but he commanded Sumantra to drive
on; and the heart of the driver was torn by the conflicting
orders as if it had been torn by the chariot-wheels. And

Ráma desires
Sumantra to
drive on, and to
excuse himself
by a falsehood.

Ráma said to Sumantra:—" When asked by the Maháraja
wherefore you did not rein in the horses, say that you did
not hear; my deep distress has driven me to this falsehood." So Sumantra drove on the restive horses, and the
royal Counsellors said to Dasaratha :—" O Maháraja, no one
follows far after him whom they expect to see return."
But the wretched Maháraja, with a sad countenance, stood
still with his Rání Kausalyá, watching the chariot as it was
driven further and further from his eyes.

General mourn-
ing throughout
the city and
palace of
Ayodhyá.

Meanwhile all the ladies of the royal household were
filled with distress, like cows who have been bereft of their
young. The priests who served the sacred fire made no
oblation to the gods; the householders prepared no food;
the moon forbore to shine; the sun disappeared while it was
yet day; the elephants rejected their fodder; the cows
refused to nourish their calves; mothers felt no pleasure
even in the sight of their first-born; the planets approached

the moon in evil aspects; the stars appeared gloomy and moved backwards; the clouds were driven by the wind until they resembled a troubled ocean in the air; the city was moved out of its place; and the four quarters of the heavens were in great agitation and overspread with darkness. The whole city of Ayodhyá was thrown into mourning, and resembled the earth and mountains when deprived of Indra; fathers and mothers ceased to think of their children, wives forgot their husbands, and lovers failed to remember each other.[6]

Now so long as the Mahárája beheld any vestige of his beloved and virtuous son, he raised himself up on the earth to behold him; but when he could no longer see the dust of the chariot-wheels, he fell again to the earth in the deepest misery; and the beautiful Kausalyá attended him, holding his right hand, and Kaikeyí followed him on his left side. When the Mahárája saw that Kaikeyí was there, he said to her:—"O Kaikeyí, bent on evil, touch not me! I wish not to see you, for you are neither my wife nor my friend: You, who have abandoned virtue for the sake of wealth, I now abandon for ever: Your hand which I took in the presence of the sacred fire, I relinquish for ever, both in this life and the next: If Bharata, receiving this flourishing Raj, be pleased with what you have gained for him, he may present me with what funeral offerings he will, but none shall approach me." Then the Ráni Kausalyá, wasted with distress, raised the Mahárája from the earth, and wiped the dust from off him. And he repented on account of Ráma, like one who has murdered a Bráhman, or touched fire with his hand; and he vented his grief thus :—" The foot-prints of the excellent horses that have borne away my son are still in the road, but the great one is to be seen no more: My son Ráma, who has ever slept on soft pillows perfumed

The Mahárája falls to the earth, but is attended by Kausalyá and Kaikeyí.

Refuses to be touched by Kaikeyí.

Kausalyá raises him.

His lamentations for Ráma.

---

[6] The author of the Adhyátma Rámáyana here introduces a very extraordinary scene for the purpose of enforcing the belief in the divinity of Ráma. It will be remembered that the Mahárája had two priests, namely, Vasishtha and Vámadeva. Of these Vámadeva is said to have preached a long sermon to the people of Ayodhyá, explaining how Ráma was an incarnation of Vishnu for the destruction of Rávana. The matter of the sermon is so entirely theological that it is reserved for discussion in a future volume.

with sandal wood, and been fanned by damsels adorned with costly ornaments, will this night take shelter beneath a tree, with a block of stone for his pillow ; and in the morning he will rise covered with dirt like a buffalo arising from a muddy pool : The inhabitants of the jungle will behold the valiant Ráma rising and departing like one forlorn : The beloved Sítá, ever worthy of happiness, will be wearied with the entangled thorns, and alarmed at the roar of the wild beasts of the forest : O Kaikeyí, be whatever you desire, and dwell a widow in the Raj ; I can live no longer without the presence of Ráma." Thus lamenting, the Maháraja entered his beautiful palace, like one who enters the house of mourning after he has burned a deceased kinsman.

The Maháraja returns to the palace and is conveyed to the apartments of Kausalyá.

Seeing the city bereft of its people, the Maháraja entered the palace as the sun enters a cloud, and he said :—" Carry me speedily to the apartments of Kausalyá, the mother of Ráma, for nowhere else can my heart obtain ease." Then those who were waiting on the Maháraja carried him to the chamber of Kausalyá, and he ascended a couch and sank into

Midnight scene. a delirium. And the night overspread all around, like the night of universal death ; and at midnight the Maháraja said to Kausalyá :—" O excellent Kausalyá, I cannot see you ; touch me I pray you with your hand, for my sight has gone

Lamentations of Kausalyá.

after Ráma." Then the Rání, seeing him lying on the couch mourning for Ráma, drew near and sat by the side of her afflicted lord, and thus addressed him :—" That female reptile Kaikeyí, having shed her poison upon Ráma and cast her slough, will now go about with ease, and will terrify me like a venomous serpent : Better would it have been for me, if Ráma had dwelt in the city as a wandering mendicant, or if he had been condemned to servitude ; but the wicked Kaikeyí has cast him out to be a portion to the Rákshasas, as fuel is thrown to the sacrificial fire : The hero of mighty arm, attended by his wife and brother, has been condemned by you to exile in the forest, and what can await them but the direst distress ? How can these tender ones drag on their wretched lives feeding on fruits ? Alas ! they are like the remains of a tree, which has been devoured by elephants or destroyed by the jungle fire before its fruit has ripened : Yet even now the day may come when I shall again behold Ráma, and his wife Sítá, and his brother Lakshmana ; but when will that day arrive ? When will this renowned city of Ayodhyá, hearing that the two heroes have returned from the forest, once again be filled with gladness and be decorated with banners ? When will the city be moved with joy at beholding these two heroes, like the sea at the new and full moon ? When will the thousands of people scatter sweetmeats in the streets, as the two sons enter Ayodhyá adorned with beautiful ear-rings and holding up their scimitars ?   When will the daughters of Bráhmans joyfully go round the city with fruits and flowers ? When will my son Ráma, who is old in understanding but endowed like the gods with perpetual youth, when will he return and revive us like a seasonable rain ? O Maháraja, like a cow whose calf has been carried off by a lion, so have I been deprived of my offspring by the tigress Kaikeyí."

The foregoing story of Ráma's departure into exile is replete with many touching references, which to the European would appear to be exaggerations, but which are never for a moment doubted by the Hindú.   Thus it seems difficult to understand why Ráma, Sítá, and Lakshmana should have walked to the palace with bare feet instead of proceeding thither in a chariot ; but according to Hindú ideas the conduct of the exiles would have been regarded as contumacious and defiant had they approached the palace in a more ostentatious manner whilst suffering under the displeasure of the Maháraja. Again, the sorrow of the royal household may have been exaggerated by the bard ; but still some allowance must be made for the overweening and demonstrative affections, which on all occasions are strongly manifested in Hindú families. The excitement of the

Review of the foregoing narrative of Ráma's departure into exile.

Reason why Ráma, Sítá, and Lakshmana walked to the palace with bare feet.

Demonstrative character of family affections amongst the Hindús.

Sympathies of the people with the domestic life of the Raja in ancient times.

people of Ayodhyá has also been described with much poetical extravagance and embellishment; but still it should be borne in mind that in ancient times, when the Hindú sovereignties had been as yet undisturbed by Mussulman invasion, the attachment between a people and their Raja was of a strong and patriarchal character; and the domestic incidents of palace-life were regarded with an interest and sympathy which finds but little expression in modern history, excepting in the fervent loyalty of the people of England towards the family of our sovereign lady Victoria.

Filial obedience
of Ráma, a
Hindú model
for all time.

The filial obedience of Ráma is of course intended as a model for all time; and to this day his refusal to countenance any scheme of disobedience or rebellion, his patient self-sacrifice in order that the promise made by his father should be fulfilled in its integrity, and his loyal reverence towards the Maháraja and the Ránís, are regarded as bright examples to be followed when required in every Hindú family.

The cruel and relentless conduct of Kaikeyí is in like manner intended as a solemn warning to a young and beautiful wife against exercising an undue influence over a fond husband, and causing him to commit the injustice of promoting her son at the expense of the elder branch of the family.

But inasmuch as a favourite wife is more prone to ambition than a son is prone to disobedience, the lesson involved in the tradition of Kaikeyí apparently exercises but little influence in those households in which a husband is married to more than one wife; and it is by no means unfrequent even in the present day for the youth and beauty of a favourite wife or concubine to prevail over the better judgment of an uxorious Chieftain.

CHAPTER IX.

JOURNEY TO CHITRA-KÚTA.

THE journey of Ráma with his wife and brother, immediately after taking leave of the Maháraja, is described with considerable clearness in the Rámáyana. The route lay in a southerly direction from the city of Ayodhyá to the country of Bundelkund; and the three most important stages are as follows:—

1st, SRINGAVERA, the modern Sungroor, which is situated on the left or northern bank of the river Ganges. This was an important station, inasmuch as it formed the frontier town between the Raj of Kosala and the country of the Bhíls, and appears to have been the residence of the Bhíl Raja.

2nd, PRAYÁGA, the modern Alláhabád, which is situated at a very holy spot according to Hindú ideas, being at the junction of the two sacred rivers, the Ganges and the Jumná. Prayága was the seat of a famous Bráhman named Bharadwája, who is said to have dwelt here surrounded by a band of Bráhman disciples, who led the ideal life of austerity, sacrifice, and devotion, which is so frequently described and lauded by Brahmanical bards.

3rd, CHITRA-KÚTA, a celebrated hill, which is situated to the south of the Jumná in the country of Bundelkund. This was the seat of Válmíki, the sage and bard, who became famous in after years as the author of the Rámáyana; and who was surrounded by a society of disciples, and led the same mode of life as was pursued by Bharadwája. It was on this hill that the exiles ultimately took up their abode, and passed some pleasant years.

The narrative of the journey may be related as follows:—

1st Route: from
Ayodhyá to
Sringavera.
People of
Ayodhyá follow
Ráma to the
Tamasá river.
The halt.

Now all this while, though the Maháraja had been carried back to the city of Ayodhyá, yet the people would not return from following the chariot of Ráma; and when the evening was come, Sumantra halted the chariot on the banks of the river Tamasá, and loosened the weary horses; and the horses drank of the water and rolled themselves in the dust, and then plunged into the flood, and began feeding on the banks of the river. And Ráma fixed upon a pleasant lodging on the banks of the Tamasá, and he said to Lakshmana:—"I will spend this night in feeding only on water; this is my choice, although there is abundance of wild fruits." Then, the sun being set, Sumantra tied up the horses and gave them plenty of fodder; and when all had performed their evening duties Sumantra and Lakshmana prepared a bed of leaves, and thither Ráma retired with his wife Sítá. And when Ráma and Sítá had fallen asleep, Lakshmana related to Sumantra the various excellencies of Ráma; and when the night had almost passed, the early dawn beheld Lakshmana and Sumantra still conversing respecting the merits of Ráma.

Sunrise: Ráma,
Sítá, and
Lakshmana
depart without
awaking the
people.

In this manner Ráma and the people that were with him spent the night on the banks of the river Tamasá; and at early morning Ráma arose from the bed of leaves, and seeing the people very quiet, he said to his brother:—" O Lakshmana, behold these people devoted to us, and inattentive to their own houses, locked in sleep beneath the trees; these citizens have vowed to bring us back, and will never leave us while their lives remain: Let us therefore gently mount the chariot while they are sleeping beneath the trees, and take our departure; lest they be overwhelmed with trouble on account of our distress." Then at the command of Ráma, Sumantra harnessed the horses to the chariot, and Ráma, and Sítá, and Lakshmana mounted it; and Ráma said to Sumantra :—"Turn back the chariot and drive it a short while the way we came, that the people may see the footprints of the horses, and think that I have returned to the city of Ayodhyá." So Sumantra drove the chariot back a short distance towards the city, and then turned round another way, and again came to the river Tamasá. And when the citizens awoke in the morning they were overwhelmed with sorrow at finding that Ráma had departed; but presently they saw the track of his chariot, and they followed it a little way, and then lost it, and they filled the air with their lamentations. After a while they approached the city weeping abundance of tears, and their grief broke out afresh. No one rejoiced, and no one was cheerful; the merchants ceased to expose their wares, the bazaars were empty of people, and no one was pleased at finding lost goods, or at the increase of wealth, or at the birth of a firstborn son; every house was filled with weeping, and the husbands who had returned home full of distress, were tormented by their wives as the elephant is tormented by the iron hook of his driver. And the women of the city cried out in their grief:—" What are houses, or wealth, or children, or pleasure to us, who cannot behold Ráma : Blessed are the rivers and pools which Ráma shall purify by bathing therein : The forest abounding with beautiful groves, the rivers, the lakes, and the verdant sides of the mountain will all be adorned by the presence of Ráma : The greenwood shades and hills to which Ráma may resort, will honour him as a most beloved guest : The trees laden with flowers and blossoms, and covered with humming bees, will point out Ráma to one another : The mountains, through compassion for Ráma, will display their most beautiful flowers and fruits even out of the due season, and pour forth their varied cataracts of pure water : Let us follow Ráma; and we will

HISTORY OF INDIA. PART IV.

Sumantra drives towards Ayodhyá to delude the people, and then returns by a detour to the Tamasá.

The people return to Ayodhyá.

Mournful appearance of the city.

Lamentations of the women.

attend upon Sítá, whilst you, O husbands, wait upon Ráma." Then all the women wept aloud, for Ráma was dearer to them even than their own sons.

Meanwhile Ráma and the others had crossed the river Tamasá, and journeyed far away from the place where they had slept, and viewed the villages cultivated to their utmost borders, and passed through the rich country of Kosala, which was plenteous in corn and wealth, and abounded with sacred groves and places of sacrifice, and was covered with pleasant gardens and mango trees, and filled with men generous and happy. Presently Ráma saw the divine Ganges flowing in three directions; the river which is frequented by holy sages whose hermitages adorn its banks; the river where the glad females resort at festive seasons, and lave in its cool and pleasant waters; the river which dashes against its strong banks with a terrific sound resembling a deep laugh, or smiling with its pure foam, now flows with a divided stream and anon is diversified with whirlpools; the river which abounds with the pure lotos, and where the gods perform their ablutions; the river which rolls on gently shelving shores, bordered with pure sand, vocal with geese and cranes, and adorned with flocks of playful birds; the river whose banks are decorated with trees growing in the form of garlands, and are here and there covered with the expanded lotos; the river which removing every load of impurity is itself clear and pellucid; the river whose surrounding forests are adorned with fruits, flowers, and leaves, like a damsel with excellent ornaments, and resound with the roar of elephants as mighty as those that guard the universe, and as sportive and generous as those which carry Indra, the sovereign of the gods; the river which fell from the feet of the divine Vishnu, and from the matted hair of the great god Siva, through the influence of the sage Bhagíratha; the river Gangá, wife of Sumudra, pure and destroying sin.[1] The valiant and dauntless Ráma, viewing this river full of waves

---

[1] According to the Pundits, the chariot passed over this river through the air. Between the Tamasá and the Ganges, other rivers, including the Gomatí, are said to have been crossed by Ráma and his party in like manner.

and whirlpools, proceeded towards the city of Sringavera, which is on the borders of the Raj of Ayodhyá towards the country of the Bhíls.   When he had reached Sringavera, he said to Sumantra :—" O charioteer, to-day we will lodge in this place under that Ingudí tree, which stands near the river : There I will contemplate the chief of rivers, whose waters are esteemed by the gods, the demons, and the Gandharvas, and prized by deer, serpents, and birds."   So Sumantra drove the horses to the Ingudí tree, and there Ráma descended from the chariot with Sítá and Lakshmana, exclaiming :—" This is a delightful tree."

Now Sringavera was the border town between the Raj of Kosala and the country of the Bhíls ; and the Raja of the Bhíls was Guha, who was a valiant and renowned chieftain, and a friend to Ráma.   When Raja Guha heard that Ráma had come into his dominions, he went out to meet him with all his kinsmen ; and Ráma, seeing the Raja of the Bhíls approaching, went forward with Lakshmana to welcome him.   Then Guha manifested great sorrow, and he embraced Ráma, and bowed down to his feet, and raised his joined hands to his head, and thus spoke to him :—" O Ráma, let this place be to you even as Ayodhyá !   What shall I do for you?   O valiant one, who ever was so fortunate as to obtain a guest so highly beloved ? "   Then this excellent Raja Guha brought the argha and various kinds of provisions to Ráma, and said :—" Welcome, O valiant one ; my whole Raj is yours : We are your servants and you are our lord : Provisions, beds, and provender for the horses are all at your command."   Ráma then embraced the Rája of the Bhíls, and said :—" O Guha, through my good fortune I behold you and your friends this day in good health : Is all well in your Raj ?   What you have brought through affection, that I accept, though I do not partake thereof : Know that I have assumed the dress of bark and the antelope's skin, and that my food is fruits and roots : Through my duty to my father I am become a devotee of the forest, and I request a little provender for the horses and nothing more : These are the horses of my

Border town between the Raj of Kosala and the Bhil country.

Guha, Raja of the Bhíls, entertains Ráma with great hospitality.

Ráma's moderate request.

Ráma's fasting
and devotions.

Night at
Sringavera.

2nd Route: from
Sringavera to
Práyaga.
Sunrise : pre-
parations for
crossing the
Ganges.

Ráma dismisses
Sumantra, the
charioteer.

His mild ad-
dress to Suman-
tra.

father Dasaratha, and I shall be sufficiently honoured by the attention paid to them." Raja Guha then immediately ordered his men to provïde what was necessary for the horses. Meantime Ráma bound his garment like a rope over his left shoulder and under his right arm, and performed his devotions to the setting sun, and drank a little water which Lakshmana brought to him. Lakshmana then washed the feet of Ráma, and the renowned one slept upon the ground beneath a tree, with his wife Sítá by his side. And Raja Guha, and the charioteer Sumantra, conversed with Lakshmana throughout the long night, and carefully watched Ráma ; nor would Lakshmana betake himself to sleep, though earnestly entreated so to do by the Bhíl Raja.

When the goddess Night had retired, and the sun began to rise, and the call of the shrill peacocks was heard throughout the forest, Lakshmana said to Ráma :—" O excellent one, we will soon cross the swift Ganges river that falls into the sea." And Raja Guha prepared a stout and beautiful boat, furnished with oars and a helm, and capable of crossing the holy river with ease ; and at the request of Ráma, he put the baggage and the weapons into the boat. Then Ráma took Sumantra the charioteer with his right hand, and said :—" O Sumantra, enough has been done for me ; and we will now leave the chariot and go on foot to the great forest : Do you therefore speedily return to Ayodhyá, and be cautious in the presence of the Maháraja." At these words Sumantra was overwhelmed with distress and wept aloud ; and Ráma in mild accents addressed him as follows:—" Amongst all the descendants of Ikshwáku, I esteem no friend comparable with you : As Maháraja Dasaratha has never caused me any distress, so I pray you not to distress him. Whatever the Maháraja through affection for Kaikeyí may command, do you perform without hesitation ; for sovereigns should not be resisted in the management of their affairs : O Sumantra, act so that my father may not be absorbed in fruitless sorrow, nor even think of me : Present my dutiful regards to him, and to

Vasishtha, and to all the pious teachers of Ayodhyá, and say
that I bow at their feet: Say also the same to Kaikeyí,
Sumitrá, and my other mothers, and to the unhappy Kausalyá, if she has survived my departure: Then bow down to
the excellent and aged Maháraja, and say to him from
me :—' O Raja of Rajas, it does not become you to give way
to sorrow and distress on account of me, or Lakshmana, or
Sítá : In a virtuous cause we could spend a thousand years
in the forest at the word of our father: Neither I, nor Sítá,
nor Lakshmana, are objects of regret : We have relinquished Ayodhyá, and will reside in the great jungle ; and
when fourteen years are expired you will see us return : Let
the mother of Bharata, the beloved consort of the Maháraja, enjoy happiness, and govern the Raj together with her
son :' Having thus spoken to the Maháraja in my name,
do you repeatedly say to my mother Kausalyá, and the other
Ránís, and to Kaikeyí, that we are well and bow to their
feet : And when Bharata is installed in the Raj, do you say
to him from me :—' Pay every attention to your own mother
Kaikeyí, and have regard likewise for Sumitrá the mother
of Lakshmana, and speak graciously also to my mother
Kausalyá.' "[2]

When the great Ráma had thus finished his commands to
Sumantra, Lakshmana, enraged with Kaikeyí, delivered to
the charioteer a very angry message to the Maháraja; but
Ráma forbade him, and said to the charioteer :—"Let not
the disrespectful words which Lakshmana has spoken be
mentioned to the Maháraja : The venerable sovereign ought
always to be addressed in an affectionate manner, accompanied with becoming prostration."

Lakshmana's angry message to Kaikeyí pre-vented by Ráma.

Then the faithful and distressed Sumantra prayed that
he might remain with Ráma and Sítá during their fourteen
years' sojourn in the forest ; for it was the desire of his soul
to convey them again to Ayodhyá in the chariot when the

Sumantra's re-quest to remain with the exiles refused by Ráma.

---

[2] This language addressed by Ráma to the charioteer, is generally admired as
a proof of the goodness and mildness of the divine hero. But when it is remembered that this language was addressed by a young Prince to the aged Minister
of his father, the whole speech will appear affected and priggish to European
eyes.

term of residence in the jungle had expired. But Ráma, full of compassion, thus addressed him:—" O beloved of your royal master! I know your perfect devotion to me; hear therefore the reason for which I wish to send you to the palace of Dasaratha: Seeing you returned to the city of Ayodhyá, the Rání Kaikeyí will be satisfied that I am gone to the jungle, and will enjoy the pleasant Raj governed by her son Bharata: For the sake then of gratifying both me and the Maháraja, return now to the palace and declare exactly the messages which I have entrusted to you."

Ráma and Lakshmana mat up their hair after the fashion of devotees.

After this, Ráma spoke these important words to Raja Guha:—" I will now mat my hair as a devotee and depart to the great forest of Dandaka: Bring me therefore speedily the milk of the fig tree!" So the Raja of the Bhíls quickly brought the milky juice, and Ráma formed the jatá for

Ráma takes leave of Raja Guha and embarks with his wife and brother on the Ganges.

Lakshmana and himself.[3] The two heroes, of long and mighty arm, now appeared with their matted hair like two venerable sages; and taking the road towards the river Ganges, Ráma said to his friend Guha:—" If you wish for prosperity, attend to your army, your treasuries, and your fortresses, and the affairs of your Raj!" They then approached the boat, and Lakshmana, at the command of his brother, placed Sítá in the boat and entered it himself. Ráma then entered likewise, and bade farewell to Sumantra and Guha, who saw them depart with eyes overflowing with tears; and the boat guided by the steersman and propelled by the rowers then moved away with the velocity of the wind.

Sítá's prayer and vow to the goddess Gangá.

Now when the boat reached the middle of the river, Sítá, with joined hands, thus addressed the goddess Gangá:—

[3] The jatá, or knot of hair, on the head, is peculiar to Hindú devotees. According to the Adhyátma Rámáyana, Ráma chose this opportunity of withdrawing the real Sítá from the gaze of men, and substituting a false Sítá in her room. The reason for this will appear hereafter; but the passage may be quoted as follows:—" Ráma then turning towards Sítá, said to her:—' I have for ages past, my love! found a habitation for thee in my heart; enter and dwell therein; it is not proper that thou shouldst be exposed to view.' Sítá in obedience to her husband's order entered into his heart. Ráma, through his own power, created a form resembling Sítá, which he placed by his side; this form was so exact a resemblance of Sítá that there was not a single hair different."

"May this son of Dasaratha, keeping the commandments of the wise Maháraja, be preserved by thee, O Gangá; and after residing fourteen years in the forest, may he return again to the palace at Ayodhyá, with his brother Lakshmana and myself: Then, O excellent goddess Gangá, when we shall have returned in prosperity, with all our wishes gratified, we shall worship thee with great joy: Thou, O goddess, art one who flowing in three directions came from the world of Brahma: I bow to thee, O goddess; I offer praise to thee, O beautiful river: When Ráma, through your favour, returns and obtains possession of the Raj, I will, in gratitude to you, give to the Bráhmans a hundred thousand cows, besides raiment and ornaments: Having returned, O goddess, to the palace at Ayodhyá, I will offer to you a thousand jars of spirituous liquors, and rice mixed with flesh;[4] I will sacrifice to all the gods who inhabit your banks, and make offerings at all the sacred places whether small or great: O excellent goddess, may this sinless and valiant Ráma, together with his brother Lakshmana and myself, return from residing in the forest and again enter Ayodhyá!"

Whilst the beautiful Sítá was thus praying to the goddess Gangá, the boat reached the south bank of the river, and the two heroes bowed to Gangá, and quitted the vessel accompanied by Sítá. And Ráma said to Lakshmana:— "This day will Sítá have to experience the pains of sojourning in the forest, and endure the roaring of lions and tigers, and the grunting of wild hogs; so do you go on before, and I will follow Sítá." Then the two heroes entered the forest with their bows in their hands, whilst Sítá walked between them, having Lakshmana in front and Ráma behind; and at length they came to the sacred fig tree, with its numerous roots descending from its branches, and they sat underneath the shade of the fig tree. And as they sat there at their ease, they saw a beautiful lake of water thickly set with water lilies, and covered with geese and various kinds of

The trio land on the south bank of the Ganges.

Order of march through the forest: Lakshmana in front and Ráma in the rear, with Sítá between them.

---

[4] This vow of an offering of flesh-meat and spirituous liquors to Gangá, is in accordance with the idea that a female delights in these things. In the Adhyátma Rámáyana, Sítá is represented as vowing an offering of cow's milk and sugar.

Halt beneath a
fig tree and
partake of
venison.

ducks; and they drank of the water [and killed a deer, and
kindled a fire, and prepared a repast; and when they had
dressed the deer, and given a portion to their ancestors and
the gods, the two brothers and Sítá partook of the meat]
and prepared for lodging beneath the tree.[5] And Ráma
said to Lakshmana:—" This will be our first night in the
forest, freed from our attendants; and we shall now resemble
true devotees: Fear not, O hero, at being without attendants in this uninhabited forest, nor be dispirited at the departure of Sumantra: From this day it is my duty and yours
to be ever careful to protect Sítá: Bring some grass, O

Beds of grass
and leaves pre-
pared by
Lakshmana.

Lakshmana, and prepare a bed for me here, and a bed for
yourself at a little distance from me." Lakshmana then
prepared the beds of grass and leaves beneath the lordly

Lamentations of
Ráma.

tree; after which Ráma addressed him as follows:—" Assuredly the Maháraja sleeps at ease to-night, attended by
Kaikeyí; but what wise man is there upon earth, who for the
sake of a woman would abandon an obedient and beloved
son? Perchance, Kaikeyí, intoxicated with the wine of
prosperity, has abused my mother Kausalyá, and your
mother Sumitrá: Wherefore,. O Lakshmana, go you to
Ayodhyá, whilst I alone go with Sítá into the forest; Go, O
sinless one, and be the protector of our mothers: Wretch
that I am! my mother Kausalyá obtained me in her old age,
and brought me up with difficulty; and now she has been
deprived of me just as she was beginning to enjoy the fruits
of her labour: What is she the better for having a son that
assists her not?" Thus lamenting, Ráma gave way to his

Lakshmana
administers
consolation.

tears and wept aloud. Then Lakshmana said:—" O excellent hero, it is unworthy of you to grieve; your weeping
answers no purpose, and fills Sítá and myself with sorrow:
Suppress your feelings, O excellent one, and dismiss grief:
It is for little minds when sunk in the mire of distress, to
lament like an aged elephant sinking down in a muddy

---

[5] This passage in which the illustrious trio are represented as eating flesh-
meat, as well as others of a similar character, are placed in brackets because they
are omitted in the North-West recension. They are, however, of undoubted
authenticity.

HISTORY OF
INDIA.
PART IV.

pool: Myself and Sítá, seeing you thus distressed, must soon expire like two fishes taken out of the water: O hero, I feel no desire to see my father Dasaratha, nor my brother Satrughna, nor my mother Sumitrá, nor heaven itself." Ráma, hearing these weighty words of Lakshmana, dismissed distress and embraced his brother, and said to him:— "I abandon grief!"

The two heroes and Sítá then passed a pleasant night under the fig tree; and when the cloudless sun had risen, they plunged into the vast forest, directing their course towards the hermitage of the sage Bharadwája at Prayága, where the holy Ganges unites with the river Jumná. When the day was nearly at an end, Ráma said to his brother:— "O Lakshmana, behold that smoke which ascends from the sacred fire at Prayága: We have assuredly found the junction of the Ganges and Jumná, for the murmuring sound can be heard of the two fierce streams dashing together, and I can already see the trees around the hermitage of Bharadwája." Then Ráma, and Lakshmana, and Sítá proceeded along, and when the sun cast a long shadow they arrived at the confluence of the two rivers, and approached the hermitage of Bharadwája; and they beheld the great sage offering the sacred fire, surrounded by his disciples and engaged in devotion. Ráma then advanced a little way, and bowed his head respectfully, and related his story to the sage; and Bharadwája having courteously inquired of Ráma respecting his journey, brought water and argha, and presented his guests with food, and wild roots, and fruits of various tastes, and prepared a lodging for them.[6]

Marginal notes:

Sunrise in the jungle: progress from the fig tree to Prayága, the modern Allahabád, at the junction of the Ganges and Jumná.

Arrival at the hermitage of Bharadwája.

Hospitality of the sage.

---

[6] The meeting between Ráma and Bharadwája is somewhat differently described in the Adhyátma Rámáyana, for the purpose of imparting a religious significance to the interview. The passage is as follows:—"When Ráma, Sítá, and Lakshmana came near to the abode of Bharadwája, they beheld one of his disciples, and Ráma directed the disciple to inform Bharadwája of their arrival, and of their desire to pay their respects to him. Bharadwája was delighted. He selected such articles as were proper for religious ceremonies towards Ráma, and then went out to meet the three, and fell at their feet and worshipped them. He praised Ráma as the Supreme God, and incarnation of Vishnu, and said:—' I have passed through a long series of years in religious contemplation and worship in the hope of beholding thee, but without success; this day have I obtained the reward of my faithful adoration of thy name; I now see thee." Ráma, gratified at his ex-

HISTORY OF
INDIA.
PART IV.

Bharadwája
counsels Ráma
to dwell at
Prayága.

Ráma desires a
more lonely
locality.

The sage recom-
mends the hill
of Chitra-kúta
in Bundelkund
on the opposite
bank of the
Jumná.

And the sage said to Ráma :—" This place is large, uninhabited, and pleasant, and rendered pure by the confluence of the two great rivers : I pray you therefore to dwell
here at ease." But Ráma replied :—" O divine one, the
people of the city of Ayodhyá and Raj of Kosala will often
come hither to see us, and therefore I do not approve of
staying here : O holy one, look out for a pleasant hermitage
in a lonely place where Sítá may enjoy herself." Hearing
these pleasant words of Ráma, the sage said to him :—" At
a short distance hence, O my lord, is a mountain on which
you may reside ; a mountain prized by sages, and pure and
beautiful to the sight : It is named Chitra-kúta : As long as
men behold the peaks of Chitra-kúta they have prosperity
and clearness of mind : Many sages, after spending hundreds
of years there, have ascended by their austerities to heaven :
I esteem this a proper residence for you, O Ráma, if you
will not stay here and reside with me." Thus Bharadwája
received Ráma and his wife and brother with every attention ; and Ráma and Sítá spent the night pleasantly in the
delightful hermitage of the sage.

3rd Route : from
Prayága to
Chitra-kúta.

Departure from
Prayága.

Directions given
by the sage for
crossing the
Jumná.

At the dawn of morning Ráma presented himself before
Bharadwája, and respectfully requested to be favoured with
his commands ; and the sage said :—" O most powerful one,
depart to the pure and pleasant mountain of Chitra-kúta,
which abounds with fruits and roots : There wandering with
Sítá your mind will be gladdened with the view of rivers
and springs, hills and valleys, greenland slopes and cool
cascades." Then the two Princes bowed to the feet of the
great sage, and prepared to depart, and the sage directed
them as follows :—" At a short distance hence you will see
a great number of huts ; thence you will reach the river
Jumná, and then you should make a raft and pass the great
river which constantly abounds with crocodiles : On the
opposite shore you will see a large green-leaved fig tree ;
let Sítá, joining her hands there, implore a blessing : A

pressions, said :—' We, priest ! are Kshatriyas ; thou art a Bráhman : It is our
duty to serve thee, to obtain thereby our reward : He who serves the Bráhmans
faithfully, will easily pass over the waters of this transitory world."

short distance further you will see a dark forest ; that is the
way to the hill Chitra-kúta."

The two Princes then bowed their heads, and went forward with Sítá to the river Jumná ; and there they collected
much wood, and made a large raft, and covered it over with
dried bamboos ; and Lakshmana cut down branches of trees
and made an easy seat for Sítá ; and Ráma placed his
beloved upon the seat on the raft. Ráma then put the garments, the ornaments, and the spade and basket by the
side of Sítá ; and the two brothers took a pole each and
pushed the boat across the swift stream. When they
arrived in the midst of the river, Sítá thus addressed the
river goddess :—" O goddess Jumná, blessings attend thee,
I am passing over thee : May my lord accomplish his vow !
I will offer to you a thousand cows, and a hundred jars of
spirituous liquor, when Ráma returns in peace to the city
which is protected by the race of Ikshwáku." Having
crossed the river and arrived at the sacred fig tree, Sítá
went up to it with joined hands, and thus addressed the
tree :—" Salutation to thee, O great tree ! May my husband accomplish his vow ! May we again see Kausalyá and
the renowned Sumitrá." Sítá then walked round the tree
with joined hands. And Ráma beheld his beloved spouse
devoted to his interests, and he said to Lakshmana :—" Do
you take Sítá and proceed in front, whilst I will follow
behind with the weapons ; and whatever fruits or flowers
Sítá may desire, do you collect them for her." Sítá then
advanced between these two brothers like a female elephant
guarded by two males ; and she asked Ráma about every
new flower and shrub and climbing plant which she beheld ;
and at her request Lakshmana brought her very many
pleasant plants full of flowers. [Meantime, as Ráma and
Lakshmana wandered on their way, they slew many animals
that were fit for sacrifice and food.]

Having passed one night on the banks of the river
Jumná, the two brothers, together with Sítá, set forward at
early dawn on the road to Chitra-kúta ; and as they beheld
the trees bending with fruits and flowers, and the large

HISTORY OF
INDIA.
PART IV.
───────────
Hermitage of
Válmíki.

honey-combs covered with bees, and the multitude of deer
and birds, they rejoiced greatly, for they saw that there
would be abundance of food.   And they went on until they
came to the hermitages on the hill where resided the great
Válmíki and other distinguished sages; and they advanced
with joined hands, and bowed to the feet of Válmíki; and
the wise sage, full of joy, returned their salutation and bade
them welcome; and Ráma related to Válmíki all that had
occurred.[7]   Ráma then determined to take up his abode on

Hut of branches
and trees con-
structed by
Lakshmana.

the hill of Chitra-kúta; and at his command, Lakshmana
brought various kinds of wood and erected a hut of branches
and leaves.   Ráma then said to Lakshmana:— "Bring
venison that we may sacrifice to the god of the dwelling:
Those who desire long life should propitiate the god of their
dwelling: Having killed a deer, bring it speedily, O Lakshmana."   And Lakshmana did as his elder brother commanded; and Ráma again said to him:— "Dress the
venison that we may sacrifice·to all the other gods who pre-

Propitiatory
sacrifice to the
god of the
dwelling.

side over dwellings."   And Lakshmana brought an excellent
antelope that he had killed, and cast it on the fire; and
when it was separated from the blood, and thoroughly
dressed, the devout Ráma, skilled in sacrificial rites, per-

───────────

[7] The interview between Ráma and Válmíki is thus described in the Adhyátma
Rámáyana:—" When the three exiles came to the river Jumná, Ráma put on a
religious habit.   He then proceeded to Chitra-kúta, at which place dwelt a holy
saint named Válmíki, a fervent adorer of the deity.   They arrived at his house,
where they found a pleasant garden, in which water-fowl sported in the tanks;
the trees were loaded with delicious fruits and sweet-smelling flowers; thousands
of birds sang enchanting songs, especially those in praise of Ráma.   Bráhmans
were seated in all quarters reading the Vedas.   Here were sages sitting with their
eyes closed, absorbed in meditation on Ráma; others with rosaries of Tulsi leaves
in their hands were calling on the name of Ráma.   Others again with both hands
raised towards heaven were performing the penance.   Some held in their breath
with religious fervency; others performed various ceremonies in honour of Ráma.
Thus were all the sages engaged in contemplation on Almighty God.   Válmíki's
soul was filled with holy rapture on the approach of the three; especially when
he perceived that Ráma had on a religious habit,—his hair braided in a knot on
the crown of his head, a deerskin round his loins, his body rubbed over with the
yellow earth, and having a bow and arrows in his hands.   Válmíki was overcome
with surprise at the brilliant appearance of the three, but led Ráma into his
house, worshipped him, walked three times round him, and set before them the
choicest fruits, of which they partook."

Válmíki is also represented as delivering a long religious discourse to Ráma,
which will be considered hereafter.

formed the sacrifice according to the Sastras, and repeated the secret prayers, and performed his ablutions in the river. Ráma then made a place for an altar, and planted a grove; and he and his brother Lakshmana, and his wife Sítá, entered the delightful hut, as the gods enter their sacred assembly. Thus having arrived at the pleasant mountain Chitra-kúta, and at the river Mandákiní, that excellent place which was frequented by deer and birds, Ráma was filled with joy, and relinquished all grief on account of his exile.

HISTORY OF INDIA. PART IV.

Sacrificial rites performed by Ráma.

Residence of Ráma, Sítá, and Lakshmana in the hut at Chitra-kúta.

The foregoing narrative does not call for much remark. Sumantra, the charioteer, seems to have been directed to conduct the exiles to the frontier town of Sringavera; and this duty he accomplished, crossing the rivers Tamasá and Gomatí on the way. At Sringavera he took his leave and returned to Ayodhyá, whilst the exiles crossed to the southerly bank of the Ganges, and proceeded due eastward to the celebrated station at Prayága. At Prayága the exiles crossed the river Jumná, and proceeded southward into the country of Bundelkund, where they finally took up their abode on the hill Chitra-kúta; which is said to have abounded in game, fruit, honey, and other products of the jungle which were suitable for food.

Review of the foregoing narrative of Ráma's journey to Chitra-kúta.

The exiles part with Sumantra at the frontier town of Sringavera.

Cross the Ganges to Prayága, and cross the Jumná for Chitra-kúta.

The worship paid by Sítá to the rivers Ganges and Jumná, and to the sacred fig tree, is well worthy of notice. It may be a relic of the old fetische worship which undoubtedly prevailed in ancient India, and which, as such, will have to be considered hereafter; but still the picture of the faithful wife offering up prayers and vows on behalf of her beloved husband is ever regarded with deep admiration by the Hindús; and indeed the worship is

Worship of the Ganges and Jumna, and the sacred fig tree, by Sítá.

Bráhman set-
tlements, or
hermitages,
scattered
amongst the
aboriginal
population.

Bráhman set-
tlements at the
junction of the
Sarayú and
Ganges; at
Buxar; at the
junction of the
Ganges and
Jumná; and at
Chitra-kúta.

Question of
whether the
hermitages
really existed in
the time of
Ráma post-
poned.

perhaps as largely practised by Hindú women in the present day as at any previous period.

Another important circumstance connected with Ráma's exile must also be duly noticed, namely, the assumed fact that a number of Brahmanical settlements, or hermitages, each under a distinguished sage, were scattered amongst the aboriginal population beyond the frontier of Kosala. Notice has already been taken of two of these settlements much further to the eastward, in the narrative of Ráma's expedition against the Rákshasas; namely, first, the hermitage at the junction of the Sarayú and Ganges rivers, which was famous as the spot where Siva was smitten by Káma, the Indian Cupid, with the arrows of love; and secondly, the hermitage of Viswámitra in the neighbourhood of Buxar, which was famous as the spot where Vishnu, incarnate as a dwarf, took the three steps which terminated in the overthrow of Bali. In the present narrative of Ráma's exile two other Brahmanical settlements are described, namely, the hermitage of Bharadwája at Prayága, and the hermitage of Válmíki at Chitra-kúta. Whether these hermitages did or did not exist in the days of Ráma, is a question which can scarcely be settled definitely; but the tradition that Brahmanical settlements were formed in the midst of an aboriginal and hostile people is highly significant; and illustrates an important phase in the history of the Bráhmans, namely, the mode by which their influence was extended throughout India. This subject, however, will be discussed hereafter.

CHAPTER X.

DEATH OF MAHÁRAJA DASARATHA.

THE exiles having been settled down in quiet residence on the hill of Chitra-kúta, the story of the Rámáyana once more reverts to the city of Ayodhyá; and the melancholy events are related which followed the return of Sumantra, and the delivery of Ráma's dutiful message to the Mahá-raja. The narrative comprises four distinct scenes, namely :—

1st, Palace scene, including the conversation between the Maháraja and Kausalyá after the return of Sumantra with Ráma's message.

2nd, The death of the Maháraja at midnight.

3rd, The morning scene without and within the palace.

4th, The summoning of the Council, and des-patch of messengers to bring Bharata to Ayodhyá.

These events are highly suggestive of ancient Hindú life, but demand no preliminary explanation ; and the narrative, therefore, may be reproduced from the Rámáyana as follows :—

Meantime the charioteer Sumantra had taken leave of Raja Guha, and returned with a heavy heart to the joyless city of Ayodhyá. The people seeing him return without

HISTORY OF
INDIA.
PART IV.

Distress of the
people, the
ladies of the
palace, and the
Maháraja.

Sumantra de-
livers Ráma's
message.

Prostration of
the Maháraja.

Kausalyá re-
proaches the
Maháraja.

Ráma filled the air with their cries; and he drove his chariot through the chief street, with his face covered, until he came near to the palace of Maháraja Dasaratha. Then Sumantra descended from his chariot, and passed through the seven enclosures of the palace; [1] and all the ladies of the Maháraja, seeing him return without Ráma, were filled with anguish, and their bright eyes streamed with tears. And Sumantra quickly entered the eighth enclosure of the palace, and beheld the wretched Maháraja in the white house, wasted with grief on account of his son; and he approached the Maháraja and bowed to his feet, and delivered the message which had been entrusted to him by Ráma.

When the Maháraja heard the dutiful words of his eldest son, he fell down in a swoon; and the Rání Kausalyá, with the aid of Sumantra, raised him up, and thus addressed him :—" Arise, O Maháraja, for no help can come out of this sorrow ! O my lord, Kaikeyí is not here, and you need not fear to converse about Ráma." Kausalyá then began to heap bitter reproaches upon Dasaratha, saying :—" Who ever abandoned a beloved and innocent son after having engaged to install him in the Raj ? If you had promised to grant two boons to Kaikeyí, why did you promise to give the Raj to Ráma ? If you exiled your son for fear of violating your word, why did you not fear to break the promise that you had made to your Counsellors to install Ráma ? Enslaved in your old age by the love of a woman, you break your promise either way; by giving Ráma the Raj you would have broken your promise to Kaikeyí, but by sending him into the jungle you have broken your promise to your Counsellors : The oath given to a favourite wife, and the exile of Ráma to the forest, are crimes which I rank with the murder of an unborn infant : Happy is it for me that Kaikeyí did not solicit the death of Ráma, for you would have granted that also without hesitation : Then Ráma would have been seized by the strong arm of power,

[1] Five courts or quadrangles are specified on a previous occasion. See *ante*, p. 109.

like a victim bound by its owner for a sacrifice; for in this world the weak sink beneath the grasp of the strong, as elephants in the forest are seized in the grasp of lions: Should Ráma return after his exile is accomplished, I cannot expect that Bharata will abandon the Raj and the treasures, nor would Ráma receive them at his hand: If people first entertain their new friends at a funeral feast, and afterwards invite the Bráhmans, they will find that the Bráhmans will not look with pleasure even on amrita when it has been left by others: Will Bráhmans sit down before other Bráhmans have finished their meat, and eat that of which they have eaten? Will an elder brother accept of a Raj which has been enjoyed by a younger brother? Will a tiger eat the prey which has been caught by another? No oblations, nor ghee, nor sacrificial articles, nor sacred kusa grass, nor sacrificial posts, are ever again employed in a new ceremony; and in like manner Ráma will never look with pleasure on a Raj which resembles stale wine at a feast, or spoiled homa at a sacrifice: Ráma will no more endure such disrespect than a fierce tiger would suffer his tail to be pulled with impunity."[2]

The Maháraja, hearing this angry speech of Kausalyá, thus spoke to her:—" O Kausalyá, I entreat your forgiveness with joined hands: Tenderly affectionate toward your son, do not pour salt into my wounds! My heart is bursting with sorrow for my son, and your words are to me as thunderbolts: The husband of a chaste wife, whether virtuous or worthless, is her deity, her refuge, and the grand object of her veneration: Pardon my transgression, O Rání; in excess of agony do I supplicate you: Do not again wound me, who am already smitten and wounded by the gods: O goddess, I know you to be wise, and acquainted with the different passions of men; let me not again hear these bitter reproaches from you! "

*The Maháraja
implores the
forgiveness of
Kausalyá.*

---

[2] This speech which has been put into the mouth of Kausalyá contains several similes which may be regarded as so many inferential lessons in Brahmanical law. The most important is that which refers to the especial claim of the Bráhmans, which is still observed at all feasts, of being served before those of any other caste, and of being served all at one time.

Kausalyá acknowledges her transgression in having reproached her lord.

When Kausalyá, ever affectionate towards her husband, heard those words of the afflicted Maháraja, she abandoned her distress on account of her son, and applying her joined hands to his, she bowed her head even to his feet, and replied:—"O Raja of Rajas, pardon my transgression! Through distress for my son, I have said what I ought not to have said: She who is supplicated by her husband with joined hands, and does not relent, is cursed both in this life and in the life to come : Pardon, O Maháraja, this fault of a distressed woman; you are the lord and deity both of myself and Ráma: I know what is right, I know that you are acquainted with your duty, and are a speaker of truth; and what I have spoken has been through my affliction on account of my son : Grief destroys the understanding, and the memory, and the patience; there is no enemy more destructive than grief: The touch of fire may be borne, and the stroke of a dreadful weapon; but, O Maháraja, the distress which arises from grief is not to be endured; even the sages when smitten with grief have sunk beneath the stroke : These five days which have passed away since the departure of my son, are to me, by reason of my sorrow, even as a thousand years : My grief for my exiled son increases like the waters of the Ganges after the departure of the cold season."

2nd, Last words of the Maháraja to Kausalyá at midnight.

Whilst Kausalyá was thus speaking, the day declined and the sun set; and the Maháraja, composed by her words and wearied by reason of his mourning, sunk into the arms of sleep. And in the middle of the night the Maháraja awoke weeping and terrified, and said to his wife:—"O Kausalyá, I am now giving up the ghost through grief for my son : My eyes are unable to see you, so do you come near and touch me ; those men can perceive nothing who are departing to the mansions of Yama : Could Ráma once touch me, and receive the Raj from me, I might even yet live : O Kausalyá, I cannot behold you ; my eyes and memory are gone, and the messengers of Yama are hastening me away : What affliction can exceed this, that when my soul is departing I cannot behold Ráma : My grief dries up my heart as the heat of the sun dries up pools of water: They are not men but gods who see the shining face of Ráma adorned with his beautiful ear-rings; and happy will they be who shall again behold his fragrant face after he shall have returned from exile: O Kausalyá, my heart is dying away; I am sinking into imbecility like the expiring light of a lamp which has been exhausted of its oil." While thus *Death of the Maháraja.* lamenting, the eyes of Maháraja Dasaratha became fixed in death, and he gave up the ghost in the presence of Kausalyá the mother of Ráma, and of Sumitrá, the mother of Lakshmana; and the two Ránís swooned away until the morning, and no one knew what had occurred.

Now when the night had passed away, the bards and *3rd. Morning scene without and within the palace.* eulogists assembled, according to their custom, at the palace of the Maháraja. And they sounded aloud the praises of *Bards and eulogists praising the Maháraja.* the Maháraja, and invoked the gods for blessings on his head; and the sound of these hymns and prayers spread through the whole palace; and louder than all was the noise of those who declared the great deeds of the Maháraja and clapped their hands in harmony. The birds who were sleeping on the branches of the trees, or in the hedges, or on the roofs of the palace, were awakened at that mighty sound, and began to utter their cheerful notes. The Bráh- *Bráhmans chaunting the Vedas.* mans also filled the palace with the music of the Vedas, and the sacred chaunting of the Vedic hymns. The servants were *Servants, male and female, performing their morning duties.* assembled in great multitudes; the men-servants brought water in golden jars mixed with the fragrant yellow sandal wood for the morning ablutions; whilst a number of chaste young damsels brought articles of food, and those for ornament, all prepared according to the ordinance, and all of excellent appearance and quality. After a while the sun arose, *Appearance of the Maháraja anxiously expected.* and every one stood with great respect and attention, waiting for the coming of the Maháraja; and when they saw that he did not appear, they looked with anxiety one at the other and said:—"Why does he not come forth?" Then the ladies, who attended near the bed of the Maháraja, approached to awaken him; and they touched his bed with becoming reverence; but even then they knew not what had

Palace ladies
discern that the
Maháraja
is dead.

Kausalyá and
Sumitrá
awake from
their swoon.
Lamentations
of all the
women.

The Ministers
hasten to the
chamber of the
dead Maháraja.

Funeral cere-
monies delayed.

Royal corpse
preserved in a
bath of oil.

4th, Council of
Bráhmans and
Chieftains con-
vened by the
Ministers.

Address of the
assembly to the
priest
Vasishtha.

occurred. At length they saw that his eyes were fixed, and that his pulse had ceased to beat, and they began to tremble for his life. They also saw that Kausalyá and Sumitrá, overcome by distress, were lying in a swoon, their eyes swollen with grief. Then they wept with a loud voice, like that of female elephants when their leader has disappeared; and Kausalyá and Sumitrá awoke from their heavy slumber, and seeing that the Maháraja was dead, they fell to the earth with loud cries. Then Kaikeyí and all the other Ránís came forward and filled the palace with their lamentations; and they all wept and screamed, and smote themselves with their hands. The Ministers, hearing that the Maháraja had died during the night, hastened to the chamber of death, and removed the distressed and devoted Kausalyá, who was embracing the lifeless body of her lord, and pouring bitter words upon the cruel and remorseless Kaikeyí. But no funeral ceremonies could be performed at that time for the dead Maháraja, for all his four sons were dwelling at a distance from the city of Ayodhyá. So the Ministers, directed by the Bráhmans, would not burn the royal body, and they placed it in a bath of oil, whilst all the Ránís wept aloud and cried :—" Our lord is dead ! " And the illustrious wives of Dasaratha, overwhelmed with sorrow, walked up and down as if bereft of their all ; and Ayodhyá appeared as a widowed city, like the sky without the sun, or a night without the stars ; and the sun having finished its course suddenly retired, and darkness fell on all around.

When that night had passed away in Ayodhyá, and the sun had again risen, the Ministers of the Raj called together an assembly of Bráhmans and Chieftains ; and those renowned sages and courtiers delivered their opinions in the presence of the chief and excellent priest Vasishtha, as follows :—" The past night has been to us like a hundred years : Distressed on account of the exiled Ráma, the Maháraja has given up the ghost : Dasaratha is now in heaven, but none of all his sons remain in the city of Ayodhyá : Ráma has departed to the forest, and the illustrious Lakshmana has gone with him ; and Bharata and Satrughna are dwelling in

Girivraja, the royal city of the Kaikeyas : It is necessary this
day to appoint some one to be our Maháraja, that our
widowed country may not fall into ruin : In countries desti-
tute of a Raja the rain-cloud ceases to pour forth its showers *Necessity for the immediate*
upon the earth, and the husbandman fears to sow his seed ; *appointment of a Maháraja.*
the sons and women of the deceased sovereign are under no *Poetical de-*
scription of a
subjection ; no man is secure of his wealth, nor even of his *country with-*
out a Maháraja.
life ; all becomes anarchy ; no councils are held ; the pleasant
houses and gardens are destroyed by the dissolute ; the
Bráhmans make no offerings ; the sacrificing Bráhmans refuse to give the others their share of the sacrificial fees ; the
glad leaders of the sacred song and dance cease to exalt the
fame of the Raja by their social and joyous assemblies ; dis-
putants are no longer gratified with pleasing discussions ;
renowned orators are no longer surrounded with applauding
audiences ; young damsels adorned with gold do not flock to
the gardens in the evening for the sake of amusement ; rich
men, even when well-guarded, are unable to sleep with their
doors open ; husbandmen and those who attend cattle are
unable to enjoy repose ; young men and maidens can no
longer repair in swift chariots to the grassy plains ; elephants
adorned with bells can no longer walk at large on the high
roads ; those who are joyfully practising with the sword and
bow, the mace and the spear, are no longer to be heard ;
merchants travelling to distant places cannot carry their
goods in safety along the high-way ; the holy and subdued
sage goes not out of his house meditating with his mind
fixed upon the all-pervading spirit ; soldiers cannot overcome their enemies in war ; the people do not assemble in
rich attire, and ride on chariots, or on excellent horses ;
men learned in the Sastras are not found conversing with
each other in the roads and gardens ; garlands of jewels,
and portions of choice viands, are no longer offered to the
gods : O Vasishtha, a Raj without a Raja is like a river *Vasishtha im-*
plored to ap-
without water, a forest without vegetation, or a cow without *point a success-*
or to the Raj.
a keeper ; and men mutually devour one another like the
fishes of the sea : O chief of the twice born, this day our
Raja has departed to the mansions of Indra, and our Raj is

becoming a wilderness; do you appoint another Prince to be Raja, a son of the family of Ikshwáku."

Vasishtha despatches messengers to bring Bharata from the city of his grandfather.

The sage Vasishtha having heard these words, replied thus to the Counsellors, the Bráhmans, and all the friends of the deceased Mahárája :—" As Bharata, to whom the Raj is given, remains at ease with his brother Satrughna in the house of his grandfather, Aswapati, speedily send swift messengers to bring the two brothers hither : Why look ye on the ground ? " All present then replied to Vasishtha :—

Directions to the messengers.

" Let messengers be sent ! " Vasishtha then appointed certain messengers, and said to them :—" Attend to what it becomes you to do : Go with all speed on swift horses to the royal city of Girivraja, and dismissing all signs of grief, speak thus to Bharata :—" Vasishtha the priest, and all the Counsellors, send to you salutations of peace, and entreat you to hasten without delay to the city of Ayodhyá : But do not inform Bharata that Ráma is in exile, that the Mahárája is dead, and that the royal race is ruined by this woman Kaikeyí : Bring out of the treasury with all speed the excellent apparel and jewels for the new Raja, and then depart

Departure of the messengers.

for the abode of Bharata." Then the messengers, being provided with victuals for the journey, mounted their horses, and going by the way of the river Malini, they crossed the Ganges at Hastinápur, and proceeded through the country of Panchála, and at length approached the excellent city of Girivraja, which is the royal city of the Kaikeyas.

Review of the foregoing tradition of the death of the Mahárája Dasaratha.

The foregoing narrative of the death of the Mahárája, and of the events which immediately preceded it and followed after it, contains some valuable illustrations of ancient Hindú life and manners.

Exaggeration of the dialogue between the Mahárája and Kausalyá.

The dialogue between the Mahárája and Kausalyá is perhaps too much exaggerated for modern tastes ; but yet the touching resignation of the mother of

Resignation of Kausalyá.

Ráma, and her self-reproach at having used bitter words towards her husband, is highly significant of the perfect subordination which is expected to be displayed by Hindú wives to their husbands. The description of the death of the Maháraja is, however, exquisitely true to human nature. The old sovereign, bowed down by deep sorrow, wakes up at midnight weeping and terrified, and with a certain presentiment that his last hour has arrived. His eyes are dim with approaching death, and he begs his wife to touch him as he cannot see her; and in this manner he feels his soul dying out of his body, until he at last gives up the ghost, and the timid surviving women swoon away until the morning.[3]

The description of the palace at sunrise, when the death of the Maháraja is still a secret confined to a single chamber, is graphic in the extreme. The bards and eulogists are there, all sounding the praises

---

[3] There is a curious episode in the original, in which Dasaratha declared that all his misfortunes had arisen from his having been cursed by a pious recluse whose son he had accidentally slain. The story is told at considerable length, but the main points are comprised in the following extract from the Adhyátma Rámáyana:—" Being in his younger days fond of hunting, the Maháraja went one night to the side of a pond, where the sage Serwan was procuring water. Serwan attended on his father and mother with the purest affection. Both parents were blind, and Serwan was in the habit of placing each of them in a separate basket, and slinging them across his shoulders; and in this fashion he conveyed them to all the places of worship then existing in the world. On the present occasion his parents had complained of thirst, and Serwan had slung the baskets over the branch of a tree and gone down to the pond with a vessel to procure water. The Maháraja, hearing the footsteps, thought it must be a deer, and shooting an arrow in the darkness towards the sound, it pierced the breast of Serwan, who thereupon fell to the ground. The Maháraja, perceiving he had shot a man, hurried to the spot and was at once thrown into the deepest affliction. Serwan, however, said:—' Be not distressed, O Maháraja, I am a Vaisya, and not a Bráhman, so that the heinous sin of the murder of a Bráhman will not fall upon thy head: My parents, however, have performed sundry religious observances, and should their anger be raised against thee, they would reduce thee to ashes : Give them first a little water to allay their thirst, and then address them with humility and respect.' The Maháraja then drew out the arrow and Serwan expired. The Maháraja then did as he was directed, and explained the circumstances to the bereaved parents, and expressed his deep contrition. At the request of the parents he then collected wood for the funeral pile, and they then sat upon it and, directing the Maháraja to fire it, were consumed with their son. Before this was accomplished, however, the old man uttered the malediction that he, like them, would die out of sorrow for the loss of a son."

of the Maháraja, in order that at the moment of awakening his ears may be greeted with pleasant words. The birds on the roofs of the palace, and on the branches of the neighbouring trees, are pouring forth their cheerful notes. The Bráhmans are said to be chaunting Vedic hymns. Meantime, the servants are engaged in their customary morning avocations. The men are bringing in jars of water; and the women are ready with the light food, and the articles of decoration, which are required upon awakening. Suddenly a wild cry of lamentation is heard from the inner apartments, and very speedily it is known that the Maháraja is dead. Another commotion soon prevails throughout the palace. The Ministers assemble and take the necessary steps for preserving the body of the sovereign, until the funeral rites can be performed by one of the sons, who at that moment are all absent from the city of Ayodhyá. But otherwise the scene is one of weeping and desolation; and the author of the Rámáyana indulges in the poetical license of declaring that the sun became suddenly eclipsed, and that darkness prevailed throughout the melancholy day which followed the decease of the Maháraja.

Constitutional
form involved
in the conven-
ing of the
Council.

On the second day, the Council was summoned, in accordance with those constitutional forms of which many traces are observable in both the Mahá Bhárata and Rámáyana. The proceedings are so intelligible as scarcely to call for remark. The greatest possible stress is laid upon the fact that the Raj was without a Raja; and upon this point the author has given wings to his imagination, and described the desolation of a country without a

sovereign in language which could scarcely have
found expression amongst the Counsellors themselves. Meantime the claims of Ráma are ignored.
His exile is accepted as a disqualification, and messengers are sent to bring Bharata, the son of Kaikeyí, who was nominated by the Maháraja to succeed
to the Raj.

CHAPTER XI.

BHARATA REFUSES THE RAJ.

Five leading
events in the
narrative of
Bharata's re-
fusal of the
Raj.

THE narrative of the return of Bharata to the city of Ayodhyá, and his subsequent refusal of the Raj, contains nothing which seems to demand a preliminary explanation. It comprises the following events :—

1st, The ominous dream of Bharata.

2nd, Bharata's departure from Girivraja and arrival at Ayodhyá.

3rd, Scene between Bharata and his mother Kaikeyí.

4th, Scene between Satrughna and the nurse Manthará.

5th, Scene between Bharata and Satrughna and the mother of Ráma.

The story of these events may be related as follows :—

Now in the night, when the wearied messengers entered the city of Girivraja, an ominous dream was seen by Bharata, and he was greatly distressed. His beloved companions, youths of his own age, seeing that he was melancholy, endeavoured to remove his trouble ; some repeated jests and mirthful stories, whilst others danced, and played on musical instruments ; but Bharata received no pleasure therefrom. Then the youths said to him :—" Why are you troubled, and why will you not join in our mirth ?" And

Bharata answered :—"I have had a dream, and in that
dream I saw my father standing with his head downwards,
immersed in oil; and then the earth was rent in great grief,
and women dressed in black placed my father on a seat of
black wood; and he also was dressed in black, and adorned
with garments of red flowers, and went towards the south
in a chariot drawn by asses; and a woman clothed in
blood-red garments was also deriding my father, and I saw a
female Rákshasí of deformed visage fastening upon him:
Either myself, or Ráma, or the Maháraja, or Lakshmana will
certainly die; for when men are seen in a dream riding in
vehicles drawn by asses, the curling smoke of their funeral
pile will soon ascend."

Whilst Bhárata was relating this dream, the messengers, 2nd. Bharata's return. The Messengers arrive from Ayodhyá with the message from Vasishtha.
with their weary steeds, were crossing over the deep moat
which surrounded the royal city of Girivraja; and being
received with all respect, they embraced the feet of the
Raja, and afterwards addressed Bharata thus :—" Vasishtha
the priest sends you the salutation of peace, as do all the
Counsellors: Speedily depart from hence, for there is im-
mediate occasion for your presence at Ayodhyá: O lotos- Presents sent to Bharata's grandfather and uncle.
eyed! taking these costly clothes and ornaments, present
them to your maternal uncle: These, O Prince, to the value
of twenty crores, are for your grandfather the Raja, and
those to the value of ten crores are for your uncle Yudhájit."
Bharata accepted the presents, and was congratulated by
his friends; and he entertained the messengers with all
they could desire, and said to them :—" Is my father the
Maháraja well? Are Ráma and Lakshmana well? Are
my mothers well ? " The messengers replied :—" O Prince,
all are well whose welfare you desire; the goddess Lakshmí,
who dwells in the lotos, is favourable to you: Speedily yoke
the horses to your chariot." Then Bharata, urged by the Bharata takes leave of his grandfather.
messengers, spoke thus to his grandfather :—" O Raja,
entreated by these messengers, I wish to return to my
father: I will come back again when you shall call for me."
Then Raja Aswapati kissed the head of his grandson, and
said :—" Go, O beloved, at my command: In thee is my

HISTORY OF
INDIA.
PART IV.

daughter Kaikeyí blessed with an excellent son : Give my blessing to your mother, and bow down at her feet : Salute also your father and the priest Vasishtha, and the other excellent Bráhmans ; and give my blessings to the two great archers, your brothers Ráma and Lakshmana."

Presents given
to Bharata by
his grandfather.

Raja Aswapati then gave to Bharata excellent elephants, variegated woollen cloths, deer-skins, and other presents ; he also gave him certain large dogs, brought up in the inner apartments of the palace, which were as strong and ferocious as tigers, and well armed with teeth ; together with twenty-two thousand pieces of gold. The Raja also appointed chosen Counsellors to attend him. But Bharata was in no way elated at the sight of these riches, for his mind was filled with fear on account of his dream, and because of the great haste of the messengers in coming from Ayodhyá.

Seven days'
journey of
Bharata and
Satrughna to
the city of
Ayodhyá.

Bharata then mounted the full-wheeled chariot, together with his brother Satrughna, and setting his face towards the east, he departed out of the palace of the Raja, followed by hundreds of cattle, kine, asses, and servants, guarded by an army, and attended by the Counsellors of his grandfather. When seven nights had been passed upon the road, Bharata beheld the city of Ayodhyá ; and he said

Bharata's sur-
prise at the
desolate state of
the city.

to his brother :—" O Satrughna, this is Ayodhyá, but it excites no pleasure in me : I do not hear the noise of the men and women, nor see the people sporting about in the gardens : To-day the city appears to me like a wilderness ; I hear not the voices of the joyful birds and beasts, nor the glad sounds of the drum and the tabor : I see portentous signs and tokens, and my heart sinks within me." Thus

Bharata sus-
pects that his
father is dead.

fearing evil, Bharata entered the city ; and the people who were sitting at the gate inquired after his welfare, and rose to salute him ; and he spoke again to his brother, saying :—" O Satrughna, my heart is full of apprehension : All the appearances which portend the death of Rajas I behold here : The houses of my kinsmen are not cleansed, and the

Picture of the
popular sorrow.

doors are open : I perceive no signs of enjoyment, no sacrifices, and no incense ; and the people seem to be bereft of all cheerfulness: The temples of the gods are deserted and their courts are unswept: The images of the gods, the places of sacrifice, and the shops where garlands are sold, are all neglected and desolate: The bankers and merchants appear dejected, as if in pain at the stagnation of trade: The birds which inhabit the temples and sacred groves appear to be wretched: I behold the people of the city, men and women, their eyes filled with tears, absorbed in thought, and wasted with grief." So saying, and filled with anguish, Bharata entered with a downcast countenance the palace of the Maháraja.

When Bharata saw that his father the Maháraja was not in the palace, he went to the apartments of his mother Kaikeyí, and kissed her feet. Kaikeyí, seeing him returned after his long absence, rose with glad heart, and kissed his head, and clasped him to her bosom, and said:—" How many nights have passed since you left the house of your grandfather? Are you not wearied with the speed of your coming? Is your grandfather in health and prosperity, and is your uncle well? Tell me, O son, all the pleasures you have enjoyed during your visit!" Bharata replied:—" O mother, this is the seventh night since I left the house of my grandfather: My grandfather and uncle are both well; the wealth which they gave me as presents are on the road, for the beasts were weary, and I came on before: But, O my mother, the family of Ikshwáku wears not the face of cheerfulness, and I cannot find the Maháraja: Is he at the house of my chief mother Kausalyá?" Then Kaikeyí related to him the unwelcome news, as though it had been glad tidings. She said:—" That which is the lot of all creatures has befallen your magnanimous father!" At these words the pious and pure Bharata instantly fell to the ground in an agony of grief; and he wept very bitterly and covered his face with his garment. Kaikeyí raised him up, saying:—" O Prince, why are you prostrate? The pious, who like you are honoured in the assembly, should not give way to grief." Bharata, filled with sorrow, replied thus :— " I was joyful when I asked leave of my grandfather to

3rd. Scene between Bharata and his mother.

Kaikeyí's affectionate address to Bharata.

Bharata's reply.

Kaikeyí explains with gladness that the Maháraja is dead.

Bharata's grief at the news.

return to Ayodhyá, for I thought that the Maháraja desired to install Ráma and perform a sacrifice; but suddenly deprived of the sight of my father, my soul is torn with anguish: O mother, by what disease was the Maháraja carried away! Happy are Ráma and the others who have performed his funeral rites! If the great and renowned Maháraja knew of my return, would he not kiss me, gently bowing his head? Would he not with his soft hand have cleansed my face from the dust? But where is Ráma, my elder brother, who has now become my father?"

Kaikeyí informs
Bharata of the
exile of Ráma.

Kaikeyí, asked thus particularly, related the mournful story as though it had been pleasant news. She said:— "Ráma has undertaken a long residence in the jungle, and has gone with Sítá to the wilderness of Dandaka, and Lakshmana has followed him." Hearing these words, Bharata was greatly alarmed on account of his brother, and concerned for the glory of his family, and he replied:—

"What! Has Ráma taken away the wealth of a Bráhman? Has he injured a poor man who is worthy and innocent? Or has he fixed his mind upon the wife of another? Wherefore is he exiled to the wilderness of Dandaka, like one who has killed a Bráhman?" Then the feeble Kaikeyí, vainly esteeming herself as able and wise, thus addressed the mag-

Kaikeyí ex-
plains her in-
trigues, and
entreats him to
perform the
funeral rites and
take the Raj.

nanimous Bharata:—"No Bráhman has been deprived of his wealth by Ráma; no poor man, worthy and innocent, has been injured by him; and never has he fixed his eye upon the wife of another: But when I heard, my son, that the Maháraja proposed to install Ráma in the Raj, I requested him to give the Raj to you, and to send Ráma into exile; and your father, having formerly made me a promise to grant whatever I desired, did according to my request: The renowned Dasaratha has now resigned his breath, and royalty is to be sustained by you: For your sake have I done all this: O my son, this is not a time to grieve; the city and Raj are now yours; and when you have performed the funeral rites for the dead Maháraja, you will be quickly installed in the Raj by Vasishtha and the Chiefs of the Bráhmans."

When Bharata heard of the death of his father and the exile of his two brethren, he was deeply afflicted, and said:—"What will a Raj avail me who am mortally wounded with grief? Me, who am bereft of a father, and of a brother equal to a father? You have added affliction to affliction, as if you had rubbed salt upon my wounds: You have placed the Maháraja among departed souls, and the exiled Ráma among the devotees of the forest: Are you come hither for the extinction of the family, like the darkness which destroys the universe? My father, the Maháraja, who suspected no one, has embraced burning coals, and met his death through you! O you, who are bent upon evil! through your infatuation has happiness been taken away from this family! Wherefore is my father destroyed? Wherefore is Ráma exiled? The pious and excellent Ráma has never acted improperly towards you; viewing you as entitled to the highest respect, he has ever treated you as a son should treat a mother: In like manner my eldest mother, the prudent Kausalyá, has ever acted towards you as a sister: How can I ever govern the Raj, now that I am deprived of Ráma and Lakshmana? The Maháraja ever reposed all his confidence in Ráma, even as the sun rests on Mount Meru: The eldest among the sons of a Raja is ever anointed to the Raj; and this is the rule amongst all Rajas, and particularly among those of the race of Ikshwáku: But I will bring back Ráma from the wilderness of Dandaka: I will bring from the forest the darling of the people of Ayodhyá." Thus speaking, the illustrious Bharata roared aloud, like a lion in the caves of Mandara; and he fell upon the ground breathing like a serpent, his eyes red with sorrow, and his ornaments shaken from his body.

Meanwhile, Satrughna, the younger brother of Ráma, had been informed of all that had occurred, and he spoke out his indignation in hot words; when suddenly there appeared at the eastern gate of the palace the wicked nurse Manthará, who had caused Kaikeyí to request the exile of Ráma. This deformed old woman was adorned with glittering ornaments, and perfumed with sandal and aloes wood,

HISTORY OF
INDIA.
PART IV.

Bharata bitterly reproaches his mother.

Proclaims the virtues of Ráma and declares his superior right to the Raj.

His deep affliction.

4th, Scene between Satrughna and the nurse Manthará.

Sudden appearance of the wicked nurse.

and arrayed in costly garments; and she had small bells tied on with parti-coloured ribbons, and resembled an elephant in its trappings. The porter at the gate, seeing this wicked and deformed slave, instantly seized her, and said to Satrughna :—" This is that cruel wretch through whom Ráma is gone to the forest, and your father has resigned his life; do to her according to your will." Satrughna was then filled with rage, and he seized Manthará by the neck, and threw her upon the ground, and dragged her along the earth; and he said to the other women in the inner apartments :—" This contemptible wretch, the cause of the troubles of my father and my brethren, I will send to the mansions of Yama ! " The aged slave, being thus threatened, set up a loud cry; and all the women of the palace were greatly distressed, and entreated Satrughna not to kill her. But the eyes of Satrughna were red with wrath, and he dragged her along the ground hither and thither, while all her trinkets and jewels were scattered on the floor. At length he drew her with great fury into the presence of Kaikeyí, and poured forth bitter reproaches; and Kaikeyí was filled with terror, and fled for safety to her son Bharata.

And Bharata said to his brother Satrughna :—" Among all creatures, women are those who are not to be killed : Desist, therefore, I pray you ! I would myself kill the wicked Kaikeyí, were it not that the pious Ráma would forsake me as a matricide : Restrain your rage, and she will be destroyed by her own deeds : If the pious Ráma hears that this deformed creature has been killed, he will never converse more with me or you." So Satrughna listened to the counsel of Bharata, and restrained his anger, and released Manthará; and she went away full of alarm, and took refuge at the feet of her mistress Kaikeyí.

Bharata and his brother Satrughna then went, afflicted and weeping, to the apartment of the distressed Kausalyá; and the excellent Kausalyá, prostrate with anguish, spoke thus to Bharata :—" The Raj now belongs to you, who are so desirous of the royal dignity, easily obtained by the cruel deed of Kaikeyí ! " The guiltless Bharata was pained with

5th, Scene between Bharata and Satrughna, and Kausalyá, the mother of Ráma.

Kausalyá reproaches Bharata.

these reproaches, as if a tumour had been opened with a knife;[1] and he fell at her feet, and bewailed himself in many ways, and thus replied to Kausalyá :—"O xcellent one, why do you reproach me who am guiltless and even ignorant of this matter ?   Know that my affection towards Bharata declares his loyal attachment to Ráma. Ráma is great and firm : If I have ever consented to the exile of the renowned Ráma, may I become the messenger of the wicked : May I kick my foot against a sleeping cow : May all the injustice of a master, who withholds the wages of his servant, be imputed to me ; May the guilt of those, who are traitors to a virtuous Raja, fall upon me : May the guilt of that Raja, who takes the sixth part of the harvest without protecting his subjects, fall upon me : May the guilt of those, who withhold the sacrificial fees which they have promised to the devotees, fall upon me : May the guilt of those cowards, who will not face the enemy upon the field, fall upon me : May the guilt of those who pervert the Sastras, fall upon me : May the guilt of those magistrates, who unjustly favour one party, fall upon me : May the guilt of him, who gives no gifts on the pure days of Ashara, Kartika, and Magha, fall upon me : May I eat sweetmeats alone in my own house, surrounded by my children, wives, and servants : May I die childless, without having married a wife of my own caste, and without having performed a virtuous action : May I support my family by selling wine, flesh, iron, or poison : May I be taken by enemies in the heat of battle, and be killed when about to fly : May I wander about with a skull in my hand, covered with an old dirty cloth, and begging my subsistence like a fool : May I be given up to liquor, women, and gaming : May I never have my mind set on right things : May I always practise that which is wrong, and present all my gifts to improper persons : May my wealth be destroyed by robbers : May I incur the guilt of one who sleeps both at the rising and at the setting of the sun ; or of one who sets fire to the property of another ; or who commits adultery, or betrays a

---

[1] This is a curious simile, but tumours are not unfrequent in India, and are extremely painful.

friend : May I never serve the gods, or my ancestors, or my immediate parents : May I speedily fall from the heaven of the righteous, and lose the merit of all the good deeds I may have performed : May I be poor, old, and diseased, and have a large family to support : May I be deceitful, profligate, impure, and the companion of those who constantly riot in vile pleasures : May I destroy the articles designed as a gift for a Bráhman : May I milk a cow which has a young calf." Bharata, having thus comforted Kausalyá, fell down in distress; and Kausalyá embraced him who loved his elder brother, and wept aloud.

Bharata comforts Kausalyá.

The foregoing narrative is characterized by so much exaggeration in reference to Bharata's affection for Ráma, that it may be dismissed with little consideration. His dream that his father was dead, and the presentiment of evil which troubled him on his return to Ayodhyá, are all in accordance with Hindú ideas, but have almost grown out of date in more enlightened countries. His wrath against his mother Kaikeyí is carried beyond all bounds, and is altogether unnatural; especially when he declares to his brother Satrughna that he would have slain her, only in that case he feared Ráma would forsake him as a matricide. Satrughna's conduct towards the nurse Manthará may perhaps have some foundation in fact ; but if so, his treatment of the old woman was savage and cowardly, and merited a far severer reproof than was administered by his brother Bharata.

Exaggerated references to Bharata's affection for Ráma.

Hindú ideas as regards dreams and presentiments.

Exaggerated representation of Bharata's wrath against his mother.

Barbarous character of Satrughna's treatment of Manthará.

CHAPTER XII.

FUNERAL RITES FOR THE MAHÁRAJA.

THE question of the succession was thus virtually settled by the refusal of Bharata to supplant Ráma; but before any further steps could be taken for inducing Bharata to change his mind, or for appointing one of the other brothers to the throne, it was necessary that Bharata, being present on the spot, should perform the funeral rites for the deceased Mahárája. The description of these ceremonies is very interesting, as it evidently refers to an ancient period in Hindú history, when animal sacrifices were still largely in vogue; but the narrative requires no preliminary explanation, and may now be related as follows:—

Necessity for the immediate performance by Bharata of the funeral rites for Mahárája Dasaratha.

Ancient date of the funeral ceremonies.

After this Vasishtha the sage addressed Bharata as follows:—"The man who cannot restrain himself under misfortune is without wisdom; but that man is regarded as truly wise who attends to his duties whilst under affliction: It becomes you, therefore, to restrain your grief and shake off distress, and set yourself to perform the funeral rites of your father." Bharata replied:—"O sage, how can the Raj devolve on me while Ráma is living? But take me whither my father lies, and I with you will perform his obsequies." All the Counsellors of the deceased Mahárája, with Vasishtha at their head, then conducted Bharata to the place where lay the body of the Mahárája; and all the Ránís of Dasaratha went in like manner to behold the

Vasishtha requests Bharata to perform the funeral rites for the Mahárája.

Bharata's reply.

Procession to the chamber of the royal corpse.

remains of their deceased lord; and Bharata filled the air with his lamentations, whilst all the women wept aloud. The two excellent sages, Vasishtha and Jáváli, then said to Bharata :—"O wise Bharata, grieve not for the departed Maháraja : He is no longer an object for grief, and too many tears from his friends may bring him down from that heaven to which he has gone : Rise, therefore, and cast aside your sorrow, and perform the funeral rites according to the ordinance." Then Bharata directed the Counsellors of his father to bring all the articles that were necessary for the funeral ceremonies; and he passed the whole of that night conversing with the Counsellors and priests of his father; and the night appeared to him as though it had been lengthened out to a hundred quarters. When it was morning the eulogists and bards, whose duty it was to awaken the sleeping sovereign, began with melodious voices to utter the praises of Bharata ; and the kettle-drums, and the shrill shell, and the flute, and the loud trumpet filled the palace with their sounds. But Bharata was disquieted thereby, and forbade the exhilarating sounds, saying :—"I am not the Raja !"

Then the sage Vasishtha, eminent in the knowledge of the Vedas, desired to consult with Bharata on what was proper to be done ; and, accompanied by Bharata, he entered the Council hall, which was adorned with a hundred golden pillars, and with gems wrought in various devices, as Vrihaspati, accompanied by Indra, enters the assembly of the gods.[1] Having taken their seats on a carpet ornamented with jewels, and overshadowed with a splendid canopy, Vasishtha caused all the Counsellors to be summoned, and all the chief servants of the Maháraja. A large multitude of citizens also came together from all quarters to see the young Princes ; and beholding Bharata, with the priest Vasishtha, in the assembly, they shouted for joy as if they had seen Dasaratha himself. The sun being now risen, Vasishtha thus addressed Bharata and the Counsellors :—

Bharata hailed
at sunrise as
the Maháraja,
but declines the
dignity.

Vasishtha de-
clares that all is
ready for the
funeral cere-
monies.

---

[1] Vrihaspati was the priest and preceptor of the gods. Here Vasishtha is compared to Vrihaspati and Bharata to Indra

"The principal citizens are here present with the articles necessary for the funeral ceremonies of the Maháraja: Arise, O Bharata, and perform the rites according to the ordinance: The sacrificing priests of your father, well versed in the Vedas and Vedángas, have brought hither the sacred fire, and are standing here with Jáváli at their head: The servants have already been sent on with the fragrant woods collected for the funeral pile, and are now expecting us: Jars of ghee, and oil, and wine, are all prepared; and so too are the chaplets of sweet-smelling flowers, the sweet ointment, the perfumes, the incense, and the aloes: The litter for your father is also ready, adorned with jewels: Place, therefore, the body of the Maháraja upon the litter, and speedily carry. him to the place of burning."

Meanwhile the dead body of the Maháraja had been adorned according to the precepts in the Sastras, and wrapped in cloth of the finest description. And Bharata and Satrughna, with loud lamentations, placed the body of the Maháraja on the litter, and threw the garlands over it, and sprinkled it with incense of the best kind, and went forward, repeatedly exclaiming :—"O Maháraja, where art thou gone?" The royal servants, commanded by Vasishtha, took up the litter, and a great procession moved on towards the place of burning. First went the eulogists, bards, and musicians, chaunting in melancholy tones the praises of the deceased Maháraja. Next walked all the royal widows, with their black hair falling dishevelled over their shoulders, filling the air with their shrieks and screams. Then came the royal servants bearing the litter, whilst Bharata and Satrughna took hold of the litter and followed it weeping. Other royal servants carried the ensigns of royalty; the white umbrella over the litter, the jewelled chámara to wave over the dead Maháraja, and the sacred fire, brightly flaming, which had been daily fed by Jáváli and the Bráhmans. After them came many chariots filled with gold and jewels, which the servants scattered amongst the multitude that had gathered together,

HISTORY OF INDIA. PART IV.

Adornment of the royal corpse.

The body placed on the litter.

Procession from the palace to the place of burning.

The eulogists, bards, and musicians.

The royal widows.

The royal servants bearing the litter.

Bharata and Satrughna.

The ensigns of royalty.

The chariots of funeral gifts of gold and jewels.

The people of
the city.

The place of
burning.

The funeral pile.

The body on the
pile.

The sacrifices of
the Bráhmans.

Sacrificial ar-
ticles cast on
the pile.

Sacrifice of an
animal.

Body covered
with rice.

Sacrifice of the
cow and calf.

Bharata fires
the pile.

Lamentations
of the widows
and citizens.

Prostration of
Bharata.

as funeral gifts of the Maháraja; and all the people of the
city of Ayodhyá went out with their wives and daughters,
and followed the remains of the Maháraja.

When they came to the bank of the river Sarayú, where
no man dwelt, and which was covered with green grass, they
raised the funeral pile of the Maháraja with fragrant woods;
and the friends of the deceased sovereign took the body
with distressed minds, and laid it upon the pile. The
Bráhmans then placed the sacrificial vessels upon the pile;
and they put fire to the sacrifice, and repeated the mantras
in their minds, and took up the sacrificial ladles to pour
clarified butter thereon. Then the Bráhmans cleansed all
the sacrificial vessels, and cast them on the pile; and also
the ladles, and the rings of the sacrificial posts, and the
wooden mortar and pestle, and the pieces of wood by which
the fire was produced, which were all perfectly pure. And
they took a purified beast, which had been consecrated by
the proper formulas, and slew it and threw it on the funeral
pile. And they threw boiled rice on all sides of the royal
body; and they made a furrow round about the place where
the pile was erected according to the ordinance; and they
offered the cow with her calf, and scattered ghee, oil, and
flesh on all sides.

After this, Bharata and his friends set fire to the pile;
and the fire instantly blazed up and consumed the body of
the Maháraja. Thus the Maháraja, consecrated by his
spiritual teachers, went to the blissful abodes of those who
perform meritorious deeds; and the widows seeing the
blazing pile, renewed their shrieks and screams; and the
thousands of citizens burst out with lamentations, together
with the friends and sons of the Maháraja, exclaiming:—
" O great protector, O sovereign of the earth, why have you
departed and left us helpless here ? " And Bharata walked
round the pile, and staggered like one who had drank
poison; and bowing at the feet of his father, he tried to
prostrate himself, but fell to the earth; and his friends took
hold of him tenderly, and raised him up; and when he saw

the fire kindling round every part of his father's body, he HISTORY OF INDIA. PART IV.
threw up his arms and lamented aloud, saying :—" O my
father, since you have gone to heaven, and Ráma is gone to
the forest, I have no wish to live, and I will enter the fire :
I will not return to the empty city which is bereft of my
father and my brother, but I will perish on the funeral pile."
Then the sage Vasishtha said to Bharata :—" Everything in Vasishtha consoles Bharata.
this world is ever attended with pain and pleasure : What is
to be will come to pass, and it is not therefore becoming of you
to grieve : The death of everything that is born, and the
reproduction of everything that dies, must of necessity take
place ; and it is improper for you to bemoan what cannot be
prevented."

Bharata and Satrughna then wiped away their tears, and Rite of sprinkling water for the soul of the Maháraja.
were directed by the Counsellors to perform the funeral
libations of water for the refreshing of the soul of the
deceased Maháraja. They proceeded with all their friends
to the pure and sacred river Sarayú, which is frequented by
the great sages; and there having bathed in the stream,
Bharata poured water with the palm of his hands in
memory of his father, and refreshed the soul of the Mahá-
raja in heaven. Thus having performed the rite of fire and Return to the city of Ayodhyá
the rite of water, the mourners all returned to the city of
Ayodhya. And the city was full of distressed persons, and
resounded with the cries of the wretched ; and its courts
and streets were empty, and the bazaars were destitute of
wares. Thus the afflicted Bharata, surrounded by his kinsfolk, entered the palace of his father, which, bereft of the
Maháraja, was overspread with gloom.

After this, Bhárata spread a mat of kusa grass and lay Ten days of mourning on a mat of kusa grass.
thereon until the tenth day of his father's death ; and on the
tenth day of the mourning he purified himself according to
the ordinance ; and on the twelfth day he performed the Sráddha performed on the twelfth day.
Sráddha, and offered cakes and other articles of food to the
soul of his deceased father, and gave abundance of provisions to the Bráhmans. Bharata also gave to the Bráhmans, as funeral gifts, very many goats and multitudes

HISTORY OF
INDIA.
PART IV.

Purification of
the thirteenth
day.

Bones thrown
into the river.

Funeral rites
completed.

Review of the
foregoing nar-
rative of the
burning of the
royal corpse.

Picture of the
funeral proces-
sion.

Sacrifice of a
cow and her calf
an ancient rite.

Remaining cere-
monies still per-
formed by the
Hindús.

of cows, and many male and female slaves, and much silver, and horses, and chariots. Then on the thirteenth day, at early dawn, the mighty Bharata returned again to the bank of the Sarayú for the purpose of purification; and seeing the place where the body of his father had been consumed, strewed with ashes and burnt bones, he broke out afresh into lamentation. The excellent and wise Vasishtha, the priest of Dasaratha, then said to Bharata: —" This, O Prince, is the thirteenth day since the death of your father: Do you collect the bones which now remain, and throw them into the river." And Bharata and Satrughna did so, and thus finished the funeral rites of their deceased father.

The foregoing description of the burning of the royal corpse furnishes a graphic picture of the funeral rites which were performed in honour of a deceased sovereign. The procession from the palace of the dead Maháraja to the desolate place of burning is singularly suggestive. In front were the bards, eulogists, and musicians, filling the air with melancholy strains. Next followed the widows with dishevelled hair, shrieking and screaming. After them, the royal corpse was carried upon a litter surrounded by the ensigns of sovereignty, the umbrella and the chámara. Lastly followed the chariots, from which the servants of the deceased Maháraja scattered the funeral gifts, and which appear to have been surrounded by the whole body of citizens.

The sacrifice of a cow and her calf, probably for the purposes of feasting, is an ancient rite which has long fallen into disuse ;[2] but in other respects, the ceremonies are much the same as those which are performed in the present day. The funeral pile is

---

[2] At marriage ceremonies a cow and her calf are still always present, and probably in ancient times were sacrificed for the purposes of an entertainment.

set on fire by the son, or nearest kinsman, of the deceased ; and after the burning is over, the mourners bathe in the river for the purposes of purification, and then sprinkle water to refresh the soul of the dead man. The days of mourning and the performance of a Sráddha are still observed in the manner described.

CHAPTER XIII.

BHARATA'S VISIT TO RÁMA.

Thirteen days of
mourning be-
tween the burn-
ing of the royal
corpse and the
Council at
which Bharata
declines the
Raj in favour of
Ráma.

ON the thirteenth day after the burning, the time of purification and mourning seems to have been accomplished; and on the fourteenth day a great Council was held at Ayodhyá, at which Bharata was formally requested to accept the Raj. Bharata, however, again declined the throne, declaring that it belonged of right to Ráma, and announcing his intention of proceeding into the wilderness and installing Ráma as Raja of Kosala.

Route followed
by Bharata in
his journey from
Ayodhyá to
Chitra-kúta.

The narrative of Bharata's journey from Ayodhyá to the hill of Chitra-kúta, where Ráma was residing, is exceedingly interesting and curious. Bharata was accompanied by his army, and apparently by a large caravan of people, as well as by his mothers and Counsellors; and he followed precisely the same route which had been taken by Ráma himself when going into exile. In the first instance, a new road was constructed through the jungle, by which Bharata proceeded to the frontier town at Sringavera. On arriving at Sringavera, he had a curious interview with the Bhíl Raja, and then crossed the Ganges, and proceeded to the hermitage of Bharadwája at Prayága. Here the holy sage entertained Bharata, and all the army and people who accompanied him, in a most extravagant fashion ; and the description of this feast will demand special consideration hereafter. From Prayága the party proceeded across the Jumná river, and thence marched towards Chitra-kúta, where they ultimately discovered the residence of Ráma.

The narrative of these transactions comprises the eight following incidents :—

1st, The great Council held at Ayodhyá, at which Bharata formally declined to accept the Raj, and announced his intention of going into the jungle and installing Ráma.

2nd, The construction of a great road through the jungle.

3rd, March from Ayodhyá to Sringavera.

4th, Proceedings of Raja Guha on seeing Bharata's army encamped at Sringavera.

5th, Passage of the river Ganges.

6th, March along the southern bank of the Ganges towards Prayága.

7th, Grand entertainment given by Bharadwája to the army and people of Bharata.

8th, Passage of the Jumná and journey to Chitra-kúta.

The story of these circumstances, as recorded in the Ramáyána, is as follows :—

Now on the morning of the fourteenth day, when the time for mourning was over, a great Council was held in the Court hall of the royal palace ; and when all the Counsellors had gathered together, they thus spoke to Bharata :— "Our most venerated sovereign, Mahárája Dasaratha, having sent his eldest son Ráma, together with Lakshmana, to the great forest, has now departed to the mansions of Indra : We therefore pray you, O illustrious Prince, to become this day our Raja ; for as long as you delay accepting this office, our Raj is without a head : O descendant of Ikshwáku, all the articles for the installation are now ready ; and your kinsmen and all orders of men look up to you : Accept therefore, O Bharata, the Raj which has so long pertained to your paternal ancestors, and cause yourself to be installed

Bharata's re- Raja, and become the protector of us all." The illustrious
fusal to set
aside the su-
perior claim of
Ráma.

Bharata, who was now purified, walked round all the jars designed for the installation, and thus addressed the Council :—" O excellent men, it is improper for you to address me thus : In our family the Raj has ever been esteemed the inheritance of the eldest son, and it is right that my elder brother Ráma should become your Raja, and that I should reside

Announces his
intention of pro-
ceeding to the
jungle and in-
stalling Ráma
in the Raj.

fourteen years in the forest : Therefore prepare a large army, and I will fetch my elder brother Ráma from the wilderness : Preceded by all the sacred articles requisite for the installation, I will go to the forest and there install Ráma, and he shall be your Raja : Let the rough roads be made smooth by the proper artisans ; and let pioneers go forward and ex-

Acclamations of
the people.

plore the difficulties of the way." Then all the people were filled with joy, and replied to Bharata in these auspicious words :—" May the goddess of prosperity, even Lakshmí, ever attend you, who are thus desirous of giving the Raj to your elder brother." And big tears of joy fell from the eyes of Bharata ; and the glad Counsellors dismissed their grief, and said to him:—" O chief of men, your devoted servants, the artisans, are preparing the road at your command."

2nd, Construc-
tion of a great
road through
the jungle.

Now when it was fully known that Bharata was determined to bring back his brother Ráma, and install him in the Raj, a mighty crowd of mechanics and labourers of all descriptions were sent forward to prepare the way for Bha-

Labourers em-
ployed.

rata through the great wilderness. There were men acquainted with the ways frequented by former travellers, accompanied by strong men who were diggers of the ground, wheelwrights, carpenters, pioneers, hewers of trees, workers of bamboos, cooks and confectioners ; and the vast multitude moved along with great haste for this joy-

Clearing of a
way through the
jungle.

ous purpose, resembling the sea at a spring tide. Some

began to form the highway, cutting through trees, brush-wood, and rocks, with hatchets, axes, and bill-hooks; some planted trees in places where there was no shade; whilst those skilled in the use of engineering, and the making of machines, emptied the ponds, and turned streams, and removed every obstruction. Others levelled the difficult places, setting fire to the clumps of long grass, and filling up pits and ravines. Others constructed bridges, and cut their way through large rocky masses which they reduced to powder. Some made canals which contained abundance of water; and where there was no water they dug wells, and surrounded them with benches. Houses and booths were erected at different places for the accommodation of the army; and stately palaces for the reception of Bharata, and his kinsfolk, and friends. The road abounded with trees adorned with flowers, and was enlivened with gladsome birds, and decked with gay banners; and thus decorated, the way through the wilderness resembled the highway of the gods.

Meanwhile the pious Bharata had commanded Sumantra to assemble the army in order for the purpose of bringing back Ráma; and all the officers and soldiers, and all the people of the Raj, rejoiced in the hope of bringing back Ráma. And all the women of Ayodhyá hastened their husbands in every household. And horses, and bullock carriages, and chariots were prepared as swift as thought, together with camels, and asses, and elephants; and an abundance of excellent provisions was likewise provided to subsist the vast multitude in their journey to bring back Ráma.

Now on the eve of this auspicious journey, it came to pass that the bards and eulogists praised Bharata in congratulatory strains; and striking the kettle-drums with golden sticks they played melodiously thereon; whilst hundreds of others blew the shrill-sounding shell and the piercing trumpet, until the air was filled with the noise. But the clangour of the music only excited the distress of Bharata, and he commanded them all to cease, saying :—"I am not the Raja!"

At the dawn of morning Bharata ascended his chariot,

HISTORY OF INDIA. PART IV..

Levelling.

Bridges.

Canals and wells.

Booths and palaces.

Decoration of the road with flowers, birds, and banners.

3rd, March from Ayodhyá to Sringavera.

Assembling of the army. Preparations for the march.

Bharata refuses to be treated as the Raja.

Departure of Bharata, accompanied by the Counsellors, priests, and army.

and commenced his journey to the abode of Ráma. All
the Counsellors and priests preceded him in carriages
vying in splendour with the chariot of the sun; and he
was attended by nine thousand elephants richly capari-
soned, and sixty thousand chariots with archers, and a hun-

Kaikeyí, Su-
mitrá, and
Kausalyá.

dred thousand horsemen, and a million of footmen. Kaikeyí
and Sumitrá, together with the renowned Kausalyá, also
accompanied Bharata in splendid vehicles, being greatly

People of all
ranks and con-
ditions.

pleased to bring back Ráma. All the people of the city
went out in like manner with Bharata, to meet Ráma. There
were potters, jewellers, garland-sellers, weavers, and those
who lived by practising arms; also husbandmen, tamers of
peacocks, snake-catchers, charmers, tanners, carpenters,
workers in gems, workers in glass, workers in ivory, per-
fumers, goldsmiths, wool-manufacturers, boilers of water,
bathmen, physicians, dealers in incense, distillers, fullers,
tailors, dancing-men and dancing-women, fishermen, and
thousands of Bráhmans of subdued minds, learned in the
Vedas, and contented with their incomes. All were apparelled in clean raiment and mounted on vehicles newly

Halt at Sringa-
vera.

painted.[1] This mighty multitude proceeded in chariots, and
on horses and elephants, until they arrived at the bank of
the Ganges, near the town of Sringavera, where dwelt the
friend of Ráma, the renowned Guha, the Raja of the Bhíls.
Bharata then said to his Counsellors:—" Let the army halt
at this spot, and rest for the night, and on the morrow we
will cross this river Ganges." So the army encamped
near the town of Sringavera, on the northern bank of the
Ganges.

4th. Proceedings
of Raja Guha.

Now it so happened that Raja Guha was dwelling on the
southern bank of the river, and seeing the army of Bharata en-

---

[1] That the description of the camp of Bharata is in accordance with Hindú
ideas, may be gathered from the following description of a Mahratta camp in the
last century, extracted from Forbes's " Oriental Memoirs :"—" Ragoba's encampment covered a space of many square miles; the bazaar, or market-place, belonging
to his own division and to the principal Generals, contained many thousand tents,
where every trade and profession was carried on with as much regularity as in a
city. Goldsmiths, jewellers, bankers, drapers, druggists, confectioners, carpenters,
tailors, tent-makers, corn-grinders, and farriers, found full employment; as did
whole rows of silver, iron, and coppersmiths; but those in the greatest and most
constant requisition, were cooks, confectioners, and farriers."

camped on the opposite shore, he said hastily to his kinsmen :
—"This vast army appears to me like an ocean overflowing
its bounds : I cannot guess wherefore this foolish Bharata has
come hither : I am afraid he is desirous of obtaining the complete possession of the Raj, and is going to kill Ráma, who has
been sent into exile by his father : But Ráma is both my protector and my friend, so on his account do you, my kinsmen,
remain here in arms on this side of the Ganges ; and let all
my servants remain here lining the bank of the river ; for I
will not allow Bharata to cross over until I know his intention as regards Ráma : Let the strong keepers of the river,
who feed on flesh, roots, and fruits, remain here : Let a multitude of fishermen, young, stout, and armed, the crews of
five hundred boats, be also commanded to remain here : If
however Bharata be at peace with his brother Ráma, his
army may cross the Ganges this day."

His alarm lest Bharata should contemplate the death of Ráma.

Preparations of Guha for opposing Bhara-ta's passage over the Ganges.

When Raja Guha had thus explained his intentions to his
Counsellors, he took presents of fish, honey, and flesh, and
crossed over to the northern bank of the river to wait upon Bharata ; and when he approached the Prince, the charioteer Sumantra, who was well acquainted with the proper forms of
address, spoke thus to Bharata :—" This Raja of the Bhíls is
eminent in his knowledge of the forest of Dándaka, and he is
the friend of your elder brother Ráma : Therefore, O Bharata,
let Raja Guha be admitted to your presence, for he assuredly
knows where Ráma and Lakshmana are abiding." So Raja
Guha was introduced to Bharata, and he bowed his head, and
said :—" This country is covered with jungle, and your coming has taken us by surprise ; but still we entreat you to
stay with all your army and attendants at the house of your
servant : I have fruits and roots, both fresh and dry, which
have been laid up in store by my Bhíls ; and I have also
flesh meat, and everything that is produced in the forest :
I pray you therefore to remain here to-night with all your
army ; and to-morrow, when you have been furnished with
all you desire, you can cross the river and go onward."
Bharata replied :—" O my friend, your kindness towards me
is very great, since you desire to entertain so vast an army
as that which accompanies me : But tell me the way by

Raja Guha crosses to the northern bank with presents for Bharata.

Interview be-tween Guha and Bharata.

Bharata desires to know the way to the her-mitage of Bha-radwája.

Guha offers to
accompany
Bharata.

Rejoices at hear-
ing that Bhárata
is going to con-
duct Ráma to
Ayodhyá.

Night passed in
conversation re-
specting Ráma.

5th. Passage of
the river
Ganges.

Embarkation of
Bharata and
Satrughna, and
the three chief
widows of the
Mahárája.

which I should proceed to the hermitage of Bharadwája ! This country is very difficult to traverse, for it is full of thickets and deep forests ; and this side of the Ganges is marshy and flooded with water : Every road abounds with difficulties, and is infested with serpents, and filled with thorns and trees." Then Raja Guha, who was well acquainted with the forest, replied to Bharata with joined hands, as follows :— " O valiant Prince, my servants armed with bows shall carefully attend you, and I also will accompany you : But tell me, I pray you, are you going forth in anger against Ráma ? This mighty army which accompanies you, leads me to fear that you are an enemy to Ráma." Bharata said :—" O Guha, may the time never come in which I shall give distress to Ráma ! There is no cause for you to be afraid of me ; Ráma is my eldest brother, and I esteem him as equal to my father : I go to bring back Ráma to the throne of Ayodhyá." Guha replied :—" Happy are you, O Bharata ! In the whole world I do not know one who is equal to you, since you desire to relinquish a Raj which has fallen to you without any scheming of your own ; and on this account your fame will spread throughout the whole universe."

While Guha was thus conversing with Bharata, the sun began to decline in the heavens, and Bharata encamped his army, and rested that night with Satrughna. And Bharata, filled with solicitude for Ráma, said to Guha :—" I wish to hear particularly from you where Ráma was lodged, together with his wife Sítá and his brother Lakshmana : What words did he speak, and what food did he eat, and in what place did he lie with Sítá ? " And Guha told him the whole of what had occurred whilst Ráma halted at Sringavera, and how Lakshmana kept watch for the protection of Ráma and Sítá. And when Bharata and Satrughna had heard the whole of the sorrowful story, they wept aloud, and their mothers wept with them.

Now when it was morning, Bharata was desirous that his army should be conducted across the river Ganges to the southern bank ; and Raja Guha presented himself to Bharata, and said :—" My people have brought five hundred boats, adorned with flags and great bells, and furnished with oars and rowers." And Guha brought a boat on which a chamber had been erected : and the chamber resembled a temple, and was lined with white, and filled with a band of joyful musicians ; and Bharata ascended that boat, together with Satrughna, and all the widows of Mahárája Dasaratha. Then Vasishtha the priest, and the other Bráhmans, entered the boats set apart for them ; and the female attendants entered their boats, together with the baggage which had been brought on carts. Meanwhile the noise of those who were burning the booths and huts of the encampment, and the uproar of those who were plunging into the river, and of those who were carrying the baggage to the boats, ascended to the very sky. The boats adorned with flying streamers, on which the servants had embarked, sailed swiftly over the river ; some being filled with women, others with horses, and others with carriages, cattle, and treasure ; and when they had reached the opposite bank they landed the people, and returned for more. The elephants, also adorned with flags, swam across the broad stream like winged mountains. But the mighty army and the multitude of people could not find sufficient room on the boats which Raja Guha had prepared ; and some crossed on rafts, and others upon jars and pots, whilst some swam over the river with their hands and arms ; and thus every one that came with Bharata was conveyed over the river Ganges by the care of the servants of Raja Guha.

Now when they all had passed over the river, Bharata marched his army some distance into the jungle, towards the hermitage of Bharadwája at Prayága, and then he commanded it to halt. And he laid aside his arms and ornaments, and put on two silken garments, and proceeded with Vasishtha the priest, and the Bráhmans and Counsellors, to pay his respects to that great sage, who was the chief of Rishis, and the priest of the gods. And when he beheld the delightful hermitage of Bharadwája, and the huts made of leaves, he left the Counsellors, and, preceded by the priest Vasishtha, he went forward and entered the presence of the great Bráhman. Then Vasishtha and Bhárata saluted Bharadwája in the most respectful manner, and Bharadwája rose

HISTORY OF INDIA. PART IV.

Vasishtha and the Bráhmans. The female attendants.

Stirring scene upon the river.

Swimming of the elephants.

Crossing of the people on rafts and jars.

6th, March along the southern bank of the Ganges towards Prayága.

Vasishtha and Bharata proceed in advance to the hermitage of Bharadwája.

Their hospitable reception.

HISTORY OF
INDIA.
PART IV.

Courteous ex-
change of in-
quiries.

from his seat, and commanded his disciples to bring the argha ; and he then presented them both with the argha, and with water to wash their feet, and refreshed them with fruits. Then Bharadwája inquired separately of Bharata and Vasishtha respecting their welfare, and also about Ayodhyá, and the army, the treasury, and the Counsellors of the Maháraja ; but knowing that Dasaratha was dead, he made no inquiries concerning him. In return, Vasishtha and Bharata inquired respecting the health of Bharadwája, and how far his body had been wasted by his austerities ; and also regarding his sacred fires and his disciples, and the trees, beasts, and birds by which he was surrounded. After

Fears of Bha-
radwája respect-
ing Ráma
allayed by Bha-
rata.

this the renowned sage, fearful lest Bharata contemplated the slaughter of Ráma, questioned Bharata as to the reason of his coming ; and Bharata replied that he came " to bring back Ráma to the city of Ayodhyá, and to bow at his feet." So Bharadwája rejoiced, and said :—" I know Ráma and his wife Sítá, and his brother Lakshmana, and they dwell on the famous hill of Chitra-kúta : Go thither on the morrow, but to-day do you stay here with your army and Counsellors."

7th, Great en-
tertainment
given by Bha-
radwája to the
army and people
of Bharata.

After this, the great Bharadwája commanded Bharata to bring his whole army to the hermitage, that he might feast them ; and the sage then entered the house where the sacred fire was kept, and having sipped water and wiped his lips,

Invokes Vis-
wakarma, the
architect of the
gods.

he invoked Viswakarma, the architect of the gods, as follows :—" I invoke the great artist Viswakarma to acquaint him that I desire to entertain guests, and I pray that all

Invokes the
gods, with Indra
at their head.

things may be made ready for me ! I invoke the gods, with Indra at their head, to acquaint them in like manner that I desire to entertain guests, and I pray them to supply me

Invokes the
rivers, the Gand-
harvas, and the
Apsaras.

with all that is necessary ! Let all the rivers which flow towards the east come hither ! Let some flow with wine and sweet liquors, and let others bring cool waters as sweet as the juice of the sugar-cane ! I call upon the Gandharvas, the divine musicians, to come hither with all their instruments of music ! I call upon the beautiful Apsaras, the divine nymphs of paradise, to come hither with all their dresses and ornaments ! Let a beautiful grove be formed resembling that of Kuvera, the leaves of which shall consist of jewels, and fine apparel, and lovely damsels shall be the fruit thereof! Let some prepare every kind of food that can be eaten, sucked or licked! Let garlands appear ready formed upon the trees; and let intoxicating liquors be produced in great abundance, together with flesh of various kinds!"

Thus spoke in words of authority the mighty sage who had all his passions under perfect control, and who was invested with divine power. All the celestials then entered his presence, together with the fragrant zephyrs; and flowers fell in showers from heaven, and the divine kettledrums were heard in the sky, filling the air in every direction; whilst the Apsaras danced, and the Kinnaras sang, and the Gandharvas played sweet music. Then when the divine harmony had ceased, Bharata beheld the wondrous deeds which were wrought by Viswakarma and the gods. For many miles on every side the ground became level, and was covered with a carpet of tender grass, and enamelled with sapphires and onyxes; and in it were trees loaded with every variety of fruits. A forest abounding with enjoyments came from the mansions of Indra. Many excellent rivers also came attended by the various productions of their banks; whilst other rivers came flowing with various liquors. White houses, with four apartments to each, rose from the ground to receive the immense number of guests; together with stables for elephants and horses, and great numbers of palaces, and temples, and arched gateways.

Then Bharata, the valiant son of Kaikeyí, entered a palace which was as resplendent as a white cloud; and the portals thereof were adorned with white garlands, and sprinkled with fragrant perfumes; and the square courts of that palace were covered with excellent carpets, and furnished with beds, couches, and every kind of seats. And there was an abundance of agreeable liquors of every kind, and sweetmeats of every variety, and provisions of all sorts, as well as clean dishes and new apparel. There also was the royal throne, with the white umbrella, and chámara of white hair; but Bharata and the Counsellors walked round the

Marginal notes:

The celestials obey the commands of Bharadwája.

Wondrous works of Viswakarma and the gods.

The enamelled plain.

The forest of Indra.
The rivers flowing with liquors.

The white houses.

Beautiful palace prepared for Bharata.

Preparations for the feast.

Respect paid to the royal throne in honour fo Ráma.

HISTORY OF
INDIA.
PART IV.

throne, and bowed respectfully towards it, in honour of
Ráma; and Bharata took the chámara and placed himself on
one of the seats set apart for the Counsellors. All the
Counsellors and priests then seated themselves according to
their respective rank, and last of all the general of the army

Vasishtha and the Bráhmans eat first. took his seat with a reverential bow. Then Vasishtha and
the Bráhmans partook of the entertainment, and when they

Feasting of Bharata and the Counsellors. had finished, Bharata and the Counsellors sat down to the
feast. And all the rivers, which ran with choice liquors,

Wonderful rivers. passed before Bharata at the command of the sage Bharadwája; and the beds of the rivers were so clean and pure that
the white earth could be perceived at the bottom as well as
at the sides. And the banks of the rivers were adorned
with excellent houses produced by the prayers of the great

Beautiful women sent by Brahma, Kuvera, and Indra. Bráhman. At the same instant came twenty thousand
women adorned with excellent ornaments, who were sent by
Brahma; and twenty thousand more, adorned with gold, and
gems, and coral, who were sent by Kuvera; and twenty
thousand more issued from the forest of Nandana, which is

Performances of the Gandharvas and Apsaras. the garden of Indra. And the Rajas of the Gandharvas, as
resplendent as the sun, played and sang before the assembly,

Performances of the trees. whilst the Apsaras danced with great joy. And many trees
came hither and played on musical instruments, whilst some
beat time and others danced; and the clusters of fruits in
the forest assumed the form of beautiful damsels, and cried:
—"O you that are thirsty, drink strong wine! O you that
are hungry, eat juicy meat!"

Feasting of the army and people. Meanwhile the army of Bharata and the people of
Ayodhyá were feasted in like manner. Eight beautiful

Beautiful damsels. damsels waited upon each man, and these damsels and the
men caused each other to drink liquid honey. And there
were other beautiful damsels, and many excellent musicians,
all with garlands round their necks; and they danced, and
played, and sang, until the warriors, horsemen, and footmen, cried out:—"We will not go forward to the wilderness of Dándaka, nor will we go back to the city of Ayodhyá,
but we will remain and dwell here: Peace be to Bharata,

Intoxication of the soldiery. and happiness attend Ráma!" And the soldiers ran about in crowds, and they danced, and laughed, and sang songs, and adorned themselves with the garlands which had been given them by the damsels; and they were so drunken that the elephant-keepers could no longer discern their elephants, nor the grooms behold their horses. The messengers also, and the servants, and the wives of the soldiers, and those who followed the army, dressed themselves in every kind of fine cloth, and were completely filled. The elephants, horses, asses, cows, goats, sheep, deer, and birds, were likewise all completely satisfied, and none wished for more. No one was there whose clothes were not white; no one who was dirty or hungry, or whose hair was defiled with dust. Innumerable couches were supplied, furnished with excellent coverlets and rich carpets. By the side of the soldiers were wells filled with páyasa, made of milk, rice, sugar, and spices; and there were cows yielding every desire of the heart, trees dropping honey, as well as large oblong ponds full of spirituous liquors, and bordered with sweetmeats and choice viands. There were thousands of dishes of various metals, garnished with flowers and ornaments, and filled with venison, peacocks, partridges, mutton, and pork, accompanied with the proper sauces, and boiled in pots, or roasted on ivory spits. There were likewise thousands of plates, and millions of golden vessels, and of pots well cleansed, together with lakes of butter-milk three hours old; and other lakes of milk, and white curds, and prepared butter, with large heaps of sugar round about resembling mountains. There were also all the vessels and articles necessary for ablution, and great numbers of white tooth-picks with their ends bruised, and vessels filled with the powder of white sandal wood; together with thousands of mirrors, and clean garments in abundance, and shoes and sandals in endless quantity, and combs for the head and beard. There also were mountains of betel, and lakes full of liquors to promote digestion, and lakes abounding with lilies of a sky-blue colour, into which the descent was easy, and in which it was grateful to bathe. Thus passed away the night, while these men enjoyed themselves in the pleasant hermitage of

HISTORY OF INDIA.
PART IV.

Servants, followers, and animals of all kinds, completely satisfied.

General cleanliness.

Couches.

Wells of páyasa.

Exhaustless cows.
Trees dropping honey.
Ponds of wine.
Flesh meat.

Plates, vessels, and pots in abundance.

Lakes of butter-milk, milk, curds, and butter.

Tooth-picks and sandal wood.

Mirrors, clean garments, shoes and combs.

Betel.

Lakes for bathing.

Sudden return
of all things to
their previous
state.

Bharadwája, like a night spent by Indra in his garden of
Nandana.   At length at the command of Bharadwája, all the
beautiful females and musicians and singers returned to the
places from whence they had come; and the flowers com-
posing the various kinds of garlands, and those scattered
round and trampled under-foot by men, returned to their
former state as if the whole had been a dream.

Bharata ac-
knowledges the
hospitality of
Bharadwája.

At early morning, Bharata went to the sage Bharadwája;
and when the sage saw the Prince approaching him with
joined hands, he came out of his hermitage and said :—" O
Bharata, was every one gratified with this mighty entertainment ? "   Bharata then bowed his head, and replied :—" O
divine one, myself with all my army, and the very animals,
were made completely happy : Servants and all have been
lodged in the most agreeable manner, and have lost all
sense of fatigue and pain : We have been plentifully
feasted, and have slept in excellent houses : But I ask of
you one favour more : O divine sage, look with a friendly
eye upon me, and tell me how far it is to the hermitage of

Bharadwája
points out to
Bharata the
road to Chitra-
kúta.

my pious brother, and which is the way thither."   Bharadwája said :—" At a short distance from here, in an uninhabited forest, is the delightful mountain Chitra-kúta : On
its north side is the river Mandákiní, overshadowed with
trees, covered with blossoms, and skirted with flowery
woods : O my lord, beyond that river, at the mountain
Chitra-kúta, your two brothers are residing in their leafy
hut on the south road."

8th, Passage of
the Jumná and
journey to
Chitra-kúta.

Order of march.

The Captains in
chariots.

The elephants.

Bharata having thus accomplished his wish, bowed at
the feet of the sage, and took his leave.   And Bharata and
all his army crossed over the river Jumná in like manner that
they had crossed the Ganges ; and when they had reached
the opposite bank every preparation was made for marching
to the hill Chitra-kúta.   The various Captains commanded
their horses to be yoked, and mounted their excellent
chariots adorned with gold.   Male and female elephants,
furnished with golden howdahs, and decorated with beautiful flags, stood roaring like clouds in the rainy season ;
and the various kinds of vehicles, small and great, went

forward, whilst the footmen marched on foot.   The ladies of the royal house, with Kausalyá at their head, were filled with joy; and went forward in different vehicles, earnestly longing to see Ráma.   Bharata likewise ascended a beautiful litter, as resplendent as the moon or the rising sun, and began his march with the priests and Counsellors.   The innumerable army, accompanied by a multitude of elephants and horses, covered the earth like a vast cloud rising in the south.   At the sight of that great army marching with banners flying, the herds of wild animals and the flocks of birds fled away in great consternation.   The bears, the wild boars, and the spotted antelopes, which appeared in view on all sides grazing among the hills and rivers, were terrified, and hastened into the depths of the jungle.   Greatly pleased, the pious son of Dasaratha marched on, whilst this large army filled the air with their shouts, and covered the earth like a widely-spreading sea, or as the clouds cover the sky in the rainy season.   At length, having advanced a long way, Bharata said to the sage Vasishtha:—"We must be now approaching the dwelling-place of Ráma: Yonder hill must be Chitra-kúta, and this river must be the Mandákiní: The forest appears in the distance like a blue cloud, and my mountain-like elephants are even now treading upon the pleasant table-lands of Chitra-kúta: The trees are shedding their flowers upon the mountain, as the dark clouds pour forth their store of rain when the hot season is passed: Behold the mountain-side covered with horses, as the sea is covered with crocodiles: The swiftly running deer, driven away by my army, appear like the clouds which are driven away in autumn by the winds: The soldiers putting flowers on their heads, resemble the people of the south who cover their heads with blue shields: The forest, which was silent and dreadful to behold, is now through my coming suddenly filled with men like the city of Ayodhyá: The bamboos, shaken by the winds, send forth a pleasant noise, and shade the heavens from view: The beautiful peacocks run about on the mountain, whilst the joyful birds hop from spray to spray: How captivating does this country appear to me !

HISTORY OF INDIA.
PART IV.

The infantry.
The ladies.
Bhárata's litter.

Alarm of the beasts and birds at the advance of the army.

Description of Chitra-kúta.

HISTORY OF
INDIA.
PART IV.

Halting of the
army and dis-
covery of Ráma's
dwelling.

It is the abode of holy devotees, the manifest road to heaven: Let the army halt at this spot and make a search throughout the forest, that the two chiefs of men, Ráma and Lakshmana, may be found."

Hearing the words of Bharata, the many warriors, with their weapons in their hands, entered the forest, and they beheld smoke ascending; and they returned and carried the news to Bharata, saying:—" Fire is not seen in a place that is destitute of men ; and doubtless Ráma and Lakshmana are dwelling there." Then Bharata, pleased at the news, said to the whole army:—" Let the soldiers remain here perfectly silent: Ráma and Lakshmana cannot be far from hence, and I will go with my brother Satrughna and the charioteer Sumantra and Raja Guha, and find out Ráma."

Bharata pro-
ceeds, accom-
panied only by
Satrughna, Su-
mantra, and
Guha.

Review of the
foregoing nar-
rative of Bha-
rata's visit to
Ráma.

The great high-
way.

Probably a
reconstruction
of the old road.

Poetic embel-
lishments.

The foregoing narrative comprises some graphic pictures of Hindú life well worthy of consideration. The account of the Council at which Bharata declined the Raj includes perhaps no details requiring special notice ; but the description of the construction of the great road by which Bharata and his army passed through the jungle, is very curious and suggestive. With the exception of one or two trunk lines, the absence of roads was a peculiar feature of India until a comparatively recent period ; and it was generally impossible for wheeled carriages to proceed, especially after the rainy season, without sending precursors to level the hills of sand and mud, and fill up the chasms and ravines. The road constructed by Bharata cannot be regarded as altogether a new one, as Ráma was driven by Sumantra in a chariot along the entire distance when going into exile. Neither can it have been carried all the way to the frontier, as Bharata complained at Sringavera of the badness of the way. Moreover, the story of the construction of the road has apparently received some considerable embellishments HISTORY OF INDIA. PART IV. from the Hindú bard. But even if the description is not literally true, it indicates the difficulties to be overcome in constructing a road through the jungle, and the ancient custom of preparing the way for distinguished personages which finds full expression in Messianic prophecy:—" Prepare ye the way of the Lord, make straight in the desert a highway for our God. Every valley shall be exalted, and every mountain and hill shall be made low; and the crooked shall be made straight, and the rough places plain."[2]

Ancient custom of preparing a new road for the advance of distinguished personages.

The march from Ayodhyá to Sringavera calls for no remark; but the proceedings of Raja Guha on perceiving the army of Bharata encamped on the opposite bank of the Ganges, furnishes a curious picture of ancient life. Fearing that Bharata was pursuing Ráma for evil purposes, he ordered his fishermen and servants to line the banks of the river, whilst he himself carried over propitiatory presents of fish, flesh, and honey, with the view of learning the real object of Bharata's expedition. The passage of the river is very picturesque, and perfectly true to modern Hindú manners in the north-western quarter of India. The burning of the booths on leaving the encampment, the uproar of embarkation, the boats adorned with gay streamers and enlivened with musicians, the sing-song of the rowers, the multitude crossing the river on rafts or empty jars, and the elephants swimming slowly from shore to shore, are all scenes which will be readily realized by those who are familiar with the

Curious picture of ancient life presented by the proceedings of Raja Guha.

Picturesque description of the crossing of the Ganges.

[2] Isaiah xl. 3, 4. Forbes's " Oriental Memoirs," Vol. II., p. 59.

conditions of Hindú life under similar circumstances.

Extraordinary
character of the
entertainment
miraculously
furnished by
Bharadwája.
But the most extraordinary picture connected with this expedition, and perhaps the most extraordinary in the whole of the Rámáyana, is the weird-like entertainment given by the sage Bharadwája to

the army and followers of Bharata. The whole scene is one of enchantment, and consequently has special charms for the Hindú. All that he can desire or imagine, as a source of pleasure and gratification, are here said to have been produced in abundance at

the mere prayer of a holy Bráhman. The jungle was not merely transformed to a level plain covered with soft grass, but the turf is said to have been radiant with precious stones; whilst the plain was shaded by trees loaded with fruits, and watered by rivers running with the choicest liquors. White and beautiful palaces rise upon the enamelled plain in all the glory of oriental magnificence or gorgeous pantomime. Garlands of flowers are hanging on the portals; sweet odours are issuing from the rooms; whilst the inner courts are furnished with everything that can please and gratify the senses. There are rich carpets and soft couches on which to repose, whilst exquisite wines, choice viands, and delicious sweetmeats are served up in abundance. There, too, are divine musicians to please the ear, celestial dancing-girls to gratify the eye, and beautiful women without number to enliven the guests by their potent charms. Even

Distinction be-
tween the
dreamy luxury
of Bharata and
his Counsellors,
and the uproar-
ious conviviality
of the soldiers
and common
people.
the clusters of fruits that hang from the trees take the form of bewitching damsels, who press every one to eat the juicy meat and drink the strong wine.

But such a picture of dreamy luxury is only pleasing to the confirmed voluptuary, and consequently is confined to the palace in which Bharata and his Counsellors are entertained. In feasting the soldiers and camp-followers it was necessary to introduce coarser elements, indicative of profuse hospitality and a more uproarious conviviality ; and in this respect it must be confessed that the bard has described a scene equally true to Hindú ideas and to a lower order of human nature. Here are couches, clean garments, new shoes, mirrors; combs, and toothpicks, for every one. Here are ponds full of spirituous liquors, bordered with sweetmeats; thousands of dishes of meat, either boiled in clean pots or roasted on ivory spits ; together with lakes of butter-milk and curds, and mountains of betel. The female element was much the same as at the more aristocratic banquet; but the men grew more intoxicated and noisy ; and to repeat the language of the poem, the soldiers ran about in crowds, and danced and laughed, and sang songs, and adorned themselves with the garlands which were given to them by the damsels, until at last they were so drunken that the elephant-drivers could no longer discern their elephants, nor the grooms behold their horses.

But the most extraordinary fact connected with these scenes, is not their truthfulness to human nature, but the anomaly that they should have been described by a Brahmanical bard, and have found their way into what the Hindús believe to be inspired writ. If, however, the narrative is critically examined, it will be seen that a Kshatriya tradition of a feast in which juicy meat and strong drink formed the prominent features, has been partially overlaid by Brahmanical details, in which more stress

Strange anomaly that the description of the feast should be deemed a portion of inspired writ.

The Kshatriya tradition partly overlaid by Brahmanical details.

Opposition be-
tween rice and
milk food and
flesh meat.

The feast re-
ferred to the
Tretá-yuga.

Miraculous
powers of enter-
tainment
ascribed to
Bráhman sages.

is laid upon wells full of rice and milk, and lakes of butter, curds, milk, and butter-milk. Here the opposition is manifest, for the same revellers who feasted on venison and peacocks, mutton and pork, are scarcely likely to have feasted on rice, milk, and curds. The anomaly that flesh meat and spirituous liquors were served up at a Brahmanical feast given by a holy sage, is explained away by the assertion that the event took place in a former age, known as the Tretá-yuga, when such indulgences were allowable. In other respects the miracle is intelligible; and indeed the idea of a Bráhman sage being able to entertain armies through the supernatural powers which he had acquired by the force of his devotions, seems to have been a favourite fancy with Hindú bards, and finds expression in more than one myth of a Brahmanical origin and character.

CHAPTER XIV.

RÁMA REFUSES THE RAJ.

THE narrative of the interviews which took place at Chitra-kúta between Bharata and Ráma contains some highly interesting scenes which throw a curious light upon the inner life of the Hindú, and upon the standing-point from which he contemplates the world around. The general aim of this portion of the poem is to exhibit the noble self-sacrifice which Ráma firmly carried out in obedience to the expressed commands of the deceased Mahárája. The narrative opens with a poetical description of the hill Chitra-kúta, and the river Mandákiní, accompanied by a pretty, but somewhat child-like, picture of Ráma and Sítá taking their pleasure among the flowers, during which Ráma frequently declares that he cares not for the Raj so long as he can enjoy the society of his wife upon so pleasant a mountain. This disclaimer, however, must be accepted with some reservation. The Hindú bard was evidently desirous of furnishing an ideal picture of conjugal happiness and affection, and in doing so was perhaps compelled to represent the possession of the Raj as a minor consideration. But that Ráma should have literally preferred a jungle to a throne, a leafy hut surrounded with perils and deprivations, to the luxury of a palace and pride of sovereignty, seems never to have

Interesting character of the interviews between Bharata and Ráma.

Stress laid upon the self-sacrifice of Ráma in order to fulfil his father's commands.

been understood by the Brahmanical bard for a moment. Indeed, the greatest possible stress is laid by
Válmíki upon the filial obedience of Ráma in refusing to accept the Raj. In three distinct interviews between Bharata and Ráma, the former appears to exhaust every argument to induce his elder
brother to accept the Raj; and in so doing is supported by his mother Kaikeyí, and by the sages
Jáváli and Vasishtha; but Ráma never hesitates for
a moment as to the duty which he owes to his deceased father, and at length the people and the great
sages acknowledge the righteousness of his resolution.

The incidents and speeches which arise in the
course of the narrative are very significant, and well
worthy of consideration. In the present place, however, it will be sufficient to indicate the seven leading events as follows:—

1st, Description of the hill Chitra-kúta and the
river Mandákiní, and of the sports of Ráma and Sítá
amongst the flowers.

2nd, Approach of Bharata's army and description of Ráma's hermitage.

3rd, First interview between Ráma and Bharata,
comprising Ráma's inferential speech upon the duties
of Rajas.

4th, Ráma's offering of oblations of water and
funeral cakes to the soul of his deceased father.

5th, Second interview between Bharata and
Ráma on the bank of the Mandákiní river, comprising Jáváli's atheistical speech against the belief in a
future state, and Ráma's reply.

6th, Third interview between Bharata and Ráma,
comprising Vasishtha's appeal.

7th, Return of Bharata to Ayodhyá, and residence at Nandigráma, where he subsequently ruled the Raj under the authority of Ráma's shoes.

The narrative of Ráma's refusal of the Raj may be reproduced from the Rámáyana as follows:—

Now on the very day that the army of Bharata was approaching the hill of Chitra-kúta, the heroic Ráma, who was attached to the pleasant hill, and who was as desirous of gratifying Sítá as Indra is desirous of gratifying his spouse Sachí, was showing Chitra-kúta to his beloved.   And Ráma said to Sítá :—" O excellent woman, neither my fall from the throne of Ayodhyá, nor the separation from my friends, give me any pain so long as I behold this pleasant mountain : See this hill, O my beloved, frequented by various kinds of birds, adorned with peaks, abounding in metals, and penetrating the skies : It is covered with trees and flowers, and filled with spotted deer and tuneful birds, as well as with tigers, leopards, and bears : Behold the charming retreats !   The mountain with its cool cascades, and bubbling springs, and purling streams, appears like an elephant spouting up inebriating liquors : Who would not feel delight, whilst the zephyrs, coming from the valleys laden with fragrance, salute and gratify the senses ? O peerless one, were I to spend an age here with you and Lakshmana, still grief would never consume me : In this mountain, O beautiful one, radiant with fruits and flowers, and vocal with tuneful birds, I feel awakened to all the tender emotions of love : O Sítá, rejoice with me on Chitra-kúta : The royal sages have declared that retiring to the forest from the cares of royalty, is as delightful as amrita : The stones of different colours, of blue, yellow purple and white, adorn the mountain on every side : The medicinal herbs upon this prince of mountains shine in the night like the flames of a burnt-offering : Some portions of the mountain resemble palaces, others are like gardens, and others are wrapped in deep gloom : Chitra-kúta fixes its foundations deep in the earth, and exalts its head on high : See here and there the beds of the celestial damsels, devoted to soft delights, formed

1st, Description of the hill Chitra-kúta and the river Mandákini, and of the sports of Ráma and Sítá amongst the flowers.

Ráma descants on the beauties of Chitra-kúta.

of the leaves of the lotos and covered with various flowers: See here the garlands of water-lilies pressed down, which have been thrown at each other by these damsels: This mountain Chitra-kúta, abounding with roots, fruits, and water, excels the garden of Kuvera and the abode of Indra: O beloved Sítá, having spent the appointed time with you and Lakshmana, I shall have accomplished a work which will exalt the family of Ikshwáku."

Ráma descants on the beauties of the river Mandákiní.

Descending from the rock, the godlike son of Dasaratha then showed his beautiful wife the pleasant river Mandákiní. He said:—" Behold the river Mandákiní, with its various islands frequented by geese and crows, and abounding with flowers: See the pleasant fords where the herds of deer have drank, and where for a moment they have made the water muddy! There at stated seasons the holy sages bathe in the stream, wearing matted hair, clothing of bark, and the thong of leather rolled up like a cord, which passes over the left shoulder and under the right arm; and there, bound by their vows, they stand with uplifted hands repeating hymns to·the sun: The trees, agitated by the winds, scatter their flowers and leaves on every side of the river, and cause the mountains to appear as though they were dancing: Behold, O slender-waisted, the heaps of flowers, shaken down by the wind, spreading abroad upon the earth or driving through the air! See the red geese sitting on the shallows and uttering their pleasing sounds! O lovely one, the sight of Chitra-kúta and of Mandákiní, in company with you, I esteem far beyond a residence in a palace: Bathe with me in the stream which is constantly frequented by perfect men, who are washed from their sins, and who are devoted to austerities and self-denial: O charming Sítá, do you bathe in the river Mandákiní, and throw red and white water-lilies into it, as one companion throws flowers at another! O beloved spouse, esteem this mountain as Ayodhyá, this river as the Sarayú, and these animals as the people of the city: The virtuous Lakshmana, who is devoted to my commands, and whose heart, O Sítá, is ever in union with mine, constitutes all my happiness: Performing the appointed duties of religion

The fords.

The holy sages worshipping the sun.

The trees.

The flowers.

The red geese.

Ráma invites Sítá to bathe.

three times a day, and living with you upon honey, roots, and fruits, I feel no wish for the Raj of Kosala: Where is the man whose fatigue is not removed, and whose mind is not exhilarated by bathing in this pleasant river, which is frequented by monkeys, elephants, and lions, and adorned with such a profusion of flowers?"

Thus Ráma showed to Síta the river Mandákini flowing through the villages, and the beds of water-lilies, and the mountain Chitra-kúta; after which he saw on the north side of the mountain a pleasant cave, which abounded with stones and metals, and was covered with a profusion of trees in flower, and afforded a delightful shade, and was frequented by joyful birds. Beholding this cave, and the thicket which concealed it from the view of every creature, Ráma said to Sítá:—" O my beloved, if this cave is pleasing to your sight, sit here a little while and rest from your fatigue: These smooth stones by the side of this tree loaded with flowers are placed here for you." Sítá, devoted to her lord, humbly replied in tender words:—" O my lord, it becomes me to regard your words: In order to show me the beauties of this mountain, you have this day wandered a long way, and must be much fatigued." The beautiful one, filled with tenderness, then seated herself upon the stone; and Ráma, conversing with her as she sat by him, said as follows:— " O goddess, see this climbing plant, bending with blossoms, clasping this blooming tree! Do you, my beloved, imitate this charming plant and cling to me with your arms." Then Sítá, resembling a daughter of the gods, sitting in the arms of her husband, clasped her lord, rejoicing the soul of Ráma, who was filled with unutterable affection. Now there was a red clay, washed by the mountain stream, which yielded a crimson dye; and Ráma rubbed his finger on the dye and adorned the forehead of his beloved; and Sítá appeared like the newly-risen sun, or like the ruddy sky at the close of day; and the affectionate Ráma, rubbing the flowers of Káma in his hand, completed the ornament on the forehead of his spouse.[1] Then Ráma arose, and taking

Ráma and Sítá rest in a beautiful cave.

Ráma requests Sítá to cling to him as the climbing plant clings to a tree.

Ráma paints a red tiká on Sítá's forehead.

---

[1] The tíká, or mark on the forehead, is very general amongst the Hindús. It

HISTORY OF
INDIA.
PART IV.

Sítá alarmed by
monkeys.

The tíká on her
forehead is
stamped on
Ráma's chest.

Wanderings in
the asoka
grove.

Ráma and Sítá
adorn each
other with
flowers.

Ráma and Sítá
return to the
hermitage.

Met by Laksh-
mana, who has
slain ten ante-
lopes.

Sacrifice and
supper of
venison.

Sítá with him, went to another place; and there a troop of monkeys came up, and Sítá in her alarm took refuge in the arms of her husband, and closely embraced him; and Ráma embraced Sítá, and consoled her, and drove the monkeys away. Then the bright ornament on the forehead of Sítá appeared imprinted on the breast of the full-chested Ráma; and Sítá laughed to see the mark on her own forehead imprinted on the breast of her lord. Presently Sítá beheld a grove of asoka trees loaded with flowers; and desirous of an asoka flower, she said:—"O my lord, let us go to that grove." The happy Ráma, devoted to the pleasure of his beloved, went with her to the asoka grove; and they traversed the grove as the great god Siva traverses the wood of Himavan with his beloved Párvatí, the daughter of the mountain. The two lovers, the bright grass-complexioned Ráma and the ruddy slender-waisted Sítá, now adorned each other with asoka flowers; and they wreathed garlands, and made floral ornaments for their ears, and for the tuft of hair on the crown of their heads; and their presence seemed to heighten the beauty of all the mountain.

At length the amiable Ráma, having shown various scenes to his beloved Sítá, returned at length to their leafy hermitage. And Lakshmana came out to meet his brother, who, adorned with flowers, was walking with his arm round the neck of his tender spouse; and Lakshmana showed them what he had done during their absence, and how he had killed ten pure antelopes with a clean arrow, and was drying their flesh in the sun. And Ráma was pleased, and said to Sítá:—"Let the offering be made to the gods." Then the beautiful Sítá first offered a portion to the gods and Pitris, and gave plenty of honey [and flesh to the two brothers; and Ráma said to Sítá:—"This is juicy flesh; it is of delicious taste, and has been well roasted by the fire." When

---

consists of a round painted spot, or a patch of gold, placed on the centre of the forehead, either as an ornament, or as a sectarial distinction, or as a mark of high rank. Amongst the Rájput Princes, the conferring the tíká upon a subordinate or feudatory Chief is the privilege and indication of supremacy.—See Wilson's *Glossary*.

Sítá had satisfied the two heroes she took her own meal; and then at the desire of Ráma she guarded the remainder of the flesh, which had been cut into pieces and laid out to dry, from being devoured by the crows.]²

At this moment, the noise and dust of Bharata's army approaching the leafy hut arose even to the sky. The wild elephants of the forest left their afflicted companions and fled on all sides, being affrighted at the great uproar. Ráma heard the noise and beheld the wild elephants of the forest running away; and he said to Lakshmana:—" O excellent son of Sumitrá, do you not hear this warlike sound, as deep and terrible as thunder? The herds of elephants, and the buffaloes and startled deer, are hastily running off in every direction; are they affrighted by lions, or is some Raja come hither to hunt? Then Lakshmana hastily mounted a tree, and looked around, and saw coming from the northern quarter a large army composed of elephants, chariots, horsemen, and well-armed infantry; and he said to Ráma:—" O chief of men, this must be the army of Bharata, the son of Kaikeyí: Being desirous of enjoying the Raj without a rival, he is coming to destroy us both: I see his flag upon the chariot, the selfsame chariot in which we left Ayodhyá: We must certainly kill him, and then you may govern the Raj in peace." Ráma replied:—" What evil has Bharata ever done to you, or what fear have you of Bharata, that you desire to kill him? I have engaged to fulfil my father's promise, and what should I do with the Raj? Perchance Bharata has been drawn hither by affection only; or he has come hither to surrender the Raj to me; and it is improper for you to speak so harshly of him." Thus addressed by his pious brother, Lakshmana was abashed, and said:—" Perchance, our father the Maháraja has come to see you." Ráma, seeing that Lakshmana was ashamed, replied:—" Dasaratha may have come to see us, and to take us home again: I see

2nd. Approach of Bhárata's army and description of Ráma's hermitage.

Terror of the beasts of the jungle.

Lakshmana mounts a tree and sees the army.

Advises the slaughter of Bharata.

Reproved by Ráma.

Conjectures that the Maháraja is approaching.

---

² The passage in brackets has been omitted in the North-West recension. Its genuineness, however, is undoubted.

Bharata approaches the hermitage.

Description of the hermitage.

The golden bow.

The quiver.

The two scimitars.
The two shields.

The altar.

Rama attired as a devotee, seated near the altar on kusa grass.

3rd, First interview between Ráma and Bharata.
Lamentations of Bharata on beholding Ráma.

the great and aged elephant marching before the army, but I cannot see the white umbrella of my divine father."

Meanwhile, the army commanded by Bharata had prepared their lodgings on every side; and Bharata entered the forest on foot, and seeing the smoke arising from the hermitage of Ráma, he rejoiced like one who has passed a dangerous stream. Presently he descried a large and pleasant hut, sacred to some devotee, made of branches of trees, and covered with wide-spreading leaves, as an altar is covered with kusa grass. It was adorned with a large bow, covered with gold, resembling the bow of Indra; and with a large quiver of arrows, as bright as the rays of the sun, and as keen as the faces of the serpents in the river Bhagavatí. This hermitage, which filled an enemy with dread as deer are frightened at a lion's den, was likewise adorned with two scimitars wrapped in cloth of gold; and with two shields which were studded with gold, and the guards for the arm and the fingers were also covered with gold. In that hermitage Bharata also saw a large pure altar sloping towards the north-west, and on it was a blazing fire; and after a little time he beheld his elder brother Ráma sitting in the hut of leaves on a seat of antelope's skin, dressed in the garb of a devotee, with a weight of matted hair on his head. And Ráma was seated near the altar, within a sacrificial enclosure strewed with kusa grass, and he was attended by Sítá and Lakshmana; and he was as resplendent as the fire, and his shoulders resembled those of a lion, and his eyes were like the water-lily; Ráma, the nourisher of the sea-girt earth, the valiant one of mighty arm, the righteous one resembling the eternal Brahma!

When Bharata thus beheld Ráma, he wept bitterly, and said :—"This is my elder brother, who in former times was ever attended by his faithful subjects, but who is now the associate of beasts: This magnanimous one, who formerly had thousands of suits of apparel, now wears two vestments of bark : This Ráma, whose head was so delicate that he felt pain even when adorned with flowers, now endures the weight of matted hair : He whose meritorious deeds were increased by costly sacrifices, has now embraced a course of bodily austerities: The body of that excellent one, which was formerly perfumed with costly sandal wood, is now covered with the dust of the forest: Ráma, worthy of all happiness, has undergone all this distress because of me."

Meanwhile Ráma recalled to mind his brother Bharata, and embraced him, and clasped him to his bosom, and said :—" O beloved brother, where is your father Dasaratha that you are come to this forest ? What, my dear brother, is the cause of your coming ? Is the Maháraja alive, or has he departed from the world.[3] O Bharata, do you regard the words of our preceptor Sudhana, who is alike skilled in the science of arms and eminent in the law ?[4] Have you appointed those men to be your Counsellors, who are like yourself heroic, learned, masters of their senses, noble, and capable of understanding a nod ? Counsel which is kept secret by the Counsellors is the source of the good fortune of Rajas: Have you overcome sleep ? Do you awake at proper times ? Do you at the close of night think upon the way to become prosperous? Do you consult with yourself when alone, and do you also take counsel of many ? Does your decision, when determined upon, spread abroad throughout the Raj ? When, O Bharata, you have determined upon any affair, small in its origin but great in its consequences, do you speedily begin it ? Do you not put it off to a future day ? Are other Rajas acquainted with your opinions as to what is most proper to be undertaken ? Are they acquainted with the works which you are about to undertake ? Are the secret plans concerted in the Councils of other Rajas, known to you and your Counsellors ? Do you prefer one learned man to a thousand of the illiterate multitude ? In difficult situations a learned man may prove of infinite advantage to a Raja ; but if a Raja retain about

Marginal notes: Ráma recognizes Bharata and embraces him. Delivers a speech on the duties of Rajas. Selection of Counsellors. Avoidance of sleep. Decisions. Procrastination. Secrecy. Value of learned men.

---

[3] The remainder of Ráma's speech is apparently an interpolation, inserted for the purpose of enforcing the duties of Rajas. That Ráma should have delivered such an oration at his first interview with Bharata in the jungle is scarcely in accordance with human nature.

[4] Ráma here speaks of his preceptor Sudhana. Now his real preceptor was Vasishtha, and Sudhana seems to have been a Buddhist.—See Prof. H. H. Wilson's Works, Vol. II. p. 24.

Incorruptible
Counsellors.

Respect of the
people.

Selection of a
Minister.

Selection of a
General.

Public rewards.

Regular pay to
the army.

Selection of an
Ambassador.

Self-indulgent
Bráhmans.

Ignorant and
presuming
Bráhmans.

him thousands and tens of thousands of ignorant people, he derives no assistance from them : Do you employ excellent servants in great affairs, lower ones in common business, and mean ones in a mean capacity ? Do you appoint Counsellors to great employments who will not open out their hands to receive bribes, and who were engaged in the service of your father and grandfather ? O son of Kaikeyí, do the people, oppressed by severe penalties, despise you ? Do your own Counsellors disregard you in your Raj ? Do the priests contemn you as one who has fallen into sin, or as a virtuous woman contemns one who is drawn after a harlot ? He who does not destroy a Minister, who is deep, artful, and ambitious, and who delights in accusing other Ministers, is himself destroyed : Have you appointed one who is heroic, patient, determined, pure, noble, able, and devoted to your person, to be your General ? Have you honoured with proper rewards those persons who are valiant and distinguished, eminent in war, and of tried abilities ? Do you issue the pay and food of your troops in proper manner, and immediately they have become due ? When the distribution of pay and provisions is protracted beyond the proper time, servants become enraged against their masters, and great undertakings are often frustrated : Are all those who are of good family and the chief among the people, well affected towards you? Would they unite in sacrificing their lives for you ? O Bharata, is your Ambassador learned and active, able to reply on the spot to any question ? Is he a man of judgment, and one who will repeat a message in the terms in which it was delivered to him ? Do you know the officers of Government to be on your side when you send them to a foreign country, and when they are unacquainted with each others' commission ? Do you think lightly of foes who are weak and driven away, and who are yet always returning ? Do you disregard those Bráhmans who are given up to the pleasures of the senses, and who are so much engrossed in the pleasures of the world that they have no time to look after things divine ? Do you disregard those who are eminent in useless knowledge, babes

esteeming themselves learned, who whilst they have all the HISTORY OF
chief treatises on the duties of men before them, are stupidly
ignorant; who having gained a smattering of logic, proclaim
themselves to be wise without learning? Do you protect Protection of
the fair and extensive city of Ayodhyá, justly termed invincible; which was inhabited in former times by our heroic
predecessor, whose name is truth; and which is defended by
strong gates, and filled with horses, and with thousands of
excellent Bráhmans, Kshatriyas, and Vaisyas, all cheerful,
intent upon their proper calling, and superior to their appe-
tites; which city is also adorned with temples of various
forms, and inhabited by men skilled in the Vedas? O Bha- Protection of
rata, are the country districts duly protected? Are the hus- districts.
bandmen and herdsmen duly esteemed by you? Are their
circumstances easy? Are they protected by officers of
justice duly appointed by you? Are all the householders
duly protected? Do you behave with courtesy to all women?
Do you disregard the counsel of women and refrain from Female counsel.
communicating your secrets to them? Is the forest well Stock of ele-
kept where the royal elephants are maintained? Have you a and horses.
stock of new milch cows? Are you well furnished with
female elephants and horses? Do you rise at the early dawn,
and constantly show yourself adorned to the people? Are
all the workmen in your presence without fear, and do they
attend to their business when you are absent? Are your Forts.
Forts well stored with riches, grain, arms, water, and
machines; and are they well furnished with artificers and
bowmen? Is your expenditure smaller than your income? Finances.
Are your treasures spent among persons unfit to receive
them? Do you expend your wealth among the Bráhmans,
and needy strangers, and the soldiers, or do you squander
it amongst your friends? If a Chieftain be apprehended is Corrupt ad-
he set at liberty by a bribe? In a cause between a rich man justice.
and a poor one are the learned judges above the desire of
gain? O Bharata, the tears which fall from those who are unjustly condemned will destroy the children and the cattle of
him who governs with partiality? Do you seek to gain the
affections of young and old, and try to increase your Raj, and

HISTORY OF
INDIA.
PART IV.

acquire land and wealth by every lawful means ? Do you
bow to your spiritual guide, to the aged, to devotees, to the
gods, to strangers, to sacred groves, and to all Bráhmans
who are perfected by education ? Do you sacrifice wealth
to virtue, or virtue to wealth, or both to favouritism, avarice,
and sensuality ? O Bharata, do you divide your time with
due regard to recreation, public business, and moral duties ?
Do the Bráhmans, as well as the citizens and people of the
country, express their wishes for your good ? Do you abhor
atheism, deceit, and anger, and guard against any neglect of
your own affairs ? Do you perform all the duties of Rajas ?
A Raja who governs with justice a Raj which is surrounded
with difficulties, will gain heaven when he leaves this
world."

Ráma demands
the reason of
Bharata's com-
ing.

When Ráma had thus addressed Bharata, he began also
to say :—" I wish to hear on what account you have come
into this country in the habit of a devotee: Tell me, I pray
you, why you have abandoned the newly-acquired Raj, and
entered the forest with the antelope's skin and matted

Bharata in-
forms him of
the death of
Dasaratha.

hair ? " Bharata replied with joined hands :—" O excellent
one, my valiant father, having sent you into exile at the
instance of my mother Kaikeyí, has departed to heaven
overwhelmed with grief : O chief of men, I pray you to
accept the Raj, but first arise and perform the rites of water
for thy father: Satrughna and myself have already offered
water: O Ráma, you were indeed the beloved of your
father ; through grief on your account, and the desire of
seeing you, he has departed to the mansions of Indra."

At this afflicting account of his father's death, as dreadful as the thunderbolt cast by Indra at the Dánavas, Ráma
sank upon the ground like a tree which has been felled by the
axe. Sítá and his brothers sprinkled him with water, and
when he was somewhat revived, he said to Bharata :—

" What shall I do in Ayodhyá now that my father has gone
to heaven ? Who shall nourish Ayodhyá, now that she is
bereft of the best of Rajas ? Happy are you, O Bhárata
and Satrughna, by whom his funeral ceremonies have been
performed ! When my forest residence is over, from whom

shall I hear the words with which my father was accus-
tomed to cheer me?" Ráma then turned to Sítá, and
said:—"O Sítá, your father-in-law is dead! O Laksh-
mana, you are fatherless! Bharata has related the afflict-
ing story of the departure of the Mahárája to heaven!"
And whilst Ráma was thus speaking, the tears fell in
abundance from all eyes.

At length the younger brethren said to Ráma :—"Let
the funeral libations of your father, the Mahárája, be now
performed!" Then Ráma, accompanied by his brethren,
walked down into the beautiful river Mandákiní, and
descended into that sacred stream which is free from mud,
and sprinkled water on account of the Mahárája, saying :—
"O Dasaratha, may this be thine!" Ráma then filled his
two joined palms with water, and turning his face to the
south quarter, sacred to Yama, he said :—"O Raja of Rajas,
may this pure imperishable water given to you by me always
quench your thirst in the region of spirits!" Afterwards,
the renowned Ráma came out of the sacred waters of the
river, and performed the customary offering together with
his brethren. Having made a cake of the pulp of the fig-
tree, and of such other materials as could be procured in
the forest, he spread it upon the sacred kuśa grass, and
said :—"O Mahárája, eat with pleasure the viands which
we eat ourselves; for that which is the nourishment of man
is likewise the nourishment of his deity." Ráma then left
the bank of the river, and returned to the door of his hut,
taking hold of Bharata and Lakshmana with both his
hands.

Meanwhile the army of Bharata heard the lamentations
of the brethren and of Sítá re-echoed from the mountains
like the sound of roaring lions; and the soldiers were greatly
alarmed, and said :—" Bharata has met with Ráma, and the
brethren are bewailing their departed father." Then leav-
ing the animals and baggage, they set their faces towards
the sound, and hastened towards the place, being all with
one mind anxious to behold Ráma. The noise of their
chariot-wheels was like the rolling of thunder; and the

HISTORY OF INDIA. PART IV.

4th, Ráma's offering of obla- tions of water and funeral cakes to the soul of his de- ceased father.

The funeral cake made of the pulp of the fig-tree.

Approach of the army to behold Ráma.

Ráma's con-
descension.

Grief of
Kausalyá at
seeing the
coarse cake
which Ráma
had offered to
his father.

Grief of the
other Ránis.

Kindness of the
Ránis towards
Ráma, Laksh-
mana, and Sítá.

Ráma embraces
the feet of
Vasishtha.

5th, Second
interview be-
tween Bharata
and Ráma on
the bank of the
Mandákini.

beasts and the birds were terrified with fear and fled away. At length those soldiers beheld Ráma sitting on the sacrificial ground; and they all execrated Kaikeyí and Manthará, and burst into tears. Ráma, viewing them all deeply afflicted, embraced them like a parent; and treated all his ancient friends with the respect due to each. Meanwhile, the priest Vasishtha, being eager to behold Ráma, proceeded with the widows of Dasaratha to the place where the heroes were. Presently the Rání Kausalyá saw upon the ground the funeral cake laid in order which Ráma had prepared for his father Dasaratha, together with the kusa grass laid with their points towards the south; and Kausalyá said :—"Behold this coarse cake which the magnanimous Ráma has prepared according to the ordinance! How should the great Dasaratha, who on earth was equal to Indra, relish such an offering as the pulp of the fig-tree? There does not appear to me to be a greater wretchedness than that the mighty Ráma should offer a cake made of the pulp of the fig-tree to the spirit of his deceased father! Verily it is a true saying :—'The food which is eaten by a man is the food also of his god.'" All the widows of the deceased Maháraja then went forward and beheld Ráma, who was like a god who had fallen from heaven : and when they saw him they wept aloud overpowered with grief. The heroic Ráma then arose and fell down at the lotus-like feet of his mothers ; and the Ránís with their fair and soft hands, pleasing to the touch, wiped the dust from his back. Then Lakshmana, also beholding his afflicted mothers, bowed slowly to their feet with great affection; and all the Ránís manifested the same respect towards him as they had previously shown to Ráma. Sítá also, filled with grief, bowed down to the feet of her mothers-in-law, and stood before them; and the afflicted Ránís embraced her, who was emaciated by her residence in the jungle. Meanwhile Ráma embraced the feet of the priest Vasishtha, even as Indra embraces the feet of Vrihaspati.

Now when the night had passed away and the morning had dawned, and the brethren and their friends had performed their religious devotions on the bank of the river Mandákiní, they all sat down in a profound silence, no one uttering a word. At length Bharata addressed Ráma in the presence of all assembled, and said :—" My mother Kaikeyí having given the Raj to me, is now satisfied : This Raj, which is like a bridge broken down by a violent stream in the rainy season, I now give to you : O Ráma, wipe off the guilt of my mother's anger, and deliver your father from sin : I entreat you with my head bowed : Show that pity to me which the great Supreme shows to all his creatures : But if you turn your back upon me, and persist in going hence to the forest, lo, I will go with you ! "

Bhárata offers the Raj to Ráma.

Ráma then replied to Bharata, in the presence of all his friends and kinsmen, as follows :—" O Bharata, our father Dasaratha, at the request of your mother Kaikeyí, has appointed that I should go into exile and that you should possess the Raj : O Bharata, release the Maháraja from his obligations ! Save your father and rejoice your mother : Go with Satrughna to Ayodhyá and console the people ; whilst I with Sítá and Lakshmana enter the forest without delay : Be you, O Bharata, the Raja of men ; I will be the Raja of the wild beasts : Go you this day to the chief of cities, and I will enter the thickets of Dandaka : The royal umbrella shall shade your head from the sun, while mine shall be shaded by the trees of the wood : Satrughna of unequalled understanding will be your attendant ; and Lakshmana, renowned for fidelity and friendship, shall be mine.

Ráma refuses to depart from the arrangement ordered by his father.

At this time the sage Jáváli, the renowned logician of the deceased Maháraja, and a pious Bráhman of the highest rank, came forward, and expressed the following vicious sentiments to Ráma :—" O chief of men, may prosperity attend you : Let not the understanding of a pious devotee such as you are, be rendered as useless and centemptible as that of common people ! Having obeyed the commands of your father, you have already fulfilled all that was incumbent upon you : It ill becomes you now to prefer a life of sluggishness and stupidity, merely through attachment to virtue and austerities, and contempt for the possession of a Raj : Attend,

Atheistical speech of Jáváli the logician.

"Whilst your father was alive you obeyed his commands, but now that he is dead they are no longer binding.

my lord, to my words ! Bharata, to whom the Raj was given
by your father, himself entreats you to take possession of
it : Kaikeyí, on whose account this injury was done to
you by your father, herself gives the Raj to you : Accept,
therefore, the Raj in the presence of your subjects, and
render your own people happy : It is not right for you
to cherish any longer this false idea of obedience to the
dead, which is disapproved by the wise, and is the mere

"The relation-
ship of parents
to their children
is only tempor-
ary, like that of
the inn to the
passing travel-
ler.

offspring of your own imagination : It is not becoming
that your father, who has departed to heaven, should be kept
in continual expectation of your performing the duties of a
son : His soul has left this body and now resides in another ;
how then can he who inhabits another body have any claim
upon you ? A man is born alone and perishes alone ; his
parents resemble an inn, at which he resides for a time and
then departs ; and silly is he who fixes his heart upon a
temporary abode : As a traveller sleeps for one night under
a mango tree and next morning takes his departure ; so the
parents, and the possessions, and the wealth of a man are as
a mere temporary residence : Why then, O Ráma, forsake a
road which is smooth, free from dust, and secure from all
danger, for an evil road abounding with thorns ? Cause
yourself to be installed in the rich city of Ayodhyá : The
city, like a wife whose husband is absent, is anxiously expecting your return ; and it is for you to taste the choice

"Take your
pleasure in this
mortal life of
which we know
something, and
trouble not
respecting the
life hereafter of
which we know
nothing.

delights of the Raj : Take your pleasure then, O hero, as
Indra takes pleasure in his celestial abode : Dasaratha is
nothing to you, nor are you anything to him, he is one
person and you are another ; follow therefore the advice of
your friends : A father is the production of an animal, man
is produced by his father and mother : Our mortal life in this
world is the whole of our being, and by your refusal of the
Raj you are destroying yourself in vain : I grieve not for
those who aspire to wealth and happiness in this world, but

"I grieve for
those who
sacrifice the
substantial hap-
piness of this
life for a vision-
ary happiness
hereafter.

I grieve for those who despise these solid blesings whilst
living, and waste their time for the sake of happiness in a
future life which has no existence ; for after a life of trouble
and distress they only sink at death into utter annihilation :

Men, it is true, offer funeral cakes in honour of their departed ancestors, but this is merely a spoiling of food : Say, what will a dead man eat ? Can what is eaten by one go into the body of another ? How can the soul of a father eat the funeral cakes which are offered by a son ? It will not stand to reason, and is merely the work of fancy : If the soul is immortal, the moment it leaves one body it goes to animate another : How then can it eat the cake when it inhabits another form, and when that cake is in commemoration of the old form ? If you say that the cakes being eaten by the cows is tantamount to their being eaten by the soul of the father, then a cake offered to the memory of a friend who is still living but in a remote country, and afterwards given to a cow, and eaten by it, will thereon satisfy the hunger of that distant friend : Books have been written by learned men for the sake of inducing others to make offerings and presents, and their doctrine is : ' Perform sacrifices and make offerings, and consecrate yourselves, and undertake religious austerities, and bestow gifts : ' But a future state has no existence save in this world, and it is the present state which is the chief good : O Ráma, be wise ! That which is manifest to the senses is the grand object of pursuit, because of such things we have direct proof; and those which are not present to the senses may be thrown behind your back ; because the only proof we have of their existence is indirect and inferential : Adopting the sound judgment of the wise, and regarding that which is sought by all, do you accept the Raj : Rajas and heroes of great renown have left their beloved children and wives, and sunk under the stern hand of death ; but we have no assurance, O Ráma, whether they have become Gandharvas, or Yakshas; we know not what they are nor whither they are gone : Their names and lineage are rehearsed, and wherever any one would fain have them, there he conceives them to be : The whole universe is involved in uncertainty : Men eminent for virtue fail to obtain happiness : The virtuous suffer great afflictions, while the wicked appear to be happy indeed : Everything that exists will pass away, and the whole world is in a state

HISTORY OF INDIA.
PART IV.

" Men, it is true, offer cakes to their dead ancestors, but how can those ancestors eat them ? If the soul is immortal it must have passed into a new form which cannot eat the cake.

" If, indeed, the eating of the cake by the cows satisfies the hunger of a dead father, it might also satisfy the hunger of a distant friend.

" Our existence in this mortal life is our chief good, but we have no proof of the future, and it is therefore nothing to us.

" Of those who are already dead we know nothing.

" The whole universe is in disorder, for the wicked are often happy whilst the good are often miserable

HISTORY OF
INDIA.
PART IV.

"Therefore
accept the
Raj!"
Wrathful reply
of Ráma:—
"I will not
disobey my
dead father,
whom I obeyed
when living.

of disorder : Therefore, O Ráma, do not despise the good
fortune which has approached so near to you, but take possession of this great Raj, which has no equal in all the
world."

Ráma, slow to anger, was filled with wrath at these atheistical arguments of the subtle Jáváli ; and thus he answered
the skilful Bráhman :—"Trained up to filial obedience, I will
no more depart from my father's commands than a well-disci-
plined horse leaves the road, or an obedient wife forsakes her
lord : If, after obeying the words of my father while he was
living, I were to act otherwise now that he is dead, should I
not be deemed devoid of all principle ? But I can no more
be moved by your vain words than a mountain can be

"Your words
are as deleteri-
ous as wine.

moved by the wind : Your words resemble a pot of wine,
which is pleasant and delicious to the taste, but most
injurious in its effects : You have even pleaded that there is
no such thing as future happiness ; that all the happiness we

"If there is no
future state,
why are the
vicious cen-
sured ?

can enjoy we enjoy in this mortal life : If that be the case,
why should men censure the vicious and the debauched, for
they are only carried away by their love of pleasure, that
most contemptible of all the affections : Why do the sages
then live upon roots and fruits, instead of enjoying flesh and

"If you demand
direct proof, a
woman is a
widow in her
husband's
absence, and
astronomy
teaches nothing.
"But Indra
obtained
sovereignty by
his sacrifices,
and sages have
been glorified
through their
austerities.

wine ? If you admit of no inferential or indirect proof, a
woman ought, according to your notions, to be a widow the
moment her husband is out of her sight : Astronomy and
other sciences would fall to the ground, for most of their laws
are based upon inference : Did not Indra, the sovereign of
the gods, obtain his celestial Raj by the performance of a
hundred sacrifices ? How can this proof be evaded by you ?
Kusika, the son of Atri, is another proof ; he and other great
sages have obtained an eminent degree of glory by the performance of sacrifices and practice of religious austerities,
which, according to what you say, are useless pursuits : But

"I will obey my
father!"

be it even as you say, I will still adhere to the commands of
my father, as a great sage inflexibly adheres to his vows :
Let Bharata govern the Raj which has been given to him !
I desire not the Raj which has been prohibited to me by the
Maháraja."

Whilst the sons of Dasaratha were thus conversing, surrounded by their friends, the day was spent and the night also passed away ; and when the brethren had separately performed their morning devotions, Bharata went again to Ráma, and entreated him to accept the Raj. Then Ráma, still bearing in mind the words of Jáváli, thus spoke :—" Jáváli applauds as right both the noble and the ignoble, the real hero and the pretended one, the pure and the impure : According to him the bad man is equal to the good one, the evil disposition with the good disposition : If I, deceived by false reasoning, were thus to confound good and evil, I should abandon that which is good, and sink into a state of lawless confusion : Who would then look with approval upon me, and how should I obtain heaven ? Moreover, the whole nation would then have no other rule but their own passions ; since the principles of a Raja, whatever they may be, become the principles of his subjects : Truthfulness and benevolence are the eternal duties of a Raja ; by these virtues an example is set to the whole Raj, and the nation is established in truthfulness : The gods and sages esteem truth as invincible ; and the man who always speaks the truth in this world obtains an imperishable reward : I recollect with pain, O Jáváli, the act of my father which accepted you, a man of grovelling mind, who art governed by these infidel ideas ; an atheist who has fallen from the path of rectitude ! As a thief is, so is a Buddhist ; after them are the Hastikas or atheists. He who is seeking the good of his subjects, will not, if he be a man of understanding, stand in the presence of an atheist : The Bráhmans, constantly setting before them this life and the next, offer peace offerings and burnt offerings : Those sages also are revered by men, who are zealous in the cause of virtue, the companions of the good, full of sacred energy, pre-eminent in charity and every good quality, never doing evil towards others, and purified from all moral defilement."

The frank and magnanimous Ráma, having thus spoken words full of conviction, the Bráhman Jáváli thus addressed to him a speech fraught with propriety and religion :—" I

HISTORY OF
INDIA.
PART IV.

6th, Third interview between Bhárata and Ráma.

Ráma renews the discussion.

"Jáváli confounds right and wrong, and if I did the same I should be censured by all, whilst the people of the Raj would follow my example.

"Truthfulness and benevolence are the eternal duties of a Raja.

"I regret that my father should have promoted a Buddhist and an atheist.

"No virtuous Rája will stand in the presence of an atheist."

Jáváli, convinced by Ráma's reasoning, recants his atheistical opinions.

by no means speak the sentiments of an atheist, for I am no atheist: Now that the fitting opportunity offers I will lay aside my atheistical disguise : As atheistical sentiments were introduced by me, O Ráma, for the sake of turning you from your purpose, so sentiments of piety and religion are now uttered to conciliate your favour."

Vasishtha then said to Ráma :—" Jáváli is deeply versed in the customs of the world; he has thus spoken, O Ráma, through his desire of turning you back to Ayodhyá : You are known to be the son and heir of Maháraja Dasaratha ; accept therefore your own Raj, O Sovereign of the world, and look upon us with compassion : Amongst all the race of Ikshwáku, the eldest son is constantly Raja : A younger son cannot be anointed Raja whilst the elder son lives ; the eldest must be Rája : It is not proper for you to violate this day the sacred custom of the family of Ikshwáku : There are three persons to whom every one who is born is bound to yield implicit deference ; namely, his father, his mother, and his preceptor : A father begets, a mother nourishes, but a preceptor instructs ; the preceptor is therefore said to be entitled to implicit regard : I was the preceptor of your father, and now I am your preceptor ; and you will not transgress the Sástras if you obey my directions : Moreover, it is not right for you to disobey your pious and aged mother : O Ráma, in obeying her words you will not step out of the path of virtue ; nor in acceding to the prayer of Bharata, will you violate truth, or justice, or abuse your power."

Ráma dilates
upon the claims
of parents to the
obedience of
their sons, and
refuses to dis-
obey the Ma-
hárája.

Ráma, thus mildly addressed by his preceptor Vasishtha, who was seated near him, replied as follows :—" What parents constantly do for a son can never be recompensed : The tenderness of a father and a mother in rearing their children, in bathing and clothing them, in constantly giving them excellent counsel, and in training them up in virtue, can never be repaid : What, therefore, my father has commanded me, shall not be rendered ineffectual."

When Bharata heard these words of his elder brother, he said to Sumantra :—" O Charioteer, speedily spread kusa grass on this spot which has been prepared for sacrifice : I will sit opposite to Ráma until he be gracious to me: As a Bráhman, deprived of his wealth, lies before the door of a creditor, without food and without beholding any one, so will I sit here until Ráma return with me to Ayodhyá." Then looking at Sumantra, who was spreading the kusa grass, Bharata seated himself upon the ground.[5]

Then Ráma said to his brother :—" O beloved Bharata, *Ráma reproves Bharata.* what evil am I perpetrating that you thus seat yourself against me? For a Bráhman thus to confine a debtor by sitting down before him is right; but for Rajas to sit in dharná against each other, is not according to the law : Rise then, O chief of men, and abandon this cruel vow, and quickly return to the city of Ayodhyá." Then Bharata *Bharata appeals to the people to compel Ráma to accept the Raj.* turned to the citizens of Ayodhyá, and the people of the Raj, who had accompanied him to Chitra-kúta, and said :— " Why, O people, do you not lay your injunctions upon Ráma?" The citizens and subjects replied :—" We well *The people hesitate.* understand what is said by the magnanimous Ráma : You, O Bharata, also speak with reason : But Ráma is engaged in performing his father's word; and we are unable to say anything in haste." At these words Ráma said to Bharata :— " Rise, O valiant one, and touch me and also touch water, that you may be purified from the guilt of sitting down to starve out your brother." And Bharata arose and touched *Bharata offers to go into exile in the room of Ráma.* water, and said :—" Hear, all ye counsellors, and ministers, and people ! I do not desire the Raj of my father, nor did I desire my mother to ask it for me, nor was I the cause of the exile of Ráma : If some one must fulfil my father's word and reside in the forest for fourteen years, let it be me." Then *Ráma refuses to alter his determination, but promises to govern the Raj after his exile.* Ráma spoke in like manner to the people and citizens, as follows :—" Whatever was bought, pledged, or sold by my

---

[5] Dharná was a strange custom, by which a creditor sat at the door or tent of a debtor, to compel payment of an ordinary debt, or of arrears owing by a public officer or prince. The person so sitting observes a strict fast, and under such circumstances the person from whom he demands payment is compelled to fast also, and abstain from his usual occupations and amusements. If the suitor perished, the guilt of murder fell upon the debtor. Originally, the person sitting in dharná was necessarily a Bráhman, either on his own behalf or on that of another, and the sin of Brahmanicide would be incurred by his death. The practice is obsolete in British territory, having been made a punishable offence.

father whilst alive, cannot be annulled by me or by Bharata :
I have no occasion for a substitute to dwell in the forest in
my place, for what was advised by Kaikeyí was well done
by my father : I know Bharata has resigned his right, and
seeks the good of his superiors ; and after my return from
my exile, I shall be able with this pious brother to govern
the Raj with honour : The Maháraja will then be discharged
from his obligation to Kaikeyí, and his words will have been
fulfilled by me."

The sages confirm the resolution of Ráma.

The great sages who were present at the meeting of the
two most illustrious brothers, were astonished at the words
of Ráma, and their hair stood erect with joy ; and they came
to Bharata, and said :—" O Bharata, if you regard your
father, you must respect the words of Ráma : We wish that
your father's Raj may be absolved from every debt : Dasaratha has ascended to heaven through his determination to
discharge his obligation to Kaikeyí." Bharata then took a

Bharata presents Ráma with a pair of shoes, and requests him to wear them.

pair of new shoes, adorned with gold, and turned to his
brother Ráma, and said :—" Put on these shoes, I pray you,
and they shall furnish the means of securing the good of
all." The heroic Ráma then put on the shoes, and pulled
them off, and returned them to the magnanimous Bharata.

Declares he will rule the Raj through the shoes.

And Bharata bowed to the shoes, and said to Ráma :—" O
Ráma, I will for fourteen years assume the matted hair and
the habit of a devotee, and subsist on fruits and roots :
Waiting your return, I will commit the management of the
Raj to your shoes, and reside without the city : and unless
you return to Ayodhyá within five days of the completion of
the fourteenth year I will enter the fire."[6]

7th, Return of Bharata to Ayodhyá.

Ráma dismisses Bharata and Satrughna.

Return of Bharata to Ayodhyá.

Ráma then embraced his two brothers, Bharata and
Satrughna, with great respect, and dismissed them ; and
Bharata took the shoes on his head, and mounted the chariot
with Satrughna, preceded by Vasishtha, and Jáváli, and all
the counsellors. In this manner they left Chitra-kúta, and
after visiting the sage Bharadwája in their way, they at

---

[6] In the Adhyátma Rámáyana, Bharata is represented as yielding only because
Ráma privately imparted to him the mystery of his incarnation, and the divine
necessity that existed for his destroying Rávana.

length came near to the city of Ayodhyá; and the dark and melancholy city resembled a gloomy night, and was traversed by cats and owls, and bereft of elephants.   It was like the bright Rohini, when the hostile Ráhu is devouring her husband Chandra; or a mountain stream whose shallow waters have been dried up by the heat, when birds are faint with thirst, and when fishes have all disappeared; or the smokeless quivering flame of a sacrificial fire, after the sacrificial articles have been consumed; or an army stripped of its weapons, with its elephants, horses, and chariots destroyed, and all its valiant men slain; or the sea, when the foaming and roaring waves are hushed into silence by a calm; or an altar stripped of the sacrificial implements, and deprived of all its fat fruits after the sacrifice is ended; or the glad herds of kine feeding in their pasture upon young grass, when suddenly deserted by the bull; or a necklace stripped of all its most precious stones; or a star which has fallen to the earth when its merits are expended; or as a climbing plant, loaded with flowers and redolent with bees, when burnt up by a sudden fire in the jungle; or a troubled sky, when the traders fly from the bazaars in alarm, and leave their merchandise behind; [or a tavern, when the liquor is all expended, and the house broken down and nothing remains but the fragments of broken pots[7]]; or a resting-place where water is given to the thirsty traveller, when the building is levelled with the ground, and the water all spent; or a bow-string which drops from the bow when cut with a swifter arrow; or a war-horse ridden by a warrior eager for the battle, which is suddenly slain by an enemy; or a fiery colt heavily laden and fallen under his burden; or the clear light of the sun when obscured by a dark cloud in the rainy season.   The afflicted Bharata, having thus brought all his mothers back to Ayodhyá, then said to his preceptors:—"I will now go to Nandigráma, which is without the city, and there I will dwell until Ráma returns and takes possession of the Raj" And the words of Bharata were praised by his mothers and his preceptors;

HISTORY OF INDIA.
PART IV.

Gloomy appearance of the city described in a succession of Hindú similes.

Bharata resides at Nand gráma in the guise of a devotee, and rules the Raj under the authority of Ráma's shoes.

---

[7] This passage in brackets does not occur in the North-West recension.

and he speedily proceeded to Nandigráma with the shoes upon his head, and said to his assembled subjects :—" Bring hither the State umbrella ! By these shoes of my elder brother is justice established in the Raj." Thus lamenting, the renowned but afflicted Bharata, together with his Counsellors, governed the Raj at Nandigráma. Assuming the bark dress and the matted hair of a devotee, the hero Bharata dwelt with the army at Nandigráma. Bharata, thus faithful to his word and promise, being installed together with the shoes, continued to reside at Nandigráma, waiting for the return of Ráma ; himself holding the royal umbrella over the shoes, whilst the chámara was taken by Satrughna ; and all affairs of the Government were transacted under the authority of the shoes. The fortunate Bharata, installed with the shoes of his elder brother, and paying homage to them, thus governed the Raj. All the presents that were brought, and all the business of State which occurred, he first laid before the shoes, and afterwards did as occasion required.

Review of the
foregoing nar-
rative of Ráma's
refusal of the
Raj.

The incidents in the foregoing narrative are so valuable and suggestive, as to demand a careful consideration. Fresh traces will be found of the process by which a Kshatriya tradition has been converted into a Brahmanical legend ; whilst the vivid expression of ideas, which are as prevalent amongst the Hindús of the present day as at any former period, imparts a peculiar significance to the entire story.

Hindú idea of
wedded hap-
piness involved
in the amuse-
ments of Ráma
and Sítá upon
the hill Chitra-
kúta.

The first picture presented to the eye is that of Ráma and Sítá taking their pleasure upon the mountain. The description of the amusements of the happy pair upon this occasion is undoubtedly pretty from a Hindú point of view, but it indicates the low conception which the Hindús have formed of the married state. A pair of lovers, to say nothing of newly-married couples, may doubtless find much pleasure in wandering together in the country amongst trees and flowers; and under such circumstances they are highly susceptible of the beauties of natural scenery. But the language of Ráma is that of a priggish youth to a very young girl; whilst that of Sítá illustrates the utter want of mental culture in Hindú wives, beyond the rare art of listening with patience to the self-satisfied remarks of an ignorant and self-sufficient husband. But still wherever nature asserts herself through the affections, she always excites a sympathetic admiration; and the scene in which Sítá is called upon to embrace her spouse, as the climbing plant clings to the tree, and the gentle mirth of the young wife at seeing the painted ornament on her forehead impressed upon the chest of Ráma, are touches of nature which make the wide world kin. The scene in which Ráma and Sítá wreathe ornaments of flowers for each other to wear, is equally admired by an oriental audience, but falls far short of the European ideal, in which more rational pleasures are expected, even on a holiday, from all who have outgrown the age of childhood.

The description of Ráma's hut as it appeared to Bharata, is a curious specimen of that strange mixture of military pursuits and religious worship which finds expression in the Brahmanical conception of the Kshatriya hero. The bows and arrows, the scimitars and the shields, are all in perfect accordance with what is known of Kshatriya tradition, and conformable to the idea of Ráma as a warrior; but they will scarcely harmonize with the Brahmanical conception of a devotee with matted hair, arrayed in the garb of an ascetic, and sitting by the altar on

Puerile character of the dialogue.

Pretty touches of nature.

Mixture of military pursuits and religious worship involved in the description of Ráma's hut.

HISTORY OF
INDIA.
PART IV.

which the fire of sacrifice is supposed to be ever burning. Clergymen may have fought for King Charles, and Cromwell's Ironsides may have spent their leisure in preaching and prayer; but in the

Character of a devotee super-added to that of an archer.

present instance it is obvious that the character of a devotee is superadded to that of the archer, for the artificial purpose of representing the hero who slew the Rákshasas as the divine incarnation of Vishnu.

Generous contest involved in the interviews between Bharata and Ráma.

The interviews between Bharata and Ráma are intended to exhibit a generous contest between the brothers, in which Bharata entreats the elder brother to accept the Raj, whilst Ráma insists upon the paramount duty of filial obedience which compels him to remain fourteen years in exile. The outline of the story comprises much graphic description. The approach of the army and alarm of the wild beasts; the blue smoke arising from the hermitage; the doubts and fears of Ráma and Lakshmana; and the approach of Bharata, accompanied only by Satrughna, Sumantra, and Guha;—are all described with considerable truthfulness to nature.[8] But the dia-

Strained and artificial character of the dialogues.

logues are strained and artificial, and are marred by the introduction of much extraneous matter. In the original also there is much repetition, which has, however, been cut away from the foregoing version. The speech of Ráma to Bharata at the first interview contains many suggestive references, but is altogether out of place under the circumstances in which it is

---

[8] The march of an army through an Indian jungle, which perchance has never been entered by soldiery within the memory of man, frequently excites the most ludicrous alarm in what are called great game. A huge beast will suddenly rush out of its lair, and face the advancing lines, in evident astonishment. It will then move on in front, occasionally turning round and gazing in wonder and indignation at the unexpected invaders, and then running on again, tossing its head in wrath and perplexity at the sudden intrusion.

said to have been delivered. The rules for the right conduct of Rajas are indicated in the form of questions with sufficient clearness, and in strict accordance with Brahmanical ideas. They include the necessity for appointing wise, intelligent, and trustworthy Counsellors; the evils of untimely sleep; the necessity for secresy; the advantage of employing learned men; the duty of appointing a good Minister and punishing a bad one; the duty of appointing an able General; the duty of giving rewards for eminent services; the very important and significant duty of issuing the pay and provisions with due punctuality and regularity to the troops; the qualifications necessary in an ambassador; the worthlessness of self-indulgent, ignorant, and heterodox Bráhmans; the duty of treating all women with courtesy, whilst neglecting their advice, and withholding from them all secrets. But to represent a young Prince of seventeen as questioning a brother of his own age as to the fulfilment of these duties, and this too at the moment of meeting him unexpectedly in the jungle, is an extravagance for which the Brahmanical bard is alone responsible.

HISTORY OF
INDIA.
PART IV.
____
Ráma's speech
on the duties of
Rajas an inter-
polation.

The distress of Ráma on hearing of the death of his father, and his simple offerings to the soul of the deceased Maháraja, are more appropriate to the occasion. The sprinkling of water, and the offering of a funeral cake or ball to the spirit of a deceased parent, are regarded as a paramount duty throughout India, and are supposed to refresh the soul of the departed, and ultimately release it from the hell or purgatory known as pát. The speciality in Ráma's case is, that in his wretched life in the jungle, he could find nothing better than the pulp of the fig-

Simple cha-
racter of the
sprinkling of
water and offer-
ing of a cake to
the soul of the
deceased
Maháraja.

tree from which to make his funeral cake; a circumstance which seems to have specially excited the
sympathy of his mother Kausalyá.   It is, however,
difficult to reconcile the account of the misery and
privations endured by Ráma and Sítá in the jungle,
with the pretty picture of their sports upon the hill,
and evening meal upon venison, which is described
in the opening of the present chapter.

Character of
Jáváli as a
Bráhman of the
Niyáya or logical
school of
Gótama.

The second interview between Bharata and
Ráma, at which Jáváli, the free-thinking Bráhman,
endeavours to shake Ráma's resolution to refuse the
Raj, is apparently an interpolation, but is also one
of a very valuable character.   Jáváli is said to have
been a logician, and therefore seems to have belonged to the Niyáya, or logical school of Gótama;

A representa-
tive of Budd-
hism and
atheism.

and he is put forward as a representative of Buddhism
and atheism, whose false doctrine is exposed by
Ráma, and who is ultimately compelled to recant.

Drift of Jáváli's
reasoning.

The drift of Jáváli's reasoning appears to be to the
following effect.   There is no proof whatever of a

No proof that
death is any-
thing but anni-
hilation.

future state of existence; as far as we know, death
is nothing but annihilation; consequently man is not
justified in sacrificing the substantial pleasures of this
life for the sake of a visionary happiness after death.

If the soul ex-
ists hereafter it
must be in
another form,
which destroys
the relation-
ship between
parents and
sons.

Even granted that the soul does exist hereafter, it
can only exist in a form different from that of its
earthly body.   In other words, if death does not an-
nihilate the soul, it certainly destroys the relationship between parents and children; so that a parent
who is dead, and who consequently has become some-
body else, can have no claim to the obedience of his
living sons, who remain as they were.   Therefore it
is absurd for Ráma to refuse the pleasures of sove-

reignty merely for the sake of fulfilling a duty to a father who has ceased to be a relation.

In the course of his argument Jáváli finds it necessary to indicate the utter uselessness of the general custom of performing a sráddha; that is, of offering funeral cakes to the souls of dead men. A dead body, he seems to say, cannot possibly eat cakes; and as for the soul, if it exists at all, it can only exist in another body; and how can the new body eat the cake which is offered up in commemoration of the old body? Jáváli next alludes to the custom of disposing of the cakes in question, by giving them to be eaten by cows; which custom was in accordance with a popular belief that the eating of the cakes by so sacred an animal was tantamount to their being eaten by the deceased ancestor. He says with some truth and considerable smartness, that if the eating of a cake by the cows will satisfy the hunger of a dead man, it might in like manner be made to satisfy the hunger of a friend in a distant country.

Review of the reasoning of Jáváli against the performance of a sráddha.

Absurdity of supposing that the eating of cakes by cows is tantamount to the eating of the cakes by the soul of the deceased relative.

Some expressions, however, appear to have been put into the mouth of Jáváli, which such a philosopher could scarcely have uttered, and which were probably introduced for the purpose of rendering Ráma's subsequent refutation the more conclusive. Thus he is made to rail against sacrifices, not from the Buddhist point of view that the slaughter of animals was contrary to the eternal principle of benevolence; but because sacrifices and all other religious observances were utterly useless, inasmuch as they referred to a future state of the soul which had no real existence. Then again he is represented

Expressions put into the mouth of Jáváli to render his refutation more conclusive.

Peculiar argument against sacrifice.

Inutility of virtue.

by inference as impugning the utility of virtue, because the wicked were often happy whilst the good
were often miserable ; and this argument seems to be
adduced for the purpose of enforcing the view that
Ráma would be justified in accepting the Raj, or in
other words, that he would be justified in looking to
happiness alone without regarding his duty to his

Strained appli-
cation of Jáváli's
views to Ráma's
acceptance of
the Raj.

father. But this particular application of Jáváli's
views to the propriety of Ráma's acceptance of the
Raj, seems strained and artificial throughout; whilst
the form in which these views are expressed is a palpable misrepresentation of the school to which Jáváli
belonged, and could only have been adopted for the
purpose of rendering the sect hateful in the eyes of

Phenomena
that the wicked
are often happy,
and the good
often miserable,
an argument in
favour of a
future state.

the populace. Moreover the phenomena that the
wicked are often happy, whilst the good are often
miserable, are usually brought forward by the be-
lievers in the immortality of the soul as proofs of the
necessity for the existence of a future state, in which
the inequalities which prevail in this present life
might be finally corrected, and the great riddle as
to the object of human existence be finally solved.
On the other hand, a rational disbeliever in the soul's
immortality would be more inclined to defend his
scepticism by urging that a habit of virtue is a
source of greater happiness to mankind in the
present life than a habit of vice; and that the practice
of either virtue or vice was wholly unaffected by a
belief or otherwise in a future state of existence.

Dogmatic cha-
racter of Ráma's
reply to Jáváli.

The reply of Ráma is couched in that dogmatic
language which is so frequently employed in defending
a conventional belief against the objections of sceptics.
He denounces the insidious language of Jáváli ; he
dilates upon the duty of filial obedience ; and he con-

founds happiness with pleasure by insinuating that if
mankind are to devote themselves to present happiness,
the vicious would be no longer open to censure, since
they would be only carried away by a love of pleasure.
As regards the value of inferential proof, the reasoning of Ráma is of more weight.   He says, unless inferential proof be admitted, a wife becomes a widow
the moment her husband is out of her sight, and the
science of astronomy falls to the ground.   Indeed,
there can be no question that the error of Jáváli
arose from his ignoring those inferential proofs upon
which mankind in general base their belief in the
existence of the soul after death.   But the proofs adduced by Ráma of the immortality of the soul are of
an unsatisfactory nature, being drawn from the historical element in Hindú theology.   He refers to
Indra, who obtained the sovereignty of the gods by
the performance of a hundred sacrifices, and to the
sages who obtained great glory by those very sacrifices and austerities which Jáváli despised; proofs
which might appear perfectly valid to the Hindú,
but would be rejected as unduly assumed propositions by all who disbelieved in Hinduism.   Finally
he declares that Jáváli confounds virtue and vice,
right and wrong; and that if he were himself to
carry out the same views, and accept the Raj, his
subjects would henceforth follow his example and
obey no rule which interfered with the gratification
of their desires.

The important point in this controversy, and one
which will be further considered hereafter, is that
Ráma is put forward as a champion of the Bráhmans
against the Buddhists; and that this polemical character is superadded to his heroic character as pro-

Confusion of
happiness with
pleasure.

Rejection of
inferential
proof, the
source of
Jáváli's error.

Ráma's proofs
of the immor-
tality of the
soul, to be
treated as un-
duly assumed
premises.

Polemical cha-
racter of Ráma
as a champion
of the Bráh-
mans against
the Buddhists,
superadded to
his heroic cha-
racter as pro-
tector of the
Bráhmans
against the
Rákshasas.

tector of the Bráhmans against the Rákshasas.
Accordingly the question arises of whether the
Buddhists are not identical with the Rákshasas of
the Rámáyana, and this question can only be solved
by the production of further evidence which will appear in the sequel.

Exaggeration in
the account of
Bharata's pro-
ceedings on
Ráma's refus-
ing the Raj.
The proceedings of Bharata on receiving Ráma's
final determination not to accept the Raj, are no
doubt exaggerated for the sake of effect, but at the
same time are characterized by one or two incidents
Threat to sit in
dharná.
which are deserving of notice. In the first instance
Bharata threatened that he would sit in dharná
against Ráma; a Brahmanical proceeding which in
former days was a frequent source of oppression, but
which in modern times has been put down by law.
Ráma accordingly pointed out to Bharata that although a Bráhman might sit in dharná against a
debtor, yet it was contrary to rule for one Raja to
Curious adop-
tion of Ráma's
shoes as sym-
bolical of
sovereignty.
sit in dharná against another Raja. Subsequently
when Ráma agreed to rule the Raj after the expira-
tion of the fourteen years of exile, Bharata determined to govern Kosala in the name of Ráma; and
this he did by carrying away a pair of shoes which
had been worn by Ráma, and which he treated as
symbolical of Ráma's presence. This proceeding
does not appear to refer to any particular custom, but
it serves to indicate the peculiar tendency of the
Hindú mind to personify and symbolize. Thus
Bharata is said to have held the royal umbrella over
the shoes, whilst Satrughna fanned them with his
chámara; and the administration of affairs during
the remainder of Ráma's exile was conducted by
Bharata in the presence and under the authority of
the shoes.

CHAPTER XV.

RÁMA'S EXILE.

THE narrative of Ráma's exile in the jungle is one of the most obscure portions of the Rámáyana, inasmuch as it is difficult to discover any trace of the original tradition, or any illustration of actual life and manners, beyond the artificial life of self-mortification and self-denial said to have been led by the Bráhman sages of olden time. At the same time, however, the story throws some light upon the significance of the poem, and upon the character in which the Brahmanical author desired to represent Ráma; and consequently it deserves more serious consideration than the nature of the subject-matter would otherwise seem to imply.

According to the Rámáyana, the hero Ráma spent more than thirteen years of his exile in wandering amongst the different Brahmanical settlements, which appear to have been scattered over the country between the Ganges and the Godáveri; his wanderings extending from the hill of Chitra-kúta in Bundelkund, to the modern town of Nasik on the western side of India, near the sources of the Godáveri river, and about seventy-five miles to the north-west of Bombay. The appearance of these Brahmanical hermitages in the country far away to the south of

HISTORY OF
INDIA.
PART IV.

the Raj of Kosala, seems to call for critical inquiry. Each hermitage is said to have belonged to some particular sage, who is famous in Brahmanical tradition. But whether the sages named were really contemporaries of Ráma, or whether they could possibly have flourished at one and the same period, is

Existence of all the sages as contemporaries of Ráma, refuted.

open to serious question. It is of course impossible to fix with any degree of certainty the relative chronology of the several sages, who are said to have been visited by Ráma; but still it seems tolerably clear that some belonged to an age far anterior to that in which the Rámáyana was composed, and probably to an age anterior to that in which Ráma existed as a real and living personage; whilst, at least, one sage is to be found who could only have existed in the age during which the Rámáyana was produced in its present form. The main proofs of these in-

Long interval of time between the Rig-Veda and the Rámáyana.

ferences are as follows. An interval of many centuries seems to have elapsed between the composition of the Rig-Veda and that of the Rámáyana; a conclusion which has long been proved by the evidence of language, and is generally accepted by Sanskrit scholars.[1]

Sages said to have been contemporary with both compositions.

But three of the sages, said to have been contemporary with Ráma, namely, Viswámitra, Atri, and Agastya, are frequently mentioned in the hymns of the Rig-Veda; whilst Válmíki, the sage dwelling at Chitra-kúta, is said to have been himself the composer

Appearance of Atri as the first progenitor of the Lunar race.

of the Rámáyana. Again, the sage Atri, whom Ráma visited immediately after his departure from Chitra-kúta, appears in the genealogical list preserved in the Mahá Bhárata, as the progenitor of the Moon, and consequently as the first ancestor of the Lunar

---

[1] See Müller's Hist. of Sanskrit Literature, *passim*.

race; whilst his grandson Buddha is said to have married Ilá, the daughter of Ikshwáku, who was himself the remote ancestor of the Solar race of Ayodhyá, from whom Ráma was removed by many generations. These conclusions are not perhaps based upon absolute proof, because they are drawn from untrustworthy authorities; but still the chronological difficulties have been fully apprehended by the Pundits, and an attempt has been made to reconcile all contradictions by representing the sages to have lived thousands of years, and to have often re-appeared upon earth in different ages widely removed from each other. Modern science refuses to accept such explanations; and consequently it is impossible to escape the conclusion that if Válmíki composed the Rámáyana in the form of Sanskrit in which it has been preserved, he could not have flourished in the same age as the sages who are named in the Rig-Veda. The most probable hypothesis appears to be that the sages said to have been contemporary with Ráma are merely introduced as types or representatives of the Bráhmans, who seem to have established their influence throughout a large portion of Hindustan and the Dekhan during the age of Brahmanical revival which accompanied and followed the decline of Buddhist ascendancy.

Attempted reconciliation of the chronological difficulties by the Pundits.

Sages probably introduced as types of the Bráhmans of the Dekhan.

The next question that requires consideration is that connected with the real character of the Rákshasas, who appear in the Rámáyana as the especial enemy of the Bráhmans. It has already been seen that the illustrious exiles of the royal house of Kosala were always entertained with the utmost respect by the Bráhman sages; and that Ráma is put forward as the especial protector of the Bráh-

Inquiry into the real character of the Rákshasas of the Rámáyana.

Not to be con-
founded with
the aborigines,
or to be
regarded
as mere crea-
tions of the
imagination.

mans against the Rákshasas. It has also been seen
that the Rákshasas are not to be simply confounded
with the aboriginal population ; and that although
their appearance and attributes have been much
embellished and exaggerated by the Brahmanical
author, yet they are not to be regarded as mere
creations of the imagination, like the cannibal

The Rákshasa
empire seated in
Ceylon, but
having military
outposts to
the north of
the Dekhan.

Asuras who were conquered by Bhíma. They are
described as forming an empire, more or less civilized, having its capital in Lanká, in the island of
Ceylon ; but having military outposts in different
quarters of the Dekhan, and extending their operations as far to the northward as the right bank of

Religious and
sectarian cha-
racter of the
opposition be-
tween the
Bráhmans and
Rákshasas.

the Ganges. Moreover, their opposition to the
Bráhmans was of a religious character ; not a radical
opposition, like that of Christianity to heathenism ;
but a sectarian opposition, like that of Protestant-
ism to Roman Catholicism, in which there is generally less toleration, and infinitely more virulence, than
where the difference of religious belief is more

Rávana, a wor-
shipper of
Brahma.

thorough and complete. Rávana, the famous sovereign of the Rákshasas, is said to have been originally
a worshipper of Brahma; and probably the Rákshasas
may all be regarded as worshippers of the same ortho-

Identification
of the Ráksha-
sas with the
Buddhists.

dox deity. But yet the Rákshasas are described as
being violently opposed to the sacrifices of the Bráhmans, and as being utterly wanting in faith in sacred
things ; circumstances which seem to identify them
with the Buddhists, who flourished more or less in
India for a period of twelve centuries, namely, from
the sixth century before Christ, until the eighth cen-

Opposition be-
tween the
Rákshasas or
Buddhists, and
the Asuras or
aborigines.

tury of the Christian era ; and who established a
seat of empire in Ceylon which has continued to the
present day. Moreover, it will be seen by reference

to the complaint of the gods addressed to Brahma in reference to the incarnation of Vishnu, that Rávana oppressed not only the gods with whom the Bráhmans seem to be associated, but also the demons or Asuras, who were identified with the aborigines of the country.[2] Whilst, therefore, the Rákshasas and Asuras are occasionally confounded, yet in the present instance an opposition is indicated, such as might have been expected between the Buddhists and the aborigines of the country.

HISTORY OF INDIA. PART IV.

The polemical character of Ráma as an opponent to Buddhism, has already been put prominently forward in his controversy with Jáváli; and the light in which he will appear hereafter as a mortal enemy of Rávana, confirms the view that he was a champion of the Bráhmans against the Buddhists. Accordingly, it must for the future be borne in mind that Ráma appears in three characters in the Rámáyana, each of which has apparently no real connection with either of the others. These three characters are as follows :—

Three distinct characters of Ráma in the Rámáyana.

1st, Ráma as a mortal hero of an original and authentic tradition, in which the story seems to turn upon his being condemned to exile through the jealousy of a step-mother, and upon his being ultimately restored to the throne of his ancestors.

1st, Ráma, as a mortal hero.

2nd, Ráma as an incarnation of Vishnu, sent down from heaven at the instigation of Bráhma and the other gods, for the express purpose of destroying Rávana and the Buddhists.

2nd, Ráma, as an incarnation of Vishnu.

3rd, Ráma as a protector of the Bráhmans of the Dekhan against the Buddhists; in which capacity he

3rd, Ráma, as a champion of the Linga worshipping Bráhmans against the Buddhists.

---

[2] See ante, page 18.

appears to have been in reality a worshipper of the Linga as a form of Siva; for it is certain that the Buddhists were driven out of the Dekhan by the worshippers of the Linga, and compelled to take refuge in Ceylon.[3]

Contradiction involved between the incarnation of Vishnu and the worshipper of the Linga.

The most significant feature in the threefold character of Ráma is the strange contradiction implied in his being at once an incarnation of Vishnu and a worshipper of Siva. In olden time the fiercest antagonism prevailed between the Vaishnavas, or worshippers of Vishnu, and the Saivas, or worshippers of Siva, or Mahadeva. Ráma's character as an incarnation of Vishnu has already been sufficiently indicated; but his character as a worshipper of Siva will be more fully delineated hereafter, when it will be seen that he set up the triumphant Linga in the island of Ramiswaram, which stands about half way across the channel that separates the continent of India from the island of Ceylon. From the opposition existing between these three representations of one and the same individual, it may be inferred that there are three distinct elements in the Rámáyana, originating in three distinct periods, namely :—

Three elements in the Rámáyana corresponding to the three characters of Ráma.

1st, Ancient tradition of Ráma's exile.

1st, The ancient tradition of Ráma's exile, including the loss and recovery of his wife Sítá.

2nd, Myth of Ráma's incarnation as Vishnu.

2nd, The Vaishnava version, claiming Ráma as the divine champion of all India against the Rákshasas.

3rd, Tradition of the invasion of the Dekhan by the worshippers of the Linga.

3rd, The Saiva version, claiming Ráma as the especial hero of the Linga worshippers, who appear to have invaded the Dekhan at a remote period, and to have finally driven the Buddhists into the island of Ceylon.

---

3 See Colonel Sykes' learned report on the landed tenures in the Dekhan.

These points will form a subject of further discussion hereafter. For the present it will be sufficient to revert to the original narrative of the exile of Ráma, as it appears in the Rámáyana. This narrative comprises ten leading incidents, which may be indicated as follows:—

HISTORY OF
INDIA.
PART IV.

Ten principal
incidents in the
narrative of
Ráma's exile.

1st, Departure of Ráma, Sítá, and Lakshmana from the neighbourhood of Válmíki's hermitage at Chitra-kúta.

2nd, Journey towards the south, and visit to the sage Atri, and his wife Anasúyá.

3rd, Ráma engages to defend Atri and the other sages from the depredations of the Rákshasas in the forest of Dándaka.

4th, Visit to the hermitage of Sarabhanga, who burns himself alive on a funeral pile.

5th, Ráma engages to defend the ascetics in the neighbourhood of Sarabhanga's hermitage against the Rákshasas.

6th, Visit to the hermitage of Sutíkshna at Ramtek, near Nagpore.

7th, Dialogue between Ráma and Sítá as to the propriety of waging war against the Rákshasas.

8th, Ten years' wanderings amongst the sages in the neighbourhood of Sutíkshna's hermitage at Ramtek.

9th, Visit to the sage Agastya, near the Vindhya mountains.

10th, Residence of Ráma, Sítá, and Lakshmana at Panchavatí, the modern Nasik, on the river Godáveri.

The story of these events may now be related as follows:—

The narrative.

HISTORY OF
INDIA.
PART IV.

1st, Departure
of Ráma, Sitá,
and Lakshmana
from the neigh-
bourhood of
Válmiki's her-
mitage at
Chitra-kúta.

The sages at
Chitra-kúta
complain to
Ráma of the
persecutions of
the Rákshasas.

When Bharata had returned to Ayodhyá, Ráma saw that the devotees and sages who dwelt round about Chitra-kúta were sorely troubled; and an aged sage came forward and said to him :—" O excellent one, the fear of these devotees arises from the Rákshasas, for the Rákshasas feed on men and assume various forms : O Ráma, the wicked chieftain Khara, the younger brother of that mighty Raja Rávana who dwells at Lanká, occasions us much alarm : Khara is a terrible Rákshasa, daring, fearless, and cruel, a cannibal who regards neither age nor sex : O beloved one, these vile and deformed Rákshasas inspire terror by their dreadful forms, and annoy the devotees with unclean things, and continually molest them : They gambol in the woods and hermitages, and throw about the sacrificial implements, and spoil the sacrificial articles, and pollute the offerings with blood on every side : At times of sacrifice these wretches, who are void of all faith, rush hastily forward making a loud cry in the ears of the believing and pious devotees : They take away the pots, the flowers, the sacrificial wood, and the sacred kusa grass of those

Declare their
intention of
removing to
another locality.

who walk in the ways prescribed in the Vedas : The sages and devotees, haunted by these wicked ones, are anxious to leave these hermitages, and would fain consult with you respecting their departure to another place : A little way from hence, there is a beautiful forest abounding in fruits and roots, where I, with my companions, will take up our abode : But, O Ráma, when we have departed, Khara will fall upon you who are unprepared; if therefore it meets with your approbation, do you go with us." Having thus spoken, the venerable sage took his leave, and presently all the devotees humbly took their leave in like manner and departed out of

Solitude of the
hermitage after
the departure of
the sages.

Chitra-kúta. And when the hermitage was forsaken by all the devotees, it seemed to be inhabited only by deer and serpents; and after awhile it became overspread with gloom; and the heart of Ráma was saddened, and he said :—" I, too, will depart to another place." [4]

---

[4] In the Adhyátma Rámáyana the departure of Ráma is ascribed, not to the Rákshasas, but to the constant visits of the people of Ayodhyá in large numbers, which greatly disturbed the divine hero.

So Ráma departed out of Chitra-kúta, together with Sita and Lakshmana; and they journeyed towards the south until they came to the hermitage of the sage Atri. And Atri received them with great joy, and commanded that he should be hospitably entertained; and he called to his aged wife, the virtuous and devout Anasúyá, who had also chosen the life of a devotee, and he said to her:—"Receive Sítá, and conciliate her by giving her everything that she desires."

HISTORY OF INDIA. PART IV.

2nd, Ráma journeys southward to the hermitage of Atri.

Atri introduces his aged and devout wife Anasúyá.

Atri then said to Ráma:—"O sinless one, this my wife is a Bráhmaní renowned for her vows, devoted to severe mortification, and ever performing pious deeds: Do you regard her as your mother: By the power of her austerities, fruits and roots were produced during a ten years' drought, and the holy Gangá was brought near to our dwelling; and by her interference ten nights passed without a rising of the sun: O sinless one, regard the gentle and aged Anasúyá as your own mother, and let Sítá come into her presence." Then Ráma said to Sítá:—"Do you hear the words of the sage? Go now into the presence of Anasúyá." And Sítá approached the aged and pious wife of Atri and eagerly bowed to her feet, and with hands most respectfully joined, inquired with joyful mind respecting her health. The venerable matron said to Sítá:—"Through your good fortune, O honourable Sítá, you have abandoned your kinsfolk, and followed your husband Ráma in his exile in the wilderness: That woman who loves her husband, whether he be in the city or in the forest, in prosperity or in adversity, will obtain a great reward hereafter: O Sítá, a husband is esteemed by a virtuous woman as her supreme deity; even though he be stripped of wealth, or possess an evil disposition, or go after other women: O Sítá, there is no friend greater than a husband; an incessant attention to a husband is everywhere comely: She who is unchaste, ignorant of right and wrong, and domineering over her husband, obtains only dishonour: She who is under the dominion of evil habits, and distinguished only by her uselessness, is ruined both here and hereafter."

Miracles wrought by Anasúyá through the force of her austerities.

Interview between Anasúyá and Sítá.

Anasúyá praises Sítá for her devotion to her husband, and dilates on the duty of wives.

Thus addressed by the divine Anasúyá, Sítá replied as

Sítá replies, praising Ráma.

Ráma's virtuous
conduct towards
the Maháraja's
women.

Anasúyá gives
Sítá an oint-
ment which will
render her ever
young and
beautiful, to-
gether with
jewels and
ornaments.

follows :—"What you have said to me I have known already : Though a husband be poor and wicked, he should
ever be to his wife an object of the highest regard : But
how much more ought she to reverence him when he is applauded for his virtues, compassionate and self-subdued,
steady in his affection and loving as a parent : The virtuous
Ráma conducts himself towards the other women of the deceased Maháraja, as he does towards his own mother Kausalyá :
That hero, who bears the most affectionate regard to the
memory of the Maháraja, has ever regarded as a mother the
woman who was only once viewed by his father : The words
of my mother-in-law, when I was coming to the desolate
forest, are firmly fixed in my heart ; and so, too, are the ad-
monitions given to me by my mother when I gave my hand
to my lord in the presence of the fire : The precept incul-
cated in me that 'a woman has no greater religious duty
than that of honouring her husband,' has never, O pious
Anasúyá, been forgotten by me : She who is assiduously attentive to her husband is as sure of heaven as if she were
already there ; such a one is the chief among women, a goddess in heaven ; she resembles the goddess Rohiní, who is
never seen for a moment without her husband Chandra."
At these words of Sítá, Anasúyá was greatly pleased, and
kissing the head of Sítá, she replied exultingly :—"Through
my many religious austerities I have acquired great powers:
Depending upon these, O Sítá, I desire to confer a blessing
upon you : O beloved wife of Ráma, anoint yourself with
this divine ointment, and constantly adorn yourself with this
apparel and these ornaments, and the bloom of youth shall
remain with you for this day, and for ever : O Sítá, beauti-
fied by this ointment which is given to you by me, you shall
ever be as charming as the goddess Lakshmí, and shall ever
enrapture your husband with your beauty." [5]   Then Sítá
accepted the ointment and the jewels and the bracelets and
the apparel, which were thus given to her as tokens of

---

[5] The ointment given by Anasúyá to Sítá, which was to render her ever beautiful, is supposed by some Pundits to mean piety, or faith in Ráma, which renders
all women beautiful.

friendship; and raising her joined hands to her forehead, she did honour to the pious devotee. After this, at the request of Anasúyá, Sítá related to her the whole story of her birth and marriage; and Anasúyá, having heard the pleasing narrative, embraced and kissed Sítá, and said:—"You have related the story to me in the most delightful language: [6] The sun is set, O bright one; the pleasant night, bespangled with planets and stars, has already commenced; the birds, who were scattered abroad throughout the day in search of food, are now softly murmuring in their nests; the sages, who have been to bathe, are now returning in wetted garments; the sacrifices of the sages have been offered according to the ordinance, and the blue smoke is rising tinged with the colours of the neck of the pigeon; the trees clothed with leaves are darkening on every side, and distant objects cease to appear; the wild beasts of the night are prowling on all sides, and the deer of the forests are sleeping on the altars and sacred places; the night adorned with stars has commenced; the moon clothed with brightness has risen in the sky; I therefore now give you permission to depart, but first gratify me by adorning yourself with the divine ornaments, and then go and attend upon Ráma."

Sítá, resembling a daughter of the gods, then put on the ornaments, and bowing her head to the feet of the aged matron, she went towards Ráma; and Ráma was highly pleased at the honour done to her by the pious devotee, and rejoiced as he beheld the celestial beauty of his wife Sítá.

When the night had passed away, Ráma and Lakshmana bathed according to the ordinance, and then inquired of the devotees respecting the forest. The sages replied:—"O Ráma, the paths of this forest are overrun by man-devouring Rákshasas, and savage beasts thirsting for blood, who molest the devotees whenever they wander abroad: O Prince, depart in peace and put a stop to their depredations; and when you have returned after accomplishing your design, we shall behold you from this hermitage." Then the magnanim-

Marginal notes:
HISTORY OF INDIA. PART IV.

Anasúyá describes the approach of night in poetic language, and requests Sítá to adorn herself with the divine ornaments.

Ráma's delight at his wife's beauty.

3rd, Ráma engages to defend Atri and the other sages from the depredations of the Rákshasas in the forest of Dándaka.

Ráma, Sítá, and Lakshmana enter the forest of Dándaka.

---

[6] The ordinary conversation of Hindú women may be inferred from the delight with which Anasúyá heard the story of Sítá's marriage.

HISTORY OF
INDIA.
PART IV.

Picture of a
cluster of
Brahmanical
hermitages.

The courts.

The groves.

Flowers and
pools.
The sages.

The sages joy-
fully entertain
Ráma, and de-
clare that he is
their Raja.

Description of
the forest of
Dándaka.

ous and valiant Ráma, together with Sítá and Lakhsmana, entered the great forest of Dándaka; and after a while Ráma saw a cluster of hermitages, strewed with kusa grass, and illuminated with the habits of devotees, and the tokens of Brahmanical devotion, as the air is illuminated by the dazzling light of the sun. The courts before the several huts were laid out with all neatness, and were kept perpetually clean, and frequented by various kinds of deer, and by numerous flocks of birds; and they were constantly enlivened by the gambols of the Apsaras, and adorned with large sacrificial fires, ladles, pots, antelope skins, kusa grass, sacrificial wood, fruits and roots. The hermitages were surrounded with large forest trees, which yielded pure and delicious fruits; they were rendered sacred by oblations and sacrifices, and cheered with the sound of the Vedas; they were strewed with wild flowers, and supplied with pools abounding with water-lilies; they were inhabited by ancient sages who lived on fruits and roots, who were men of subdued passions, who wore the habits of devotees, and who were as bright as the sun or as the sacred flame. Thus adorned the hermitages resembled the habitation of Brahma. The illustrious Ráma, seeing this cluster of hermitages, unstrung his mighty bow, and went towards them, attended by Sítá and Lakshmana. The devout sages received those renowned ones with every mark of gladness; and they beheld with astonishment the striking symmetry, the beauty of face, the delicacy of form, and the amiable countenance of Ráma; and all were filled with wonder as they gazed upon the three, as though their eyes could never be satisfied. Those truly fortunate sages then led their guests into a hut of leaves, and brought water for them all, and offered them roots, flowers, and fruits; and they said to Ráma:—"You are the protector of the devotees, the renowned refuge, the object of our honour and regard, our Raja and our Governor: O sovereign of men, whether you are in the forest or in the city, you are still our Raja."

Having been thus entertained by the sages, Ráma rose at sunrise on the following morning, and departed into the

forest of Dándaka with Lakshmana and Sítá. And that
forest was full of different kinds of deer, and was frequented
by large bears, and abounded with thickets of broken trees,
and with climbing plants and bushes, and with lakes inhabited by ducks and water-fowls, and it was rendered
vocal by the sweet warblings of various kinds of birds. In
that deep wood full of wild beasts, there appeared a cannibal as tall as a mountain-top, with a deep voice, hollow
eyes, a widely extended and monstrous mouth, and a
tun belly. That cannibal was named Virádha, and he was
hideous to the sight, and the terror of all beings ; and he
was seated on a tiger's skin, and was smeared with raw fat
and blood, and continually cried out with a dreadful cry ;
and his mouth was widely gaping like that of Yama ; and
before him, spitted on a large iron spit, were three lions,
four tigers, two wolves, ten deer, and a large elephant's head
with the tusks smeared with fat. This Virádha, seeing
Ráma and Lakshmana and Sítá, ran towards them as fierce
as death, and he sent forth a roar which caused the earth to
move, and he seized Sítá in his arms, saying :—" O little
dwarfs, why do you come with your wife into the forest of
Dándaka, clad in the habits of devotees, and armed with
arrows, bow, and scimitar ? Why do you two devotees
remain with one woman ?[7] Why are you, O profligate
wretches, corrupting the devout sages ? Know you not that
Virádha, the Rákshasa, constantly traverses this forest,
clothed in armour, and feeding on the flesh of sages ? "
Saying these words, Virádha leaped up into the air with
Sítá in his arms, exclaiming :—" I have obtained a woman,
who will be a delicious meal: Tell me instantly who you
are, and whither are you going ? " The magnanimous
Ráma replied :—"Know you that we are two brothers, born
of Kshatriyas and abiding in the forest: But who are you
traversing Dándaka in this dreadful form, and perpetrating
every abomination ? " Virádha said :—" I am the son of
Kala, and all the Rákshasas call me Virádha: By religious

HISTORY OF
INDIA.
PART IV.

Horrible ap-
pearance of
Virádha, the
cannibal
Rákshasa.

Virádha seizes
Sítá.

Taunts the two
brothers with
having only one
wife.

---

[7] It is not impossible that this charge brought by Virádha referred to the polyandry which undoubtedly existed in India at an early period.

HISTORY OF INDIA. PART IV.

Virádha rendered invulnerable by Brahma in return for his religious austerities.
Alarm of Sítá.

Lamentations of Ráma at seeing his wife in the grasp of Virádha.

Wrath of Lakshmana.

Lakshmana threatens Virádha.

Description of the battle between Ráma and Lakshmana and the Rákshasa Virádha.

austerities I have obtained the promise from Brahma that I shall be invulnerable to all weapons: Give up your joint wife to me and expect her no more, but fly with haste wherever you choose! This beautiful woman shall be my wife, and I will drink the blood of you ill-favoured wretches unless you fly at once." Hearing the impious words of the cruel Virádha, the terrified Sítá trembled like the leaves of a plantain-tree shaken by the wind; and Ráma, seeing his beautiful wife in the grasp of Virádha, exclaimed to Lakshmana:—" See, O excellent one, the fearless daughter of Raja Janaka, my virtuous spouse, who has been brought up with the greatest delicacy, enclosed in the arms of this Rákshasa! O Lakshmana, see what evil Kaikeyí has brought upon us! There is no affliction greater to me than that Sítá should be subjected to the touch of another man: O Lakshmana, neither the death of my father, nor the loss of the Raj, affects me like this." While Ráma was thus lamenting, Lakshmana was distracted with rage, and snuffing the air like the serpent Rudra; and he replied to his elder brother:—" O Ráma, why do you, who are the lord of all, and the equal of Indra, suffer Sítá to be taken away, and grieve yourself thus as though you were unable to rescue her? Why are you thus afflicted while I am at your command? The earth shall drink the blood of this Rákshasa, who shall be slain by my arrow: The rage I felt towards Bharata for desiring the Raj, I will pour forth on Virádha, as the thunderbolt suddenly strikes the mountain." Lakshmana, his eye inflamed with anger, then said to Virádha:—"You base and diminutive wretch! By your evil act you are certainly seeking your own death! You shall not obtain Sítá, nor shall you depart alive from me." So saying, Lakshmana discharged seven arrows, golden-shafted and peacock-feathered, and as bright as fire; and they pierced the body of Virádha, and he fell upon the ground bathed in blood. Then the Rákshasa uttered a dreadful yell, and drew forth a bright and green dart, and hurled it in anger at Lakshmana; but Ráma, expert in arms, drew out two darts with heads resembling sharp

knives, and cut in twain the dart of Virádha. Then
Virádha seized a spear as terrible as the flag-staff of Indra,
and brandished it in the air, like Yama breathing universal
ruin. Then the two brothers rained a shower of bright
arrows upon the Rákshasa, but they fell harmless from his
body, and he stood before them laughing. Next Virádha
hurled his spear, but Ráma cut it by two darts, and it fell to
the ground like a rock torn by a thunderbolt from Mount
Meru. Then the two brothers drew their scimitars, which
resembled two black serpents, and they ran upon Virádha,
and struck him with all their might. Upon this the terrible
Rákshasa seized the intrepid heroes forcibly with his two
arms, and threw them over his shoulders as though they had
been children; and uttering a horrid yell he rushed into the
depths of the jungles. Then the beautiful Sítá set up a
loud cry, and Lakshmana broke the left arm of the Rákshasa, and Ráma broke the right arm; and Virádha fell to
the ground; and the two brothers beat him with their fists,
and their arms, and their feet, and lifted him up and dashed
him against the ground, but he could not give up the ghost
because of the blessing he had received from Brahma.
Then Ráma, seeing that the mountain-like monster would
not die, said to Lakshmana :—" This Rákshasa, reaping
the fruit of his religious austerities, cannot be conquered
with weapons in battle; therefore we will bury him
alive: O Lakshmana, dig a large grave for this terrible
Rákshasa!" Lakshmana replied :—" Let us burn this
Rákshasa!" But Ráma said :—" The proper death of a
Rákshasa is to bury him alive, and not to burn him." So
Lakshmana took a spade and dug a large pit by the side of
the huge Virádha; and Ráma who had kept his foot upon
the neck of the Rákshasa now removed it; and the two
brothers took up the loud-roaring Virádha, and threw him
with mighty force into the pit, whilst the forest resounded
with his fearful yells. Thus Virádha was put to death by
being buried alive, but as soon as he was dead there arose
from the grave a very beautiful person who began to ascend
to heaven; and on his way he prayed to Ráma with joined

HISTORY OF
INDIA.
PART IV.

The two
brothers unable
to slaughter
Virádha, be-
cause of the
blessing he had
received from
Brahma.

Burial of
Virádha alive.

Virádha as-
sumes a beauti-
ful form and
rises out of the
grave and as-
cends to heaven.

HISTORY OF
INDIA.
PART IV.

Legend of his
being originally
a Gandharva,
but cursed by
Kuvera, on
account of his
love for Ramb-
há, to be a
Rákshasa until
delivered by
Ráma.

hands, as follows :—"I wish you all success, O Ráma, the son of Kausalyá, the protector of Sítá, and the fulfiller of the wishes of all your worshippers : I knew you from the first, and spoke to you harshly in order that I might excite your anger and die by your hands: I am a Gandharva ; my name is Kosharee, and I used to sing in the court of Kuvera : One day Kuvera, perceiving that I was inspired with a passion for the beautiful Apsara, named Rambhá, cursed me for my misconduct, saying :—" Go and assume the shape of a Rákshasa, and live in the forest of Dándaka ; and remain so until you are killed by Ráma, when you will resume your previous form :[8] This day I have been relieved by you :

---

[8] In the Adhyátma Rámáyana, the Rákshasa Virádha is represented as a female ; and the following significant account is given of her life and resurrection :—When the soul of Virádhá quitted her body, a beautiful figure, resembling a celestial nymph, rose from the corpse adorned with jewels and rich garments. She prostrated herself at Ráma's feet, and walking three times round him she thus addressed him :—" Condescend, O Lord ! to listen to an account of my former state : I was originally a dancer in the assembly of the gods : no one ever equalled me in beauty : I was once engaged in admiration of myself when the sage Durvása accidentally came that way. I, being so much taken up with my own charms, omitted to pay my respects to him. At which negligence his anger being roused against me, he uttered a curse on me, in consequence of which I became a demon. I was overwhelmed with distress, confessed my folly, and prayed him to have compassion upon me ; on which Durvása, taking pity on my misery, said :—' In the Tretá-Yuga, the Almighty and Eternal God, the Supreme Soul, Vishnu, will assume an incarnation of the flesh in the house of Maháraja Dasaratha at Ayodhyá, and will take the name of Ráma : He will come to this forest, where you will be slain by his hand, then will you quit this shape and assume your own proper form. From that period I have been steadfast in the recollection of thy name, and in the worship of thee : This day I have been pre-eminently great, for I have seen thee ; the dust from thy feet has fallen on my head : Thou art the only pure light ; thou art one, there is nothing like unto thee : I praise, I adore thy name. Thou art styled the protector of the poor, take pity on me ; consider the misery of thy slave. Grant that I may not forget thy name, and that I may sing thy praises."

Ráma said :—" I will bestow on thee, O dancer ! this blessing ; the forgetfulness of my name shall not take possession of your mind : From beholding me this day great benefit will accrue to thee ; faith in me will be engendered in your heart, and from that faith pure worship will be produced : It is difficult to acquire this faith ; the Vedas and Sástras declare that I do not bestow it on every one : This honour have I conferred on thee, that you may enjoy faith, wisdom, and meditation, and at the last day I will remember thee : Depart to your own abode, and when you shall quit this corporeal frame you will be absorbed into me."

In obedience to Ráma's orders, Virádhá departed singing his praises, and from that time was a faithful worshipper of Ráma.

HISTORY OF INDIA.
PART IV.

Accept my prayers and thanks, and permit me to return to my master Kuvera." So saying, Virádha vanished away from the presence of Ráma.

Having thus killed the terrible Virádha, the heroic Ráma embraced Sítá and comforted her, and he said to Lakshmana :—" This forest is full of dangers, and we are not acquainted with it; we will therefore proceed to the hermitage of Sarabhanga." Then Ráma and his spouse and his brother proceeded to the hermitage, and as they approached the magnanimous god-like devotee Sarabhanga, they beheld a wonderful appearance in the heavens. The mighty Indra, the Raja of the celestials, mounted on a car as splendid as the sun or as a glowing fire, passed through the air followed by all the gods; and Indra was adorned with splendid ornaments, and arrayed in shining garments, and received the adoration of multitudes of the celestials, who were arrayed with equal splendour. And near unto the car of Indra was another chariot drawn by horses, resembling a thick cloud illuminated by the sun. And over the head of Indra was a splendid umbrella, adorned with a garland, and two beautiful Apsaras held each a golden chámara in her hand, and fanned the sovereign of the gods. Then Indra entered the hermitage of the sage, and conversed with Sarabhanga; and Ráma addressed his brother as follows :—" See, O Lakshmana, that wonderful and glorious chariot, resembling the descending sun! Surely these horses are the steeds of Indra! Behold also those celestial youths of ample chests, and arms like maces, who stand in hundreds on every side, with rings in their ears, and scimitars in their hands; and whose apparel is of the colour of topaz! They are terrible as tigers, and the necklaces on their breasts are as bright as the glowing fire: They all appear to be youths of twenty-five years of age, and that is the constant age of the gods."

At this time the mighty Indra took his leave of the sage, and departed to heaven in his car. Ráma and his spouse and brother then approached Sarabhanga, who was offering a burnt offering, and with his permission, they

4th. Visit of Ráma, Sítá, and Lakshmana to the hermitage of Sarabhanga.

Visit of Indra to the sage Sarabhanga.

Description of Indra.

Ráma admires the chariot, horses, and attendants of Indra.

Indra departs, and the trio enter the hermitage.

The sage explains that
Indra had come
to take him to
heaven, but that
he waited to
behold Ráma.

advanced and kissed his feet. Being then invited to a repast, and to a lodging which was prepared for them, Ráma asked the reason of Indra's coming; and Sarabhanga said :—" O Ráma, the sovereign of the gods is desirous of taking me to the heaven of Brahma, which I have gained by my severe austerities; but knowing, O my beloved guest, that you were not far off, I would not depart to heaven until I had seen you : Having now beheld you, O chief of men, I will go to the highest heaven : Receive, O Ráma, the worlds I have acquired by the merits of my austerities." Ráma replied :—" I am highly honoured by you, and I return to you the worlds you have acquired : Depart hence to the realms of bliss, but tell me, I pray you, where I may now take up my own abode ? " Sarabhanga

Directs Ráma to
proceed to the
hermitage of
Sutíkshna.

replied :—" O Ráma, a highly illustrious sage named Sutíkshna resides in this forest; he will point out where it is best for you to abide." Sarabhanga then said :—" Behold now, whilst I put off this body, as a serpent casts his

Sarabhanga
burns himself
alive, and
ascends to the
heaven of
Brahma in a
youthful form.

slough ! " Then the sage prepared a fire, and offered ghee, and entered the flame; and the fire consumed the hair of his body, and the skin, flesh, bones, and blood; and a youth bright as the fire was instantly produced; and in this shape Sarabhanga sought the heaven of the sages, who had devoted their lives to religious austerities, and passing by the heaven of the gods, he ascended to the heaven of Brahma.[9]

---

[9] The following account of the death of Sarabhanga is extracted from the Adhyátma Rámáyana :—" I have been engaged, O Lord ! a long period of time in religious penances at this place in anxious expectation of beholding thee, who art the Supreme God, the Lord of all hearts, and from whom nothing is concealed : This day have I obtained the fruits of my pious austerities in having seen thee : I lay before thy feet the worship, charity, pilgrimages, and indeed every good work upon which I have been engaged throughout my whole life; I shall in thy presence depart from this transitory world." Having thus spoken he collected a quantity of wood, with which he erected the funeral pile, and seating himself thereon he set fire to it with his own hands. He prostrated himself before Ráma, Sítá, and Lakshmana; he worshipped them in silence, conceiving in his own mind that he should become like unto Ráma, with his hair braided in a knot on the crown of his head, a cloth made from bark of trees on his body, the colour of his body like the lotos, his eyes resembling the red and white lily, and attended by Lakshmana and Sítá in full beauty. While he thus represented himself to his

When Sarabhanga had thus departed from this world, the whole body of sages gathered together, and came before Ráma at the hermitage. There were those who possess no goods, those who feed on the rays of the sun and moon, those who subsist on raw food, those who feed on leaves, those who eat rice with its husks, those who stand in the water immersed to the neck, those who sleep on the bare ground, those who do not sleep at all, those who always stand on one leg, those whose food is water alone, those who feed on air, those who live always in the open air, those who sleep in places of sacrifice, those who reside on the peaks of mountains, those who always wear wet clothing, those who spend their whole time in repeating the name of some god, those who pass their lives in repeating the Veda, those who perform worship with fire on each of their four sides, and the sun over their heads, those who eat but four months in the year, those who never take food, those who remain suspended by their heels to the branches of trees, those who stand on their heads, some standing in the air upon nothing, or only supported by the thread of their meritorious deeds, and those who stand only on the point of one of their great toes. All these sages stood before Ráma with their hands respectfully joined, and addressed him as follows :—" You are the chief of the race of Ikshwáku, a great warrior, supreme on earth even as Indra is supreme among the gods : Your power and renown are celebrated throughout the world; filial obedience, truth, and justice reside in you : We, your subjects, would fain speak to you, and it becomes you not to disregard us : Great indeed is the injustice of that Raja who receives the sixth part of the harvest as his revenue, and yet protects not his people with paternal care : The stupid wretch who does not preserve his subjects as his own life, or as the lives of his own beloved offspring, is an object of detestation throughout the world : The Raja who governs his subjects by justice, as though they

HISTORY OF INDIA.
PART IV.

5th, Ráma engages to defend the ascetics against the Rákshasas.

Extraordinary description of the different ascetics who mortified the flesh.

The sages pray Ráma to preserve them from the Rákshasas.

own imagination, and while he was pronouncing the name of Ráma, his mortal body was consumed. He obtained a new and pure frame, and ascended on a celestial car to the dwelling-place of Vishnu in the highest heaven.

were his own family, and who reduces the wicked by the terror of his power, obtains universal renown in this life, and an imperishable reward hereafter : The sage who lives on roots and fruits, and performs the exalted duties incumbent upon him, confers a sixth part of the merits of his good deeds upon that Raja, who governs his people with righteousness : O Ráma, the multitude of Bráhmans, who are devoted to a religious life in the jungle, are destroyed by the Rákshasas, and consider you as their only protector : The sages who reside near the river Pampa, and those on the border of the river Mandákiní, and those in the mountain Chitra-kúta, have been devoured by these cannibal Rákshasas : We cannot endure these dreadful persecutions, and have come to you for protection : O hero, we pray you to

preserve us from these Rákshasas." Ráma replied :—" It ill becomes you to supplicate me, as I ought to be supplicating you, for I am at the command of the Bráhmans : I have entered the forest to fulfil the words of my father, and to remove the persecutions which you endure from these Rákshasas." Ráma having promised to defend the devotees then accompanied them to the hermitage of Sutíkshna.

Now when Ráma and his brother and his wife had travelled a great distance into the forest and crossed many rivers, they at length saw a hermitage which was purified with the clothing and garlands of devotees. There they beheld Sutíkshna covered with mud; and his head covered with matted hair ; and he was without flesh in consequence of his austerities, and his body was reduced to bones and skin ; and he was absorbed in deep meditation. And Ráma paid his respects, and the sage Sutíkshna embraced him, and addressed him as follows :—" O Ráma, has your journey been pleasant ? The hermitage of which you have taken possession now enjoys its true owner : Waiting for you, I have forborne to relinquish the earth for the habitation of the gods : O hero, Indra, the chief of the celestials, and the great god Siva, also, have desired me to deliver to you all the worlds I have subdued by my merits : Enjoy yourself then, with your spouse Sítá, and your brother Lakshmana, in the god-frequented

worlds which have been conquered by my austerities." Ráma
replied :—" I accept all the worlds, O great sage, and desire
you to appoint me a place of residence in the forest." Sutíkshna said :—" Attended by the holy sages, and constantly
supplied with fruits and roots, enjoy yourself in this pleasant
hermitage." So Ráma took up his abode for that night in
the pleasant hermitage of Sutíkshna, together with Sítá and
Lakshmana.

HISTORY OF
INDIA.
PART IV.

Now when it was morning, and the ablutions had been duly
performed, Ráma went to Sutíkshna, and said :—" O divine
one, we have had a most refreshing night, and now ask permission to take our leave : The sages who have accompanied
us are hastening to depart, and we are desirous of beholding the whole circle of hermitages belonging to the devoted Rishis who inhabit this forest; and we would fain
commence our journey before the heat of the sun becomes as
insupportable as an obstinate person in pursuit of gain."
Sutíkshna replied :—" Go, O beloved one, and having
viewed the pleasant hermitages of the pious inhabitants of
the wilderness of Dándaka, do you return to this abode."

*The trio depart
to visit the
other hermit-
ages in the
neighbourhood.*

The brothers then departed accompanied by Sítá; when
Sítá, full of tender affection, thus addressed her spouse
Ráma :—" O beloved one, a great mind may contract guilt
through the almost imperceptible distinctions of right and
wrong; but he may avoid the danger by subduing the first
risings of evil desire : O hero, you are devoted to truth,
and never regarded the wives of others, but the vice of anger
has been produced in you through inadvertence, and is now
attendant upon you : You have come into the forest as a
devotee, but now you have engaged to compass the death of
the Rákshasas, for the sake of preserving the sages who inhabit the forest of Dándaka; and you and your brother have
come into the wood for this purpose armed with your bows
and arrows : O hero, this is not pleasing to me; for when
the bow of the Kshatriya and the sacrificial fire of the Bráhman are placed near each other, their power and energy will
increase exceedingly : If you say that as a Kshatriya you are
bound to punish the wicked and protect the good, I say that

*7th, Dialogue
between Ráma
and Sítá as to
the propriety of
waging war
against the
Rákshasas.*

*Sítá reproaches
Ráma.*

*A Kshatriya
bound to punish
evil-doers only
when he is a
Raja, and not
when he is a
devotee.*

this duty belongs to a Kshatriya who is a Raja, and not to one who has adopted the life of a devotee : When you have recovered your Raj, and become sovereign of Ayodhyá, then you may draw your bow for the sake of punishing the Rákshasas ; but so long as you are a devotee, you ought not to wish injury to any fellow-creature : In ancient times there was a certain devotee, and Indra sought to interrupt his austerities, by assuming the form of a warrior, and leaving his scimitar as a deposit with the holy sage ; and that devotee carried the scimitar ever with him as a sacred trust, until after awhile he too acquired a love of war, and ceased to perform his devotions, and at last through his connection with the weapon he sank into hell : O hero, the slaughter of Rákshasas in the forest of Dándaka, when they are without enmity towards you, will never be approved by the wise : In this sacred grove I pray you to constantly practise religious austerities, for happiness never springs from self-gratification : O excellent one, this has been spoken by me in the feeble language of a woman ; you alone are able to understand your duty."

Ráma, hearing these words of the devoted Sítá, replied thus :—" O goddess, you have given me good advice becoming your present situation ; but I will mention one rule which has been stated by you.: You have said that a Kshatriya must carry a bow, that the voice of distress be not heard : Now the sages are distressed by the cannibal Rákshasas in the forest of Dándaka, and relying upon me they have taken refuge with me : I said :—' It is a great shame to me, that Bráhmans should stand before me when I ought to stand with joined hands before them ; ' and having heard the address of the sages to become their protector, I cannot turn a deaf ear to them while life remains : I can relinquish life, and even you, O Sítá, with Lakshmana ; but having once plighted my promise to these Bráhmans, it is my duty to protect them : But you have spoken to me through affection and friendship, and I am delighted with your frankness : O Sítá, a person who is not beloved is not admonished : You have spoken sentiments becoming your family, and you are my companion in virtue, and dearer to me than life itself."

Having thus spoken, Ráma entered the wood armed with his bow; and the beautiful Sítá went after him, while Lakshmana followed with his bow in his hand. And they beheld many mountains, and groves, and pleasant rivers, together with cranes and red geese; and they saw ponds covered with lilies and water-fowl; also herds of sportive deer, and buffaloes and hogs, and wild elephants. When they had proceeded far upon their way, and their shadows had become long on the ground, they beheld a sheet of water which was many miles round; and it was skirted with green meadows, and adorned with herds of elephants, and covered with the red and white lotos, and with cranes, geese, wild ducks, and other animals that live on water. Presently they heard the sounds of songs and music, but they saw no musician; and Ráma inquired of the sage Dharma-vrita respecting the cause of what they heard. The pious sage then related the wonders of the lake thus:—"This ancient lake, called Mandakarni, was formed by the sage Mandakarni through the powers of his religious austerities: Standing in a pool, and feeding on nothing but air for ten thousand years, the sage Mandakarni performed so severe a course of mortification, that all the gods were distressed, and assembled together with Indra at their head. And Indra said:— 'This sage is bent on supplanting me, and obtaining the sovereignty of the gods:'—Indra then sought to tempt the sage from his devotions by sending to him five chosen Apsaras, the brightness of whose beauty exceeded that of the lightning; and the damsels came hither, singing and playing, and employing every act of fascination to entice the devotee: After awhile, the sage was ensnared into a love for the Apsaras; and the five damsels all became his wives, and still inhabit a concealed house in this lake; and there they pass their time in pleasure with the sage, who by his previous mortification and subjection, had again obtained youth; and the captivating sound of their songs and instruments of music is what you now hear." At these words,

HISTORY OF
INDIA.
PART IV.

8th, Ten years' wanderings amongst the sages in the neighbourhood of Sutikshna's hermitage at Ramtek.

Mysterious lake abounding with music and song.

Legend of the lake being the abode of the sage Mandakarni and five Apsaras.

HISTORY OF
INDIA.
PART IV.

Hermitages of
the sage
Dharma-vrita.

Ráma was full of thought, and exclaimed :—" This is marvellous, indeed ! "

After a short while, Ráma beheld a pleasant cluster of hermitages which belonged to the sage Dharma-vrita, with whom he had been conversing; and the hermitages were bestrewed with kusa grass, and with garments worn by the sages, and were full of Brahmanical glory. Ráma then entered with Sítá and Lakshmana, and was received with due honour by all the sages, and looked around upon the pleasant place which adorned the forest. After this the mighty Ráma visited in succession those hermitages of the sages in which he had formerly lodged; and he remained two months with one, and a year with another, and four months with another, and five or six months with others; and thus he went on, sometimes abiding only a fortnight at one place,

The trio remain
ten years in the
neighbourhood,
visiting the
different her-
mitages.

and sometimes remaining for more than a full year. Thus passed away ten years of exile, whilst Ráma resided in the hermitages of the sages and enjoyed great happiness therein;

The trio return
to the hermitage
of Sutíkshna
after the ten
years.

and when the ten pleasant years of exile had expired, Ráma returned with Sítá and Lakshmana to the hermitage of the sage Sutíkshna, and took up his abode there many days.

9th,* Visit to the
sage Agastya,
near to the
Vindhya moun-
tains.

After awhile, Ráma said to Sutíkshna :—" I continually hear that the sage Agastya resides in this forest of Dándaka, but through the extent of the forest, I know not the spot where he has taken up his abode. Sutíkshna replied :—" I wish to send you to Agastya with your brother and your wife : Go from hence towards the south, and you will behold the glorious hermitage of the brother of Agastya : There stay one night, O Ráma; and then, going forward, still towards the south, you will find at the skirt of the forest the hermitage of Agastya." Hearing these directions,

Journey
through the
forest towards
the south.

Ráma bowed to the feet of the sage, and set out in company with Sítá and Lakshmana to search for Agastya. Seeing the variegated forest, and the mountains at a distance resembling clouds and lakes, and the rivers running beside the roads, Ráma went pleasantly along the road pointed out

Halt at the
hermitage of the
brother of
Agastya.

by Sutíkshna. At length he said to Lakshmana :—" This hermitage, which appears in view, must certainly be that of

the pious brother of Agastya: The trees of the forest in
thousands are bowed down by the weight of fruits and
flowers; the scent of the pepper trees, wafted hither by the
breeze, creates a pungent sensation: Bundles of sticks
and kusa grass are thrown hither and thither on the road;
the black smoke, resembling the peak of a mountain, rises
from the sacrificial fires; and the leaves of the trees are
black and oily from the smoke of the sacrificial homa: The
Bráhmans, having bathed in these lovely and sacred retreats,
are preparing offerings of flowers in blossom, which they
have collected: In former times, two cruel Rákshasas, the
devourers of Bráhmans, resided here, and their names were
Vátápi and Ilwala; and Ilwala was accustomed to assume
the form of a Bráhman, and speak the sacred tongue, and
invite the Bráhmans under pretence of solemnizing a
Sráddha: Then his brother Vátápi assumed the form of a
ram, and was consecrated for the sacrifice by Ilwala; and
when the Bráhmans had eaten the ram, Ilwala called to his
brother to come forth, and Vátápi came forth out of the
stomachs of the Bráhmans, bleating like a sheep, and tear-
ing his way through their bodies: Thousands of Bráhmans
were thus destroyed, when Agastya came to this spot, and
accepted the invitation to a Sráddha; and Agastya had not
eaten for many years, and he devoured the whole of Vátápi
in the form of a ram, and then prayed to Gangá; and the
goddess appeared in his alms dish, and he touched the
water, and pronounced her divine name: Then when Ilwala
called on his brother to come forth, Agastya laughed and
said:—'Your brother has been eaten by me in the form of a
ram and has now gone to the abode of Yama, and for him
there is no coming forth:' Ilwala in a rage began to assail
Agastya, but was immediately consumed by the fire which
flashed from the eyes of the sage: This hermitage, which
formerly belonged to the two Rákshasas, is now inhabited
by the brother of Agastya."[10]

---

[10] This absurd myth is preserved here chiefly because it is widely known
amongst the Bráhmans, who make a point of praying after a meal that they may
be blessed with a digestion equal to that of Agastya.

Ráma, Sítá, and
Lakshmana
spend one night
with the brother
of Agastya.

Reach the
hermitage of
Agastya.
Miracles per-
formed by
Agastya.

Lakshmana
informs a dis-
ciple of Agastya
of the arrival of
Ráma and Sítá.

Joy of Agastya
at the coming of
Ráma.

While Ráma was thus conversing with Lakshmana, the sun set, and the evening came on; and the brothers performed their evening devotions towards the west, and entered the hermitage of the brother of Agastya, accompanied by Sítá, and spent the night there. The next morning they took their leave, and departed towards the abode of Agastya himself; and as they went they beheld the trees of the forest in full flower, surrounded by climbing plants, broken by the trunks of sportive elephants, enlivened with playful monkeys, and vocal with joyous birds. Ráma, as he viewed the beautiful wilderness, said to his brother Lakshmana :—" The hermitage of Agastya appears in view : This is the abode of that sage who freed the southern quarter from the Rákshasas ; at whose command the Vindhya mountain forbore to rise higher in the sky; who drank up the sea abounding in crocodiles and great fishes ; who was entreated by the gods, with Indra at their head, to destroy the Dánavas : O Lakshmana, here will I spend the remainder of my exile : Here the perfect men, the great sages, cast off their old bodies, and ascend in new bodies to heaven on chariots as resplendent as the sun."

Ráma, having arrived at the hermitage, said to Lakshmana :—" Enter the hermitage, I pray you, and inform the sage that I have arrived with Sítá." And Lakshmana entered, and said to one of the disciples of Agastya :—" Behold, the mighty hero Ráma, the eldest son of Maharaja Dasaratha, is come hither with his wife Sítá, to visit the sage ; perchance their fame may have reached your ears." The disciple, having heard the words of Lakshmana, entered the house where the sacred fire was kept, and gave the information to the great sage ; and Agastya replied :—" The coming of Ráma has been long desired by me, and now through my good fortune he is here this day to see me : Go, let the highly honoured Ráma, with his spouse and Lakshmana, be introduced to me ! " Then the disciple bowed to the feet of the sage, and with joined hands spoke his ready acquiescence ; and he brought in Ráma and Sítá and Lakshmana, in the manner prescribed in the ordinance.

And they entered the abode of Agastya, and saw the places sacred to Brahma, to Agni, to Vishnu, to Indra, to the Sun, the Moon, and the other gods; and they beheld the sage Agastya, surrounded by his disciples, clothed in the skin of antelopes and vestments of bark. Then Ráma, seeing Agastya, the devotee, severe in austerities, and resplendent as the fire, said to his brother Lakshmana:—"He, who is Agni, Soma, Dharma, yea, the Eternal himself, is coming forth: Let us approach him with the greatest reverence; for he is without doubt the sage Agastya; he is the abode of sacred austerities, a mass of consecrated glory." With these words Ráma approached with devout affection and kissed the foot of the Bráhman; and the great sage kissed the head of Ráma. Agastya then inquired respecting their health and welfare, and said to his disciples:—"First offer oblations on the fire, and then present the remainder with appropriate ceremonies and the consecrating formulas to Ráma; and let it be eaten by him according to the statutes of the Vanaprasthas: Ráma is Raja over the whole universe, steady in the paths of virtue, a mighty warrior, and worthy of the highest respect and adoration: Come in, O beloved guest! Ráma is the asylum and the lord of all: I will worship the lord of the world who has arrived here, according to the ordinance." Thus Agastya and his disciples yielded due honours to their guest, saying:—"As a false witness feeds in the next world upon his own flesh, so he who fails to entertain a guest to the best of his ability, is stripped of all his merits, and receives all the sins of his visitant.[11]

Sacred places in the hermitage of Agastya.

Ráma's profound respect for Agastya.

Agastya directs his disciples to offer oblations to Ráma.

Acknowledges Ráma as Raja of the universe.

---

[11] The Adhyátma Rámáyana contains the following highly spiritualized description of the hermitage of Agastya and his reception of Ráma:—"The house of Agastya was a spacious building surrounded by pleasant gardens, abounding with fruits and flowers of every description, and resembling the bowers of paradise or Brahma's heaven. There thousands of sages, such as Bramharishya, or Bráhman saints; Deva-rishya, or heavenly spirits; and Raja-rishya, or princes turned saints, were engaged in religious pursuits. Such was the sanctity of that place, that lions, tigers, deer, sheep, and other animals fed promiscuously therein without fear of each other. Ráma remained at the gate of the garden, while Sutíkshna went in to inform the saint of his arrival. When Sutíkshna entered the gardens he beheld the saint surrounded by his disciples, to whom he

HISTORY OF
INDIA.
PART IV.
—————
Agastya pre-
sents Ráma
with the bow
of Vishnu, the
arrow of Brah-
ma, two inex-
haustible
quivers, and a
scimitar.

After this, when Agastya had entertained Ráma with fruits, roots, and flowers, he said to him :—"Receive, O Ráma, this divine bow of Vishnu, adorned with gold and diamonds, the work of Viswakarma ; this excellent in-fallible arrow of Brahma, given to me by Indra ; these two quivers of inexhaustible arrows resembling the glowing fire ; and this golden-sheathed scimitar : O Ráma, with this bow Vishnu smote innumerable Asuras, and obtained the most splendid honours among the gods." The Bráhman, having thus given Ráma the bow, the arrow, the scimitar,

The coat of mail
given to Agastya
by Indra.

and the two quivers, presented him also with an excellent coat of mail which had been given to the sage by Indra.

Agastya's
encouraging
words.

Agastya, having thus entertained his guests, discoursed with them in the most encouraging manner, saying :—" O Ráma, I am gratified ! Peace attend you, O Lakshmana ! I am greatly pleased with you both for having come with Sítá to bow at my feet : You are greatly fatigued by the length of the

Agastya praises
Sítá.

road : The weary Sítá is evidently afflicted : She, a delicate princess, who has never experienced privations, has come to a forest abounding in hardships out of love for her spouse :

Evil nature of
women in
general.

O Ráma, such is not the nature of women : They will fawn upon a husband in prosperity, and forsake him in adversity : They are as sudden and uncertain as the lightning's flash, as keen as the sharpest weapon, as swift in their course as the bird Garura, as fickle as the wind, and as fatal as the

---

was expounding the actions of Ráma, of whom he was a strenuous adorer. Sutíkshna paid his respects to the saint, and said :—' Ráma, my spiritual guide ! the exalted son of Dasaratha, with Sítá and his brother Lakshmana, is waiting at the gate ; he is desirous of paying his respects to thee.' Great was the surprise and sincere the joy of Agastya when he heard these words. He said to his disciple :—' Auspicious indeed, Sutíkshna ! is your destiny ; the intelligence you have conveyed to me is equal to the wholesome breeze of the morning, it affords me the highest satisfaction : That master, to behold whom I have been so long engaged in religious penances, towards whom my soul is so fervently attached, has of his own accord condescended to visit my humble mansion : Who then in this world can equal me in good fortune ? ' Having thus spoken, he rose and went out to meet Ráma ; he worshipped him with reverence and faith, and thus addressed him :—' This day, O Lord ! my destiny is most exalted, for thou hast con-descended to visit thy servant : Great and long have been my religious penances in the hope of beholding thee : this day have I obtained the reward of my piety and sufferings ; I have seen thee.' "

most deadly poison : O Ráma, your spouse Sítá is free from HISTORY OF
INDIA.
PART IV. all these evil qualities." Ráma replied :—"Happy am I, since the chief of sages is pleased with me, my brother, and my spouse."

After this Ráma said to Agastya :—"Direct me, I pray you, to a spot supplied with water and wood, where I can erect a hermitage, and constantly reside in safety." Agastya replied :—"Beloved one, at a short distance from here, near the river Godáveri, is a place called Panchavatí, which abounds with fruits and roots, and where there is water in abundance : Go thither, O hero, and fix your dwelling there." So Ráma, and Sítá, and Lakshmana took their leave, and departed out of the hermitage of Agastya, and went their way to Panchavatí.

10th, Residence of Ráma, Sítá, and Lakshmana at Panchavati, the modern Nasik.
Agastya directs the trio to Panchavati, near the river Godáveri.

Now, on the road from the hermitage of Agastya, Ráma and the others saw a vulture of enormous size, who said that he was a friend of their father Maháraja Dasaratha ; and this vulture was named Jatáyus, and he was the son of Garura, and his eldest brother was named Sampáti. And Jatáyus said to Ráma :—"When you, O beloved one, are gone abroad with Lakshmana, I will guard Sítá." And Ráma accepted his friendship, and embraced him with great joy, and he accompanied Ráma on his way to Panchavatí.

Ráma forms an alliance with Jatáyus, the great vulture, who was the son of Garura.

When the party arrived at the spot pointed out by Agastya, Ráma said to Lakshmana :—" O excellent one, this is the flowery forest of Panchavatí : Let a place for a hermitage be sought in some pleasant thicket, near a pool or a sheet of water; and where sacrificial wood, and flowers, and kusa grass, and water, may be easily procured." Lakshmana replied :—" I am your servant ! " Then Ráma showed his brother a beautiful spot facing the river Godáveri ; and there was a sheet of water near it, as bright as the sun and fragrant with lilies ; and in the distance were high mountains abounding with glens, and vocal with peacocks. In this charming neighbourhood Lakshmana built a large hut on a high floor of earth, with firm posts of bamboos wrought together with wicker work ; and he covered it and roofed it with branches of trees, and tied it with strong

Arrival of Ráma, Sítá, and Lakshmana at Panchavatí.
Ráma selects a site for a hermitage.
Lakshmana builds a large hut with four rooms.

Oblations to
the god of
dwellings.

Termination of
thirteen years
and a half of
the exile.

Commencement
of the cold
season.

Poetical
description of
the cold season.

Characteristics
of the cold
weather in
India.

The day time.

The night time.

The moon.

cords, and thatched it with grass and leaves; and he divided it into four rooms. When he had thus finished the dwelling-house of Ráma, he went down to the Godáveri and bathed, and then returned, bringing fruits and water-lilies; and he made an oblation of flowers to the god of dwellings, and sprinkled water according to the ordinance, to secure peace to the new habitation and remove all evil from it. After this, he showed the hermitage to Ráma; and Ráma and Sítá beheld the excellent habitation, and entered it with delight; and the pious Ráma dwelt in that fruitful country in perfect happiness, as Indra dwells in heaven.

In this manner thirteen years and a half of Ráma's exile passed away in delight; and at this time the rainy season had departed, and the exhilarating cold season commenced. One morning, when it was very early, Ráma went to the pleasant river Godáveri for the sake of ablution; and his brother Lakshmana, shivering with cold, followed him with a jar of water in his hand. And Lakshmana said to Ráma:—"The season so grateful to you has now arrived; and the season which crowns the year appears with peculiar beauty: Mankind are stiffened with cold; the earth is loaded with crops; water is unpleasant, and fire agreeable: The gods and ancestors are honoured with oblations of new corn: The cities are full of delicacies, and abound with the juices of the corn: Rajas eager for conquest now march forth to battle: The sun keeps on the south quarter sacred to Yama, whilst the north quarter appears with a sad countenance like a woman without her tíká: The Himálaya mountain, abounding with stores of cold, is now distant from the sun, and is rightly named the mountain of snow: The midday abounds with high pleasures, and delight attends whatever we touch: The sun is beloved in the daytime, and shade and water are not pleasing: In this season the heat is temperate, the days are short and cold, the forests are bare, and the snow is fallen: The nights forbid all sleeping in the open air; governed by the star Pushya they are whitened with hoar frost and lengthened by the cold: The full moon having gained the side of the sun esteems himself fortunate; his face is whitened with cold, and he shines dimly like a mirror covered with human breath : The west wind is impregnated with frost, and its blast is doubly keen in the morning : At the rising of the sun, the fields of barley and wheat appear covered with fog ; and the golden fields of rice, frequented by the paddy birds and cranes, appear covered with down : In the rice-fields the kine drink water with their eyes half shut, through fear of the sharp blades of the corn : The sun rises at a distance, and appears through the fog like the moon surrounded with its halo : In the forenoon he is devoid of strength, but at midday he beams with pleasure, and his countenance is ruddy : The wild elephant touches the cold water in his thirst, and then draws back his trunk in haste : The water-fowls sit upon the bank, devoid of resolution, and fear to launch themselves upon the cold stream : The rivers covered with steam are known by the voice of cranes, and their shores are indicated by borders of moistened sand : The drops of dew, through the weakness of the god of day, hang suspended from the ends of branches like globules of quicksilver : O Ráma, the pious Bharata, full of affliction, mortifies himself in the city of Ayodhyá, through devotion to you : Having relinquished the Raj, and the many enjoyments of life, he confines himself to spare diet and lives upon the ground : At this hour he is certainly going to bathe in the Sarayú, and perform his daily ceremonies : A tender youth, brought up delicately, how can he, wetted with the chilling dew of morning, again immerse himself in water ? Your brother Bharata has subdued heaven by his devout austerities, and sets his mind upon you who are in the forest : It is said that men disregard the commands of their father, and obey those of their mother ; but the reverse of this has been done by Bharata : Why is our middle mother thus cruel, whose lord was the good Dasaratha, and whose son was the excellent Bharata ? "

Lakshmana having thus spoken, Ráma replied to him as follows:—" O beloved one, it is improper for you thus to reproach our middle mother : Speak indeed of Bharata ; for though my heart is fixed upon a forest residence, it is

The west wind. The sunrise.

The wild elephants.

The water-fowls.

The cranes.

The dew-drops.

Austerities of Bharata on account of Ráma.

Cruelty of Kaikeyi.

Ráma reproves Lakshmana for reproaching Kaikeyi.

pained through affection for Bharata: I remember the tender and sweet expressions of my brother, grateful as amrita, and rejoicing the heart: When, O Lakshmana, shall I again meet the magnanimous Bharata, and the hero Satrughna?"

Ablutions in the Godáveri.

Thus conversing, the brothers reached the Godáveri and made their customary offering to their ancestors and the gods. Ráma then performed his ablutions with his younger brother and Sítá; and he appeared like the divine Siva after bathing with the daughter of the chief of mountains.

Departure of the great vulture Jatáyus.

Thus Ráma dwelt in his hermitage of Panchavatí in company with his wife and brother; and Jatáyus, the Chief of Vultures, also dwelt there. But at this time Jatáyus requested permission to return to his own abode, saying:— "After visiting all my own friends, O chief of men, I will return." So Ráma gave him permission to take his leave, and the Chief of Vultures departed out of the hermitage.

Review of the foregoing narrative of Ráma's adventures amongst the sages.

The foregoing narrative of Ráma's wanderings amongst the sages is chiefly valuable for the proofs which it furnishes of the conclusions already laid down at the commencement of the present chapter. At the outset it will be observed that the Bráhman

Religious opposition of the Rákshasas to the Bráhmans.

sages were compelled to leave the neighbourhood of Chitra-kúta on account of the opposition offered to their religious rites by the Rákshasas; and that the Rákshasas mustered strong in that quarter, and were under the command of a younger brother of Rávana.

Virádha, a worshipper of Brahma.

Again, Virádha is described as being both a terrible Rákshasa, and the faithful worshipper of Brahma; and as having received certain supernatural powers from that deity in return for his devotions. But

Significance of the dialogue between Sítá and Lakshmana.

perhaps the most significant passage connected with the identification of the Rákshasas with the Buddhists, is the dialogue between Sítá and Ráma respecting the propriety of waging war against the

Rákshasas.   The argument has evidently been
garbled, but the drift of it may perhaps be gathered
from the following facts. Buddha Sákya Muni was a
Kshatriya.   So was Ráma.   Now although Sítá is
represented as saying that Ráma ought not to fight
because he was a devotee; yet inasmuch as his
character as a devotee is altogether mythical, the
speech may be regarded as mythical likewise.   Sítá's
language may therefore have been to the effect that
Ráma was a Kshatriya, and as such was scarcely
justified in interfering in the disputes between the
Bráhmans and the Buddhists ; whilst Ráma seems to
have replied that having promised to protect the
Bráhmans, or Linga worshippers, he was compelled
to engage in war.

The other portions of the narrative contain many
descriptions which are interesting, but which scarcely
call for comment.   The pictures of the different
hermitages are generally well drawn, but with considerable sameness ; and the conversation between
Ráma and the several sages is almost always of the
same character.   The Brahmanical tone of this portion of the poem betrays however, with startling
clearness, the proclivities of the Brahmanical author.
The appearance of Indra at the hermitage of Sarabhanga ; the prominence given to the doctrine that a
seat in heaven, and the possession of worlds, may
be obtained by such merits as religious austerities ;
and the poetic effort to throw a halo of sanctity
round the emaciated forms and religious pursuits of
the Bráhmans in the jungle, whilst associating such
sages with mythic accounts of supernatural weapons;
all serve to indicate that Brahmanising of Kshatrya
traditions which has been so frequently pointed out

Married life of
Atri opposed to
the Buddhist
rule of celibacy.

Pious suicide of
Sarabhanga
compared with
the burning of
Calanus.

Idea involved
in the death of
Sarabhanga.

Strange fancy
involved in
Ráma's alliance
with the vul-
ture Jatáyus.

in the narrative. The circumstance of the sage Atri living with his wife Anasúyá is curious, and perhaps illustrates a further opposition between the Buddhist priests and the Bráhmans; the former insisting upon celibacy, whilst the Bráhmans were not only permitted but required to marry. The pious suicide of Sarabhanga is very striking; and similar incidents appear to have been not uncommon in ancient times. Arrian, in his description of Alexander's expedition, relates the story of a sage named Calanus who burned himself to death upon a funeral pile in like manner; [12] and in Strabo's description of India, it is said that the sophists or Bráhmans considered disease of the body as most disgraceful, and that if any one apprehended its approach, he prepared a pyre, and destroyed himself by fire [13] The idea involved in the account of the death of Sarabhanga is somewhat mythical, and accordingly seems to be of a different character. He had long waited for the coming of Ráma, and having at length been blessed with a sight of the incarnate deity, he had no longer any desire to live; and consequently destroyed his body upon the funeral pile, and ascended to the heaven of Brahma. The description of the ascetics in the neighbourhood of Sarabhanga's pilgrimage is illustrative both of ancient and modern times; although it may be remarked that such self-mortifications, whether real or pretended, appear to be gradually dying out in India.

The strange alliance between Ráma and Jatáyus the Vulture is one of those eccentric ideas which

---

[12] Arrian's Exped. Alexand. lib. vii. c. 2.
[13] Strabo, lib. xv. c. 1.

abound to a considerable extent in the Rámáyana; and will be further illustrated when dealing with Ráma's subsequent alliances with monkeys and bears. For the present it will be sufficient to remark that these animals, like the serpents or Nágas, are treated in every respect, excepting that of form, as human beings; and there seems reason to believe that they were originally the deities of the aboriginal populations of the south of India, whom the Brahmanical author of the Rámáyana enlisted in the service of Ráma, for the purpose of facilitating the propagation of the worship of Ráma as an incarnation of Vishnu.

The description of the cold season in India, which is put into the mouth of Lakshmana, is exceedingly poetical; and its truthfulness to nature will be readily admitted by all who are familiar with the country at that reviving period of the year. In one instance, indeed, a sense of humour is blended with truthfulness of description; and it is difficult to avoid a smile at the picture of the wild elephant who put his trunk into the water to quench his thirst, and then drew it back hastily from the cold.

THE next event in the life of Ráma, was his wars against two brothers of Rávana, respectively named Khara and Dúshana, who appear to have commanded a Rákshasa army in the neighbourhood of the hermitage. The story can scarcely be regarded in any other light than that of a pure fiction. It is said that a sister of these brothers, named Súrpa-nakhá, fell in love with Ráma, and was jestingly referred by Ráma to Lakshmana, and again by Lakshmana to Ráma. In her jealousy she fell upon Sítá, on which Lakshmana cut off her ears and nose. She then fled to her brothers Khara and Dúshana, and prayed for revenge; on which ensued an extraordinary war, in which Ráma, single-handed, slaughtered a vast army of Rákshasas.

Notwithstanding the extravagance of this story, it furnishes a valuable illustration of the general character of many Hindú works of the imagination; such as the reckless sacrifice of probabilities for the sake of effect, the want of delicacy in the female character, and the frequent reference to Brahmanical ideas. These points, however, will be best considered hereafter. The narrative is as follows:—

After this, while Ráma was sitting in his pleasant four-roomed abode conversing with Sítá, a certain female Rákshasí happened to come to the hermitage. The name of this Rákshasí was Súrpa-nakhá, and she was sister of the ten-headed Rávana, the mighty Raja of Lanká; and her two other brothers were Khara and Dúshana; and these two were mighty Chieftains, and had been appointed by Raja Rávana to command all that country. This woman Súrpa- nakhá approached the leafy hut, and beheld Ráma of re- splendent countenance and substantial arm; and he appeared like a god in heaven, and his eyes resembled the lotos, and his step was as firm as that of an elephant, and on his head was a load of soft but matted hair; and he was evidently a great Raja, bearing all the marks of royalty; and his com- plexion was green like the new grass, and he was captivat- ing as the god of love. [1] Seeing Ráma, the heart of the Rákshasí was smitten with the arrows of Káma, and she was distracted with the flame of desire. And she was of an evil and malignant disposition, of a base family and base in mind, and she was a female only in appearance. This damsel was very ugly, whilst the countenance of the portly and well- formed Ráma was most lovely; this one was squint-eyed, whilst the eyes of Ráma were beautifully elongated; her locks were the colour of copper, whilst his locks were black and curly; she was deformed in figure, whilst he was shaped with the most perfect symmetry; her voice was a horrid yell, while his accents were most melodious; she was rash and vague in speech, whilst his discourse was ever apt and prudent; her conduct was notoriously vile, whilst his conduct was ever exemplary. This Rákshasí, seeing that Ráma was a perfect model of beauty, began to reflect within herself:— " This is a most beautiful person, proud of his youth and blooming as a god: I am smitten with love, and will there- fore assume another form, which shall be very beautiful: I will induce him to abandon his lawful and happy spouse Sítá, though she is in the bloom of beauty and prime of youth, and

Admires the beauty of Ráma.

Contrast between Súrpa- nakhá and Ráma.

Súrpa-nakhá determines to induce Ráma to marry her and desert Sítá.

[1] Ráma is frequently represented in Bengallee pictures as having a bright- green complexion; although as an incarnation of Vishnu his proper colour would appear to be blue. Indeed, in pictures procured from the Upper Provinces Ráma is painted blue.

Súrpa-nakhá
assumes a cap-
tivating form,
and asks Ráma
who he is.

Ráma relates
his story, and
asks why she is
wandering in
the forest.

Súrpa-nakhá
replies that she
has left her
brothers out of
love for him,
and invites him
to marry her.

lovely as Lakshmí; and I will cause him to direct all his attentions to me, whom he shall behold clothed with loveliness."

Súrpa-nakhá then assumed a most captivating form, and approached the valiant Ráma, and thus addressed him :—" O devotee, with matted hair, why are you come bearing a bow and arrow, and accompanied by your spouse, to this place which is haunted by the Rákshasas? I presume that the sages on the banks of the Godáveri, who are as bright as flame, are trusting in the strength of your arm." Ráma replied with the utmost simplicity, for never did he utter a falsehood, especially near his hermitage, or in the presence of a woman :—" There was a Raja named Dasaratha : I am his elder son, known among men by the name of Ráma; yonder is my younger brother Lakshmana who is devoted to me ; and this is my spouse Sítá : At the command of my father and mother, bound by a vow and desirous of fulfilling my duty, I am come to dwell in the woods; why do you in the bloom of youth and beauty, as charming as Lakshmí, wander about without fear in this most dreadful forest of Dándaka ?" To these words Súrpa-nakhá replied as follows : —" O Ráma, I am a female Rákshasí, and my name is Súrpa-nakhá, and I can assume any form at will: Rávana is my brother, of whom you may have heard ; my other brothers are Vibhishana, the virtuous, and Kumbha-karna, the sleepy, and the two mighty heroes, Khara and Dúshana : I have left my brothers, O Ráma, from the time I saw you ; through desire I have come to you, O my spouse: Clothed with power, I traverse the woods with the greatest ease ; do you become my husband by a lasting union : What occasion have you for Sítá ? She is deformed and ugly, and not a fit match for you : But I am a spouse worthy of you, clothed in beauty and possessed of every accomplishment : Behold me of charming mien, adorned with glorious ornaments, elegant in form and plump in size : I will eat this unchaste creature. and then devour your second brother : O my spouse, with me you shall wander through the wilderness of Dándaka, and view the lofty mountain-peaks and the verdant woods."

Having heard the words of Súrpa-nakhá, Ráma cast a meaning look towards Sítá and Lakshmana, and then for the sake of the jest replied to her, with a smile, in smooth and gentle words, as follows:—" O Súrpa-nakhá, I am already married; this is my beloved spouse, and the presence of a rival wife would be painful to one like you:. But, O charming female, my younger brother Lakshmana is youthful and engaging; he is intelligent, beautiful, fortunate, heroic, unmarried, and desirous of a wife; he is a fit match for you, and will become your husband: O full-eyed one, do you wait upon my brother as your husband, who is without a rival spouse, and attend him as the sun attends the Meru mountain."

HISTORY OF INDIA. PART IV.

Ráma jests with Súrpa-nakhá by advising her to marry Lakshmana.

Thus addressed by Ráma, the infatuated Rákshasí left the hut, and immediately addressed Lakshmana thus:—" I am very beautiful, and a fit wife for you; come and roam with me at your ease in the forest of Dándaka." Lakshmana replied with a smile:—" How can you desire to become a slave, the wife of a slave like me? O delicate fair one, I am the property of another, even of this my excellent brother Ráma: O full-eyed one, you should aspire to a higher station: Do you become the wife of my brother in whom is to be found every accomplishment: He will abandon his present wife, and devote all his attention to you."

Súrpa-nakhá offers herself as a wife to Lakshmana. Lakshmana refers her back to Ráma.

Súrpa-nakhá, considering that Lakshmana was serious, began to smile with studied art, and again addressed Ráma:—" Do you prefer Sítá to me? I will instantly devour her in your sight, and then I will roam the forest with you without a rival." Súrpa-nakhá then rushed towards Sítá in her rage, with eyes glaring like burning coals, when Ráma repelled her, and said to Lakshmana:—" O brother, it is not always proper to jest with those who are cruel and base: See Sítá is scarcely alive! O excellent one, disfigure this ugly Rákshasí!"

Súrpa-nakhá again offers herself to Ráma, and rushes upon Sítá to devour her.

The valiant Lakshmana then became exceedingly angry, and he seized his scimitar, and in the sight of Ráma he cut off the ears and nose of Súrpa-nakhá. Disfigured by the loss, the dreadful Rákshasí uttered a horrid shriek, and ran

Lakshmana cuts off the ears and nose of Súrpa-nakhá.

Súrpa-nakhá
flies for refuge
to her brother
Khara.

into the wood from whence she came. Smeared with blood, she threw out her arms, and yelled aloud, like the roaring of the clouds in the raining season. In this state she hastened to her brother Khara, who was surrounded by a multitude of Rákshasas, and she fell at length upon the ground like a star that has dropped from the sky.

Wrath of Khara.

When Khara saw his sister smeared with blood and fainting on the earth, he exclaimed in great wrath :—"Arise and tell me plainly who has done this : Who is there, who, even in sport, would vex with his finger's end a black serpent full of venom ? Who would take the rope of death and bind it round his own neck ? Yet that man has done this who has approached you this day ; that man has drank the deadly poison : What mighty one among the gods, or the great sages, can have disfigured you thus ? I see no one in this world, who would dare to do a thing displeasing to me : To-day with mortal arrows I will drink up the blood of the thousand-eyed god Indra; as a crane drinks up milk that is mixed with water : There are none of the celestials who can preserve themselves in fight from my drawn scimitar ! "

Súrpa-nakhá
relates the story
of her dis-
figurement.

At these words Súrpa-nakhá, in great grief, thus related the cause of her disaster :—"There are two brothers, Ráma and Lakshmana; they are young and beautiful, tender and yet strong, their elongated eyes resemble the water-lily ; they are clothed in the habit of devotees, and feed on fruits and roots, and have subdued their passions, and practise devout austerities, and are of royal appearance, but whether they be Davatas or Dánavas I cannot say : Between them I beheld a beautiful young woman, of waist elegantly slender, and adorned with every ornament : By these two brothers have I thus been treated for the sake of that woman : I long to drink the frothing blood of that human female, and of these two brothers ; and I pray you to accomplish my grand wish."

Khara sends
fourteen Rák-
shasas to bring
Ráma. Sítá, and
Lakshmana
before him.

While Súrpa-nakhá was thus speaking, the enraged Khara called fourteen powerful Rákshasas, as terrible as death, and said to them :—"Go and bring me two men, who are armed, and clothed in the habit of devotees, and who, with a woman, have entered the forest of Dándaka." The four-

teen Rákshasas thus commanded by Khara, went to the
hermitage of Panchavatí accompanied by Súrpa-nakhá, like
dark clouds driven before the wind; yet these Rákshasas,
armed with sharp weapons, could no more subdue the valiant
Ráma, than a wild elephant could oppose a forest when it is
burning. Inflamed with rage, and filling the air with their
terrible yells, they rushed upon the hermitage. Ráma with
his arrows cut their weapons in twain, and then seizing
fourteen arrows of iron, bright as the sun and sharpened on
a stone, he discharged them fledged with golden feathers;
and the arrows sped through the air like meteors, and pierced
the hearts of the fourteen Rákshasas; and they fell dead
upon the ground, whilst the arrows of their own accord returned to the quiver of Ráma.

Then Súrpa-nakhá uttered a tremendous yell, and fled
back to her brother Khara, and writhed upon the ground
before him like a serpent. When Khara heard that the
Rákshasas were slain by Ráma, he cried aloud in a voice of
thunder:—" Wipe away your tears, and shake off your terror! This day I will send Ráma and his brother to the
abode of Yama: This day you shall drink the blood of this
feeble mortal Ráma." Then Khara said to his brother
Dúshana:—" Equip the fourteen thousand Rákshasas, whose
courage and heroism are equal to your own; who are as
dreadful as the thunder-cloud and as valiant as tigers:
Bring also my chariot, my bows, my arrows, my scimitars,
my sharp javelins, and my iron clubs: I will myself go in
front of the children of Pulastya[2] and kill the abominable
Ráma." Then the white horses were harnessed to the
chariot of Khara, which was as dazzling as the crest of Meru
mountain, adorned with gold, fixed upon shafts of onyx,
blazened with golden moons, set with various jewels, spacious as a city, painted with fishes, flowers, trees, rocks, birds
and stars, and other devices expressive of joy. It was
decked with banners, and hung with a hundred bells; and it
moved at the will of him who rode thereon. Khara and
Dúshana mounted the chariot, and the mighty army of

[2] The Rákshasas were said to be descendants of Pulastya the sage, and are consequently sometimes alluded to as the children of Pulastya.

Rákshasas went forth with a noise like the roaring of the sea, and they were armed with every kind of weapon dreadful to behold.

Evil omens on
all sides.

But as the army of the Rákshasas marched out against Ráma, there were fearful omens on all sides. A large cloud in colour resembling an ass, poured down a shower of blood; the swift horses yoked to the chariot fell down of their own accord; the edges of the sun's face appeared of a bloody hue, and the middle of it was black; and a huge vulture came and perched on the flag raised on a golden staff in Khara's chariot. The flesh-eating birds and beasts shrieked and howled in various ways. At the rising of the sun, the jackals in the south quarter vomited fire and uttered dreadful yells; and the sky appeared red as blood, and the birds of the air uttered horrid screams. A sceptre without a head appeared near the sun. Ráhu seized the sun, and there was a great eclipse without the intervention of the new moon. The wind blew furiously; the stars twinkled like fire-flies; the water-lilies in the pools closed their flowers; the trees became destitute of flowers and fruits; the dust arose like a grey cloud; the minas uttered their plaintive notes; and meteors fell from the sky with a loud noise. The left hand of the experienced Khara trembled as he sat in his chariot; his sword fell from him; the tears dimmed his eyes whilst he was looking around, and his head began to be seized with pain.

Khara in his
infatuation
disregards the
omens.

But Khara was infatuated, and would not return; and he laughed aloud and said to the Rákshasas:—"These omens, which are so terrifying to behold, are nothing in my eyes: To me, who am full of strength, they are but trifling things; with my sharp arrows I can smite even the stars from the sky; I can kill even Yama, and conquer death itself: I never will return until I have pierced Ráma and Lakshmana with my keen arrows, and my sister has fulfilled the wish of her heart and drank their blood: In my rage I can transfix the mighty Indra, the sovereign of the gods, who rides the inebriated elephant Airávata, and holds the thunderbolt in his hand: How much more easily then can I subdue two mortals!" The army of the Rákshasas rejoiced as they heard the extravagant boasting of their chief Khara; and rushed on eager for the fight to the hermitage of Ráma.

Meanwhile, the dreadful omens which Khara regarded so slightly, had greatly troubled the minds of Ráma and Lakshmana. And Ráma said to his brother:—" Behold, O Lakshmana, these portentous omens which are intended for the destruction of the Rákshasas : All my arrows emit a smoke as if anxious for the battle, and my golden bow begins to stir of its own accord : The birds of the forest are uttering their mournful notes, as if calamity and fear of death had already reached them : The trembling of my right arm tells me that a dreadful war and a great war are near : I hear the roaring of the Rákshasas, and the loud beating of their drums : O Lakshmana, take your bow and arrows in your hand and conduct Sítá to a cave in the mountain, which is difficult of access, and covered with trees : There shall she witness at a distance the alarming tumult of the battle, and you shall hear the sound of the bowstrings filling the air : Reply not to my words, O Lakshmana, but go without delay : You are a powerful hero, and are doubtless able to destroy all these Rákshasas, but it is my desire to kill them all myself." Thus addressed by Ráma, Lakshmana took his bow and arrows and conducted Sítá to an inaccessible cave.

Then Ráma girt on his coat of mail, bright as the glow- ing flame; and he resembled a column of fire blazing in the midst of darkness. Drawing forth his mighty arrows, that heroic one stood filling all the quarters of the heavens with the sound of his bow. The gods, the Gandharvas, the Siddhas, and the Charanas, came down from heaven to behold the combat. The sages illustrious in this world, and the sages who inhabit the mansions of Brahma, said to each other :—" May peace attend the cows, the Bráhmans, and the various worlds : May Ráma subdue the night-prowling sons of Pulastya in the battle, as that mighty Vishnu, who wields the chakra, conquered the great Asuras." Vain of their powers, the shouting army of the Rákshasas had now

HISTORY OF
INDIA.
PART IV.

Fearful appear-
ance of the
Rákshasas
before the her-
mitage of Ráma.

arrived at the hermitage of Ráma; and they collected together like a vast herd of elephants thronging each other, while Khara their Chief halted his chariot. Their shields and standards appeared on every side, while their loud roarings, screaming yells, and hideous laughter filled the whole forest. The beasts of the jungle fled away without looking behind them. The sun became dim and shrouded with darkness, and the wind blew furiously against the Rakshasas. The vast army poured down swiftly upon Ráma like the

Tranquillity of
Ráma.

raging sea; but Ráma stood still with a smiling countenance, filling the heavens with the loud twanging of his bow-string.

Wrath of Ráma.

The face of Ráma blazed with the burning of his wrath, as terrible as the conflagration of the universe; and the gods and Dánavas were stricken with fear, as when the great god Siva arose with his bow to destroy the sacrifice of Daksha. The celestials in the air beheld with astonishment the face of the angry Ráma, which resembled the face of Yama at

Recoil of the
Rákshasa army
at the sight of
Ráma.

the end of a Yuga. The Rákshasas, eager as they were for the battle, were turned to stone with surprise, and stood immovable as mountains. Khara then said to his brother Dúshana:—"There is no river to be crossed, yet the army are all standing on one foot: Inquire, O great one, the cause of this!" Then Dúshana went forth and saw Ráma standing armed before him, at the sight of whom the whole army of the Rákshasas had recoiled on one foot from fear; and he returned to Khara, and said:—"Command me to combat with Ráma, that I with my arrows may send him to the abode of

Khara leads the
Rákshasa army
to the first
charge against
Ráma.

Yama." At these words Khara himself drove his chariot towards Ráma, as Ráhu rushes upon the god of day. The army of the Rákshasas were goaded to the battle by the sight of Khara, and they ran forward with a deep roaring; and their bows and ornaments, their chariots, and their fire-resembling coats of mail, appeared like a rushing of dark clouds at the time of sun-rising. Then Khara assailed Ráma with a thousand arrows, while all the Rákshasas poured on the dread-inspiring archer a mighty shower of iron clubs, javelins, darts, scimitars, and battle-axes. Then Ráma was surrounded by Rákshasas of horrid aspect, as the clouds

surround the Raja of mountains with streams of rain, or as
the great god Siva is surrounded on the lunar days by all
his servants and courtiers. He received all the arrows of
the Rákshasas as the sea receives all the rivers; and
although wounded by their dreadful shafts, the hero felt no
pain.

Like a huge mountain pierced with many flaming
thunderbolts, Ráma stood with his whole body streaming
with blood, but shining like the evening sun surrounded by
fiery clouds. Seeing the hero hemmed round by so many
thousands, the gods, the Gandharvas, the Siddhas, and the
great sages began to lament. At length Ráma, filled with
anger, drew his bow even to a circle, and discharged keen
arrows by thousands. The fatal shafts, dreadful as the snare
of death, winged with the feathers of kingfishers and
adorned with gold, were discharged by Ráma as if in sport.
They pierced the bodies of Rákshasas, and then mounted
the air and shone there with the splendour of fire. Some of
the arrows cut in pieces the bows, the flag staffs, the shields,
the coats of mail, and the long arms of the Rákshasas which
were like the trunks of elephants adorned with various
ornaments. Other arrows mangled and pierced the golden-
saddled horses, the chariots and their drivers, the elephants
and their attendants, and sent all the footmen to the abode
of Yama. The Rákshasas, wounded by the sharp and burning bolts, uttered fearful yells, which reached the sky; and
they found no more quarter from the heart-piercing arrows
of Ráma, than a dry forest receives from a merciless fire.

*Ráma dis-
charges his
terrible arrows.*

Then some of the Rákshasas ran to Khara for refuge, and
Dúshana, foaming with rage, led them on to another attack
upon Ráma. Some were armed with trees, some with staves,
spears, and clubs, and some with platted ropes or nooses;
and they discharged thousands of arrows, and trees, and
large stones at the dauntless Ráma; and the tumult of that
dreadful battle made the hair of men stand erect from fear.
Then Ráma uttered a tremendous shout, and fitted to his
bow a brightly shining weapon named Gandharva, at which
a thousand arrows flew from his well-drawn bow. The sun

*Second charge
of the Rák-
shasa army
against Ráma.*

*Ráma again
effects fearful
destruction.*

was shrouded by those arrows and the air was darkened; whilst the earth was covered with wounded Rákshasas and fallen weapons. The exhausted, the killed, the wounded, and the mangled were scattered here and there in thousands. The field of battle, dreadful to behold, was strewed with turbaned heads, with hands and arms and legs adorned with ornaments, with horses and elephants and broken chariots, with chámaras and fans and flag staffs, with broken spears and scimitars, and with innumerable arrows and other weapons; and the few remaining Rákshasas fled deeply afflicted before the conquering Ráma.

Third charge of the Rák-shasa army against Ráma.

After this the weakened remnant of the Rákshasas again put their trust in Khara and Dúshana, and arose in battle a third time against Ráma. The mighty hero, humble but stead-fast in mind, once more stood against the arrogant few who still urged the fight. He received the dreadful shower of weapons like a bull catching the large drops of autumnal rain. At length, he seized a divine weapon to destroy in one mo-ment the whole of the Rákshasas. Blazing like the fire, he scattered in an instant the whole of the forces of Khara and Dúshana. Then with his arrows he cut asunder the great bow of Dúshana, and slew the horses that were harnessed to his chariot; and with three more arrows he smote Dúshana on the breast, and took off the head of his charioteer. Then Dúshana seized a club which resembled a mountain-peak; it was encompassed with a golden band like that on the staff of Yama, and was full of sharp iron spikes, destructive to the armies of the gods, besmeared with the flesh of foes, rough to the touch, dashing gates and doors to pieces, and terrific to all beings. Grasping this mighty club Dúshana flew at Ráma, but Ráma cut off both his hands; and Dúshana, de-prived of his club, fell to the ground like an elephant of the Himálayas deprived of his tusks; and he was instantly killed by the heroic Ráma.

Slaughter of the Rákshasas.

Combat be-tween Ráma and Dúshana.

Death of Dúshana.

Combat be-tween Ráma and Khara.

Then Khara, seeing his brother slain, roared like the roar of a kettle-drum which has been wetted with water; and rushing towards Ráma, he discharged flaming arrows of iron as fatal as enraged serpents: but Ráma stopped the shafts with his own arrows, as the foot-rope stops the elephant. Khara in his own chariot then approached Ráma, as a grasshopper leaps into the fire; but Ráma seized the bow of Vishnu, which had been given him by Agastya, and discharged innumerable arrows, and broke the chariot of Khara, and killed his horses and charioteer. Khara then leaped forward with a mighty club in his hand, and hurled it at Ráma like a flaming thunderbolt; but Ráma turned it back again and shivered it to pieces with a fire weapon of divine powers. Ráma now smiled at Khara, and said :— *Ráma threatens and abuses Khara.* "You vile Rákshasa, your boasted might has now been seen, and you roar aloud in vain: You promised to wipe away the tears of these slain Rákshasas, but your promise has been broken: To-day I will take away the life of so mean a liar, even as Garura seized the amrita: To-day the earth shall drink your blood bubbling in foam from your throat: Your carcase shall roll in the dust, and you shall embrace the earth as a man embraces a beautiful spouse: To-day all the sages shall hear that you have been killed, and shall traverse the forest of Dándaka without fear: To-day all the women of the Rákshasas shall tremble with alarm at being deprived of their lords; they shall taste of the grief which they deserve for being united to such husbands: You ever cruel wretch, the terror of the Bráhmans, apostate from all virtue, saturated with every crime, you shall receive to-day the reward of your vile actions." Thus *Death of Khara.* speaking, Ráma fought with Khara for the last time, and discharged a flaming arrow which pierced his mail armour even to the bone; and Khara fell upon the earth burnt up as with fire, and gave up the ghost. Then the sound of the *Rejoicings of the gods.* divine kettle-drums was heard in the heavens, and flowers fell from the sky upon the head of Ráma; and the gods and sages, and all the celestial beings, poured praises and benedictions upon the conqueror of the Rákshasas. And *Sítá returns to Ráma.* Lakshmana and Sítá came out of the cave, and Sítá embraced her husband with great joy; and Ráma embraced the fawn-eyed Sítá, and appeared among the adoring sages as glorious as Indra in heaven.

HISTORY OF
INDIA.
PART IV.

News of the
defeat of the
Rákshasas
carried to
Rávana.

Rávana per-
suaded by the
messenger to
carry off Sitá.

Rávana consults
his minister
Márícha.

Márícha dis-
suades Rávana
from the at-
tempt.

Now a certain Rákshasa escaped from that dreadful battle, and hastened to Lanká, and told the melancholy tidings to the ten-headed Rávana.   Then the eyes of Rávana were red with anger, and hearing that his two brothers, Khara and Dúshana, had been killed by Ráma, he snuffed up the air like the Raja of Serpents; and he said :—" I will go myself and kill Ráma and Lakshmana."   And the Rákshasa replied :— " O ten-headed one, Ráma can no more be overcome by you in battle, nor by the world of Rákshasas, than heaven can be obtained by sinful men : Not all the gods and Asuras united can accomplish his death : But listen to my plan for his destruction : He has a beautiful wife whose name is Sitá; she is a woman of delicate shape, of golden complexion, and the most exact symmetry: Adorned with jewels, no goddess, nor Apsara, nor Nága can be compared with her ; where then could be found her equal among mortals ?   Carry off this beautiful woman, and Ráma will be crushed in the great forest, for he cannot exist without Sitá."   Rávana was pleased with this counsel, and said :— " To-morrow I will go with my charioteer, and bring Sitá to this great city."   Then Rávana ascended his chariot which was drawn by asses, and was as splendid as the sun, and he went to the dwelling of Márícha who was his minister, and told him all that the Rákshasa had said; and he entreated Márícha to counsel him concerning his carrying away the wife of Ráma.   Márícha however replied :—" What enemy in the guise of a friend has mentioned Sitá to you?   The man who has thus stirred you up is undoubtedly your bitterest foe : He wishes to engage you in plucking out the fangs of a venomous serpent !   O Rávana, Ráma is a furious elephant inebriated with energy; his tusks are full grown ; he is the fierce man-lion destroying the wounded Rákshasas as though they were trembling deer : O Rávana, rouse not this sleeping lion whose body is full of arrows, and whose teeth are sharpened scimitars : Return in peace to Lanká, and enjoy yourself among your own wives, and let Ráma enjoy his spouse in the forest."   So the ten-headed Rávana

listened to the words of Márícha, and returned to his stately HISTORY OF INDIA. PART IV.
palace at Lanká.

The foregoing narrative, as already indicated, is Review of the foregoing narrative of Ráma's wars on account of Súrpa-nakhá.
essentially Hindú. No one but an oriental bard
would have ventured to depict a woman making
such proposals to two men in succession, as were addressed by Súrpa-nakhá to Ráma and Lakshmana;
and no audience, excepting an oriental one, would
have appreciated the jesting replies of Ráma and
his brother, or have applauded the savage proceed-
ing of Lakshmana. The description of the wars Brilliant imagination displayed in the details.
that ensued is apparently the work of pure imagin-
ation, whilst the similes are often far-fetched; but
still the details exhibit some brilliant coruscations of
fancy, which although altogether unreal, serve to
amuse the intellect in much the same manner as a
display of fireworks amuses the eye. The slaughter
of fourteen Rákshasas with fourteen iron arrows,
bright as the sun and fledged with golden feathers,
is an exploit on the part of the leading hero which
would have satisfied most romance writers. But Divinity of Ráma manifested in his victories over the Rákshasa army.
Ráma was to be represented as a god, and conse-
quently the story was told of his triumphantly re-
sisting three distinct charges of an army of fourteen
thousand Rákshasas, as dreadful as the thunder-
cloud and as valiant as tigers, and ultimately slaying
them all. Such a narrative, half heroic and half Impression of the story upon a Hindú audience.
divine, never fails to create a deep impression upon
a Hindú audience. The fantastic character of the
omens which preceded the battle, and the extravagant idea that the gods came down from heaven to
witness the conflict, are perfectly understood and
fully accepted by every Hindú. The descriptions Reality of the descriptions to the Hindú.

Reality of
Khara's
wonderful
chariot.

The Rákshasa
army.

Deep personal
interest taken
by the audience
in Ráma's
single combats.

Exulting chorus
of "Glory to
Ráma!"

again are very graphic, although exuberant beyond
measure; and the pictures which they bring before
the mind's eye are real and substantial forms to the
Hindú, although they must appear as mere idle
dreams to the European. Thus every Hindú audience accepts as a grand reality the marvellous
chariot in which Khara and Dúshana ride to battle.
Each one realizes the appearance of the vast car,
spacious as a city, and moving at the will of its oc-
cupants, sparkling with jewels and golden moons,
decked with banners and hung with bells, and
resplendent with pictures of fishes, flowers, trees,
rocks, birds, and stars. In like manner each one
can perceive the army of Rákshasas rushing with
yells and roarings upon the quiet hermitage of
Ráma, and pouring a shower of iron clubs, javelins,
darts, scimitars, and battle-axes upon the dauntless
hero; whilst Ráma stands as bright and unmoved as
a pillar of fire, and replies with countless arrows
which carry death and destruction amongst the
advancing host. Lastly, the audience always takes a
deep personal interest in the single combats between
Ráma and Dúshana, and Ráma and Khara. Every
one exults and sympathizes in the abusive language
which Ráma lavishly employs against Khara, and
which is scarcely compatible with the divine character of the incarnation of Vishnu, although in strict
accordance with the ancient usage of the Kshatriyas.
Finally, when the story is told that Khara is slain
by the flaming arrow amidst the rejoicings of the
gods and sages, one and all rejoice in like manner,
and the air is filled with the pious chorus of "Glory
to Ráma!"

CHAPTER XVII.

RÁVANA'S ABDUCTION OF SÍTÁ.

THE defeat of Khara and Dúshana now brings Rávana himself upon the scene. This powerful sovereign is said to have been not only a worshipper of Brahma, but a grandson of a Bráhman sage named Pulastya; consequently he does not appear as an aboriginal monarch, but as a heretic, a renegade, an apostate, who was employing against the Bráhmans the very powers which he had acquired by the worship of Brahma.

The narrative of the carrying away of Sítá by Rávana requires but a brief introduction. The design was first suggested to Rávana, as already seen, by a Rákshasa who had fled from the dreadful battle with Ráma; but he is said to have been dissuaded from the attempt by his Minister Márícha, the very Rákshasa whom Ráma had driven into the sea in the great battle near the hermitage of Viswámitra. Súrpa-nakhá, however, was resolved to be revenged alike on Ráma and Sítá; and she accordingly stirred up the rage of Rávana against the one, and excited his desires for the other. The story requires no preliminary explanation. It will be sufficient to bear in mind that according to the popular belief the Rákshasas had the power of as-

HISTORY OF
INDIA.
PART IV.

Extraordinary
conception that
Rávana had
ten heads and
twenty arms, a
substantive
belief with the
Hindús.

suming any form at will; and that Rávana in his normal shape possessed ten heads and twenty arms. However wild and unnatural this idea may seem to the European, it is a substantive conception to every Hindú, for it is formed in boyhood, and strengthened by the frequent sight of numerous pictures of the terrible Rákshasa. From the narrative Rávana would appear to be only a mortal sovereign of the ordinary human type as regards appearance and shape; and indeed, in his character as a lover of woman, it is difficult to conceive of him as any other than a mortal man. But the Hindú realizes him as a huge being moving along the earth like a vast tower, with ten crowned heads rising on separate necks, and twenty arms stretching out on either side. Such a monstrosity is the pure creation of a disordered

Probable origin
of the con-
ception.

brain; an unmeaning mass of incongruities; and probably arose from some childish idea that by multiplying the arms the physical strength of the demon was increased tenfold, and by multiplying the number of heads, the intelligence or cunning of the Rákshasa was increased in the same ratio.

The narrative
of the capture
of Sítá by
Rávana.

The narrative of the circumstances connected with the capture of Sítá by Rávana is as follows:—

Súrpa-nakhá
carries the news
of Khara's
defeat to
Lanká.

Now when Súrpa-nakhá, the sister of Rávana, saw that her brothers Khara and Dúshana, and the mighty army of Rákshasas, had been slain by the single mortal Ráma, she set up a horrid yell like the roaring of a thunder-cloud. She then hastened to Lanká, and beheld Rávana seated in front of his palace upon a throne of gold, as bright as the sun and as glowing as flame; and he was surrounded by his Counsellors as Indra is surrounded by the Maruts. He had

Description of
Raja Rávana.

ten heads and twenty arms; and his eyes were of the colour of copper, whilst his teeth were white like the new moon.

His form was vast like a mountain, and his ten faces were each as terrible as that of the all-destroying Yama. He was a tall and heroic Rákshasa, possessing all the signs of royalty, and invincible to the gods. His body was as smooth as a polished onyx, and his ears were adorned with earrings; but his breast was scarred by the thunder-bolt of Indra, the tusks of Airávata, and the chakra of Vishnu. He could *His mighty powers.* shake the seas with his strides, and rend asunder the tops of mountains with his brawny arms. He was the breaker *His wickedness.* of all laws, the ravisher of the wives of others, the murderer of the Bráhmans, the obstructor of sacrifice, the enemy of sacred vows. This was he, who went to the city of *His exploits.* Bhagavati, the great city of resplendent serpents, and conquered Vásukí, and carried away the beloved wife of the *Conquered Vásukí and Kuvera.* snake Takshaka. This was he, who conquered Kuvera on the Kailása mountain, and carried away the chariot Pushpaka, which constantly obeys the will of the rider; who in his rage destroyed the divine forests of Chitra, Nalina, Nandana, and all the gardens of the gods; who by the strength of his mighty arms stopped the sun and the moon in their course, and prevented their rising. This was he who performed *His religious austerities.* religious austerities in a vast forest for ten thousand years, standing on his head with his feet uppermost in the midst of five fires; who by permission of Brahma traversed the air in an instant, and assumed any shape at will; who offered his ten heads as a sacrifice to Siva; who caused the affrighted sun to rise upon his city with a subdued lustre. He was the cruel one, the wicked, and the furious; who by *Invulnerable to all excepting beasts and men.* the blessing of Brahma was invulnerable to gods and demons, and to every being excepting beast and man.

When Súrpa-nakhá saw her brother Rávana, adorned *Súrpa-nakhá's angry address to Rávana.* with excellent ornaments and beautiful flowers, she approached him flaming with rage; and with wide-stretched fiery eyes, and a dejected countenance, and mad with fear and terror, she yelled out these horrid accents:—"Intoxicated with the pleasure of sense, you disregard the dreadful danger which has arisen: The Raja who is devoted to his lusts, even though he be lord of the world, is detested by his subjects, as men detest a fire in which the dead have been burned : The Raja who does not in due time attend to his own affairs, will perish together with his Raj : The Raja who listens not to his spies, and is incapable of governing himself, is avoided by men, as elephants avoid the swampy edge of a river : Know you not that Khara and Dúshana, with fourteen thousand fiery Rákshasas, have been slain by the single mortal Ráma ? Know you not that Ráma has become the saviour of the sages, and has rendered the forest of Dándaka secure from the Rákshasas ? O Rávana, you can discern nothing, since you have not learned from your spies of the terrible slaughter of the Rákshasas ? "

Súrpa-nakhá describes Ráma to Rávana, and dilates on the beauty of Sitá.

Sitting among his courtiers, Rávana was enraged at these abusive speeches of Súrpa-nakhá, and cried out :—" Who is Ráma ? " Súrpa-nakhá replied :—" Ráma, the son of Dasaratha, is of long arm and elongated eye ; he is the chief of all those who wear the habit of a devotee ; he is equal in form to Káma ; he carries a bow resembling a rainbow, and discharges blazing iron arrows as fatal as poisonous serpents : I saw not the valiant Ráma draw his bow, but I saw the army falling by his arrows, as a full crop of corn is smitten by the rains sent by Indra : O Rávana, this Ráma has a beautiful wife, of charming face, and slender and delicate form, and complexion as bright as molten gold : He who is embraced by Sítá enjoys a felicity beyond that of Indra : O Rávana, it was because I wanted to bring away this beautiful woman to become your wife that my nose and ears were cut off by the cruel Lakshmana : When you behold Sítá, you will instantly be pierced by the arrows of the god of love : O Raja of the Rákshasas, revenge the death of your brothers upon Ráma and Lakshmana, and take the beautiful Sítá to be your wife."

Counsels Rávana to carry away Sitá.

Rávana again visits Máricha, and desires Máricha to assist him in carrying away Sitá.

Having heard these roaring words of his sister Súrpa-nakhá, Rávana ordered his chariot, and again proceeded to the abode of Máricha. And Rávana said :—" O Máricha, my father, I am distressed and you are my great refuge : That contemptible Ráma, the meanest of the Kshatriyas, expelled by his father, has been the murderer of my army : This tame and ignorant fellow, intent on the evil of all creatures, by whom my sister was disfigured to show his powers in taking away her ears and nose, has a wife named Sítá, who is in the prime of youth and beauty, resembling Lakshmí without her lotos : Her I will bring away this day, and you must be my helper ! Do you assume the shape of a golden deer studded with silver spots, and go to the hermitage of Ráma : Sítá, seeing your beauty, will ask Ráma and Lakshmana to procure you for her ; and when you have beguiled the brothers from the hermitage, I will carry off Sítá through the air, as Ráhu takes away the light of the moon."

Entreats Márícha to take the form of a golden deer.

Hearing these words respecting Ráma, the countenance of Márícha became withered ; and he licked his parched lips, and stared with fixed eyes at Rávana ; and spoke with joined hands, as follows :—" O Raja of the Rákshasas, you have been deceived : Ráma is magnanimous and highly renowned ; he was not abandoned by his father nor ever disgraced : He is not covetous, nor evil disposed, nor a mean Kshatriya ; his subjects were not in distress nor were the Bráhmans averse to him : He is Chief of the universe, as Indra is sovereign of the gods : How can you desire to carry off his wife Sítá, whose virtue is her preservation, and whose splendour is equal to that of fire ? If you carry away the wife of Ráma, your destruction is certain : In former times I traversed the wilderness of Dándaka with the might of a thousand elephants ; and Ráma, then a boy of fifteen, came to the hermitage of Viswámitra to protect the Bráhmans : I assumed a form as vast as a mountain, and went to the hermitage without fear ; but this beardless boy shot a dreadful arrow at my breast, and I was cast far away into the sea : My life was preserved because he desired not to kill me ; but if when a child he overcame me, how shall I engage against him now ? O Maháraja, if in wantonness you carry away Sítá, you will involve yourself in the most dreadful misery ; the city of Lanká will be reduced to ruins ; your Rákshasas will be slain in battle by Ráma ; and your women

Alarm of Márícha.

Márícha dilates on the power of Ráma.

Remonstrates with Rávana against carrying away Sítá.

Relates the story of his being cast by Ráma into the sea.

Prophesies utter ruin if Rávana carries away Sítá.

will run away in all directions: Engaged in war with Ráma, you will soon lose your honour, your prosperity, your Raj, your wives, and your own life."[1]

Rávana contemptuously replies that he requires no advice.

When Rávana heard these words, he slighted the wise reasoning of Márícha, as one who is desirous of death refuses medicine. Considering Márícha as one.speaking for his hurt, Rávana, impelled by his fate, thus contemptuously replied :—" Why, Márícha, speak these silly things to me ? Your speech is as useless as seed sown upon salt : I cannot be affrighted by your words ; I cannot fear Ráma ; and most assuredly I will carry off the wife of the murderer of Khara : The sovereign of the world is not to be contradicted, but to be addressed in gentle and pleasing language : I did not ask you, O Rákshasa, respecting the good or evil of the undertaking, nor about my own ability, but I re-

Commands Márícha to take the form of a golden deer and gambol in the presence of Sítá.

quested your assistance only : Assuming the form of a golden deer studded with silver spots, do you go into the view of Sítá and gambol in her presence : After performing this service, go where you will ; and I will then give you the half of my Raj."

Márícha unwillingly obeys.

Márícha was sorely perplexed at the commands of Rávana, for he knew that his death was near ; and he sighed repeatedly, and said :—" I will go, but I shall be slain ; nor will you, O Rávana, return alive ! " Rávana replied : —" Now I see that you are Márícha, but from your former speech I thought you must be some other Rákshasa :

Invited by Rávana to ascend his chariot.

Speedily mount with me this resplendent air-traversing chariot, drawn by asses with the heads of Rákshasas : Having allured Sítá, go where you will ; I will speedily carry her off from her protectors."

---

[1] These events are differently described in the Adhyátma Rámáyana. Both Márícha and Rávana are there said to have acknowledged that Ráma was an incarnation of the deity ; and each is said to have believed that if he fell by the hand of Ráma he would obtain everlasting salvation. Rávana therefore argued that if conquered by Ráma he should obtain paradise ; whilst if he became conqueror he would retain possession of Sítá. Márícha had another alternative. If he refused to comply with the request of Rávana, he would be killed by him, and would consequently go to hell. If on the other hand he assumed the form of a deer he would be killed by Ráma and go to heaven.

Rávana and Máricha then mounted the chariot which resembled a palace, and flew through the air over the forests, the mountains, the rivers, the countries, and the cities on their way, until they came to the wilderness of Dándaka, where stood the hermitage of Ráma.   There the Raja of the Rákshasas alighted with Máricha from the gold-adorned chariot, and he looked round, and took Máricha by the hand, and said :— " Here is the hermitage of Ráma surrounded by plantain trees : O my companion, speedily do that for which we came hither." At these words of Rávana, the sage Máricha assumed the shape of a deer, and went to the door of the hut ; and his horns were tipped with sapphire, his face was variegated with black and white, his mouth resembled the red lotos, and his azure eyes were like blue water-lilies.   In this captivating form, adorned with various jewels, and grazing at its own will, the silver-spotted deer cropped the tender shoots of the trees, and at length entered the plantain grove to attract the eye of Sítá.

Journey of Rávana and Máricha to the hermitage of Ráma at Panchavatí.

Máricha assumes the form of a very beautiful deer.

Now while this lovely deer was grazing and gamboling near the hut, the charming-eyed Sítá, eager to pluck flowers, went forth among the trees.   There the beautiful one beheld that deer covered with fine hair, and adorned with jewels, and bespangled with pearls ; its sides presenting a beautiful mixture of gold and silver colour.   Then Sítá was filled with surprise, and repeatedly called to Ráma :—" Come, my beloved, and behold this golden deer with variegated sides : I long to repose at ease on the golden skin of this deer." Then Ráma was highly pleased, and said to his brother :— " Observe, O Lakshmana, the strong desire of Sítá for this deer-skin : Be on your guard this day respecting Sítá, while I go and pierce the deer with an arrow :   Having killed it, I will speedily bring its skin hither; go not from home until I return :   Obtaining this skin, Sítá will repose this day as magnificently as she did at Ayodhyá."   The ardent hero then threw his golden bow over his shoulder, but Lakshmana, profoundly reflecting, said to him :—" It was formerly told us by the sages that Máricha, the mighty Rákshasa, who assumes illusive forms, sometimes assumes that of a deer ; and

Sítá sees the deer and requests Ráma to procure its skin for her.

Ráma leaves Sítá in charge of Lakshmana, and prepares to chase the deer.

Lakshmana reminds Ráma that Máricha could take a deer's form.

in this form he has slain many Princes : O Ráma, consider if a deer exists made of gold, with horns of coral, and gems for its eyes ! I believe this to be a factitious animal, or a Rákshasa in the form of a deer." But Sítá continued to pray Ráma to bring her the lovely deer, and he was equally desirous of securing it, and taking his bow and quivers he went forth into the jungle.[2]

Ráma chases the deer and slays it.

When Ráma approached the deer it bounded forwards, and sometimes it appeared before his eyes, and then it re-tired to different parts of the wood, until it had drawn him to a considerable distance from the hermitage. After a long time Ráma discharged a deadly arrow which pierced the heart of the deer-formed Márícha. Pained with the wound,

Márícha returns to his proper form, and dies crying for Sítá and Lakshmana in a voice resembling that of Ráma.

Márícha leaped from out of the body of the deer to the height of a palmyra tree, and fell down in the shape of a monstrous Rákshasa with vast teeth, and adorned with a golden necklace and various ornaments. Márícha then cried out with a voice resembling that of Ráma :—" O Sítá, save me ! O Lakshmana, save me !" With these words Márícha expired, and Ráma, perceiving the illusion, ex-

Rámá takes the skin and returns to the hermitage.

claimed :—"I have killed Márícha !" Then he took the beautiful skin from the body of the deer, and remembering what Lakshmana had said, and pondering over the last words of the Rákshasa, he felt great alarm, and returned in all haste to his hermitage.

Sítá hears the voice of the deer, and desires Lakshmana to assist Ráma.

Meanwhile Sítá had heard the voice of Márícha in the forest, which resembled the voice of Ráma ; and she said to Lakshmana :—" Go and learn how it is with Ráma : I have heard the piercing sound of his groan, and it becomes you to

---

[2] The following curious comment upon this event occurs in the Adhyátma Rámáyana :—" Should any one say Ráma hath forgotten himself, he, with his eyes open and knowing the consequences, followed the stag, the answer is, Ráma being distinct from all things, no injury can occur to him. What power can delusion have over him ? He hath performed various actions in this world for the sake of those who worship him ; he fulfils the desires of those who adore him with sincerity : Besides, it was necessary Rávana should commit some crime that, when his guilt was confirmed, Ráma might slay him. Ráma then had no other object in view, for he is never influenced by worldly objects ; he is the Supreme Soul, the everlasting Great One. Sítá loved him ; for her sake therefore he undertook this task."

save your elder brother :   Run quickly to Ráma who craves
succour, and who lies in the power of the Rákshasas like a
bull among lions.''[3] Thus addressed Lakshmana forbore to
go, and said :—'' Why, O goddess, are you thus distressed ?
My elder brother cannot be vanquished by the three worlds ;
the Rákshasa cannot give pain to his little finger.''   Then
Sítá was filled with wrath, and exclaimed :—'' O Lakshmana,
you are the enemy of your brother if you run not to his assistance : Surely you must be pleased with your brother's
distress, or you would not stand here so carelessly : Is it
for my sake that, disregarding my words, you desire the
death of Ráma ? Know, O hero, that I will not survive the

---

[3] The death of Márícha furnishes the author of the Adhyátma Rámáyana,
with a further text for expatiating on the divinity of Ráma.   It is said that when
Márícha had uttered the dying words quoted above, he obtained salvation in the
following manner :—'' When Márícha had uttered these words his soul departed
from his mortal frame ; and a small flame issuing from his body entered into the
foot of Ráma.   So great, so exalted is the name of Ráma, that even this
perpetrator of evil deeds, under the form of a demon, obtained salvation by being
absorbed into the essence of the deity.   Such a lot was his, as others who have
passed thousands of years in religious penances could not attain.   If any man,
who may have committed during any of his lives the most heinous crimes, shall
at his death with sincerity pronounce the name of Ráma, his sins, of whatever
nature they may be, shall be forgiven ; he will be absorbed into the divinity.
Thus Márícha obtained his death from the hand of Ráma ; he beheld him ; what
doubt then could exist, after pronouncing his name, that he should attain this
heavenly bliss free from future birth and regeneration.
   '' Brahma and the spirits of heaven assembling in the heavens above showered
down Parijáta flowers on Ráma.   They conversed together, saying :—' Behold,
brethren ! how this sinner has been saved ; such is the benevolence of Ráma.
What good actions had this demon performed that he could deserve such happiness ?   Behold what supreme bliss Ráma hath conferred on him who was peculiarly guilty, who destroyed numbers of saints : Such is the reward granted to
those who worship Ráma, who call upon his name : Great indeed is the excellence
and purity of Ráma's name.'   Brahma then said to the gods :—' This demon
who has been slain by the hand of Ráma, during former births worshipped Ráma
with sincerity and faith ; even during his late existence he entertained the greatest dread of him : By the blessing of Ráma's name, and of his former faith, his
sins have been remitted : He has, from having resigned his life at Ráma's feet,
and beholding him, been absorbed into him : Attend to me, ye heavenly spirits !
while I explain the cause of these things : If a Bráhman, or Chandála, or demon,
or any other person, be he a Mahárája or a beggar, shall have been guilty of the
most enormous crimes, if at his death he pronounce the name of Ráma, it is expressly stated in the Vedas that that person's sins will be remitted, and that he
will obtain everlasting salvation.''   Brahma and the gods, having thus conversed
together, paid their adorations to Ráma, and departed to their own abodes.''

Lakshmana
assures Sitá
that Ráma is in
no danger, and
that the voice
was that of a
Rákshasa.

death of Ráma an instant; why then do you hesitate to go in quest of Ráma?" To Sítá, suffused with tears and timid as a doe, Lakshmana replied thus :—" O goddess, there is no apprehension to be felt for Ráma; he is invulnerable in battle : O Sítá, it ill becomes you to speak to me thus : You are a charge committed to my care by the faithful and magnanimous Ráma, and I cannot leave you : It was not the voice of Ráma that was heard by you, but the voice of some hostile Rákshasa : Were his danger ever so imminent, Ráma would never utter accents so despicable and so unworthy of him; never would the saviour of the celestials exclaim :—

Sítá charges
Lakshmana
with desiring to
marry her.

' O Sítá, save me.' " Sítá, her eyes reddened with rage, replied to Lakshmana as follows :—" You cruel wretch, do you aspire to obtain me for yourself ? Have you followed Ráma into the jungle for my sake, or as a secret emissary from Bharata ? But I tell you that I will never leave my husband Ráma, nor desire another man : I will enter the blazing fire, but not even with my foot will I touch any man beside Ráma." Sítá then began to beat her breast with both her hands, when Lakshmana filled with agitation, thus replied with joined hands :—" O Sítá, I cannot reply to you who are my deity : Such language from a woman is not surprising, for women are regardless of what is right, and often rouse discord between brothers : O Sítá, your words are like red-hot iron in my ears." Then repenting of this harsh language, Lakshmana said :—" O beauteous one, I will go to Ráma : May good attend you, and all the gods protect you; I tremble at the necessity to which I am reduced ! When I return may I see you with Ráma ! " Sítá, drowned in tears, replied :—" O Lakshmana, if I am deprived of Ráma I will enter the river Godáveri, and hang myself, or take

Lakshmana
reluctantly
leaves Sitá alone
and goes in
search of
Ráma.

Ravana visits
the hermitage
of Ráma in the
guise of a
religious
mendicant.
His address to
Sitá.

poison, or enter the blazing fire, but never will I touch any man save Ráma." Having thus vowed to Lakshmana, Sítá continued to beat her bosom in an agony of distress; and Lakshmana tried to console her, but she would not speak another word; and he bowed to her feet and went out in the forest to seek for Ráma.

When both Ráma and Lakshmana had thus been drawn

away from Sítá, the wicked Rávana left his chariot, and assumed the form of a mendicant, and went speedily towards the hermitage. He was clothed in a thin red garment, with a tuft of matted hair on the crown of his head, an umbrella in his hand, shoes on his feet, a trident, a bag hanging by his side with his provisions, and a dish to receive alms.[4] In this garb the evil one approached Sítá, and said:—"You pleasing fair one, whose smile and eyes are captivating, you shed a radiance around you: You timid one in full flower, dressed in yellow silk and adorned with garlands, how came you to reside in this forest? Who are you and whither have you come?" Seeing Rávana in the guise of a Bráhman, Sítá showed him every respect, and welcomed him with all that was proper to entertain a stranger, and related to him the story of herself and her lord, saying:—"Expelled from the Raj by the word of Kaikeyí, we roam about the thick forest guarded by our power: Be content and remain here until the return of my husband: Ráma will receive you with great respect, for he is pleasing in speech and a lover of devotees."

Sítá, seeing Rávana in the guise of a Bráhman, treats him with respect.

When Sítá had thus spoken, the mighty Raja of the Rákshasas replied in these heart-appalling words:—"Hear who I am, and whence I come; for I have taken this assumed form to see you: I am that Rávana, the tormentor of the world, by whom gods and men have been driven hither and thither; and it was by my order, O beautiful one, that Khara guarded this wilderness of Dándaka: I am the brother of Kuvera, and grandson of Pulastya, who was the son of Brahma: I have received a blessing from the self-existent Brahma: I am able to assume any form, or go to any place: My name is Rávana, and I am known throughout the universe by my power: Your beauty, O smiling one, arrayed in yellow silk, eclipses in my eyes the beauty of all my own wives: O Sítá, numerous are my wives, be you my Rání, and the chief of them all: Lanká, my delightful

Rávana makes himself known to Sítá.

Invites Sítá to become his chief Rání.

Describes his city and palaces.

---

[4] This is an accurate description of a religious mendicant such as may often be seen in the present day.

city, is an island surrounded by the sea, situated upon a mountain-top adorned with seven elevated peaks, encircled by a deep moat, filled with palaces and magnificent edifices, and renowned throughout the three worlds like Amarávati, the city of Indra : This capital of the Rákshasas is a charming place built by Viswa-karmá : There, O Sítá, you shall walk with me among the groves, and feel no wish to return to this forest : You shall be the chief of all my wives, and five thousand handmaids, adorned with every ornament, shall attend you ! "

Wrathful reply of Sítá.

The slender-waisted Sítá, enraged at this address of Rávana, replied to him with contemptuous words as follows : —"Know that I am the daughter of Raja Janaka, the daughter-in-law of Maháraja Dasaratha, the beloved wife of Ráma, and that I esteem my husband as a deity : Know that, faithful to my vows, I am the devoted follower of my husband, who at the command of his father resides in the forest of Dándaka : Know that I rest upon Ráma, who is as great as the sovereign of the gods, and the source of all happiness, as Sachí rests upon her husband Indra : Know that I am devoted to that great and fortunate one, the chief of devotees, as Arundhatí is devoted to Vasishtha : As a lioness attends a strong lion, so am I the constant attendant of the strong, the full-chested, and the majestic Ráma : Do you, a pitiful jackal, wish to obtain a lioness, who am to you as a ray of the sun is to a fire-fly ? Do you wish to snatch a fawn from a furious lion and hastily devour it ? "

Rávana assumes his proper form.

Having heard the words of Sítá, the ten-headed Rávana twisted his hands together through rage, and spoke as follows :—"Infatuated as you are, O Sítá, I can only suppose that you know not my heroism and power : Standing in the air I can sustain with my hands both the earth and the sea, and am able to kill Yama himself in battle : I can torment the sun, or pierce through the earth with my arrows : O foolish one, behold me changing my form, and assuming any shape at pleasure ! " Saying this, the angry Rávana threw off the form of a mendicant, and assumed his own shape, as vast as a mountain and as terrible as Yama. He had red

Description of Rávana.

eyes, a vast breast, huge arms like the fore-legs of a lion, HISTORY OF
huge shoulders like those of a bull, and a spotted body. The INDIA.
PART IV.
hair on his ten heads emitted streams of fire, whilst his body
was covered with black bristles like a mountain covered with
the skins of black antelopes ; and he was arrayed in garments
of a blood-red colour, and monstrous earrings of heated gold
flamed in all his ears. Thus with ten heads and twenty
arms, and eyes glaring with rage, Rávana, Raja of the
Rákshasas, stood before Sítá like a huge black cloud, and
again spoke to her thus :—" Why are you attached to Ráma, Rávana remon-
strates with
Sítá.
who is clothed in the habit of a mendicant, and weak in un-
derstanding ?   If, O fair one, you desire a husband renowned
throughout the three worlds, recline on me !   I am a spouse
worthy of you :   O excellent one, abandon all thoughts of
Ráma, and think upon me with affection, and I will never
do that which is painful to you : It is foolish to reject me
because I am a Rákshasa : I will, O timid one, be constantly
under your control ; and for a full year whilst your heart is
affected for Ráma I will not speak a word to you that shall
be unpleasing to your mind." [5]

. Then that most wicked Rákshasa, intoxicated with evil Rávana carries
Sítá through
the air and
places her in
his chariot.
desire, approached and seized Sítá as Chandra seized Rohiní
in the air.   With flaming eyes, and bending his frightful
brows, he grasped the lotos-eyed Sítá by the hair of the
head, whilst she cried out :—" O Ráma !   O Lakshmana !
save me ! "   Then that wicked wretch mounted with her in
the air, as Garura carried off the wife of the Raja of the
serpents ; and he seized her by the hand, as a Súdra seizes
the Veda, and placed her on his chariot which was near by,
and carried her away.   Meanwhile Sítá cried out, like one
distracted, for Ráma and Lakshmana ; and threatened death
to the evil-minded Rávana.[6]

---

[5] The appearance of Rávana on this occasion is even more graphically
described in the Adhyátma Rámáyana :—" Rávana in his rage extended his form
to an immense size ; his heads seemed shrouded in the heavens ; his feet to
descend to the bottomless abyss ; his ten heads were as ten mountains ; his twenty
arms as the branches of the largest trees ; his eyes as the caves in a rock."

[6] The story of the illusive deer, and the outrage committed upon Sítá, is so
beautifully treated in the Dwipada Rámáyana, or Telugu version of the Rámá-

At this time the mighty Jatáyus, the Chief of Vultures, of vast energy and god-like strength, lay asleep on the

Cries of Sitá.
Jatáyus, the
Chief of
Vultures, hears
the cries of
Sitá.

yana, as to be well worthy of notice, as exhibiting some of that charming play of language which frequently characterizes Telugu poetry. The following English translation of the passage is from the pen of a well-known Telugu scholar, Mr C. P. Brown, late of the Madras Civil Service, and is extracted from the Madras Journal of Literature for 1839 :—

"The fairy hind was of extraordinary beauty; as it rambled about, chewing the cud, with a tail as freakish as that of the peacock; the whiteness of the belly gleamed through the bowers; again its reddish sides glistened like amber; when vaulting it looked like the rainbow; or, as it sprung up it flashed like lightning. The forest herds of deer were startled at its singular appearance; for it lay as in ambush, and its form was suddenly seen, now here, now there; one while it drew near, and then as though startled it bounded aloft, rushing through the thickets; then with a leap it took refuge in a bower. One while it put its nose to the ground, wagging its tail and pricking its ears at distant sounds. Then it pricked one quivering ear and flew like the wind; then it reposed on a grassy spot; then rising it drew near the hermitage; it scratched its ear with one foot, and shook the high flowering boughs with its horns so as to pour the blossoms on the soil.

"While it thus strayed among the bowers of the recluses, the blooming Sitá with tinkling anklets came out of the arbour to collect the opening flowers. At the sight of this fairy fawn she was filled with surprise; she called to the lord of men, her spouse, and thus addressed him :—'Never till this day did I see so charming a creature as this! how I long to recline, O Prince, on a couch formed of its skin : O thou leader of the solar race, pursue this creature, strike it, and bring me its hide; yet why? I wish thou couldst catch it without frightening it, which would be far better : O my spouse, we should keep it at our leafy dwelling, and when our appointed term finishes let us take the golden fawn home to the city and show it to the Mahárája, and to my aunts and cousins; how they will be delighted at such a present.'

"Thus spoke Sitá in affectionate tones; Lakshmana listened to her, and thus addressed Ráma :—'Was there ever, brother, seen so bright-hued a fawn? Can it be that a brute creature has such wondrous colours? It must be a mere delusion, unfit to be credited! Surely it must be a vision raised by (Asuras) demons; besides, possibly it is the hermit Máricha who lives here, for he is a cruel demon and continually roams the forest in a superhuman form : Have not we heard so? possibly it is that fiend; perchance he has come here to tempt us into ruin : Do not then set your gentle heart on this and be disquieted, or entertain the thought of catching the fawn : Besides, though the lady of Mithilá (i.e. Sitá) should be so simple, be not thou so foolish, O prince of men!'

"At these words Ráma looked on the bright countenance of Sitá; he smiled, and thus addressed Lakshmana :—'Why be agitated at this, O son of Sumitrá? Though even it were a giant-raised vision, certainly will I bring the deer home, and I will slay the mightiest giants that can come : Believe these two points; one or the other will I do; for I will chase it, I will slay it, and give the hide to Janaka's daughter : After so long a time she has made only this one request : Can I neglect Sitá? Can I decline the deed she points out? Stay thou with her affectionately, and neglect not the lady of the bower.'

"He said and committed all to Lakshmana; and gently taking his bow from

beautiful peak of a mountain, with his back towards the resplendent god of day; and the cries of Sítá reached his

his brother's hand, he bent it, and duly set out, like Siva when he set out in pursuit of the *Lion-giant* who carried off the sacrifice.

*   *   *   *   *

"He went on slinking behind the bush stooping as he walked, bending and running alongside; whenever the deer looked back, he stood concealed; he was on the point of catching it, it escaped, and he was vexed. He held the bow and arrows ready to shoot, he laid his footsteps softly on the soil so as to make no sound, as he observed its traces; he eyed its path, and goings, and concealed himself. 'Here it is! I'll catch it! Here it comes! See! It's mine!' cried he merrily.

"Thus thought he, but the deer caught a glimpse of him from afar; it let him draw near; but as he stretched to seize it, it bounded from him and fled. 'Alas!' cried he in anger, as it stood to gaze at Ráma. Then it fled to the horizon, while the foam flowed from the corners of its mouth; it seemed out of heart; then looking at the huntsman it sprung up elastic and fled at speed, while the skies seemed to flash with its brightness; then it vaulted away; its tongue flashing like lightning bright as a waving torch; for it moved as rapid as a potter's wheel circling at speed. Then it paused as though faint; it seemed to drop close to him; then like a goshawk it flew up to heaven. Ráma was now wearied as well as astonished; he paused, he looked around; but now the creature to cajole him stood still; but as he formed the idea of shooting it, again it vanished; then as he gave up the hope and turned homewards, behold it was again at his side, like a vision; and carried him who was now wearying, farther and farther, for deluding his glance, it fled into inaccessible hills.

"Seeing this Ráma perceived that this was a fairy hind; he exclaimed :— 'Where, O my foe, wilt thou hide from me?'. . . .

"So saying he levelled the celestial arrow at the prey; which instantly rolled over, and now laying aside the fairy form, uttering a delusive shriek, cried :—'O Lakshmana! O Sítá!'

"Then stretching his prodigious giant corpse on the soil, the wretch gave up his life; it seemed as though all the giants and their prince Rávana fell; as though their capital, Lanká, perished.

"When this fairy deer fell on the earth, the lord of Sítá was well pleased; for he clearly saw it was indeed Márícha; he remembered with approbation the words of his brother. How deeply, thought he, will he and the bright-eyed daughter of Janaka grieve at hearing their names uttered in the dying shriek of this deluder: for he imitated my voice exactly; I marvel where they are and what has become of them.

"So saying he mournfully pondered. But the dreadful cry reached the ears of Sítá, and struck her with horror to the earth; then when she recovered her senses, she gazed wildly around and was utterly downcast.

"Then in her agitation she raised the weeping cry, and gazing on Lakshmana, she exclaimed :—'Alas! son of Sumitrá, what may this be that has befallen us this day; surely Ráma cries on thee with weeping voice: O hero, listen to that voice! Wilt not thou give ear to it? or does it not reach thy ear? thou shrinkest not; thou showest no terror, or horror, thou grievest not; what is this? while my heart heaves violently with horror and despair! Alas! he went alone into the forest: It is late, and he cometh not; surely he hath this day fallen into the hands of the giants: Delay not! go, I pray thee, to the prince!'

ears as though he had heard sounds in a dream, and they
rent the heart of the Raja of Birds like the stroke of a

"She spoke pouring floods of tears, and Lakshmana replied thus to the child
of Janaka :—'Mother, why art thou alarmed ? Surely no evil shall ever befall thy
spouse Ráma : Dost not thou know the valour of thy beloved lord ? Is it right to
give vent to words so agonizing ? Surely this is the scream of some demon who
wishes to terrify thy heart : What hath such a pitiful shriek to do with the hero of
the solar race ? O daughter of Janaka, wherefore art thou thus agitated ? I will
without hesitation follow the prince Ráma ; and shall the giants who oppose him
maintain their footing ? They are no more than crickets that exult against wild-
fire.—They will in the end fall into it and turn to ashes ; or like the mighty serpents that raise themselves against the eagle and perish in his talons ; or like a
herd of elephants that rush upon the lion : No, I am afraid to leave thee, no, be
not weary of me ; plant these my words in thy heart : Be not grieved, O daughter
of the king of men.' At these words the fires of wrath arose in the heart of the
lady, and grieved, she thus addressed the son of Sumitrá :—'Thou ! art thou
faithful towards Ráma ? Why art thou this day so base ? Even though thou
hearest Ráma calling on thee by name, thou art, like a foe, filled with hatred in
thy heart. Is this becoming ? '. . . . .

"Thus spoke Lakshmana with his eyes filled with tears, and as his heart
could bear no more he exclaimed :—'Mother, I am gone, I will without delay
bring thee thy lord ; grieve not ! '

"He said and departed. But first he drew seven circles round the bower, and
said :—'Mother, pass not these limits, and should any one venture to cross these
lines, the intruder shall instantly pay for it with his head.'

"Then he addressed the god of fire, saying :—'Be not careless. I commit
the dame to thee ! '

"Then he respectfully bowed to the dame, and anxiously bent his way towards
Ráma. The god of purity (fire) guarded Sítá, and to delude her foes he formed
a fairy image of her which shone most glorious ; so that all would have taken her
for the real Sítá.

"At that moment Rávana the giant arose with agitated heart. In one hand
he bore a staff, in the other a scrip ; in his forehead was an upright mark, and on
his fingers he wore large rings of blessed grass with the sanctified thread across
his broad breast ; his right hand carried a large rosary ; he was robed in clayed
dust-colour vest, with a necklace of the blessed tulási tree, and he walked along
stooping with the weight : His body was emaciated ; he wore sandals, and a
weather-beaten umbrella ; his hair was rolled up in a large bunch ; in all points
indeed he was a Sanyási, and walked along counting over his beads and mutter-
ing his breviary : He dreaded lest the real Sanyásis should see and detect him ;
his head tottered with hoar antiquity ; he sidled and stole along peeping to see
where the fair one lay concealed. Then he would halt and exclaim Hari ! Hari !
Then a little recovering he drew near the skirts of the bower. At this sight the
rural deities filled with alarm exclaimed :—' Alas, this sinful wretch is come to bear
away the innocent Sítá ! ' He now stood at the door in the exact garb of a Sanyási. The daughter of Mithilá instantly arose, supposing that this hypocrite was
in truth a real hermit ; she folded her lily hands (and incautiously crossed the
magic circles drawn around her. *These words are spurious.*) The lady paid him
all due reverence, which he shuddering received, and as he viewed the damsel, he
spoke thus :—' Lady, how is it that thou dwellest in this desolate retreat of the

thunder-bolt. Instantly arousing himself through the affection he bore towards Ráma, he heard the noise of

forests; how art thou left here alone? Art thou a goddess, or how can loveliness so divine be found among the dames of earth-roaming mortals. . . . Who art thou, O fair one, why art thou wearing away life in this wilderness? O tell me.'

"He spoke, and Sítá reverently replied:—' I am the spouse, O saintly one, of the stainless hero Ráma: My sire is Janaka, and Dasaratha is my uncle; my name is Sítá: As the exalted Dasaratha hath banished us, Ráma hath come to this wilderness, with me and Lakshmana; we three have taken up our abode in this retreat as steadfast recluses: But a golden hind appeared to me, and looking at the Prince I requested its hide; he is gone to seek it; after which I heard a dreadful cry of "O Lakshmana," which pierced and dwelt in my ear: In my grief I reviled Lakshmana and bade him begone: He is gone, and returneth not; I know not which way to turn.' She spoke, and looking at the hermit said:— ' Reverend Sir, tell me your name, and why you are come to this place?'

"The prince of Lanká scrupled not to lay aside for awhile his humble guise, and thus replied:—' Lady of the gentle eyes, hear! I am the ruler of Lanká in the midst of the rolling Ocean: I am the Chief of giants, the son of Visravas, and brother of Kuvera, lord of Yakshas, and universally victorious; by name, Rávana, he who in battle faces and vanquishes both deities and giants: Lady! I heard of the riches of thy blooming face, and am come, full of eagerness, to behold it: Why, O dame, shouldst thou thus pining dwell with a paltry fellow in the wilderness? All my realm, O bright-eyed lady, shall be at thy command with its wealth; for thy comfort and pomp there are bright chariots, and all other princely vehicles; and in the palaces thou shalt be waited upon by the wives and daughters of fairies and demigods, genies and giants: When the light of thy footsteps shines on my realm it shall blaze as with a wall of rubies: O Lady, the lilies of thine eyes shall shed their radiance like a triumphal wreath over my gates: Thy sweet smiles shall shine as the summer moon over the ocean of my happiness: Come, come to my city of Lanká.'

"At these words Sítá was indeed filled with alarm, but like a spirited woman she looked upon him with scorn, and plucking up a blade of grass, she turned her heart to Ráma, and bending her eyes on the grass she thus spoke, without even looking at the enemy of gods: ' Fellow! is it fit for thee to address me thus? Surely ambrosia was created for deities and not for dogs! What face hast thou to dare to speak to me who appertain to the god-like Ráma? Be decent and be gone to thy noble town: If thou wilt not go away by fair means, and if thou ponderest on any iniquity, know that my noble lord is matchless in archery; it was he who burst the bow of Siva and who smote the heads of the giants: He will reduce thee and thine to nothing! Thou art to him no more than a fox is to a lion, or a fly to an elephant, or a streamlet to the ocean, or a crow to an eagle! so vast is the difference between him and thee: Be wise then and retire to thy Lanká.'

"She spoke, but the giant looked furiously at the daughter of Janaka, and throwing off his guise, in his insolence, as love stirred his heart, he shook with eagerness, and the gems that adorned his ten heads faded away; then had love more power than his twenty arms! He shone glorious in gemmed panoply, as the flames of love lighted up his visage. Dreadful was his form, and at the horrid sight as he advanced to her, poor Sítá fainted before him; she sunk down like a

Rávana's chariot more terrible than the rolling of thunder; and he looked around him, and cast his eyes towards the heavens, and presently beheld Rávana carrying away Sítá in his chariot, and heard Sítá weeping aloud. Then Jatáyus was filled with rage and soared into the air; and he stopped the chariot of the furious Rávana, and poured forth these vitu-

perations :—" O thou ten-headed monster, I am the ancient Raja of the Vultures, by name Jatáyus, of mighty strength, fixed in the path of virtue and devoted to truth : You are the famous Raja of the Rákshasas, of invincible energy, by whom the gods have been often vanquished in battle: O descendant of Pulastya, I am an aged bird, and am now destitute of strength, yet you shall see my valour in the combat, and shall not depart home alive : Ráma, the son of Dasaratha, equal to Indra and Varuna, and devoted to the good of all, is sovereign of the world : This beautiful woman is Sítá, his lawful spouse: How can a virtuous Raja dishonour the wife of another ? It behoves a Raja above all men to protect the wives of others : O despicable wretch, abandon your design of carrying away the wife of another, lest I hurl you from your splendid chariot like fruit that is torn from a tree : Instantly release Sítá, lest Ráma consume you with his flaming eye, as Vrita was consumed by the thunder-bolt of Indra : I am old,—whilst you are young, and encircled by mail, and mounted on a chariot, and armed with darts,—yet I will never permit you to carry away Sítá : As a Súdra is never permitted to touch the Vedas, so you shall never carry away Sítá."

At these words the eyes of Rávana were blood-red with anger, and he ran violently upon the Raja of Vultures. Then a mighty conflict ensued between Jatáyus and Rávana, like the conflict between a cloud and a lofty mountain. Rávana rained a tempest of winged arrows upon the Raja of Vul-

---

forest blossom before the rushing gale. The ten-faced giant beheld her drowned in tears, and with panting bosom and dishevelled tresses and broken garland, while her whole form shuddered with anguish. He instantly seized the lady of the bright eyes, and placed her on his car ; driven by fate to bear with him her who was to him the goddess of death, this foe of the gods sprung from earth, and hurried his steeds along the skyey road."

tures; but Jatáyus seized the arrows on their way, and
mounting on the back of Rávana he lacerated him with his
talons, and then destroyed his chariot and his asses.   Then
Rávana sprang from his car with Sítá in his arms, when
Jatáyus pounced again upon his back, and tore him with his
claws and beak until the Rákshasa appeared exhausted with
agony and loss of blood.   At length the ten-headed one set
Sítá upon the ground, and belaboured Jatáyus with his fists
for a full hour; and then cut off his wings and feet with a
scimitar, and the valiant Bird fell upon the earth with mortal
wounds.   Seeing his enemy bathed in blood and nearly expiring, Rávana then approached Sítá.   She with ornaments
all in confusion, and countenance convulsed with grief, clung
eagerly to the tall trees, crying out :—" Save me! Save
me ! " He, like the all-destroying Yama, seized her by her
black locks and again mounted the air.   Adorned with
golden ornaments, and arrayed in yellow silk, Sítá appeared
in the air like a flash of lightning, whilst Rávana seemed
like a dark mountain illumined with fire.   He being black,
resembled a dark cloud driven by the wind ; while she,
bright as burnished gold, appeared like the lightning within
the cloud.   The divine raiment given to her by the holy
Anasúyá, with the ointment and the necklace, shone with
peculiar radiance ; and her fair face in the arms of Rávana
resembled the moon emerging from behind a black cloud.
She, bright as the most burnished gold, appeared, while held
by the black Raja of the Rákshasas, like a thread of gold
round the loins of an elephant.

Then Sítá cried out :—" O my beloved husband, where
are you ?   Your wife is being carried off by a Rákshasa,
and why are you so cruel as to abandon her ?   If you do not
destroy this wicked Rákshasa, it will ever be a stain upon
your family and race : Where are you also, O Lakshmana,
the brother of my husband ?   If you are offended at my
bitter words in sending you for Ráma, I pray your forgiveness and implore you to deliver me from this Rákshasa ! "
Then turning to Rávana she again wrathfully reproached
him :—" You pride yourself upon being a valiant hero, but

HISTORY OF
INDIA.
PART IV.

Jatáyus
mortally
wounded.

Rávana carries
away Sítá
through the air.

Poetical con-
trast of the
black com-
plexion of
Rávana with
the golden com-
plexion of Sítá.

Lamentations
of Sítá.

Bitterly re-
proaches
Rávana.

you have acted like a mean coward: A hero never takes that which is another's, save by conquest; and if you had taken me after defeating Ráma, I would have considered you to be a hero, and would not have refused to become your wife: Even now, if you had the pride of a hero, you would wait here and fight Ráma; and if you defeated him, you might carry me where you pleased: Think not however to save yourself by flight, for rest assured that wherever you go, you must fall by the hand of Ráma: Your end is fast approaching, and the day is not far distant when you will be sent to the mansions of Yama, and float there in the river Bytarani, and be torn in pieces by the dogs of Yama, and endure everlasting misery."

Rávana approaches the mountain Rishya-múkha.

Whilst Sítá was thus filling the air with her cries and lamentations, Rávana approached the mountain named Rishya-múkha; and Sítá beheld five Monkeys seated upon the mountain, and she thought in her heart that she would throw her ornaments down amongst the Monkeys, in the hope that they might find their way to Ráma. Sítá then,

Sítá drops her ornaments amongst the monkeys on the mountain.

unknown to Rávana, threw out all her ornaments, except the jewelled flower upon her head; and they dropped down to the earth like falling stars; and she threw out her veil in like manner. And the five Monkeys saw what was taking place, and they said one to the other:—"This is the mighty Rávana, who is carrying away by force some beautiful woman, and her lamentations can be heard on this mountain: She is calling out the names of Ráma and Lakshmana; and she is throwing down her ornaments and garments that we may take care of them, and make them over

The monkeys preserve the ornaments.

to those who shall come in search for her: Be it so or not, we will keep the things until we shall hear more of this matter." So the Monkeys kept the ornaments and the veil concealed in the valley.

Rávana conducts Sítá to his palace at Lanká.

Meantime the wicked Rávana had crossed the ocean and descended with Sítá upon the island of Lanká; and he conducted her into his magnificent palace, and into one of the inner apartments. He then called for a number of female Rákshasís, and commanded them to attend upon Sítá night and day; and to allow no man to enter her apartments save himself; and to procure her everything she might desire in the way of ornaments, or perfumes, or dresses, or beds, or food, and never to say an unkind word to her upon pain of death. Rávana then went out, and sent for eight of his bravest Rákshasas, and acquainted them with his enmity against Ráma; and he commanded them to go forth and become spies upon Ráma and Lakshmana, and to put them to death by any means in their power, but to bring him with all speed the news of any attempt that Ráma might take to avenge his wrongs.

When the wicked Rávana had despatched his spies to watch Ráma, he thought himself secure against every enemy. Accordingly he returned to the apartments in which he had left Sítá; and he found her sitting in the midst of the Rákshasí women, like a deer surrounded by tigers; and her head was downcast, and the tears flowed in torrents from her eyes, for her mind was ever fixed upon her beloved husband Ráma. And Rávana approached that wretched one, and began to address her in caressing terms as follows:—" O Sítá, hear what I am going to say, for if you attend to my words, it will make us both happy: Cast aside your grief and look upon me with a favourable eye: Lament no more for Ráma, for never again will you see him in this mortal life: An impassable ocean, a hundred miles in breadth, lies between Ráma and my palace; and no human being will ever be able to take you away from this place: Even the gods fear to enter my palace without my permission; and how should a being so contemptible as a mortal man attempt to enter? I have an invincible army composed of millions upon millions of mighty warriors, so that there is no one in the three worlds who can withstand my power: Abandon, therefore, all thought and anxiety respecting Ráma, and receive me as your husband: Your youth and beauty will not last for ever, and you should make the best use of them while they last, and not waste away your life in fruitless sorrowing: If you will be my first wife, all my other wives shall be your slaves, and you shall be the chief

Points out the
beauties of his
palace and
gardens.

Ráni of this golden city of Lanká : Here you shall enjoy
the choicest delicacies without fear and without care, and
shall obtain to your heart's desire things which are rarities
even in the court of Indra : O Sítá; consider yourself very
fortunate that I have chosen you to be my spouse : See how
my palace outshines in beauty the palace of Indra : It is a
hundred miles round about, and is the work of Viswa-karma,
who is the mighty architect of the gods : Behold the lofty
mansions which reach the skies and seem to deride the
heavens ! The jewels which the gods wear upon their heads
are employed here to decorate the roads of Lanká : View
the many gardens and pleasure-grounds, compared with
which the garden of Indra is as nothing : See that beautiful
Asoka garden, which is the chief of all, and cannot be
described : The joyous season of spring reigns there
throughout the year, and the minds of all who enter it are
delighted beyond measure, and especially enlivened with
the song of bees : My chariot Pushpaka will take you wherever you please, and assume any shape you may desire :
The riches in my treasuries are beyond all that the god
Kuvera ever heard or conceived : All these shall be yours,
and I myself will be your slave, if you will only condescend
to take me for your husband."

Sítá's wrathful
and threaten-
ing refusal of
his addresses.

At these words of Rávana, the wife of Ráma was filled
with wrath, and her eyes and countenance became red as the
rising sun. Keeping some blades of grass between herself
and Rávana, she said to that wicked Rákshasa :—" No words
would have been necessary from me, O evil one, had you
endeavoured to carry me away in the presence of Ráma or
his brother Lakshmana ; for then at that moment you would
have been despatched to the abode of Yama : Even now do
not consider yourself secure, nor place too much confidence
upon the ocean which surrounds Lanká : Ráma regards the
sea as a mere rivulet of water, which he can cross over or
dry up by means of his arrows alone : For your offence you
will fall by his arrows, and your body will become the food
of dogs and crows : For your offence the whole race of the
Rákshasas will be destroyed, and no one will be left in all

your family to offer the funeral cakes: Boast not of your army; for had you the whole universe on your side, it could not save you from death: Your wicked desires will never be gratified either in this life or in the lives to come; for I will give up the ghost of my own accord rather than yield to you."

When Rávana heard this speech from Sítá, he was vexed beyond all measure ; but he called for the female attendants, and bade them conduct Sítá to the Asoka garden, saying within himself:—" The beauties of that place will excite passion in her heart, and induce her in the end to yield herself to me." Rávana then said to the females :—" I leave you now to employ four different means for persuading Sítá to become my wife: *First,* you must use sweet and endearing words in speaking to her; *secondly,* you must give her good clothes and ornaments and delicious food; *thirdly,* you must praise me in her presence, and find every fault with her husband Ráma; and *fourthly,* you must threaten her with every evil unless she consent to become my wife: If you succeed in persuading her to yield herself to me, I will reward you handsomely." So saying Rávana left the apartment, and the women began to do as he had commanded, but they could make no impression upon the mind of Sítá. Every thought of her heart was fixed upon her beloved husband Ráma, and none of the words of the Rákshasís entered the doors of her ears. She would not sleep, she refused to take any food, her beautiful form wasted away, and her golden colour became dark; and she passed her days and nights in tears for her husband Ráma.[7]

Rávana orders the female attendants to conduct Sítá to the Asoka garden, and to use four means to induce her to yield.

Sítá shuts her ears to all entreaties.

Her deep sorrow.

---

[7] The Rákshasí women, or demon attendants upon Sítá, are described in far stronger language in the Adhyátma Rámáyana, as will be seen from the following extract:—" These demons were so horrid in their forms that the souls of mortals on beholding them would quit their bodies through dismay. The female demons constantly watched over her, while Sítá seated in the midst of them, overcome with agony and despair, passed her time in silent adoration of Ráma, and in meditation on his name. She never changed her clothes, she scarcely tasted food. As a rose withers when deprived of refreshing streams, so did Sítá languish from the absence of Ráma. The surrounding demons, as an eclipse before the moon, continually terrified her with their words and looks, while they attempted to persuade her to comply with Rávana's vicious inclinations. One said :—' Consent to

Review of the
foregoing story
of the capture
of Sítá ; its
powerful effect
upon the
Hindús.

There is not perhaps in the whole range of Hindú literature any tradition which awakens so many sympathies in the minds of the people as that of the capture of Sítá by Rávana, and the subsequent efforts to procure her deliverance. The original departure of the exiles into the jungle is a powerful scene, but although it involves painful ideas of privation and distress, it is wholly disconnected with any idea of outrage or dishonour. The gambling scene in the Mahá Bhárata, in which Yudhishthira stakes and loses his wife Draupadí, is highly sensational ; but Draupadí is not really separated from her husbands, nor is she, excepting for a very brief space of time, in the absolute power of another

Harrowing
character of the
outrage.

man. But the treacherous outrage committed upon Sítá is harrowing to the last degree. Indeed the idea that a wife is at the mercy of a barbarous and unscrupulous savage, of another race and another complexion, would be equally maddening to the European and the Hindú. But still the feelings of

Peculiarly
affecting to
Hindús.

the Hindú would be wounded by a number of minor circumstances, which would scarcely enter the mind of the European whilst dwelling upon his larger sorrow. The idea of physical chastity is carried to

Fastidious idea
of physical
chastity.

such a fastidious excess by the modern Hindús, that it robs women of their personal freedom and deprives them of all mental culture, whilst it utterly fails to secure that purity of thought and feeling which finds expression in more enlightened com-

Play of the
national senti-
ment in the
story of Sítá.

munities. The play of this national sentiment is

Rávana's wishes, or I will devour thee.' Another said :—' Banish all regard for Ráma or I will plunge thee into the fathomless ocean.' Others threatened to grind her between their teeth. In this manner the demons harassed her with their persecutions."

strikingly illustrated in the story of Sítá. It will
be seen hereafter that Ráma bitterly lamented that
his wife should have been even touched by a strange
man ; whilst Lakshmana declared that he could
not identify the ornaments which Sítá had worn
upon her neck and arms, because he had never ventured to look above the feet of his brother's wife.
But yet it will already have been seen, that the
delicate Princess who had been reared in the seclusion of the zenana, and who is indeed one of the
purest creations of the Hindú bard, brings a direct
and gross charge against her husband's brother,
which could scarcely have entered the mind of a
European lady, and certainly would never be put
into her mouth in any drama or romance, without
far stronger evidence of the justice of the suspicion.

Under the circumstances indicated it will be easy *Universal popularity of the story.*
to understand that the narrative of the outrage com-
mitted upon Sítá never fails to leave a deep impression upon the Hindú mind ; and so universally
popular is the story that every scene is indelibly
fixed upon the imagination of almost every Hindú
boy and girl, husband and wife, father and matron.
The pictures follow one another with a rapidity and *Prominent scenes in the narrative.*
vigour of painting which can scarcely be realized by
a single perusal. First appears the terrible Rávana, *Rávana surrounded by his Counsellors.*
with his ten crowned heads towering in the air, and
his twenty arms glistening with jewels, and spreading out like the branches of a tree. He is seated
upon a golden throne in front of his palace, and
around him are seated his Rákshasa Counsellors ; as
Indra, the god of the firmament, is surrounded by
the winds or Maruts, who are his advisers. Next

appears the dreadful sister of Rávana, with her ears and nose cut off, roaring aloud with cruelty and rage; who kindles such a fire of sensual desire in the heart of Rávana that he refuses to listen to all counsels and all warnings. Next is to be seen the departure of Rávana and Márícha upon a chariot which rides swiftly through the air. Then follows the strange picture of the golden deer, sparkling with silver spots and jewelled eyes, gambolling before the hermitage. Next the deer is mortally wounded by Ráma's arrow, and suddenly assumes the form of Márícha, and imitates the cry of Ráma. Then the eye reverts to the quiet hut, in which Sítá is carrying on an angry and sensational dialogue with Lakshmana, which terminates in her being left alone in the hermitage, exposed to all the designs of Rávana. Then follows the climax. The pseudo Saniási presents himself clothed in a red cloth, with matted hair, an umbrella, a trident, a provision bag, and an alms dish. He finds his addresses disregarded, and suddenly assumes his own stupendous and monstrous form, and seizes the trembling wife and carries her away like a Súdra who has seized the Vedas. Then follows the desperate struggle between Rávana and the Vulture Raja, in which the Rákshasa is fearfully lacerated by the talons of the gigantic Bird, and the chariot is utterly destroyed. Lastly is to be seen the flight through the air of the golden-complexioned Sítá in the grasp of the black Rákshasa, like a golden thread round the loins of an elephant; the arrival of the hapless wife at the palace of Rávana, and her utter desolation in the inner apartments and the Asoka grove.

There is one circumstance in the narrative to

HISTORY OF INDIA. PART IV.

Appearance of Rávana's sister.

Departure of Rávana and Márícha in an aerial chariot.

The golden deer.

Sítá taunting Lakshmana.

Rávana as a Saniási.

The outrage.

The combat between Rávana and Jatáyus.

Flight of Rávana with Sítá through the air.

Sítá's desolation. Strange sentiment of Sítá that she would have yielded to Rávana had he conquered Ráma.

which allusion has already been made,[8] and which
is well worthy of consideration.   Sítá reproaches
Rávana for his cowardice in not fighting Ráma; and
declares that if he had conquered her husband she
could not have refused to become his wife.   This
strange sentiment seems to have been fully in accordance with the ancient laws of war, by which the wife
and possessions of a conquered Chieftain became the
property of the conqueror.   But although the rule
was actually laid down, yet the history of India
shows that the affections will occasionally override
all such merciless laws; and that Hindú wives have
preferred perishing by the hands of their husbands
to becoming the prey of a victorious enemy.

HISTORY OF
INDIA.
PART IV.

Hindú women
superior to the
rule.

---

[8] See Vol. I. pp. 57, 201, 203.

CHAPTER XVIII.

RÁMA'S SEARCH FOR SÍTÁ.

HISTORY OF
INDIA.
PART IV.

Narrative of
Ráma's search
for Sítá.

THE narrative of Ráma's sorrow at the loss of Sítá, and his eager search for her in the jungle, contains nothing that demands any preliminary explanation. It comprises much poetical description, and a curious story of a female devotee named Sarvarí, who was of low caste, but obtained salvation through a mantra taught her by Mantaga the sage. The narrative is as follows:—

Meantime the mighty hero Ráma had returned towards his hermitage after killing the deer-formed Máricha, and he carried the skin upon his shoulders to present it to Sítá. Presently Lakshmana appeared with a sad countenance, and told him why he had left Sítá alone in the hut. And Ráma became greatly alarmed, and said:—" O my brother, you have done wrong in leaving Sítá alone: Women are generally devoid of sense, and no wise man would attend to their words." So saying, Ráma ran with all speed to the hut,

They discover
that Sítá has
left the hut.

and his brother Lakshmana followed him; and when they came to the hut, they found that it was utterly deserted,

and that Sítá had gone they knew not where. At this sight Ráma became speechless; his bow dropped from his hand, his hair became dishevelled, his girdle became loosened, and he sank upon the earth in a swoon. Lakshmana caught him in his arms, and fanned him with branches of new leaves, and splashed his face with water; and after awhile he regained his senses and cried out for Sítá.

Then Ráma and Lakshmana both rose up and went
throughout the forest to search for the lost one; but they
found her not, and they returned in great grief to the
hermitage and saw that it was as desolate as before.   When
it was evening the full moon arose in the heavens, and Ráma
said:—" O Moon, you can gaze over the whole world, and
no corner of the earth is unknown to you; can you not
therefore tell me where my beloved is gone?"   And Ráma
passed the whole of that night in the desolate hermitage.

Early next morning Ráma and Lakshmana performed
their customary devotions, and then went forth again in
search of Sítá; and after awhile they came to the place
where Jatáyus, Chief of Vultures, had fought against
Rávana.   And Ráma said to Lakshmana:—" O brother, here
are signs that a battle has been fought in this place: Let us
search this part of the forest, and find, if possible, the track
of the conqueror."   Ráma and Lakshmana then proceeded
a little farther, and presently they came in sight of the
huge Jatáyus, with streams of blood flowing from his muti-
lated wings.   And Ráma said to Jatáyus:—" Tell me, O
virtuous and pious Vulture, whither my wife has gone, and
who it was that carried her away."   Jatáyus replied:—" O
Ráma, the wicked Rávana, the Raja of the Rákshasas, has
carried away Sítá towards the south: O Ráma, I am losing
all control over my body; I see not with my eyes, and my
life is departing from my body."   The mighty Chief of
Vultures then looked up into the face of Ráma, and his eyes
became fixed, and he gave up the ghost.   At that moment,
whilst Ráma and Lakshmana were still lamenting, a chariot
of fire descended from Vaikuntha, which is the heaven of
Vishnu, with four attendants therein; and one carried the
shell, and another the chakra, and the third the mace, and
the fourth the lotos; and the soul of Jatáyus arose from the
dead body, and mounted the chariot at the will of Ráma;
and offering up a long prayer to Ráma, he ascended to the
world of Vaikuntha, and became absorbed in Vishnu.

When Ráma beheld the happy fate of Jatáyus, he said
to his brother:—" O Lakshmana, though this Raja of Vul-

HISTORY OF
INDIA.
PART IV.

The search.

Ráma's address
to the Moon.

Ráma and
Lakshmana
discover the
body of the
dying Jatáyus.

Last words of
Jatáyus.

The soul of
Jatáyus ascends
to heaven in a
chariot of fire.

Ráma and
Lakshmana
perform the
funeral rites for
Jatáyus.

tures has ascended to heaven, still we should perform his funeral rites according to the custom of the inhabitants of the earth : Bring therefore rice and dry wood that I may prepare a funeral pile and burn the dead body." So Lakshmana did as his elder brother commanded, and the funeral pile was prepared, and the remains of Jatáyus were placed thereon; and Ráma produced a flame by rubbing together two pieces of wood, and set fire to the pile, and burned the dead body with all due ceremonies. Then the two brothers bathed in the river Godáveri, and sprinkled water for the soul of the departed. They then went into the forest and shot deer, and cut the flesh into small pieces, and gave them to all the birds of the jungle. Thus the soul of Jatáyus was secured in the enjoyments of heaven.

---

¹ The account given in the Adhyátma Rámáyana of the death of Jatáyus and his ascension to heaven, is well worthy of consideration, and is accordingly extracted as follows :—" When the funeral rites had been concluded, Ráma called out, saying :—' Assume, Jatáyus ! my form ; ascend into paradise ; I have granted salvation unto thee in my form, which is the highest rank thou canst obtain.' No sooner had Ráma uttered these words than Jatáyus became possessed of four arms as Vishnu. A car descended from heaven in which he seated himself to proceed to paradise. Such was the dignity and grandeur of his appearance, it was as if a thousand suns shone on his face. In his four hands he held a shell, a chakra, a mace, and a lotos ; a crown of pearls adorned his head ; his body was ornamented with jewels ; a veil of brocade covered his shoulders ; and four of Vishnu's attendants waved glittering chámaras over his head. The heavenly choristers sang hymns by his side ; the nymphs of paradise danced before him.

" The soul of Jatáyus in obtaining this exalted station was animated with joy and gratitude, and thus addressed Ráma :—' Thou holdest, O Lord ! a bow in thy hand, and therefore art thou distinguished by the title of the Archer,—as such I worship thee. Thou extendest thy mercy towards the oppressed, thou art the protector of the defenceless,—as such I adore thee. Brahma and the gods pour on their heads the dust that has been under thy feet, for that which thou touchest is sacred,—as such I honour thee. Thy praises are unbounded, they are beyond the powers of description : Before all things thou wert ; the creation, the preservation, and the destruction of the world are in thy hands. Thou art the only God, the fountain of benevolence, enthroned in the hearts of all things animate and inanimate,—as such I offer my adorations unto thee. Thou hast a bow and arrows in thy hands, but the archers of this world yield to thee in skill. Thou art the first among the gods, the first among mankind,—as such I praise thee. Thou art the sole object of adoration to the gods, to the saints, to the serpents, to the Gandharvas, to the heavenly spirits, who prostrate themselves at thy feet,—as such I worship thee. Thou didst punish the Kshatriyas, whose hearts were hardened with pride and obstinacy against thee ; thou didst humble their pride and they now fear thee,—as such I pay my devotions unto thee. (Here

When the day was far spent, and the night was drawing nigh, the two brethren returned to the hermitage; but Ráma passed the night in lamentations, for he knew now that Rávana had carried away Sítá towards the south.

When the morning had dawned, and the customary devotions had been performed, Ráma and Lakshmana departed out of the hermitage, and proceeded towards the south. When they had gone some distance, they came in sight of a vast and mighty demon named Kabandha, and Lakshmana beholding him, mistook him for a mountain. And Lakshmana said to his brother :—" Behold, my Lord, a great mountain resembling a black Rákshasa ! It is very high and stupendous, and dark as lamp-black : See the discoloured plants on the top, and the tall peaks on its two sides ! " Whilst he was thus speaking, Kabandha spread out his two arms of monstrous length to grasp in the two brothers ; and Lakshmana exclaimed :—" My Lord, it is not a mountain, but a real Rákshasa : The discoloured plants on the top are nothing but his hair, and I mistook his two upstretched arms for mountain peaks : I see no neck or head, but his face is within his belly, and he has one eye only, and large teeth." At this moment the monstrous arms of the fearful demon, Kabandha, began to wind round the brothers, and the two heroes seized the arms, and began to pull them. Then Kabandha cried out :—" Who are you, and what do you do here? Have you no fear of death that you come hither and seize me by the arms ? For my part I rejoice to see you, for I shall have a delicious feast this day." So saying, the demon prepared to devour them, when the two renowned heroes each cut off one of his arms with a

Ráma and Lakshmana proceed towards the south in search of Sítá.

Appearance of Kabandha.

Ráma and Lakshmana cut off his arms.

Ráma appears to be identified with Parasu Ráma ; or rather the destroyer of the Buddhists is identified with the destroyer of the Kshatriyas.)   The waters of the Ganges, which purify the souls of mankind from sin, and which Siva, knowing the excellence of them, received on his head, flowed originally from thy feet, —as such I adore thee : In taking refuge at thy feet, the terrors of future birth, regeneration, and death, are done away,—as such I worship thee : Thou art Brahma, thou art Vishnu thou art Siva, but thou art One ; the universe is comprehended in thee as an ant in an elephant : Thou art the foundation of eternal bliss, thou art neither greater nor less ; mankind are thy servants, thou art the lord of all.' "

scimitar, and the Rákshasa fell upon the ground. Then the wounded Kabandha cried out to the two brothers :—" What are your names, and the names of your fathers ? " Ráma replied :—" We are the sons of Mahárája Dasaratha." And he told the Rákshasa all that had happened to them from their exile downwards.

Kabandha then related his own story, how he had been originally a Gandharva, but in consequence of the curse of a sage, had been compelled to assume his present form until released by Ráma. And Kabandha thanked Ráma for his deliverance, and offered to serve him in any way ; and Ráma asked him to relate the story of Rávana. Then Kabandha replied :—" I am still a Rákshasa, and I cannot tell what you desire to know, unless this body of mine be burned with fire." So Ráma threw the Rákshasa into a deep pit, and covered him with dry wood, and set fire to the pile ; and while it was burning, a chariot descended from heaven, and Kabandha came out of the fire in his real shape as a Gandharva, and took his seat upon the chariot, and then spoke to Ráma, as follows :—" In the middle of the Southern Ocean is a wonderful island named Lanká, and Rávana is the owner of that island : This Rávana is a great warrior, and he has a mighty army of Rákshasas under his command ; and if you desire to conquer him you must follow my counsel : At a little distance to the north of this place is a lake named Pampá ; and near that lake is a mountain named Rishya-múkha ; and on this mountain Rishya-múkha dwells a chief among the Monkeys, named Sugríva, and by the assistance of Sugríva you will obtain the victory over Rávana : Do you, therefore, form a friendly alliance with Sugríva : He is himself suffering from an injury inflicted upon him by his own brother ; and if you assist him against his brother, he will assist you in recovering Sítá : On the road you will find the hermitage of the sage, Matanga ; and a pupil of the sage is dwelling there, and awaiting your arrival : Fulfil all the desires of this pupil, and then proceed to the lake Pampá and the mountain Rishya-múkha." Having thus spoken, Kabandha took leave of

Kabandha
burned in a pit,
and assumes his
original form.

Ráma and Lakshmana, and ascended to the heaven of Vishnu.[2]

Ráma and his brother then took the road which had been pointed out by Kabandha ; and, after travelling for some time in the jungle, they at last came to the abode of Matanga, and there they found an aged female named Sarvarí, who had been a pupil of that sage. Now Sarvarí had long been waiting to behold Ráma ; and when she saw him, accompanied by his brother, she knew directly who they were ; and she brought mats of new grass and cool water to wash their feet ; and she presented them with flowers, perfumes, and the argha, and began to offer prayers to both Ráma and Lakshmana. And Ráma rejoiced to behold her piety, and inquired of her how she came to be the pupil of Matanga, and where the sage was residing at that time, and why she lived thus alone in the forest. Sarvarí said :—" I was born of the low caste which is called Sarvarí, and one day I came to this wilderness to gather wood, when I saw the sage, Matanga : A strong desire then rose in my heart to serve the sage, but I was afraid to make known my wish, because of the lowness of my birth : I was accustomed, therefore, to come hither every night, and sweep the path leading from this hermitage to the bathing ghat, so that not a stone or pebble was left in the way when the sage went to perform his morning ablutions : Seeing the path kept so clean, Matanga asked his disciples if they had been accustomed to sweep the way, but they could give him no reply : One night after this the disciples hid themselves, and when I came to sweep the path, they caught me, and took me

Ráma and Lakshmana reach the hermitage of Matanga, the sage.

Piety of Sarvarí the female disciple of Matanga.

Sarvarí relates her story.

---

[2] In the Adhyátma Rámáyana the demon Kabandha is represented as making a long and pious address to Ráma, from which the following pantheistic description may be extracted :—" The seven upper regions are placed between thy head and thy loins ; the earth is in thy loins, the seven lower regions are from thy loins to thy feet : Thine eyes are the sun, thy mouth is a flaming fire, thy hair the clouds, thy bones the mountains, thy belly the seven waters of the ocean, thy pores the vegetable creation, thy hands Indra, thy breast the fountain of mercy, thy back the source of punishments, thy hips Death, thy lips Kama-deva, thy nose the two Aswins, thy tongue Varuna, thy whiskers lightning, thy heart the moon, thy eyelids are constantly engaged in weighing these things together. Thus are all things comprehended in thy vast form ; nothing is distinct from it."

Taught the
name of
" Ráma" as a
mantra.

before Matanga, and I related all my story to the sage :
Then the holy man took compassion upon me, and taught
me a mantra which raised me from my low caste, in the same
way that it had already raised the sage Válmikí; and that
mantra was only your name of RÁMA : From that time I have
ever remained here ; but a few days ago, Matanga told me
that he was going to the heaven of Brahma ; and he said to
me :—" Remain here but a short time longer : Your Guru,
Ráma, is come as far as Chitra-kúta, and he will be here in
due time : Then do you enter the fire in his presence, and
you will obtain the accomplishment of all your desires."

Sarvari burns
herself alive in
the presence of
Ráma.

Sarvarí having thus finished speaking, requested the
permission of Ráma to enter the fire, as she had already prepared the funeral pile ; and Ráma gave her leave, and she
set fire to the pile, and entered the bright flame with· her
eyes fixed upon Ráma. Then whilst the pile was burning, a
chariot descended from Vaíkuntha, and Sarvarí ascended
the chariot, and was carried away to the mansions of
Vishnu.

Ráma and
Lakshmana
proceed to the
lake Pampá.

Description of
the lake.

When Sarvarí had thus expired, Ráma and Lakshmana
departed out of the hermitage ; and after journeying for some
time, they came within sight of the lake Pampá. That
beautiful lake was one mile round, and the water was transparent, and covered with the blooming lotos ; and the
ducks and geese were playing upon the surface of the water,
and the bees were hovering over the lotos, and water-birds
of radiant plumage crowded the lake and the green margin
around it. And the banks on all sides were covered with
trees, and loaded with fruits and flowers, which waved to
and fro with the gentle wind, and spread a delicious perfume around. But, as Ráma beheld the beauty of the place,

Ráma's continued
affliction.

he was reminded more and more of his beloved Sítá, and his
loss lay heavy upon his soul. And Lakshmana prepared for
his brother a bed of lotos under the shade of a fig-tree, and
brought some water for his feet. Then Ráma threw himself
down upon the bed, and Lakshmana seated himself near
him, and began to press the feet of his elder brother with
his hand.

The foregoing narrative calls for but little remark.   The fanciful accounts of Ráma's sorrow, and
the lamentations which the author puts into his
mouth, are poetical according to Hindú ideas, but
too demonstrative to please European tastes.   The
description of Kabandha is simply the creation of a
distorted fancy.   He is described as a hairy mountain, without head or neck, but with one glaring eye
in his breast, and an immense mouth and teeth in
the centre of his belly; whilst his arms were more
than a mile long!   The story of Sarvarí, the female
ascetic, is worthy of consideration, because she was
of low caste, and seems to have led a life of celibacy; circumstances which would seem to denote
that she was a Buddhist, amongst whom caste was
disregarded, and female devotees were not unfrequent in ancient times.

CHAPTER XIX.

RÁMA'S ALLIANCE WITH THE MONKEYS.

Change in the
character of
Ráma from the
divine to the
human.

At this point in the Rámáyana, the character of Ráma seems to undergo an entire change. During his wanderings in the jungle he was pre-eminently regarded as a divine hero, who was received by every Bráhman sage as a deliverer long waited for, whose presence alone ensured salvation. Even the Rákshasa demons who opposed his progress, and who were slain by his arms, are said to have acknowledged his divinity in the hour of death, and to have been borne away in celestial chariots to the heaven of Vishnu. But in the narrative which now follows of the alliance formed by Ráma with the Monkeys, the divine character of the hero in a great measure disappears, and he becomes little more than a human warrior. After lamenting the loss of his wife in the language of an ordinary mortal, he seeks an alliance with Monkeys to carry on wars which he had previously sustained by his single arm. Moreover, it will be seen that his actions are not only those of a human being, but of a human being who is regardless of moral rule in the attainment of his ends; inasmuch as he killed one Monkey warrior contrary to the rules of fair fighting, and permitted another to take the widow of his deceased brother as a second wife, contrary even to the modified law of the early Bráhmans.[1] This transformation of Ráma leads to the suspicion that the son of Dasaratha was a different individual from the Linga-worshipper of the Dekhan who made war against the Buddhists; and that two distinct traditions, referring to different circumstances and localities, have been amalgamated into a single poem. But whether this hypothesis be correct or no, it will certainly be necessary to bear some distinction in mind between Ráma, the incarnation of Vishnu, and Ráma, the worshipper of the Linga, which is always associated with the worship of Siva.

Hypothesis that Ráma the son of Dasaratha, and Ráma the Linga-worshipper of the Dekhan, are different individuals.

The alliance which Ráma is said to have formed with the Monkeys, tends to confirm this view. It excites a doubt whether Ráma was so invariably the conqueror of the Rákshasas as the Rámáyana represents him; whether he did not on some occasions suffer a defeat, although the victory has been given to him by the Hindú bard in order to bring his exploits into conformity with his assumed character as a divine incarnation. Indeed if Ráma had really been so victorious in his wars against Khara and Dúshana as the Rámáyana represents, it seems difficult to understand why he should have deemed it necessary to seek an alliance with the Monkey Chieftain. It appears therefore most probable that the Ráma of this portion of the Rámáyana, namely, the representative or leader of the Linga-worshippers, had sustained such severe defeats from the Buddhists, that he was compelled to strengthen himself by an alliance before he could renew the war. But whilst

The alleged alliance with the Monkeys, a proof that Ráma must have suffered reverses from the Rákshasas, or Buddhists.

---

[1] See Colebrook's Hindú Law, p. 466, *et seq.*

Literal inter-
pretation of the
Rámáyana
believed in by
the Hindús.

this hypothesis seems highly probable, it must be distinctly stated that it has no place in the national belief. The literal interpretation of this portion of the Rámáyana is indeed deeply rooted in the mind of the Hindú. He implicitly believes that Ráma is Vishnu, who became incarnate for the purpose of destroying the demon Rávana; that he permitted his wife to be captured by Rávana for the sake of de-livering the gods and Bráhmans from the oppressions of the Rákshasa; and that he ultimately assembled an army of Monkeys, who were the progeny of the gods, and led them against the stronghold of Rávana at Lanká, and delivered the world from the tyrant Rákshasa, whilst obtaining ample revenge for his own personal wrongs.

Circumstances
which led to
the Hindú
belief in an
alliance with
Monkeys.

One other point seems to demand consideration, namely, the possibility of such an alliance as that which Ráma is said to have concluded with the Monkeys. This possibility will of course be denied by modern critics, but still it is interesting to trace out the circumstances which seem to have led to the acceptance of such a wild belief by the dreamy and marvel-loving Hindú. The south of India swarms with Monkeys of curious intelligence and rare phy-

sical powers. Their wonderful instinct for organiz-ation, their attachment to particular localities, their occasional journeys in large numbers over mountains and across rivers, their obstinate assertion of sup-posed rights, and the ridiculous caricature which they exhibit of all that is animal and emotional in man, would naturally create a deep impression upon

a credulous and superstitious people. Indeed the habits of Monkeys well deserve to be patiently studied; not as they appear in confinement, when much that is revolting in their nature is developed; but as they appear living in freedom amongst the trees of the forest, or in the streets of crowded cities, or precincts of temples. Such a study would not fail to awaken strange ideas; and although the European would not be prepared to regard Monkeys as sacred animals, he might be led to speculate as to their origin by the light of data, which are at present unknown to the naturalist whose observations have been derived from the menagerie alone.

Whatever, however, may have been the train of ideas which led the Hindú to regard the Monkey as a being half human and half divine, there can be little doubt that in the Rámáyana the Monkeys of southern India have been confounded with what may be called the aboriginal people of the country. The origin of this confusion may be easily conjectured. Perchance the aborigines of the country may have been regarded as a superior kind of Monkeys; and to this day the features of the Marawars, who are supposed to be the aborigines of the southern part of the Carnatic, are not only different from those of their neighbours, but are of a character calculated to confirm the conjecture. Again, it is probable that the army of aborigines may have been accompanied by outlying bands of Monkeys, impelled by that magpie-like curiosity and love of plunder which are the peculiar characteristics of the Monkey race; and this incident may have given rise to the story that the army was composed of Monkeys. But perhaps the most probable hypothesis is that the people of the south originally worshipped the Monkey as a deity, and adopted it as their national emblem; and thus they may have become con-

founded with the animal in the same way that the
Scythic tribe of Nágas became confounded with the
Serpent, which was in like manner their deity and
symbol. It is true that the Marawars in the present
day worship Siva, but they may have been converted to this form of religious faith by the Linga-
worshippers who are represented by Ráma. Should
this last hypothesis prove correct it would furnish
the reason why Monkey gods like Hanuman were
introduced in the Rámáyana as fighting by the side
of Ráma; namely, to represent the gods of the people as worshippers of Ráma, and subordinate to him;
just in the same way as in the Mahá Bhárata, the
Serpent-god of Manipura is represented as being
conquered by the son of Arjuna.[2] Besides, however,
the Monkeys, there are references to an army of
Bears, under the leadership of Jámbavat, who is
said to have been the father-in-law of Krishna.[3]
These Bears do not appear upon the scene apart
from the Monkeys, nor is the leader Jámbavat
as famous and important as the Monkey Hanuman. It is therefore difficult to assign a reason
for their introduction, unless it is assumed that
Jámbavat is a representative of the worshippers of
Krishna, giving counsel and support to the cause of
Ráma.

As regards the geography of this portion of the
Rámáyana, it will be observed that three localities
are distinctly specified; and although it is difficult
to identify them with modern sites, they may perhaps be referred to the territory of Mysore, or the

Reason why
the Monkey
gods of the
south may have
been repre-
sented as
fighting for
Ráma.

---

[2] See *ante*, Vol. I. page 412.
[3] See *ante*, Vol. I. pages 384, 476.

country immediately surrounding it.[4] These three localities are as follows :—

1st, Rishya-múkha mountain, the residence of Sugríva, the Monkey Raja who had been dethroned, and with whom Ráma formed an alliance.

2nd, Kishkindhyá, the Monkey city of Báli, the elder brother and enemy of Sugríva.

3rd, Malyavana mountain, the residence of Ráma and Lakshmana during the rainy season.

The narrative of Ráma's alliance with Sugríva and the Monkeys may now be related as follows :—

After Ráma and Lakshmana had passed a night on the banks of the Pampá lake, they rose early in the morning, and performed their customary ablutions and devotions, and went towards the mountain Rishya-múkha; where dwelt the Monkey Raja, Sugríva, who had been dethroned by his brother Báli, and compelled to take refuge in the mountain.   Meantime, Sugríva and his Monkey Counsellors were sitting on a bastion of a fort on the top of the mountain ; and they beheld the approach of Ráma and Lakshmana. And Sugríva turned to his Counsellors, and said :—" Behold two persons are approaching from the direction of Pampá, who are apparelled as devotees, but yet appear to carry arms : I fear they are spies who have been sent hither by my brother Báli."   But Hanuman, who was the chief of his Counsellors, said :—" Be of good cheer, O Sugríva, for these men are the sons of a Raja, and have come for our deliverance."   And Hanuman descended from the mountain, and brought Ráma and Lakshmana into the presence of Sugríva.   And when Ráma had related his story, Hanuman brought some pieces of wood, and kindled a fire ; and Ráma and Sugríva confirmed their friendship before the fire,

---

[4] Prof. H. H. Wilson remarks in a note on the Uttara-Ramacharitra, that the Rishya-múkha mountain, and the scenes in its vicinity, are said to be known by the same appellations in the neighbourhood of Anagundi in the Dekhan.

HISTORY OF
INDIA.
PART IV.

Sugríva shows
Ráma Sítá's
ornaments.

and in the presence of all the Monkeys. And when they had all taken their seats Sugríva said to Ráma:—"Some time back, when I was sitting with my Counsellors upon this mountain, I beheld a woman in the air who was being carried off by Rávana; and as she passed by she threw down her ornaments, and we have preserved them to this day." Sugríva then sent for the ornaments, and laid them before Ráma; but the eyes of Ráma were so affected with grief, that he could not tell whether they belonged to his wife or not. Then Ráma asked his brother if he could remember the ornaments, and Lakshmana said:—"Those silver bells I know, for Sítá wore them on her feet, but all the others are strange to me, for I never cast my eyes above the feet of my brother's wife." [5] At these words Ráma took the ornaments to his heart, and wept aloud; and Sugríva consoled him, saying:—"Now that we have made friendship together, vex not yourself about Sítá: Be assured that you shall soon rescue her."

When Ráma had somewhat recovered, he requested Sugríva to relate the story of his grievances. Sugríva

replied:—"O Ráma, I have an elder brother named Báli, who has deprived me of my Raj, and taken away my wife Rumá; and now he seeks to take away my life; and through fear of him I have taken refuge in this mountain: O Ráma,

I pray you to liberate me from this oppression!" [6] Ráma

---

[5] This reply of Lakshmana is taken from the modern version of the Rámáyana, and is in conformity with modern ideas. In earlier times a greater freedom of manners prevailed.

[6] A long mythical story is here related in the original respecting the origin of the breach between Sugríva and Báli, which it may be advisable to condense into a note. Báli was originally Raja of Kishkindhyá, and on one occasion he fought a certain Asura in the neighbouring plain, after which the Asura fled into a cave. Báli then directed his brother Sugríva to guard the entrance to the cave for one entire month, whilst he himself entered it in pursuit of the Asura. The month passed away, when blood issued from the mouth of the cave; on which Sugríva took it for granted that Báli was killed, and stopped up the mouth of the cave to prevent the Asura from coming out, and returned to the city of Kishkindhyá, where the Monkeys accepted him as their Raja in succession to Báli. Subsequently Báli having killed the Asura in the cave, returned to the city of Kishkindhyá; upon which he was very wroth with Sugríva, and deprived him of his Raj and wife, and would have killed him but for his escape to the Rishya-múkha mountain.

said :—" Cast aside, my friend, all fear of Báli! I promise to make you free: Báli is now dwelling in your city of Kishkindhyá: Put on your war dress, and repair to Kishkindhyá, and go to the gate of the palace, and challenge Báli to a single combat; and as soon as he shall come out against you, I will slay him with my arms."

HISTORY OF INDIA. PART IV.

Ráma directs Sugríva to proceed to Kishkindhyá and challenge Báli.

After this Sugríva set out for the city of Kishkindhyá, accompanied by Ráma and Lakshmana; and whilst the two brothers concealed themselves in the forest hard by, he went forward to the gate of the palace to challenge Báli. And Sugríva shouted with a voice like thunder; and Báli came out with all haste from the inner apartments, and saw that it was his brother Sugríva, who had challenged him to battle. Now Tárá, who was the wife of Báli, sought to prevent her husband from going out to Sugríva; but Báli refused to listen to her; and he went out to the palace gate, and abused Sugríva, and Sugríva abused him in return, and cried out :—" Vishnu is my protector, and you will fall by my hand this day." And Báli and Sugríva fought lustily against each other for a long while, and the battle went against Sugríva, and he fell down and Báli sat upon his breast. And Báli cried out :—" Where is the Vishnu who is your strong ally? Now is the time that you should seek his protection." Meantime, Ráma saw that Báli had gained the victory, and he discharged an arrow at Báli, and pierced his heart, so that he fell senseless upon the ground. Ráma and Lakshmana then came up, and Sugríva rose in great joy at seeing his enemy prostrate upon the ground.

Combat between Sugríva and Báli.

Ráma mortally wounds Báli.

Meanwhile, the sad tidings had reached the ears of Tárá that her husband had fallen in the battle with Sugríva; and

Sudden appearance of Tárá.

Báli dared not approach the Rishya-múkha mountain for the following reasons. On one occasion he had slain the great giant Dundubhi, and thrown his bleeding head upon the mountain; upon which a few drops of blood fell upon Matanga, the sage, who thereupon cursed Báli, that he should fall to pieces if he again approached the mountain. Nobody, however, could move the giant's head, until Ráma kicked it miles away, and moreover exhibited his skill in archery before Sugríva, by shooting an arrow with such force that it passed through seven palm trees, and then divided a mountain and descended to hell; after which it again returned to his quiver in the form of a shining swan.

Tárá's lamenta-
tions over her
dying husband.

she went forth out of the palace with dishevelled hair and loose garments, and all her ornaments in disorder; and she was followed by her son Angada, and a crowd of servants, Counsellors, and friends. When she beheld her husband prostrate upon the ground, she fainted for a while, and then striking her breast with her hands, she cried aloud as follows:—"O my beloved husband, sole protector of my helpless self, why do you thus lie upon the bare earth? Arise, and seat yourself, and call me your beloved as you used to do, and save me from death! You heard me not when I beseeched you not to go forth to this fatal field; and now you have fallen in battle with your enemy, and have lost your life by his dreadful arrow: Oh! why did you deprive your brother of his Raj and his wife? Surely my heart must be made of stone that it does not break at the sight of my husband! I can no longer endure to behold your pale face, and your body covered with the dust of the earth! O my beloved, look once again towards your slave, and take your son Angada to your breast! Why do you not reply, when I am weeping so bitterly at your feet?" So saying, Tárá took her husband upon her lap, and with loud lamentations addressed him thus:—"O my beloved, it is wrong for you to go to the next world, and leave me alone and helpless here: Shame be upon me that I thus be obliged to witness the death of my own husband! Shame be upon that woman who ever becomes a widow in this world! O ye ferocious birds and wild beasts of the jungle, act kindly towards me, and make me your prey, that I may follow my husband to the mansions of Yama."

Funeral cere-
monies for Báli.

Now, when it was known that Báli was dead, the city of Kishkindhyá resounded with the cries of the Monkeys and their wives, whilst Sugríva and Angada and Tárá filled the air with their lamentations: Tárá threw away all her ornaments, and the female Monkeys, seeing her deep affliction, took her by the hand, and made her sit up. Then Ráma began to console Tárá, and at his words all present began to desist from further weeping, and to make preparations for the funeral pile. And the Monkeys placed the dead body of Báli upon a litter; and they perfumed the body with sandal and other perfumes, and decorated both the corpse and the litter with garlands, and covered the body with a richly-embroidered cloth.   Then they took the litter upon their shoulders, and Sugríva and the other Monkeys followed it, crying very bitterly; while some of the Monkeys in front began to throw money to the right and left, and the women of the Monkeys walked last of all.   When they reached the place of burning, the corpse was bathed and placed upon the funeral pile, and Angada, son of Báli, set fire to the pile; and when the burning was over, they all proceeded to the lake Pampá, and bathed themselves, and made oblations of water to the soul of the deceased.

After this, Sugríva took his own wife Rumá, and also *Sugríva installed as Raja, and Angada as Yuvaraja.* took Tárá, the widow of Báli, to be his wife likewise.   And it was agreed that Sugríva should be installed as Raja of Kishkindhyá, and that Angada should be installed as Yuvaraja.   At this time the rainy season had commenced, when *Rainy season.* even the merchants stay at their own homes and go not to foreign countries; and Ráma requested Sugríva to take his pleasure until the rains were over, and then to join in the search for Sítá.   So Sugríva was installed as Raja, and Angada as Yuvaraja; and Ráma and Lakshmana departed from that place, and took up their abode in the Malyavana mountain.

The foregoing narrative of Ráma's alliance with *Review of the foregoing narrative.* the Monkeys exercises a weird-like influence upon the imagination, wholly different from that produced by an ordinary fable in which animals of different kinds are represented as speaking to each other. The mind is called upon to deal with a nondescript *Nondescript Monkeys of the Rámáyana.* being half Monkey and half man; having long tails and walking on all fours, and yet performing funeral rites for a deceased Raja, and installing a successor upon the throne, with all the form and ceremony of human beings.   It was a Monkey Raja, surrounded by his Monkey Counsellors, who beheld the approach of Ráma and Lakshmana from the Bastion of their Fort on the Rishya-múkha mountain. It was Hanuman in the form of a gigantic Monkey who carried Ráma and Lakshmana upon his shoulders up the side of the mountain. The combats between Sugríva and Báli are the combats of Monkeys; and the picture of Báli dying in the presence of his wife Tárá and son Angada, might easily be realized by those who have seen the painful caricature of a human being which a Monkey presents in a wounded or dying state. The scenes, however, are marred in the original by the lengthy dialogues which are placed in the mouths of the Monkeys, and which have been omitted in the foregoing text as being far too monotonous and artificial in tone to excite either interest or sympathy.

Traces in the narrative of an authentic tradition.

As regards the narrative, it certainly seems to refer to some real event amongst the aboriginal tribes; namely, the quarrel between an elder and younger brother for the possession of a Raj; and the subsequent alliance of Ráma with the younger brother. It is somewhat remarkable that Ráma appears to have formed an alliance with the wrong party, for the right of Báli was evidently superior to that of Sugríva; and is especially worthy of note

Ráma's breach of the laws of fair fighting.

that Ráma compassed the death of Báli by an act contrary to all the laws of fair fighting. Again, Ráma seems to have tacitly sanctioned the transfer of Tárá from Báli to Sugríva, which was directly opposed to modern rule, although in conformity with the rude customs of a barbarous age; and it

Marriage of widows and di-

is remarkable that to this day the marriage of

both widows and divorced women is practised by the Marawars, or aborigines of the southern Carnatic, contrary to the deeply-rooted prejudice which exists against such unions amongst the Hindús at large.

CHAPTER XX.

HANUMAN'S ADVENTURES IN LANKÁ.

Expansion of
the original
tradition by
the author of
the Rámáyana.

Neglect of
Sugriva to
assist Ráma.

Assembling of
the army of
Monkeys and
Bears.

Despatch of
four Monkey
armies.

THE story of the assembling of the Monkeys and Bears, and the despatch of four armies in search of Sítá, has been expanded to an inordinate length by the author of the Rámáyana; but the bare outline is extremely simple, and may be briefly indicated as probably involving an authentic event upon which the Hindú bard has based his narrative. It seems that when Sugríva had regained possession of his Raj, he abandoned himself to sensual indulgences, so that when the cold season arrived for the commencement of operations, he was devoting himself to strong drink and the society of his wives. Accordingly Lakshmana was sent by Ráma to remind him of his obligations, and to punish him for his breach of faith if he displayed any further lukewarmness or delay. Meantime, however, Hanuman had already induced Sugríva to send out messengers for assembling his armies; so that after some explanation, Lakshmana was satisfied and returned to Ráma, accompanied by Sugríva. Subsequently the armies of Monkeys and Bears were marshalled in the presence of Ráma, and sent out to the four quarters of the earth; but the army despatched to the south under the command of Hanuman, was the only one that met with any success, and brought back tidings of the lost Sítá.

The story of Hanuman's adventures in Lanká is perhaps one of the best sustained efforts of pure imagination that is to be found in the Rámáyana. The exploits of the vast Monkey hero who could swell himself to the size of a mountain, or dwarf himself to the size of a man's thumb; the strength and magnificence of Lanká with its seven broad moats and seven stupendous walls of stone and metal; the extraordinary deformities of the Rákshasa population; the marvellous palace and gardens of Rávana; the devoted love of Sítá for Ráma and the impure advances of Rávana;—are all depicted with a magnificent exaggeration which is often grand, and but for the fantastic character of some of the incidents might be said to border on the sublime.

The incidents and scenes in this portion of the narrative are so numerous, that it may be as well to indicate them under the following heads :—

1st, Hanuman's march to the sea, and leap over the channel between India and Ceylon.

2nd, Description of the city of Lanká.

3rd, Hanuman reconnoitres Lanká in the form of a cat.

4th, Meeting between Hanuman and the Genius of Lanká.

5th, Hanuman proceeds through the city to the palace of Rávana.

6th, Description of the Inner Apartments of Rávana.

7th, Description of Sítá in the Asoka grove.

8th, Rávana's night visit to Sítá surrounded by his women.

9th, Efforts of the Rákshasí women to induce Sítá to become the wife of Rávana.

10th, Interview between Hanuman and Sítá.

11th, Hanuman destroys the Asoka garden and is captured by Indrajit.

12th, Tricks played by Hanuman upon the Rákshasas.

13th, Hanuman's appearance before Rávana and his Counsellors in the Council Hall.

14th, The firing of Hanuman's tail.

15th, Return of Hanuman and his army to Ráma and Sugríva.

The narrative.

With this preliminary sketch it may suffice to reproduce the leading events in the adventures of Hanuman and his army as they appear in the Rámáyana :—

1st, Hanuman's march to the sea, and leap over the channel between India and Ceylon.

Now Hanuman was sent with the army of Monkeys to the southern quarter because of his superior intelligence, as it was known that Rávana reigned in the southern region. And when Hanuman was about to depart he prayed Ráma to give him a token, that if he should find Sítá, he might convince her that he came from her beloved husband. So

Ráma gives his marriage ring to Hanuman.

Ráma gave to Hanuman the ring bearing his name, which had been presented to him on the day of his marriage by his father-in-law Raja Janaka. Then Hanuman departed with his army of Monkeys towards the south, but one month passed away, and still no tidings could be heard of Sítá.[1]

---

[1] The adventures of the army of Hanuman are told at considerable length in the Rámáyana, but are all mythical. The following story extracted from the Adhyátma Rámáyana may serve as a specimen :—" Now while the Monkeys were proceeding towards the south, they were smitten with thirst, and searched for water on all sides, but as that wilderness was composed of sand, none could be found. At length they came to a mountain, at the foot of which they saw a grove of trees loaded with fruit, resembling the wealthy serving food to indigent travel-

And all the Monkeys were very melancholy, and began to despair. And it came to pass that after a while they came to a certain mountain, where they fell in with a Chief of the Vultures, whose name was Sampáti, and he was elder brother of Jatáyus, the mighty Bird who had given his life in the service of Ráma. And Sampáti told them that he had seen Rávana carry away Sítá, and that Rávana had taken her to his city and palace, which were situated on the island of Lanká, about sixty miles from the sea.[2] And Hanuman and all the Monkeys rejoiced greatly, and proceeded with all haste to the sea.

Now, when the Monkeys reached the shore of the sea, and beheld the island of Lanká, sixty miles from the shore,

HISTORY OF INDIA.
PART IV.

Meeting with Sampáti the Vulture Chief.

---

lers. From a cave in this mountain numberless water-fowl issued, their wings dripping with water. The Monkeys seeing this were satisfied they should find water in the cave. They followed Hanuman in a line, holding each other by the hand as the cave was dark. When they had advanced a considerable distance, the darkness was in an instant dispelled; they beheld a pond full of pure water, near to which was a palace and a garden. In this palace were deposited jewels of great value, grain, fruits, oil, clothes, and an immense quantity of provisions, with sweetmeats of every kind. There was also a large town abounding with shops, but there were not any inhabitants. They were amazed, they consulted with each other what wonderful city this could be; they resolved to enter the palace, where they might meet with some human being. In one of the apartments they beheld a woman splendidly dressed and adorned, her eyes closed in meditation. That woman was a faithful adorer of Ráma ; the veil of chastity was placed over her head; she was super-eminently pure. The Monkeys were terrified at the austerity of her penances ; they paid their adorations to her at a distance. The chaste virgin, opening her eyes and seeing them, asked who they were. Hanuman then related the story of Ráma, and the thirst of the Monkeys, concluding :—'Thou art a faithful worshipper of the divinity ; from beholding thee we are free from sin.' The holy virgin directed the Monkeys where to find food and water, with which they satisfied their hunger and thirst, and then returned to her.

"The female devotee then delivered a long discourse on the divinity of Ráma, and ultimately returned with the Monkey army to Kishkindhyá, and expired in the presence of Ráma."

[2] The real distance of Lanká from the mainland is but vaguely indicated in the Rámáyana. From shore to shore the distance is about sixty miles, and accordingly that has been set down in the text. But it would almost appear as if in times primeval the Island of Ceylon was really joined on to the main. About two miles from the Indian coast is the Island of Ramisseram, which is eleven miles long, and three centuries ago is said to have been joined to the main by a rocky causeway; whilst just off the opposite coast of Ceylon is the Island of Manar, about eighteen miles long. Moreover a low sandy ridge, impassable to ships of burden, connects the Island of Ramisseram with the Island of Manar, and is known in the present day as Adam's Bridge.

not one of them would attempt to leap across the sea excepting the mighty Hanuman. And Hanuman took a gigantic spring, and by his prodigious strength, he leaped over the wide ocean, and reached the shore of Lanká, and alighted upon the mountain which is named Subala.[3] At that moment all Lanká trembled ; and Raja Rávana sent for his Counsellors, and demanded the reason for the trembling. Some of the Counsellors then said :—" O Rávana, this trembling is an earthquake." But one Rákshasa, who was very wise, and whose name was Obindhya, said to Rávana :— " Whatever others may say respecting this trembling, I attribute it only to the presence of Sítá : From the moment that you brought Sítá into your palace, evil omens have constantly appeared in Lanká : I therefore advise you to send back Sítá to Ráma." Then Vibhíshana, who was the pious brother of Rávana, earnestly implored the Raja of the Rákshasas to follow the counsel of Obindhya ; but Rávana could not be moved, and he dismissed the Council in great anger.

Meantime Hanuman was gazing from the summit of the

---

[3] A number of absurd stories are told of the adventures of Hanuman whilst flying through the air, which are utterly devoid of meaning. It is, however, remarkable that amongst others who opposed him was a female Rákshasí named Surasá, who was said to be the mother of the Nágas, an allusion which tends to identify the Rákshasas with the Buddhists. See *ante*, page 315.

There is, however, a graphic description of Hanuman's leap in the Adhyátma Rámáyana which is worth extracting :—" Hanuman then cried out with joy in a voice of thunder as if he would rend the world with the sound ; the mountains trembled, the waves of the ocean were troubled, the earth shook, even Sesha-nája, the great Serpent on whose head the world rests, considered Hanuman's strength as equal to his own. Hanuman extended his form in size so that it equalled the Mandara mountain: his vigour and courage so agitated his soul that the hair on his head and body stood erect. He engaged to cross the sea to Lanká. He received the applause of the Monkeys, and exulting in their praises he departed to the top of Mandara. His form equalled in size that of a mountain ; the colour of his body resembled the brightest gold ; his face was as red as the rubies of Budaksban ; his arms extended as the wings of a great dragon ; his tail was so long that the end of it could not be seen. His great soul was unshaken at the danger and difficulty of the task he had undertaken ; his eyes were inflamed with fury as if he would consume his enemies, as if he would in an instant overturn the foundations of Lanká, and cast them into the ocean. He cried :—' I am the ambassador of Ráma ; his seal ring is in my hand ; every hour, every moment, I repeat his holy name ; I worship him, I entertain the fullest confidence that I shall with ease cross over this ocean.' He then roared out with a thundering voice, he extended his arms, he drew in his neck, he erected his ears, and then looking forward to the sea, he raised himself from the mountain, and sprang towards the south."

Subala mountain upon the beautiful city of Lanká.   It was situated on the middle peak of the Trikúta mountain, and was the work of the divine Viswakarma, the architect of the gods.   The city was a hundred miles in length, and thirty miles in breadth, and was completely surrounded with many walls and canals, one within the other.   Within the great outer canal was a broad belt of thick forest, which was filled with beasts and birds of different species.   Within the forest was a great wall of iron with four gates, one on each of the four sides.   Each gate was guarded by hundreds of Rákshasas, and before each of the four gates was a deep moat with a bridge upon it ; and several machines were placed upon each bridge, so that if an enemy approached the bridge, he was sure to be drowned.   Within this iron wall, and at a little distance from it, was a great wall of stone ; and within the wall of stone were five other walls, each one at a little distance from the other ; and one wall was built of brass, and another of white metal, and another of copper, and another of silver, and the innermost wall of all was built of gold.[4]   Inside these seven walls was the

HISTORY OF INDIA. PART IV.

2nd, Description of the city of Lanká.

The seven canals and walls.

Walls of iron, stone, brass, white metal, copper, silver, and gold.

The city and palace within the seven walls.

[4] The similarity between the seven-walled city of Lanká as described in the Rámáyana, and the seven-walled city of Ekbatana as described by Herodotus, is very striking (Herod. i. 98).   Herodotus, however, lays more stress upon the difference of colour, whilst Válmíki indicates only the difference of material.   Sir H. Rawlinson is of opinion that the story of the seven differently-coloured walls of Ekbatana is a fable of Sabæan origin, and he quotes a poem of Nizami, in which seven palaces are described of different colours, each of which was dedicated to one of the seven great heavenly bodies.   (Journal of Geog. Soc. vol. x. Part i.) As far as colour is concerned the walls of Lanká would appear to represent in like manner one or other of the seven heavenly bodies, as will be seen from the following comparison :—

Walls of Lanká.	Seven heavenly bodies.	Colours as described by Nizami.
Iron	Saturn	Black
Stone	Jupiter	Orange or Sandal-wood colour
Brass	Mars	Scarlet
White Metal	Venus	White
Copper	Mercury	Azure
Silver	Moon	Green, a hue applied by Orientals to silver
Gold	Sun	Gold

Herodotus has slightly deranged the order of colours.

great city of Lanká, with ponds, and lakes, and artificial gardens, on all sides; and the city was traversed by four great thoroughfares, intersected with numerous cross streets; and there were halls and high places for music, and arsenals filled with weapons and stores, and stables for horses and elephants, and places for chariots. And in the centre of that city was the great palace of Lanká, as beautiful as Viswakarma could make it by expending upon it the utmost of his skill.

3rd. Hanuman reconnoitres Lanká in the form of a cat.
Hanuman enters Lanká.

When Hanuman had thus looked down upon Lanká, and seen all its moats and walls, he assumed the shape of a cat; and when the sun had set he entered Lanká in that form, and began to observe the different parts of the city.

The gates.

The gates were protected by thousands of Rákshasas skilled in war; but every one was allowed to enter; and the guards warned all spies and enemies that if they once entered the palace, they would never be allowed to return:

The streets.

The streets were adorned with gems of every colour; but such was the rule of Rávana that no man ventured to pick up a single stone, though it were set in ever so loosely.

The houses.
The bazaars.

The houses on the two sides of the roads were beautiful beyond description, and there were large bazaars in every quarter between the houses, where everything could be obtained at any hour of thé night or day. The Rákshasas who were sleeping in the houses were of every shape and form.

Description of the Rákshasas.

Monstrous deformities.

Some of them disgusted the eye, whilst some were beautiful to look upon. Some had long arms and frightful shapes; some were very fat, and others were very lean; some were mere dwarfs, and others were prodigiously tall. Some had only one eye and others only one ear. Some had monstrous bellies, hanging breasts, long projecting teeth, and crooked thighs; whilst others were exceedingly beautiful to behold and clothed in great splendour. Some had two legs, some three legs, and some four legs. Some had the heads of serpents, some the heads of donkeys, some the heads of horses, and some the heads of elephants.

4th. Meeting between Hanuman and the Genius of Lanká.

Whilst Hanuman was beholding these things, the night became advanced, and the streets of the city were deserted;

so he descended from the wall, on which he was seated in the form of a cat. At that moment Uggra Chunda, the Genius of Lanká, stood before him in the form of a female; and she was hideous to behold, and in her right hand was a sword, and in her left was a basin containing the blood of those whom she killed. Seeing her, Hanuman resumed his Monkey shape; and she looked upon him with wrath, and said :—" Who are you, and why have you entered my city at this quarter of the night? You seem to be bent upon some evil purpose, and therefore you have come hither to fall before the fire of my anger." So saying Uggra Chunda forgot herself, and in her great wrath she gave a severe kick to Hanuman; and Hanuman dealt her a hard blow with his left hand, and she fell senseless on the ground, and vomited blood. When she recovered herself, she said to Hanuman :—" I know who you are; you are the messenger of Ráma, and have come hither to search for his wife Sítá: Go you therefore into the city, and you shall receive no further molestation."

Having thus spoken, Uggra Chunda went her way, and Hanuman again resumed the form of a cat, and proceeded through the city. He entered several houses of the Rákshasas, and examined them in every quarter; and presently he entered the house of Vibhíshana, who was the younger brother of Rávana; and he saw Vibhíshana seated near a tulasí tree, singing hymns in praise of Vishnu and other gods.[5] And Hanuman was surprised to see so much piety in a Rákshasa; and he said to himself :—"Verily this must be Vibhíshana, for he is renowned for his piety."

After this Hanuman, still in the form of a cat, entered the palace of Raja Rávana. That resplendent abode was surrounded on all sides by a deep canal, the surface of which was covered with the lotos. Within the canal was a wall of gold, so lofty that the birds could not fly over it; and the gate of that wall was of gold set with diamonds and other precious stones; and the pillars on each side

Marginal notes:

HISTORY OF INDIA. PART IV.

The combat.

5th, Hanuman proceeds through the city to the palace of Rávana.

Perceives Vibhishana, the younger brother of Rávana, worshipping Vishnu.

Hanuman enters the palace of Rávana. The canal. The golden wall, with jewelled gate, and pillars of black crystal.

---

[5] The tulasi tree is sacred to Vishnu, and its leaves are employed in the worship of that deity. The bale fruit tree is in like manner sacred to Siva.

HISTORY OF
INDIA.
PART IV.

The music
place.

The stables,
arsenals,
gardens,
kitchens, &c.

Hanuman fails
to find Sítá.

6th. Description
of the inner
apartments of
Rávana.

The walls, gates,
and gardens.

The sleeping-
room.

The couch.

The women.

Rávana sleeping
upon a crystal
throne.

of the gate were made of black crystal; and the gate
was guarded by thousands of Rákshasas, armed with spears
and swords and other weapons of war; and over the
gateway was the place for music, which ever sounded
night and day.   There also were stables for horses and elephants, and houses for chariots, and arsenals for weapons,
and places for amusements, and artificial gardens and lakes,
together with kitchens, and store-houses, and wine cellars.
Hanuman was delighted at beholding all these wonders, and
he said within himself:—"Surely this Raja Rávana must
have been a very virtuous man in his former life, and on this
account enjoys so much wealth in his present life."   Hanuman then searched every quarter of the palace for the wife of
Ráma, but could not find her anywhere.

Now, when Hanuman had grown very impatient at not
finding Sítá, he suddenly smelt a very sweet perfume; and
following the scent, he arrived at the inner apartments
of Rávana.   They were surrounded on all sides by an inner
wall of gold set with precious stones; and the gates were
formed of diamonds, and guarded by eunuchs.   Inside were
artificial gardens with lakes and ponds covered with the
white, red, blue, and yellow lotos.   In the middle of all was
the sleeping-room of Rávana; and the walls of that room
were made of gold, and adorned with precious stones, and
the floor was of black crystal.   The couch was as beautiful as
Viswakarma could make it; the pillars which supported it,
and the steps for ascending it, were all of black crystal.
The bedding was as soft and white as the froth of new milk.
Golden pots of water were placed at the four corners of the
couch, and lamps of precious stones were hung from the ceil-
ing, though the apartment was already illuminated by the
radiance of the gems.   Hundreds of beautiful women were
sleeping in that apartment.   Then Hanuman saw a very
rich carpet placed upon a crystal throne; and the carpet
was a magnificent cloth inlaid with gold; and four lamps
of gold stood on its four corners, and on one side was the
chámara and royal umbrella.   Hanuman then reduced himself to the size of a thumb, and jumped up, and sat upon the

throne; and thence he perceived Rávana sleeping upon his couch, wearing a yellow cloth; and ten crowns of gold were upon his ten heads, and his twenty hands were adorned with sandal and ornaments, and strings of rich pearls decorated his breast. A thousand women were sleeping beside him, and the chief among them was Mandodarí, who lay upon his left side; and Hanuman looked carefully among them, but he could not find Sítá, for she was not there.

When Hanuman had searched throughout the inner apartments, it was about midnight; and he was very weary, and seated himself upon the top of a wall, and was very sad at not finding Sítá, for he feared that she was no longer alive. Suddenly he heard the noise of birds in the Asoka garden, and he entered therein, and concealed himself amidst the foliage of a large cotton tree. Thence he saw Sítá surrounded by hideous Rákshasí women, like a deer surrounded by tigresses. She was as pale and emaciated as the new moon, and her body was covered with dust; but nothing could conceal her beauty, which was like a live charcoal under a cover of ashes. Her hair was tied up in a single knot, and she had only one cloth, and no ornaments whatever. Suddenly she cried out the name of Ráma, and Hanuman prepared to approach her, when at that moment the bells sounded the third quarter of the night, and the music began to play.

Now just at this time Rávana arose from his bed, and Sítá came into his mind, and he ordered all his women to follow him into the Asoka garden; and some carried lamps in their hands, and some carried the chámara, and some carried the betel pot, whilst some carried pots of water. When Hanuman saw the mighty Rákshasa coming to the Asoka grove, surrounded by his women, he concealed himself where he might hear all that passed. When Rávana entered the grove, Sítá arose up in terror, like an antelope at the approach of a tiger, and then sat down with her face turned away from Rávana.[6] Then Rávana approached her, and

HISTORY OF INDIA. PART IV.

Hánuman still fails to find Sítá.

7th, Description of Sítá in the Asoka grove.

Sítá surrounded by Rákshasí women.

8th, Rávana's night visit to Sítá surrounded by his women.

Hanuman hides himself.

Alarm of Sítá.

---

[6] The scene is still more graphically described in the Adhyátma Rámáyana, as will be seen from the following extract :—" Hanuman was preparing to address

said :—" O beautiful damsel, why do you torment yourself and shed tears for nothing ? Why are you much afraid of me, whilst I am your slave ? Fear not being discovered by others, for no man can enter this palace ; and dry up your tears, and look upon me with a smiling countenance : Let me send for women who will wash you with water, and tie up your hair in knots, and adorn you with ornaments and perfumes : Come and sit with me, and let us drink together, and pass the time in hearing songs and beholding dances : Be the mistress of all my other wives, and I too will be your slave, and do whatever you command, and give you whatever you may desire."

To this speech of Rávana, the terrified Sítá answered thus :—" O lord of Lanká, cast aside your enmity against Ráma ! You are renowned throughout the world for your wealth, strength, and valour ; and should not soil your reputation by acts of wickedness : Look upon the wives of others

Prays that she
may be restored
to her husband
Ráma.

as you do upon your own mother, and restore me to my husband Ráma, and entreat his forgiveness : My husband is my wealth, and I consider him better than anything you can offer me : I advise you to send me to Ráma, and thus save yourself and family from ruin."

Rávana said :—" O Sítá, How can you compare me with the poor and helpless devotee, Ráma ? I live in a palace of gold, whilst your Ráma dwells in a hut of leaves : I command

---

Sítá, when he heard a noise with loud acclamations ; on looking round he beheld a crowd of rosy-cheeked and lovely damsels, beautiful as fairies, ravishers of hearts, equal in splendour to the Sun and Moon, coming into the garden. This troop formed a circle, in the midst of which marched Rávana as a thorn among roses, a raven in the midst of nightingales, a giant amongst fairies, with ten heads and twenty arms as long as the branches of trees ; the colour of his body was blue mixed with black."

Then follows a singular account of Rávana's secret worship of Ráma, which is deserving of consideration :—" Rávana was constantly meditating in anxious expectation of the period when he should obtain salvation from the hand of Ráma ; that if Ráma did not come to Lanká to free Sítá from her confinement, he could not be released from his present miserable state. He worshipped Ráma in his heart, whether engaged in business, at meals, or in sleep ; he adored Ráma, nor did he at any time forget his name. Whichever way he turned his thoughts he imagined he beheld Ráma with his bow and arrows in his hands, his hair braided in a knot on the crown of his head, a deerskin bound round his body, and accompanied by Lakshmana."

a numerous army of horses, elephants, chariots, and foot-men, whereas your Ráma is without a single ally : Even my servants wear cloths which are rare to the gods, whilst your husband wears the bark of trees : My women and slaves wear ornaments which are unknown to Ráma, and live upon food which would be regarded as delicacies even by Indra, whereas your husband lives upon fruits and roots : Behold the beds and furniture of my palace ; Ráma has never even heard of their existence : How then can you prefer Ráma to me ? Moreover it is doubtful whether Ráma is alive : I think that by this time he must have been devoured by some bird or beast of prey ; but even if he is alive how is it possible for him to enter Lanká ? How then can I ever fear that Ráma will rescue you ? If thousands of Rámas were to assemble together they could not carry you away : There-fore cast aside your foolish hopes, and consent to be my chief Rání."

HISTORY OF INDIA.
PART IV.

Sítá replied in anger :—" I am now assured, O wicked Rávana, that you have not long to live : The day is not far off when your golden Lanká will be a heap of ashes, and your numberless army will fall under the arrows of Ráma : As for your bravery you need say nothing; for I know its worth from the stealth in which you carried me away : There is as much difference between you and Ráma, as there is between a mouse and a lion, a hedgehog and an elephant, a mosquito and a hawk; a glowworm and the noon-day sun, a grain of sand and a precious stone, a star and the full moon, the river Caramnasa and the Ganges, a burnt brick and a mountain, and a Chandala and the Bráh-man Vrihaspati, who is the preceptor of the gods : Boast as long as you do not meet Ráma; but the moment he is here, consider yourself and your whole family as dead per-sons : You will then remember my counsel, and repent when it is too late."

Sítá wrathfully declares Rávana's inferiority to Ráma.

Rávana was now angry in his turn, and his eyes turned round and flashed fire, and he gnashed his teeth, and said :— " O Sítá, if it were not sinful to slay a woman, I would put you to death this day : Your language is more like that of a master, than like one whom I can kill or save according to

Rávana threatens to devour Sítá unless after two months she becomes his wife.

HISTORY OF
INDIA.
PART IV.

my pleasure : I am determined, however, that you shall accept me as your husband, and I give you two months to think it over : If at the end of that time I find you still obstinate, I will devour you."

Sitá's bitter
refusal.

Sítá replied :—"Even though you gave me thousands of years I would never become your wife; I will touch no man but Ráma."

Rávana pre-
pares to slay
Sitá with his
scimitar.

At these harsh words of Sítá, the mighty Rávana was furious with rage, and he cried out :—"Never before have I heard such harsh words, and I cannot permit them to go unpunished." Then he took up a sharp scimitar, and raised it in the air to strike off her head, when his wife Mandodarí

Interposition of
his wife
Mandodarí.

suddenly appeared and caught him in her arms, and said :— "Be patient, my lord, and stain not your reputation by such a heinous offence : All the Sastras agree in condemn- ing the slaughter of a female : You have women by hun- dreds, and I pray you go and take pleasure in their com- pany : This woman is weak and melancholy, and has no inclination to become your wife : Do not, therefore, enter- tain any passion for her ; for he who forces the inclinations of a woman will die an early death, or become the prey of endless disease."

Rávana again
threatens to
devour Sitá
after two
months.

At these words Rávana was somewhat quieted, but he desired the female attendants to persuade Sítá to become his wife within two months ; and if when that time was over she still refused him, they were to cut her in pieces, and bring him the flesh for his morning meal. Having given these instructions, Rávana returned with his women to his own apartments.

9th, Efforts of
the Rákshasí
women to in-
duce Sitá to
yield to
Rávana.

Meanwhile the Rákshasí women came and seated them- selves round Sítá, and endeavoured to turn her heart towards Rávana ; but their efforts were as vain as those of a child who endeavours to turn the current of the holy Ganges with a handful of sand. They then threatened to torture her,

Sitá's terror.

and even to devour her ; and she was in an agony of terror,

Trijatá prophe-
sies the ulti-
mate triumph
of Ráma.

and a virtuous woman named Trijatá, who had hitherto been asleep, was awakened by her cries. And Trijatá arose up and said to the others :—" If you have any desire

for your own safety, you will keep your hands from Sítá, for
I have dreamed a dream which betokens victory to Ráma,
and destruction to Rávana." Then all the women left Sítá,
and crowded round the aged Trijatá to listen to the story of
her dream; and when they had heard it, they departed out
of the grove, and went to their own apartments.

HISTORY OF
INDIA.
PART IV.

Whilst Sítá was thus left alone in the grove, she heard
a voice repeating the story of Ráma; and looking up to see
whence the voice came, she beheld nothing but a very small
Monkey; and she thought that her ears had deceived her,
and became as sorrowful as before. Then Hanuman said:
—"O mother, I am not what you take me to be: I am the
slave of Ráma, my name is Hanuman, and I am the son of
Váyu; and I have been sent by Ráma to discover if you
were here." So saying, Hanuman descended from the tree,
and bowed himself before Sítá; and he put into her hand
the signet ring which bore the name of Ráma, and which
Ráma had given to him at the time of his departing with
the army towards the south. Then the grief of Sítá burst
forth afresh, and she placed the ring on her head, and then
upon her bosom; but she began to rejoice greatly when
she heard that a day of deliverance was nigh at hand.

10th, Interview
between Hanu-
man and Sítá.

Hanuman gives
Ráma's signet
ring to Sítá.

Sítá's grief.

When Hanuman had thus acquainted Sítá with all that
had occurred to Ráma after she had been carried away by
Rávana, he proposed to bear her away upon his shoulder, and
restore her to her husband Ráma. Sítá said:—"How can
so small a Monkey carry me over the broad ocean?" Then
Hanuman increased his size, until he became as large as a
mountain, and then he reduced himself to the same size as
before. And Sítá looked on with wonder, and said:—"I
now believe that you can carry me, but I will never of my
own will touch any man but Ráma: Moreover, if you took
me hence by stealth, all the world would say that Ráma is a
coward, and is unable to punish Rávana." Sítá then dismissed Hanuman, saying:—"Only two months remain to
me; and if within that time Ráma does not come and deliver
me, I shall be devoured by these dreadful Rákshasas."
She then gave to Hanuman the only jewel which she had re-

Hanuman pro-
poses to carry
away Sítá.

Proves his
strength by
swelling to the
size of a
mountain.

Sítá declines to
be touched by
any man save
Ráma.

maining, and she put on Ráma's ring in lieu thereof, and she blessed Hanuman, and permitted him to depart at the rising of the sun.

Hanuman
leaves Sítá.
11th, Hanuman
destroys the
grove.

Now when Hanuman left Sítá in the Asóka grove, he thought within himself that he had succeeded in discovering Sítá, and must now do something to injure Rávana. So he again assumed a large shape, and entered a beautiful grove of mango trees, and ravaged it in all directions, so that not a single tree remained in all the garden. The Rákshasas who watched in the garden were all fast asleep; but they were awakened by the terrible noise; and seeing that the garden was all destroyed, and that the countenance of Hanuman was fearful to behold, they went to Rávana, and told him that a large Monkey had entered Lanká, and destroyed the whole of the garden.

The guards
complain to
Rávana.

Rávana sends
eighty thousand
Rákshasas who
are destroyed
by Hanuman.

When Rávana heard what Hanuman had done, he called eighty thousand Rákshasas, and ordered them to bring that great Monkey before him, tied hand and foot. The mighty army of Rákshasas then went forth into the garden, but when Hanuman saw them approaching, he pulled down a crystal pillar, and whirled it over his head, and slew hundreds; and taking other pillars, he whirled them round also, until within a single hour he had sent the whole of the eighty thousand Rákshasas to the mansions of Yama. And Hanuman then destroyed all the guards that watched in the garden, excepting only a very few who escaped to Rávana, and told him all that the Monkey had done.

Combat be-
tween Hanu-
man and
Jambu-máli.

When Rávana heard that his eighty thousand Rákshasas were destroyed, he sent for Jambu-máli, the son of the Commander-in-Chief, and told him to go out into the garden, and not to return until he had slain this bloodthirsty Monkey. So Jambu-máli went to his own chamber, and put on a red cloth, and over it a coat of mail; and he put a helmet upon his head, a string of pearls upon his neck, earrings in his ears, and an ornament upon his arms; and he armed himself with a sword, a club, and a leathern thong. He then ascended his chariot, and proceeded to the garden, where he found Hanuman seated upon the wall; and he discharged many arrows, and pierced Hanuman upon his head, his two arms, and his breast. In return, Hanuman took up a large tree, and hurled it at the head of his enemy; but Jambu-máli cut the tree into pieces with his arrows. Then Hanuman took up a pillar and threw it at Jambu-máli, and dashed him and his chariot to pieces, and killed him and all his servants; and only one man escaped to carry the news to Rávana.

Raja Rávana was now in great dismay, and his eyes flashed fire with rage. And seven mighty Rákshasas appeared before him, and prayed that they might be sent against Hanuman; and Rávana gave them leave to go, and they went out and were all slain by Hanuman in the same manner as he had slain Jambu-máli. Then Rávana sent out five Commanders, but they too were slain by Hanuman. Then he ordered his own son Aksha to go forth, and he was slain in like manner.

Hanuman slays seven Rákshasa Chiefs, five Commanders, and Aksha, the son of Rávana.

When Rávana heard that his son Aksha was slain, he was filled with grief, and he sent for his famous and beloved son Indrajit, who had once conquered the all-powerful Indra, the sovereign of the gods. And Rávana said to Indrajit:— " O my son, nothing is impossible to you : Go you, therefore, and conquer this evil Monkey!" At these words Indrajit rose up and arrayed himself for the battle; and he ascended his chariot, which was drawn by four tigers, and went out at the head of a vast army to fight against the Monkey Chief. When Hanuman beheld Indrajit, he set up a loud shout like a roar of thunder; and Indrajit shouted in return, and drawing his bow pierced Hanuman all over with sharp arrows. Then Hanuman seized a pillar as before, and with one blow he put to death the charioteer of Indrajit. Then Indrajit took another chariot, and the battle was very hot, and lasted long. At length Indrajit thought within himself :— " This Monkey must be a god." And he loosened a powerful noose which had been given to him by Brahma, and which never failed of its object; and he threw it over Hanuman. And Hanuman thought within himself that he could break the strings of the noose, but would not do so

Rávana sends his son Indrajit, the conqueror of Indra, to fight Hanuman.

Indrajit goes out in a chariot drawn by four tigers.

The combat.

Indrajit binds Hanuman in the irresistible noose of Brahma.

lest he should offend Bráhma. And he permitted himself to be taken prisoner and bound.

Then the Rákshasas commanded Hanuman to arise and go before Rávana ; and they began to beat him with sticks to compel him to go; but Hanuman said :—" How can I arise and go before your Raja, when I am bound hand and foot ! Take me up one of you upon your shoulders, for I am unable to stir of my own accord." And one Rákshasa then came forward and tried to take the Monkey up in his arms, but he could not raise him from the ground. Then one after another came forward, but not one was able to move Hanuman. And Indrajit was in great wrath, and he abused the Rákshasas very harshly, and ordered hundreds of Rákshasas to take the Monkey up. And Hanuman lessened the weight of his body, so that the Rákshasas lifted him upon their shoulders ; but then he again assumed his former weight, and crushed the Rákshasas ; so that they fell down dead

beneath him. Seeing this, no Rákshasa would approach him, but he bade them loosen the bonds on his feet, and they did so ; and he then rose up, and walked towards the court of Rávana, and the Rákshasas followed him holding the ends of the cords in their hands. Then the inhabitants of Lanká came forward, and some of them struck Hanuman on the face, and some pulled him by the hair, and others by the tail, whilst other threw ashes upon him. In this manner he was led into the Council-hall of Rávana.

When Hanuman was brought before Rávana and all his Counsellors, Ravana questioned him in great wrath ; but Hanuman defied him to his face, and called upon him to restore Sítá to her husband, and to ask forgiveness at the feet of Ráma. Then Rávana was filled with anger, and ordered that the head of Hanuman should be immediately severed from his body. But Vibhíshana rose up and said :—" It has been laid down in all the Sastras, that an envoy is never to be put to death: He may be disfigured, or beaten with leathern stripes, or his head may be shaved,[7] for these are

---

[7] It will be remembered that the envoys of King David had the half of their beards shaved off by Hanun, King of Ammon. (2 Sam. x.) In the present instance there appears to be some confusion betwen a spy and an envoy.

the three punishments proper to an envoy: Do not therefore slay this Monkey, but let him go and make his report
to those by whom he has been sent."

Rávana replied:—"What you say, O Vibhíshana, is perfectly true, and I will not therefore kill this Monkey: But I
cannot permit him to depart unpunished: The tail is the
chief ornament of the Monkey, and I shall therefore order
his tail to be set on fire and burned." So saying, Rávana
commanded his Rákshasas to cover Hanuman's tail with old
cloths, and to dip it into ghee; and the Rákshasas did so,
but Hanuman swelled out his tail to such a monstrous size
that all the cloths in Lanká would scarcely cover it. The
Rákshasas then dipped his tail in ghee, and set it on fire.

Now, when Hanuman's tail had been set on fire, the
flame blazed very fiercely, but he felt no pain, and he knew
that he was preserved by the power of Ráma and Sítá.
Then being intent upon committing evil against Rávana, he
reduced his body to a very small size and escaped through
the meshes of the noose; and again swelling out to a gigantic height, he seated himself on the top of a wall, and took
a pillar in his hand. Then the Rákshasas hastened to re-
capture him, but with one stroke of the pillar he killed them
all; and lashing about his flaming tail, he set all the houses
in Lanká in a blaze of fire. Hanuman then went before
Sítá, and related to her all that had taken place; and having
obtained her permission to depart, he went out of the city,
and set out to return to Ráma.

When Hanuman reached the sea-shore, he set up a loud
shout which was heard by Angada and all the army of Monkeys and Bears who were encamped on the opposite side.
He then took another tremendous leap, and passed over the
ocean the same way as before; and having rejoined the
Monkey army, he related to them the story of all that had
occurred to him in Lanká. The whole army of Monkeys
and Bears then set out with great joy to return to Ráma
and Sugríva; and on their way they came to the honey
garden of Sugríva, which was guarded by his uncle, the
great Monkey Dadhi-múkha. And the Monkeys entered the

HISTORY OF
INDIA.
PART IV.

14th, The fir-
ing of Hanu-
man's tail.

Hanuman
escapes and sets
Lanká on fire.

15th, Return of
Hanuman and
the Monkey
Army to Ráma
and Sugríva.

Adventures of
the Monkeys in
the honey
garden of
Sugríva.

garden, and they drank the honey until they were all
drunken, and they made a great noise and tumult; and
Dadhi-múkha heard their shouts, and ordered his attendants
to drive them out of the garden. At this the Monkeys
were in a great rage, and they fell upon Dadhi-múkha, and
some beat him, and others kicked him, and others rubbed
his face against the ground. Then Dadhi-múkha arose and
fled to the city Kishkindhyá, and prostrated himself at the
feet of his nephew Sugríva, and informed him of all that
the Monkeys had done in the garden. And Sugríva consoled him, but rejoiced greatly, saying :—" Angada would
never have permitted the Monkeys to drink the honey in
my garden were he not returning with good news respecting
Sítá." Sugríva then requested Dadhi-múkha to forgive
Angada, and to go and bring the Monkey army with all
speed to Kishkindhyá.

Sugríva's joy at the return of the Monkeys.

Meanwhile the whole army of Monkeys and Bears, with
Hanuman in front, proceeded to the place where they were
to meet Ráma and Sugríva, and they filled the air with the
name of Ráma. And Angada and Hanuman told all. And
Hanuman said :—" Unless the army enters Lanká within
one month from this day, Sítá will have put an end to her
own life to escape from Rávana." And Hanuman gave to
Ráma the jewel which Sítá had given to him in exchange
for the ring; and Ráma knew it again, and bestowed great
praises upon Hanuman.

Meeting be-tween Hanu-man and Ráma.

Hanuman gives Sítá's jewel to Ráma.

The foregoing narrative is replete with strange
pictures which have been familiarized to every
Hindú from his childhood by nursery paintings and
dramatic representations, but which the European
must generally fail to realize by a bare perusal of
the story. Accordingly it may be advisable to
pause for awhile, and endeavour to call up the
scenes in all their grand extravagance as they flash
upon the imagination of the marvel-loving Hindú;
to leave for awhile the area of truth and nature, and

Review of the foregoing nar-rative of the adventures of Hanuman.

yield to the witcheries of the Hindú bard, until the fantastic shapes which are shadowed forth by the poet's fancy cease to be the mere phrensy of poetic painting, and become vivid and substantial realities.

The first picture is that of the mighty Monkey Hanuman, with form as vast as a mountain and as tall as a gigantic tower.   His complexion is yellow and glowing like molten gold.   His face is as red as the brightest ruby ; whilst his enormous tail spreads out to an interminable length.   He stands on a lofty rock and roars like thunder.   He leaps into the air, and flies amongst the clouds with a rushing noise, whilst the ocean waves are roaring and splashing below.   He alights upon Lanká with a bound which makes the island tremble, and fills the Rákshasa Raja and all his demon Counsellors with mysterious alarm.

Picture of Hanuman's leap.

Next the fabled city of Lanká passes before the eye like a panorama of marvels.   All that is monstrous and magnificent, all that is hideous and beautiful, are to be found in these marvellous houses and palaces, which are shut out from the outer world by lines of impregnable fortifications.   Her seven walls and moats recall the vision of the city of Ekbatana ; whilst the great streets, intersecting each other, awaken the old dream of the fabled city of Babylon, with its stupendous walls and brazen gates.

Picture of the city of Lanká, with its fortifications and monstrous inhabitants.

Through this city of marvels Hanuman stealthily creeps at midnight in the form of a cat.   The full moon is shining on the moats and battlements, the houses, the bazaars, and the gardens.   The giants, the monsters, and the fair women, are all wrapped in deep sleep.   After a strange encounter with the Genius of the city, Hanuman approaches the palace

Picture of Hanuman stealing through Lanká at midnight in the shape of a cat.

HISTORY OF
INDIA.
PART IV.

Picture of the
inner apart-
ments.

Widowed con-
dition of Sítá in
the Asoka
grove.

Extraordinary
picture pre-
sented by the
night interview
between
Rávana and
Sítá.

Favourite
pantomimic
representation
of Hanuman's
setting Lanká
on fire with his
tail.

Army of drunk-
en Monkeys
in the honey
garden.

of Rávana; and once more the Oriental bard gives full play to his imagination. The palace and garden, and especially the inner apartments, are described with a luxurious sensuousness which the European poet could scarcely reach. Contrasted with this voluptuous scene is the picture of the desolate condition of Sítá in the Asoka grove, pale, emaciated, and arrayed in the garb of widowhood, without ornament and without perfumes. It is night, but she is sitting beneath a tree, surrounded by the demon women. The bells sound the third quarter of the night, or about three o'clock in the morning. Suddenly an extraordinary incident occurs, which could scarcely have entered the imagination of any one but an Oriental. The ten-headed Rávana awakes in the night and thinks of Sítá; and accordingly descends from his couch, and goes out into the Asoka garden, surrounded by a crowd of beautiful damsels, to seek the object of his desires and induce her to become his wife.

The pantomimic action involved in the proceedings of Hanuman can be easily apprehended; and the European may even sympathize in the shouts of laughter which accompany the discomfiture of the Rákshasas. But the burning of Hanuman's tail is the prime favourite in dramatic representations, and is always hailed by a Hindú audience with a storm of delight. The false tail of the representative of Hanuman is of course stuffed with combustibles, and flares away with a display of fireworks, until the flimsy materials which indicate the streets and houses of Lanká are destroyed in the devouring flames.

The scene in the honey garden is almost equally amusing in the eyes of the Hindús. The joke lies in the presumption of the Monkeys, who consider that as they have discovered Sítá, Sugríva, will readily forgive them for revelling in his honey garden. But there is another amusing element which must not be overlooked. The Monkeys are said to have intoxicated themselves with the honey; and if the representation of a drunken man can furnish amusement to a mixed audience, it is not difficult to apprehend the intense enjoyment which is produced by the grotesque picture of an army of drunken Monkeys, playing every fantastic trick conceivable in animals that caper about sometimes on four legs and sometimes on two, whose countenances are always ludicrous, and whose very tails are provocative of laughter.

Amidst, however, all the wild extravagance of the poet's fancy, there are a few glimpses of historic truth which are well deserving of notice. Thus the picture of Rávana sleeping, surrounded by a number of beautiful women, is perfectly in accordance with the traditions of the sensuality which prevailed amongst the Buddhist Rajas, and thus tends to confirm the view that Rávana was a Buddhist sovereign. In the early life of Gótama Buddha there is a significant legend which serves to indicate the mistaken voluptuousness that appears to have been the rule, and the weary satiety which frequently followed. Gótama, like Rávana, was constantly taking his pleasure in the company of a large number of beautiful damsels; but one evening, whilst reclining upon his couch as usual, their charms failed to make any impression upon his heart. They danced, they sang, they displayed their graceful forms in every movement, but his thoughts were elsewhere, and at last he fell asleep, and they followed his example. About midnight Gótama awoke, and looking around him beneath the light of the fragrant lamps, he saw the various attitudes, and uninviting appearance of the damsels. Some were snoring, others were gnashing their teeth, others had their mouths wide open, whilst others were restlessly tumbling about in unseemly postures. Accordingly he arose from his couch, and determined from that moment to abstain from all the pleasures of sense, and to pass his life as a devotee.[8]

Part played by Vibhíshana in the original tradition.

The proceedings of Vibhíshana are also worthy of consideration, as he subsequently performed an important part in the story, and evidently belongs to the original tradition. It seems that although Ráma is represented as a god, yet he found it necessary to form an alliance with Sugríva; and in like manner it would now seem that he carried on negociations with a brother of Rávana who aspired to the throne of Lanká. A religious meaning is of course imparted to this transaction, which in itself would otherwise present a very suspicious appearance. Vibhíshana is represented as a faithful worshipper of Vishnu; and in a subsequent portion of the poem he is said to have been ill-used by Rávana for counselling submission to Ráma; and to have deserted the cause of his brother and joined that of the invaders, by whom he was at once recognized as Raja of Lanká. This arrangement, which will be further discussed hereafter, is of a singularly human character, and as such may be readily credited.

Religious significance of the alliance between Vibhíshana and Ráma.

As regards the religious aspect of the alli-

[8] See Bigandet's Legend of Gótama. The subject will be referred to hereafter.

ance, it is easy to conceive that in a religious war between the Linga worshippers and the Buddhists, an ambitious and unscrupulous brother of the Buddhist Raja would perceive the expediency of adopting the religion of the invaders, as a step towards securing their support in the effort to supplant the reigning Raja, and obtain possession of the throne. On the other hand, Ráma's genius for alliances Ráma's genius for alliances. seems to have been quite equal to that of any modern sovereign, and to have been attended with extraordinary success. By aiding Sugríva in the struggle against Báli, he secured the assistance of a powerful ally on the mainland; and by espousing the cause of Vibhíshana, he secured the support of a strong party who came over to him from the island.

CHAPTER XXI.

RÁMA'S INVASION OF LANKÁ.

HISTORY OF
INDIA.
PART IV.

Division of the
story of Ráma's
expedition into
two parts —
1st, The in-
vasion.
2nd, The war.
Narrative of
Ráma's in-
vasion.

THE story of Ráma's expedition against Rávana may be divided into two separate narratives, the first comprising the events which immediately preceded the commencement of hostilities, and the second comprising the war which followed. Accordingly the present chapter will contain the first narrative under the head of "Ráma's invasion of Lanká;" whilst the chapter immediately following will contain the second narrative under the head of "Ráma's war against Rávana."

Important inci-
dents.
Rupture be-
tween Rávana
and Vibhíshana.

Bridging of the
channel be-
tween Ceylon
and the main.

The Linga set
up in the
Island of
Ramisseram.

The story of the invasion of Lanká includes some important incidents. It will be seen that the rupture between Rávana and Vibhíshana reaches a climax, and that the Queen-mother appears to have espoused the cause of Vibhíshana. But perhaps the most interesting legend is the alleged construction of a rocky bridge over the channel which separates India from Ceylon, and which is sixty miles across. To this day the tradition of Ráma's bridge is one of the most widely celebrated in all India; whilst the islands and causeways in that neighbourhood are still pointed out as relics of the marvellous structure. The setting up of a Linga in the island of Ramisseram is a significant event that throws valuable light upon a struggle between the Linga worshippers and the Buddhists in Southern India, which appears to form the groundwork of this portion of the Rámáyana; and it is especially interesting from the fact that a magnificent pagoda at Ramisseram, containing a brazen Linga set up before an image of Ráma, exists to this day; whilst the locality is regarded as one of the most sacred in all India, and a favourite place of pilgrimage to devout Hindús from the remotest quarters of the Indian peninsula.

The narrative of Ráma's invasion of Lanká is as follows:—

After this, at an auspicious moment, Ráma and Sugríva set out for the sea-shore with an innumerable array of Monkeys and Bears; and Hanuman carried Ráma on his shoulders, and Angada carried Lakshmana in like manner; and they speedily reached the ocean, and encamped in huts made of leaves, and began to consider how they should cross the sea, and reach the island of Lanká. [1]

---

[1] The march of the army of Ráma is graphically described in the Adhyátma Rámáyana, as follows:—"Sugríva led the Monkeys, Jámbavat the Bears, and the other Chiefs took their stations at the head of their respective divisions. The troops, well armed and appointed, formed a square with Ráma and Lakshmana in the centre, who exceeded in lustre the quickly-passing sun. The Monkeys and Bears, resembling the stars of heaven round the moon, dancing on all sides and rejoicing in their strength, covered the space of one hundred thousand miles, so great were their numbers. Each Monkey was invincible in prowess ; he could in a moment assume whatever form he chose, and delighted in war. They all continually were crying out :—'Let us hasten our march that we may exterminate Rávana and his host of demons!' In this manner the armies proceeded towards the south, subsisting on the fruits and leaves of the forest, to desolate Lanká. These Monkeys and Bears were each of them an incarnation of one of the gods. Ráma in the midst of his army appeared in great splendour, as the moon among the stars. The heroic Monkeys sounded their shells, the earth trembled with the loudness of their shouts and the lashings of their tails. They passed over forests, mountains, wilds, and sands, without noticing the difficulties of the road. The race of Monkeys are always lively ; they marched along swift as the wind in sprightly conversation with each other ; they did not leave a single fruit, leaf, or root in any of the forests through which they passed.

"The vast armies of Monkeys and Bears, with Ráma and the rest, marched on day and night in the most regular order, until they reached the southern shore, where they looked with astonishment at the waves of the sea, rolling one after

Nikashá,
mother of
Rávana, re-
quests her other
son, Vibhíshana,
to interfere.

Meanwhile Nikashá, who was the mother of Rávana, began to see ill omens on every side; and she was sorely troubled; and she sent for her other son, Vibhíshana, and requested him to advise Rávana to restore Sítá to her husband. And Vibhíshana proceeded to the Council Chamber, and spoke aloud to Rávana before all his Counsellors; but Rávana was wroth and abused him sorely, and commanded him to depart out of Lanká. So Vibhíshana returned to his house, and took leave of his wife Saramá, and directed her to attend upon Sítá, and serve her as a slave.

Vibhíshana goes over to Ráma.

He then went out of Lanká, and proceeded to the camp of Ráma; and four chief men of the city went with him. And when Ráma saw the men, and discovered who they were, he ordered a pot of water to be brought from the sea, and he vowed friendship with Vibhíshana; and he took the water and poured it upon his head, and declared him to be Raja of Lanka in the room of his brother Rávana.

Ráma calls a Council.

After this Ráma called together a Council to consider how they should cross the ocean so as to reach the island of Lanká; and he invoked the god Varuna, the regent of the waters; and Varuna entered the Council, and directed that a bridge should be built over the sea. Varuna said:—

The god Varuna advises the construction of a bridge by Nala.

"There is a Monkey in your army named Nala; he is the son of Viswa-karma, and whatsoever stone he touches will float upon the water." Then Ráma rejoiced, and directed

Nala and th Monkeys build the bridge.

Sugríva to order Nala to build the bridge; and in an auspicious moment the great work was commenced by Nala. And the Monkeys filled the air with their shouts, and incessantly called out the name of Ráma; and they brought trees, mountains, stones, and other articles, and gave them all to Nala; and Nala threw them into the sea, and by

The stones float on the water. Alarm of Rávana.

virtue of his touch all the stones floated upon the waves as though they had been boats.[2] And the news was carried to Rávana that Ráma was building a bridge of stones which

---

another with a tremendous noise, and seeming as if they rose to heaven and then sank to the lowest abyss, the opposite shore being imperceptible."

[2] According to the Adhyátma Rámáyana Nala engraved the name of Ráma upon every stone; and such was the virtue of Ráma's name that the stones would not sink, but floated on the sea and were united to form a bridge.

floated on the water as though they were planks; and **HISTORY OF INDIA. PART IV.**
Rávana called together his Counsellors, but they bade him
fear nothing, for even if Ráma crossed to Lanká he would
fall in battle. Meanwhile the bridge progressed day by day, *Completion of the bridge.*
and on the last day of the month it touched the shore of
Lanká.

Then Ráma worshipped the great god Siva, who is the *Ráma worships Siva and sets up a Linga in Ramisseram.*
propitiator in all difficult undertakings; and he made a
Linga, and worshipped it, and poured offerings over it; and
when he was about to throw the Linga into the water, the
gods came down from heaven, and presented themselves
before him, and besought him to permit it to stay where it
was that they might worship it every day. And this Linga
remains to this day, and is named Ramesushur, which signifies " the lord of Ráma," or " the god whose lord is
Ráma." [3]   Then in an auspicious moment Ráma and *Ráma and Sugríva cross the bridge with the army of Monkeys and Bears.*
Sugríva, with all the army of Monkeys and Bears, crossed
the ocean upon the bridge which Nala had made, and encamped in the island of Lanká near the Subala mountain;
and Ráma sent Hanuman to tell the happy tidings to Sítá,
who was still abiding in the Asoka grove; and Sítá was
filled with joy, and exulted in the hope of her speedy
restoration to her beloved husband Ráma.

Now when Rávana heard that Ráma and all his Monkey
army had crossed the ocean and encamped without the city
of Lanká, he sent for two of his Ministers named Súka and
Sárana, and desired them to assume the shape of Monkeys,

---

[3] The setting up of this Linga is of considerable importance, as directly
associating Ráma with the worshippers of the Linga. The following account of
the circumstance is extracted from the Adhyátma Rámáyana :—" At the commencement of the work Ráma erected the Linga of Rameswara, and having
established religious ceremonies he gave it the name of Rameswara, so that even
to this day the place where the bridge commenced is termed Setubandha Ramis-
wara. Ráma issued these commands :—' Let every one born of the human race
visit this spot to behold the Rameswara ; and, having brought with him the
Ganges water, let him pour it over the Linga ; from these ablutions the most
heinous sins, even the murder of a Bráhman, will be remitted ; the performer of
these ablutions will become pure as God, and at his death he will take up his
everlasting abode in Paradise.' In this manner did Ráma establish the Rameswara on the sea-coast."

HISTORY OF
INDIA.
PART IV.

The two spies
recognized by
Vibhishana.

Ráma permits
the two spies to
survey his
army.

Ráma's message
to Rávana.

Description of
Rávana seated
upon his
throne.

Wrath of
Rávana at the
message from
Ráma.

Rávana surveys
the army of
Monkeys and
Bears.

and to go and spy out the army of Ráma, and bring him word as to the names and characters of his chief heroes and Counsellors. And Súka and Sárana did as they were commanded, but when they joined the army of Monkeys, they were seized as spies and carried away into the presence of Ráma. But Ráma said to the two spies :—" Go you and count my armies, and learn what you will of my Commanders and Counsellors : and then return and tell all to Rávana, and say that I will reduce his city of Lanká to a heap of ashes, and slaughter him and all his sons and kinsmen, so that not a single one shall be left alive to offer the cake and water to his departed soul." So Súka and Sárana were shown all the armies of Ráma, and saw that the Commanders of the Monkeys and Bears were warriors of great might and skill; and they marvelled exceedingly, and went back to the city and informed Rávana of all that they had seen and heard.

At that time Rávana was seated in pomp and magnificence on a throne studded with precious stones. Ten crowns of pearls and jewels were on his ten heads, and thousands of giants surrounded him on all sides. A rich canopy with fringes of the largest pearls was suspended over his throne. He was eating betel leaf, and held a cup of wine in his hand, whilst celestial nymphs were dancing before him. When he heard the message from Ráma he bit his lips and gnashed his teeth, and said :—" Not though all the world came out to fight against me, will I ever restore Sítá to Ráma." He then rose up and went to the roof of his palace, and saw all the armies of Monkeys encamped before his city; and Súka and Sárana pointed out to him the different armies, and told him the names of all their Commanders; and when he saw his younger brother Vibhíshana standing beside Ráma, he was filled with wrath.[4] Then Súka coun-

---

[4] In the Adhyátma Rámáyana the Monkeys are described as being of different colours,—white, black, blue, green, red, yellow, &c. The following description of the Monkey army, which is put into the mouth of Súka, is worthy of extract :—
" He who stands at the right hand of Ráma, in splendour equal to the sun, in lustre as the purest silver, over whose head the canopy and ensigns of royalty are spread, is the wise and distinguished Raja Sugríva, under whose command are myriads of Monkeys drawn up in order and battle-array; he is the brother of

selled Rávana to restore Sítá and make peace with Ráma;
but the eyes of Rávana flashed fire, and he said :—" I
would have killed you upon the spot, but for your long services : Depart out of this Lanká, and go wheresoever you
please." [5] So Súka set off for the jungle, and passed the remainder of his life as a devotee.

Báli, the conqueror in battle, of the invincible arm. He, who stands on a rock,
of mighty stature, whose body in colour resembles the water-lily, who lashes the
ground in anger with his enormous tail, who bears a war-mace in his hand, is the
valiant Prince Angada, the son of Báli; he is chief over millions of Monkeys.
The strength of his body is equal to that of ten thousand elephants; he is next in
authority to Sugríva. The next to the left is Níla, the mighty son of Agni, he
has hundreds of thousands of Monkeys under him. He who stands close to
Ráma, the colour of whose body shines like pure gold, is Hanuman, the son of
Vayu, the beloved friend of Ráma's soul, the destroyer of thy son Aksha, the
consumer of Lanká, the trusty and special servant of Ráma. He who casts his
glaring eyes towards Lanká, who shouts with a voice like a roaring lion, whose
thoughts are fixed on the destruction of the city, is the heroic Rambha; under
him are a hundred thousand Monkeys. Next is Sarambha, of the yellow body,
the commander of millions. He, with the white body, near to Sugríva, is the
daring Vanara, the chief of ten millions of long-tailed Monkeys. He who stands
by the side of Angada is the mighty Arundha, the chief of five millions. He
with the black body, red face, and yellow tail, is Darvindha, of dreadful deeds ;
he has under him seven millions. He with the green body is Nala, the son of
Viswakarma, well skilled in architecture, who built the bridge across the sea, and
to whom there is none equal in strength. These are the principal commanders of
the Monkeys. There is yet another near to Ráma, and that is the illustrious
Jámbuvat, king of the Bears, who has forty crores of Bears under his command."

[5] After the banishment of Súka many evil omens appeared in Lanká, which,
according to the Adhyátma Rámáyana, were duly reported to Rávana by the
porter of the palace in the following language :—" The heavens appear inflamed
from morning until night; the sun shows but little light, it is frequently clouded
in total darkness and invisible; heavy thunder is heard in all quarters, lightnings
flashing around full upon the city. Showers of blood and flesh drop from the
clouds, the demons are terrified, and no one enjoys his usual happiness. The
images of the gods appear sorrowful, tears fall in streams from their eyes; they
move from their pedestals, and blood sometimes issues from their bodies.
Myriads of crows, kites, vultures, and animals feeding on carcases, hover round
Lanká. The image of Kalika Bhaváni has a constant and horrible smile; she
wanders from house to house, gnashing her teeth. Asses are born from the
wombs of cows, cats from those of mice, and mice opposing cats fight with them,
while the cats fly before the mice. These things are contrary to nature, yet are
they daily seen. Serpents fight with Garuras, and though they are their food
they fear them not. A man wonderful and formidable in his appearance, his
head shaved, his body of the deepest black, his eyes yellow, a string of human
skulls strung round his neck as a rosary, his arms and legs peculiarly short, the
image of death, wanders from morn till night throughout the city, and displays

After this Rávana entered his Council-hall, and was informed by his Counsellors that Ráma was preparing to attack Lanká; and he immediately sent for Prahasta, who was his Commander-in-chief, and told him to make ready the army of Rákshasas, and to pay the soldiers whatever was due to them, and to collect all the supplies necessary for the war. Then the bugle was sounded, and all the Rákshasa soldiers came before Rávana, and bowed their heads, to receive his commands. At this moment, Nikashá, the mother of Rávana, entered the Council-hall; and Rávana rose up and paid her every respect, and gave her his own seat, and bowed down to her, and stood before her with joined hands. Then Nikashá said to him:—" O my beloved son, why have you determined to ruin your Raj for the sake of a woman? You have hundreds of women at your disposal; why do you cast them aside for the sake of a single female: I pray you to restore Sítá to Ráma, and conclude a treaty with Ráma, and tranquillize my mind."

When Nikashá had finished speaking, her father Máliavat came forward ánd spoke as follows :—" O Maháraja, since the birth of Ráma all things have become changed; the Bráhmans perform their sacrifices with impunity; they repeat the sacred hymns from the Vedas, which terrify the Rákshasas; and the smoke of the homa rises high in the air, and almost burns the Rákshasas: From all these omens I conclude that our rule is nearly over; and it is not proper at such a time for you to go to war: My counsel is that you restore Sítá, and make peace with Ráma, otherwise no good will befall you."

At these speeches Rávana was greatly enraged, and he reproached the father of his mother in harsh language; and when Nikashá and her father 'Máliavat saw that

its horrid form at every door. Earthquakes occur seven times every day; dogs and asses continually howl and bray in the streets and narrow lanes; fires hourly arise; children die before their parents. Those stars such as Saturn, planets with fiery tails, and comets, which should not be visible at this season, are seen even in the day-time. The sun and moon are under a perpetual eclipse; the circle round the moon seems a mass of blood; the sun is seen at night. Such are the evil omens which hourly are visible; their effects will, I fear, prove baneful to us."

Rávana was greatly enraged, they fled from the Council-hall.

HISTORY OF
INDIA.
PART IV.

The foregoing narrative of Ráma's invasion of Lanká prior to the actual commencement of hostilities comprises a few scenes which never fail to create a deep impression upon the imagination of the Hindú. He sees in his mind's eye the vast army of Monkeys of different colours marching to the sea-coast, accompanied by an army of Bears, and filling the air with their thundering shouts of " Victory to Ráma." He beholds the vast bridge of rock and stone stretching over the broad sea which separates the Indian continent from the Island of Ceylon; and he feels a pride, at once national and religious, in the idea that the innumerable battalions of Ráma crossed the channel upon this marvellous structure. Lastly, the Lingá which Ráma set up on the Island of Ramisseram is to him both a monument of triumph and a mysterious symbol ; and he regards it with so much religious awe that like Herodotus of old he trembles as he speaks of it, lest he should let fall any irreverent words which might excite the anger of the gods.

Flight of
Nikashá and
Máliavat.
Review of the
foregoing narrative of Ráma's
invasion.

The army of
Monkeys and
Bears on their
march.

The vast bridge
across the sea.

The Lingá, a
monument of
triumph and a
religious
symbol.

The origin of the conception of Ráma's bridge forms a curious subject of inquiry. The famous bridge of boats by which the army of Xerxes passed over the Hellespont, and the bridges constructed by Darius over the Thracian Bosphorus and river Danube, are commonplace matters of fact in comparison with a bridge of stone sixty miles long extending over a deep sea. Strangely enough a rocky causeway runs out from the Indian side of the channel, and terminates at the Island of Ramisseram ;

Origin of the
Hindú conception of the
bridge.
Bridges of
Xerxes and
Darius matters
of fact.

Physical construction of the
locality suggestive of the idea
of a bridge.
Causeway terminating at
Ramisseram.

HISTORY OF
INDIA.
PART IV.

Causeway ter-
minating at
Manar.

Adam's Bridge
connecting
Ramisseram
with Manar.

Boulders sup-
posed to have
been dropped
by the Monkeys.

Description of
the pagoda at
Ramisseram.

The gateway.

The door.

The quadrangle.

The temples.

The surround-
ing wall.

and although it is at present covered by the sea, it is
said to have been formerly above the waves. A
similar causeway runs out from the opposite shore
of Ceylon, and terminates in the Island of Manar;
whilst a sandy ridge, known as Adam's Bridge, connects Manar with Ramisseram. There can therefore be little doubt that the Hindú bard formed the
idea of a bridge from a contemplation of the physical geography of the locality; and the conception
once formed was readily believed and widely dis-
seminated. To this day the huge blocks or boulders
which are to be found in various parts of India are
universally believed to have been dropped by the
Monkeys in the attempt to carry them southwards
for the purpose of forming the bridge.

The Island of Ramisseram, and the pagoda which
appears to have been erected there as a memorial
of Ráma's crossing the sea, are naturally replete
with interest to every reader of the Rámáyana.
The pagoda is one of the most magnificent in India.
The gateway is lofty and massive, a pyramidal
oblong a hundred feet high, and covered with carvings of minute figures, amongst which the Lingá is
frequently exhibited. The door is Cyclopean in its
appearance, being forty feet high, and composed of
long slabs of stone placed together perpendicularly
with cross slabs of the same material. Beyond the
gateway is a cloistered quadrangle six hundred feet
square, the pillars of which are three feet deep and
covered with carvings. Beyond the cloisters are
several temples with brick spires profusely decorated. The whole precinct is surrounded by a
lofty wall, which is covered with minute carvings
like those on the pyramidal gateway.

The entrance to the temples is on the south side. Here stands a temple to Síva, the god of whom the Lingá is a symbol. On the right is a large temple to Ráma, in which the figure of the god is to be seen with a large brazen Lingá before it. On the left is a smaller temple to Sítá, in which the goddess is represented richly dressed; and a brazen pillar ending in a vane of three cross bars stands before it, and is surmounted by a Bird, which may perhaps be intended to represent one of those Rajas of Vultures which are introduced in the Rámáyana as allies of Ráma. Without the door are the vast chariots of the gods, profusely covered with carvings, in which the images are occasionally placed, whilst thousands of worshippers assist to draw them along.

The Island of Ramisseram is regarded by the Hindús as more sacred than the Island of Delos was regarded by the Greeks. No labour or cultivation of any kind is carried on in any part of it. The Bráhmans, safely embosomed amidst the waves, pass their time in idleness, or meditation, or in the performance of religious rites, or in attendance upon the numerous pilgrims that visit this locality. They live upon the contributions of the devout, and especially upon the large sums which the Poligar chiefs of the neighbouring provinces on the mainland expend upon the establishment in this Island.[6]

The story of the preparations for the war on either side is related at considerable length in the original, and swelled out by a number of religious discourses, similar in character to those which have already been extracted in the form of notes from

_____

[6] See Travels of Lord Valentia.

Side notes:

HISTORY OF INDIA. PART IV.

The temple to Síva.

The temple to Ráma and brazen Lingá.

The temple of Sítá with brazen pillar surmounted by a Bird.

The cars of the gods.

The sacred character of the Island of Ramisseram.

The Bráhmans supported at the public expense.

the Adhyátma Rámáyana. Angada is also said to
have been sent out with a message to Rávana, de-
manding the restoration of Sítá on pain of immediate destruction, and the transfer of the empire of
Lanká to Vibhíshana; but the narrative of the
mission has been so largely mixed up with mythical
details, that it has been omitted altogether from the
present text.